Melancholy

Melancholy
Melankólia

LÁSZLÓ F. FÖLDÉNYI

TRANSLATED FROM THE HUNGARIAN
BY TIM WILKINSON

FOREWORD BY ALBERTO MANGUEL

YALE UNIVERSITY PRESS ▪ NEW HAVEN AND LONDON

A MARGELLOS
WORLD REPUBLIC OF LETTERS BOOK

Foreword by Alberto Manguel copyright © 2016 by Yale University.
English translation copyright © 2016 by Yale University. Translation by Tim Wilkinson.
Originally published in Hungarian as *Melankólia*.
© 1984, 1992, 2003, 2015 László F. Földényi, Budapest.
© 1988, 2004 Matthes & Seitz Berlin Verlagsgesellschaft mbH.
English-language edition published by arrangement with Eulama International Literary Agency.

Yale University Press books may be purchased in quantity for educational, business, or promotional use. For information, please e-mail sales.press@yale.edu (U.S. office) or sales@yaleup.co.uk (U.K. office).

Set in Electra and Nobel type by Tseng Information Systems, Inc.
Printed in the United States of America.

Library of Congress Control Number: 2015953464
ISBN 978-0-300-16748-1 (cloth : alk. paper)

A catalogue record for this book is available from the British Library.

This paper meets the requirements of ANSI/NISO Z39.48–1992 (Permanence of Paper).

10 9 8 7 6 5 4 3 2 1

To Marianne Bara

CONTENTS

The notion that the melancholic temperament is a characteristic of the creative mind has its roots in a fragment ascribed to Aristotle, or, rather, to the Aristotelian school. Throughout the centuries, especially in the West, this notion acquired both positive and negative connotations and was explored by relating it to somatic causes, psychic inclinations, and spiritual choices, and as a reaction to certain natural or cultural environments. The variety of such ascriptions (explored in their astonishingly vast range in László Földényi's *Melancholy*) is indicative of the notion's lasting attraction. From Aristotle on (and probably long before), philosophers, artists, psychologists, and theologians have attempted to find in the almost indefinable state of melancholia the source of the creative impulse, and even perhaps that of thought itself. Every study of melancholia (notably *Saturn and Melancholy* by Raymond Klibansky, Erwin Panofsky, and Fritz Saxl, but also legions more) is, in some sense, a reflection on the intellectual act itself.

It could be said that every one of Földényi's books is a reflection on that same subject. A specialist in aesthetics and artistic theories, Földényi (who was born in Hungary in 1952) is also an essayist and philologist. His numerous books include studies of the young Georg Lukács, the Romantic painter Caspar David Friedrich, Goya, and the reading of works of art (*The Veil of the Veronica*), as well as works on Heinrich von Kleist, on William Blake, and on the contrasting ideas of history in Dostoyevsky and Hegel, this last in a short essay with the irresistible title "Dostoyevsky Reads Hegel in Siberia and Bursts into

Tears." Melancholia continues and deepens these reflections about the relationships among art, emotion, philosophy, and religion.

The Aristotelian quotation (which Földényi places in the first chapter of his book) is not a statement but a question: Why is it that all those who have become eminent in philosophy or politics or poetry or the arts are clearly melancholic? Notable in this question is the confidence implied in the words "all those" as well as in the specific "eminent": melancholia is, for Aristotle, the pervading and necessary state of every creative act that is generally recognized as important. The assumption behind the Aristotelian question is that there is indeed such a state that allows for or even fosters creation. Inspiration (the Muses, the Holy Spirit, the poetic experience of the world) might provide the external spark, yet in order to burst into creative flames, the inspired subject must be "melancholic." But what exactly is this preconditioned temperament common to all notable creators? Over the ages, the melancholic condition has been described as sad, meditative, withdrawn, reflective, morose, ailing, depressed, and bleakly ecstatic, and yet none of these epithets embraces everything that is meant by the word "melancholia."

Jorge Luis Borges, in one of his late stories, to describe the creative state in the Aristotelian question, imagined a primitive race who engage in a curious ritual of literary creation. From time to time, one of the men will utter six or seven enigmatic words. If the words excite no attention, nothing else happens. But if the words move the audience, everyone will stand apart from him in holy dread. No one will look at him or speak to him, not even his mother. He is no longer a man but a god, whom all have the right to kill. The state this privileged man has entered is that of melancholia.

A related term, *nostalgia*, was coined by the Swiss physician Johannes Hofer in his 1688 medical dissertation, from the Greek *nostos*, "homecoming," and *algos*, "pain," to describe the mental state of Swiss soldiers on postings far away from their native mountains. "Nostalgia" carries its own etymological definition; "melancholia," in spite of everything that has been written about it, continues to beg the Aristotelian question.

Though this is not part of Földényi's exploration, it can be said that not only people but also places can suffer from melancholia, and a vocabulary of poetic fallacies has emerged to characterize some specific geographic instances: the *saudade* of Lisbon, the *tristeza* of Burgos, the *mufa* of Buenos Aires, the *mestizia* of Turin, the *Traurigkeit* of Vienna, the ennui of Alexandria, the ghostliness of Prague, the glumness of Glasgow, the dispiritedness of Boston, and the *hüzün* of Istanbul, the last a Turkish word whose Arabic root (it appears five times in the Qur'an) denotes a feeling of deep spiritual loss but also a hopeful way of looking at life. For the Turkish Sufis, *hüzün* is the spiritual sadness we feel because we are not close enough to God; for Saint John of the Cross, this melancholia causes the sufferer to plummet so far down that his or her soul will, as a result, soar to its divine desire. *Hüzün* is therefore a sought-after state; it is the absence, not the presence, of *hüzün* that causes the sufferer distress.

However, as Földényi points out, it was not suffering and malaise that were first associated with melancholia, but rather excellence and extraordinariness. Two centuries after Aristotle (or earlier, if we accept Földényi's contention that there are implicit references to melancholia in Homer), the extraordinary quality of the melancholic condition was thought to stem from an excess of black bile, one of the four bodily humors described by Hippocrates in the fifth century BCE. Melancholia then becomes a psychosomatic condition.

Melancholia marks in its sufferers the quality of singularity, the extremes of an extraordinary condition in "the one whom the finger of God crushes against the wall," according to Sartre's definition of genius. One such genial extreme is madness. "Madness is a consequence of their extraordinariness," notes Földényi of the Greek heroes Ajax, Bellerophon, and Heracles, "while they owe their extraordinariness to their inherent possibility of going mad." The writers of the late Roman age and those of early Christianity agreed that this possibility did not grant the melancholics extraordinary powers. They equated madness with melancholia and argued that mad persons did not possess the gift of divination and prophecy, but were merely deprived of their common senses.

The other extreme of the melancholic condition is the despondency that comes from intellectual learning, as exemplified in the character of Goethe's Faust: a satiated sense of knowledge fostered by melancholia whose consequence is also melancholia. "A person who possesses knowledge is isolated from people who do not," states Földényi. Knowledge that lifts the spirit and its corollary, the revelation that one who is truly wise knows nothing, often lead to a state in which everything becomes questionable. This last is beautifully summed up twenty-three centuries after Aristotle in George Eliot's *Middlemarch:* "It is an uneasy lot at best, to be what we call highly taught and yet not to enjoy: to be present at this great spectacle of life and never to be liberated from a small hungry shivering self— never to be fully possessed by the glory we behold, never to have our consciousness rapturously transformed into the vividness of a thought, the ardor of a passion, the energy of an action, but always to be scholarly and uninspired, ambitious and timid, scrupulous and dim-sighted."

Because of such intellectual perversions, Christianity condemned melancholy under the denomination of acedia, for it could distance the mind from the thought of God, allowing it idly to rove in dangerous or forbidden realms. Dante condemns the melancholic to the fifth circle of Hell, together with the wrathful. There they blow bubbles of air while immersed in the marshy waters of the Styx, because, as one says to Dante, "Sullen we were / In the sweet air that the sun makes glad, / Bearing inside us the smoke of acedia." One of the many medical treatises of the fifteenth century, the *Hortulus reginae* of 1487, compares acedia to "the bite of a rabid dog." Echoes of this simile can be heard centuries later in Winston Churchill's description of his depression as "a black dog," an expression that is first recorded as "to have the black dog on one's back" in a nineteenth-century collection of proverbs and catchphrases. Modern psychoanalytic jargon has retained the expression.

It is not easy to distinguish between states of "black dog," acedia, depression, and melancholia; depending on the context, all can appear in a positive or negative light. According to legend, in the fifth century BCE, the philosopher Democritus, to escape from the follies and distractions of the world, set himself up in a hovel on the outskirts of Abdera in what appeared to be a state of melancholy. The citizens of Abdera, appalled by his conduct, asked Hippocrates to use his medical skills to cure the stranger, whom they took to be a madman. Hippocrates, however, after examining Democritus, turned to the people and told them that it was they, not the philosopher, who were mad, and that they should all imitate his conduct and retire from the world to reflect in worthy solitude. Hippocrates took sides with the man who, bitten by acedia, retired to meditate in solitude on the world of which he wanted no part.

As Földényi notes, "A person longs for solitude and at the same time is fearful of it. He can be rid of God's omnipotence only by elevating himself into an absolute. This, however, is just as depressing a state as God's solitude." Early Christians understood this conundrum. Human intellect was a faculty given to us in order to assist us in our faith — not to clarify the unclarifiable mysteries but to construct a logical scaffolding to support them. The evidence of things unseen would not, by reflection and reasoning, render those things visible but would allow the person of faith (the prerequisite of grace, as Földényi remarks) to ruminate and build upon such evidence. For that reason, the isolation of religious men and women in cells and caves and inhospitable deserts assisted the work willed by God. Sometimes the isolation was accomplished high upon a tower erected in a wasteland, such as the one in which, in the fifth century, Simeon Stylites, as Donald Atwater put it in *A Dictionary of Saints*, "despairing of escaping the world horizontally, tried to escape it vertically" by spending high above his brethren the last thirty-six years of his life.

But concomitant with this need for seclusion to nourish the inner life ran an undercurrent of guilt, a self-censuring of the very act of quiet thinking. Humankind, the Church Fathers taught, was meant to use its intellect to understand what could be understood, but there were questions that were not meant to be asked and limits of reasoning that were not meant to be transgressed. Dante charged Ulysses with a guilty curiosity and an arrogant desire to see the unknown world. Retreating into solitude with one's own thoughts might allow this same sinful desire to arise and, without counsel and guidance of one's spiritual leaders, remain dangerously unquenched. Therefore, the person seeking God in isolation was to concentrate solely on questions of Christian dogma and remain within the confines of dogmatic theology; pagan authors were dangerous because they distracted, like the Sirens, from the true course.

The thinkers of the Renaissance tried to turn what the early Christians had seen as the sin of acedia into a virtue. In "On Caring for the Health of the Man of Letters" in his *Book of Life*, the great humanist Marsilio Ficino, commenting on his own melancholia and his habit of withdrawing into solitude ("which only much playing of the lute can sweeten and soften a little"), attempted to withdraw himself from the influence of Saturn and ascribed his state to what Aristotle had called a singular and divine gift, and Plato before him a divine furor. Though warning scholars to avoid both phlegm (which blocks the intelligence) and black bile (which causes too much care) "as if they were sailing past Scylla and Charybdis," Ficino concludes that thin black bile is beneficial for the man of letters. To encourage its flow, Ficino gives detailed instructions: emulate not the energetic demeanor of the pilgrim, alert on the road, but the idling disposition of the philosopher, meditative and slow. "When you have got out of bed," advises Ficino, "do not rush right in on your reading or meditation, but for at least half an hour go off and get cleaned up. Then diligently enter your meditation, which you should prolong for about an hour, depending on your strength. Then, put off a little whatever you are thinking about, and in the meantime comb your hair diligently and moderately with an ivory comb, drawing it forty times from the front to the neck. Then rub the neck with a rough cloth, returning only then back to meditating, for two hours or so, or at least for an hour of study." And Ficino concludes: "If you choose to live each day of your life in this way, the author of life himself will help you to stay longer with the human race and with him whose inspiration makes the whole world live" (*Book of Life*, trans. Charles Boer). In certain cases and under certain conditions, as a source for philosophical enterprise, melancholy came to be seen as a privileged state, part of the intellectual condition, as well as the source of inspired creation, and the reader, locked away in a solitary tower, as a maker.

Földényi discusses as well the descent of the term *melancholia* into the boredom and mere indifference to the things of the world, and the survival of this connotation into our age. Writers such as Hobbes, Baron d'Holbach, Locke, and Swift condemned melancholia for myriad reasons. The Anglican Robert Burton (says Földényi) accused atheism, Catholicism, and Puritanism of fostering melancholia; thinkers of the French Enlightenment said that melancholia was caused by Christianity; Georg Lukács, in the twentieth century, reproached Kafka, Joyce, and Beckett for indulging in "the melancholic disdain of reality"; Walter Benjamin mocked the poems of Erich Kästner for their "left-wing melancholia." Kant saw melancholia as a sign of ethical self-consciousness. "Mention of melancholia," writes Földényi, "creates palpable unease," and adds with a certain defiance: "If psychiatry were to seek to return to the concept its due rights, . . . the closed system would be spectacularly thrown wide open."

Földényi concludes his book bravely: "With every step he takes, man tries to smuggle some goal into nothingness. The melancholic is skeptical of those goals." Rightly so, as Földényi shows. The melancholic Hamlet's remark about being in the world, bound in a nutshell but thinking himself king of infinite space, is, in spite of all our arguments, our blessed common lot.

Melancholy

The anguish of beginning signals the difficulty of the enterprise.

We have to make use of concepts to speak about something that corrodes concepts themselves in order, ultimately, to render them elusive, in the manner of a mirage. We shall turn for assistance to the grammar of words and the resonance of sentences, although what those try to articulate and render transparent is something that precedes those words and sentences themselves. Speech is sonorous, but sooner or later it falls silent: it is also an offspring of silence. Words say less than we would wish to convey—they mislead us, divert our thoughts away from their original goal to such an extent that possibly even as we speak we ourselves are amazed: we wanted to say something else, not what the words, tones, and linguistic structures imply. A word says less than we would like to communicate—however, the fact that misunderstandings cannot be eliminated from our lives is an indication that this is not a matter of faulty technique but one of the most singular paradoxes of speech, of communication. Words give little away because they contain too much. Whatever we say, whatever we speak about, our words are not just about what we wish to communicate. Deep within them lurks another, unspoken world that also sustains those words. Naturally, we may impart thoughts about this other world as well, but in so doing we do not dispose of it, merely push back its boundaries further, expanding the unreachable horizon. None of that detracts from the importance of words, concepts, and speech, but for words truly to acquire meaning and importance they must take into account their own defenselessness, advise of their own fragility. The protagonist of Cervantes' story "The

Glass Graduate" swallows a magic potion and feels that his body and soul are made of transparent glass—yet the more this delusion and fear take hold of him, the more his powers of discernment and clearsightedness grow. In a way, it is much the same with words.

An admitted weakness is an actual weakness—this needs to be laid down before juggling with concepts drives it out of our minds. In the present case, this is true on many counts. Melancholia is, among other things, a consequence of the inadequacy of concepts; that inadequacy, however, is not some kind of deficiency that can be overcome or even eliminated over time, but the sort of thing without which concept formation is unimaginable, and just as clearsightedness, measure, or definitiveness forms one of the pillars on which all insight can rest, so obscurity, gloom, incomprehensibility, and dissatisfaction form the other. Hence, perhaps, the sadness that lurks in the depths of any formulation laying claim to finality, the inconsolability that corrodes even the most closed formations. Our culture is more than happy to apply here the concept of negativity or absence, but—and of this too it is melancholia that serves us as a reminder—can we consider negativity or lack something that cannot be eliminated from human existence? Maybe one can from a kind of eschatological point of view, but—and melancholia reminds us of this as well—if eschatological faith itself is one of the manifestations of fragile human existence, then are we in the position to pass judgment, in divine fashion, drawing strict boundaries between negativity and positivity? Ultimate points and extreme boundaries do exist; this is shown not only by our finiteness, manifested in our evanescence and mortality, but also by the limits against which, sooner or later, all human endeavors come up. These ultimate human boundaries and possibilities do not encircle and embrace us from the outside, however, but rather are the most characteristic, internal foci of existence, which one may encounter anywhere, at any time. That is why what seems to be a lack from the outside (the fact that human existence is limited, not almighty) appears from the inside as fulfillment; what, from a divine perspective, seems a frailty is by human standards an internal strength and competence. Inconsolability is there even in profound perspicacity; obtuseness in the most explicit train of thought. That does not mean, however, that they extinguish each other. We live our entire lives in separate, incomparable, unique ways, and so there are no two persons with an equal share of obtuseness and perspicacity, of a desire for the boundless, and of an existence doomed to ultimate frailty. And (melancholia here warns us again) that is a precondition of life, but also of death. We do not die of weakness or strength, perspicacity or obtuseness, but of the fact that each is a lack of the other and a fulfillment of itself.

Yes, melancholia warns us time and time again; yet the beckoning does not come from outside but speaks to us from inside. It does not necessarily have any need of words, however. It is simultaneously present on this side of words and beyond them. It gives birth to words that in the end will empty it. A few centuries BCE, when mention was first made of it, the pangs that had accompanied the birth not just of melancholia but also of humankind itself had already fallen into oblivion. Melancholia stands before us in full armor (though that image is very misleading), and the words that are articulated about it are mostly descriptive and objective. Later on, as words multiplied, a time would come when the words uttered about it created melancholia, when people endeavored to become melancholic by conversing at length about it, though such a fashion had little to do with melancholia itself. Since those words, as oral expressions in general, are attended by ultimate ignorance and error, speaking about melancholia is a particularly hair-raising undertaking. It is necessary that words have a delicate balance: one must speak not only of *what* the subject of the conversation is but also of *how* the conversation proceeds. This, however, is an endless spiral: one must create words about the *how*, treated as a subject, in some form, and that form also requires that it is treated as a subject. There is no final resolution in the torrent of subject and form that grind up and erode each other:

we are talking about melancholia, yet we should be talking about the melancholic foundation of words. We are trying to pull ourselves up by our own bootstraps.

When melancholia made its first appearance as a concept, everything that might be said was said about it. From the very beginning, however, the "elusiveness" of the concept was conspicuous, and later ages were unable to alter that. No unequivocal, accurate definition of melancholia exists. The history of melancholia is an ever-inconclusive history of approximating concepts of acceptable accuracy, and that is why a doubt arises: in talking about melancholia, our true subject is not melancholia; rather, we are actually trying to assess *our own* places, with the assistance of the concepts that have been formed about it. That is why the anguish of beginning is manifold. First of all, where do we really begin? At the point where our theme first comes into sight as a concept (in antiquity), or at the point where *our own lives* latched on to the concept, being unable thereafter ever to rid ourselves of it? At the point where it dons the form of a word, or where, in backing away from words, our life reaches it all the same? We said that when mention was first made of it, it already stood before us in full armor. Caution and perhaps the fear that is at work at the bottom of all caution demand that one should start with the word and track the fate of the concept. If, as is supposed, melancholia lurks at the very back of concept formation, corroding words and belying concepts, then we shall be able to formulate more clearly the questions and doubts of our own lives, even if by doing so we won't have all the answers.

Chapter 1

THE INITIATES

> *Διὰ τί πάντες ὅσοι περιττοὶ γεγόνασιν ἄνδρες*
> *ἢ κατὰ φιλοσοφίαν ἢ πολιτικὴν ἢ ποίησιν*
> *ἢ τέχνας φαίνονται μελαγχολικοὶ ὄντες;*

"Why is it that all those who have become eminent in philosophy or politics or poetry or the arts are clearly of an atrabilious temperament [i.e., melancholic]?" The opening line (953a) of book 30 of the so-called *Problemata physica*, ascribed to the Aristotelian school, is compelling enough to stand at the head of our line of thought. It has lost none of its validity down to the present day. Since the book contains, besides undisputed Aristotelian texts, material from other sources and authors as well, it is not impossible that the thought cited stems from the pen of Theophrastus, who, according to Diogenes Laertius, wrote the first (now lost) book about melancholia. All the same, let us stay with the assumption that Aristotle is the author. It is here that the concepts of excellence and extraordinariness are first associated with melancholia, which may be surprising at first sight. Melancholia, to use the word in its original, literal meaning of "black bile" or *atra bilis* (*μέλαινα χολή*), is a quality of the body, whereas the excellence of a philosopher, politician, or artist is that of the mind, and in accordance with the modern-age view of body and mind as a duality, the two can be merged only with the assistance of a metaphor. This metaphor, however, was lacking: with Aristotle, the correspondence was direct, so one must attempt to find an internal connection between the two concepts. We must go back to the original meaning of *excellence* and *extraordinariness*. Originally, the verb *περιττεύω* meant not just "to abound in something" but also "to possess a surplus"—someone who is extraordinary and excellent possesses something that others lack: that person is the possessor of an uncommon quality. And, since pre*eminence* can refer equally to standing out in a literal, corporeal sense and to intellectual superiority, it is a secondary matter whether one regards it as a mental or physical attribute. (In most cases, extraordinariness cannot be narrowed down to one or the other.) Anyone who is preeminent, be he or she a poet, philosopher, politician, or artist, is not just intellectually so, but that intellectual preeminence per se is the consequence of some deeper-lying deviation from the norm. Naturally, not a deviation only of the body or only of the mind: one has to notice his or her particular relationship to life or, to be more accurate, his or her own fate. Facing up to fate, accepting and pursuing it mercilessly, is what is decisive. That follows from the perception of the uniqueness and oddness of life (in Greek arithmetic, περιττός also meant odd-numbered!), the intellectual and physical signs of which can be delimited from one another only inferentially and with great difficulty. (We observe that many people die of their own intellectual preeminence, or that great minds perish on account of physical causes, although we sense that it is not just a matter of body or soul.) Anyone who is preeminent has life's uniqueness (the fact that it resists division as much as multiplication) to "thank" for his or her extraordinariness; it is plain that this special gift does not bring about happiness, or even confidence, but melancholia. This goes some way in taking the edge off the apparent contradiction in the Aristotelian sentence. But what is the situation with melancholia, i.e., black bile? Having no knowledge and experience of the disunion of body and soul, a development in the past two thousand years of Western thought, the Greeks no doubt did not consider the physical nature of black bile as being exclusively a characteristic of the body, but transferred it to their assessment of the intellectual world and the cosmos as a whole, and so instead of *abolishing* it, they did not even *experience* the duality that we have defined as the antithesis of *intellectual* excellence and black bile, a characteristic of the *body*. A conceptual unraveling of melancholia, of black bile, offers a deeper insight into this approach.

One comes across the first traces of a connection between bile and spirit (temperament) in Homer, who, although not mentioning black bile, does nevertheless associate the color black with a darkening of mood. The fact that Agamemnon's "heart was black with rage, and his eyes flashed fire" (*Iliad*, bk. 1, 103) is just as much a consequence of a change in bile as of rancor on account of Calchas's prophesy. Bile and the color black make their first joint appearance in Sophocles' tragedy *Women of Trachis:* according to the poet, the arrow dipped into the "black gall" of the Lernaean Hydra was poisoned (565). Thus, the dramatist, who, as a priest, was also a physician, considered black bile—μελάγχολος—to be harmful, a poison for the body. The description and interpretation of that poison, the black bile, are linked to Hippocrates at the end of the fifth century BCE. "Now the body of man," he writes, "contains blood, pituita, and two kinds of bile—yellow and black; and his nature is such that it is through them that he enjoys health or suffers from disease" (*On the Nature of Man*, 4). Hippocrates initially derived the ailment known as melancholia from the blackening of the gall (μελαγχολία was a malady of the so-called choleric category, ὁ χολώδης), not from black bile, as in his later works. He is of the opinion that if the juices were distributed in a bad ratio, or rather—after introducing the term *black bile*—one of the juices did not mix appropriately with the other, then the organism would fall ill. The constitution of the human body was a function of that mixing; the Greeks designated mixing and constitution with the same word: ἡ κρᾶσις. The cosmocentric Greek view considered humanity to be an organic part of the universe rather than setting it in opposition.[1] Admixture, which was originally related to

---

1. The ancient Greeks, like Indian cultures, perceived a transition, not a chasm, between living organisms (plants, animals, humankind, gods), as is demonstrated by

the joining of constituent elements, was responsible for *everything*;
for the state of the cosmos as well as for the human body, constitution, and character; indeed, as Ptolemy expounds in his *Tetrabiblos*,
even for the influencing power of celestial cycles. Hippocrates pays
little attention to the spiritual aspect of constitution and much more
to the physical components, although a worldview that sees the state
of the body and the cosmos in unity contains implicitly a belief in the
unity of body and mind. Melancholia, Hippocrates avers, is an indisposition of the body: the dense humor of black bile gains ascendancy
at the expense of the other humors, and poisons the blood, which
can be the cause of maladies from headaches through diseases of the
liver and stomach to such conditions as leprosy. *Blood*, however, is
the nidus of the mind, Hippocrates says; the mental consequences
of poisoning the blood by black bile are thereby explicable. Black bile
per se is not an illness, and becomes that only as a result of bad mixing (δυσκρασία): melancholia (black bile), which primarily points to a
mental condition, is a particular case of the bad distribution of black
bile (μέλαινα χολή), in which the bodily state is coupled with fear
(φόβος) and depression (δυσθυμία). According to Hippocrates, the
so-called dry type of temperament is prone to that ailment (it is concomitant with the drying out and thickening of the bile), which is also
influenced by the weather and the seasons. In his medical treatise
On Airs, Waters, and Localities, he writes as follows: "But if the season is northerly and without water, there being no rain, neither after
the Dog Star nor Arcturus; this state agrees best with those who are
naturally phlegmatic, with those who are of a humid temperament,
and with women; but it is most inimical to the bilious; for they become much parched up, and ophthalmies of a dry nature supervene,
fevers both acute and chronic, and in some cases melancholy" (ch.
10, 84–91). The disorder caused by black bile, melancholia, may origi-

numerous mythological tales, and accordingly, in the case of man they emphasized
existence rather than individuality.

nate in the body, but in these circumstances it also affects the mood. In *The Third Book of Epidemics*, Hippocrates discusses melancholia of a physical origin as a disturbed state of the mind: a female patient he had examined was sleepless and averse to food, and "her temperament was melancholic" (τὰ περὶ τὴν γνώμην μελαγχολικά, 17.2). The word γνώμη means alike "mood," "mental ability," "mind," "heart," "frame of mind," "insight"—all these meanings are implied inseparably in that single Greek word, and that laconicism alerts one to a relative wealth: the capabilities of the mind and the spirit cannot be stowed in separate "sacks" but attest to a *uniform* stance toward and interpretation of existence, invisibly and yet firmly intertwined with the likewise manifold world of the body. Melancholia is a sickness of both temperament and constitution, of mind and body, γνώμη and κρᾶσις: the unity of the spirit and the cosmic mixture of elements defining the physical condition. Melancholia is the dissolution and indisposition of these two—can there be a more expansive, more daring medical approach to things? The origin is physical[2]—Hippocrates relates that when he visited Democritus, who was not only melancholic himself but wrote a treatise about the malady, he found the philosopher sitting under a tree and dissecting animals to find the cause of the melancholic mood—whereas the outcome is eminently intellectual. And vice versa: the origin, being physical, is cosmic and superhuman (a product of the interplay of wind, landscape, season, climate, even the planets and stars), but its effect manifests in a person's matchless and unique psychic and intellectual qualities, making him or her radically different from everyone else. Thus, in Hippocrates' view, the illness of melancholia is the result of some kind of anomaly: the balance of the micro- and macrocosm has tipped, order (the cosmos) has broken down, disorder has set in, and the affected

---

2. To the point that in the opinion of Hippocrates, melancholia, if associated with inflammation of the diaphragm (paraphrenitis), could favorably influence the healing of hemorrhoids.

person no longer obeys the indissoluble laws of the universe and his or her own fate. ἐξισταμένοισι—they have stepped out of themselves, fallen into ecstasy, Hippocrates says of melancholics at one point, and his eloquent use of the medial, reflexive form of the verb points to penetrating observation: the subjects are not only thrown upon the mercy of a will that is alien to them but they are also the objects of their own actions. Melancholics stand outside the customary rules of life; but fate, which wanted it to be so, is their own fate as well: *their life, the relationship they have evolved with fate, determines their state (malady) just as much as does the cosmos, over which they have no control.* This, however, Hippocrates does not say—voicing such ideas in the world of self-explanatory phenomena would have struck people as verging on the suspicious.

We have now got somewhat nearer the quotation from Aristotle that stands at the head of this chain of ideas. Melancholics are outstanding, the philosopher asserts, and that relates to the Hippocratic notion that the melancholic is suffering from a disturbance of balance that extends to, and points beyond, everything. Hippocrates considered melancholia to be an illness.[3] Aristotle, on the other hand, regarded it as an exalted state in which the "patient" was also capable of conjuring up healthy and durable works likely to captivate everyone. True to the Hippocratic tradition, Aristotle took the observation of the body as a starting point: he, too, held that an excess of black bile compared with the other humors was unhealthy, but he considered the *temperature* of black bile as being the ultimate causal factor. A person in whom the black bile warmed up excessively would be happy and good-natured without reason (whence the kinship of melancholia and mania in antiquity), whereas those in whom it cooled down unduly became sorrowful and depressed. It was characteristic

---

3. Although he does not dwell on it, he mentions the melancholic habitude (μελαγχολικός) and, anticipating a later point of view, regards the ailment as of general validity in the case of certain people, thereby raising it out of the sphere of illness.

of melancholics as a class that the temperature of the black bile would decrease to a moderate level (πρὸς τὸ μέσον). Since it was a *medium* type, it was therefore *healthy*, and since the hot and cold were mixing appropriately, melancholics were capable of all kinds of things and were able to achieve great things in politics, the arts, philosophy, and poetry, though they were also at constant risk of the dangers associated with the cooling down or heating up of the black bile. A person of melancholic temperament was therefore characterized by a peculiar state in which, on the one hand, the black bile was in excess, an unhealthy symptom compared with a median distribution of the humors, but on the other hand, even in that condition of excess, the medium, that is health, was still attainable. A characteristic feature of humors is poor mixing, δυσκρασία, while that of temperature is good mixing, εὐκρασία; in other words, the melancholic type was characterized by a peculiar coexistence of the medium and the extreme. The two do not rule each other out. In *The Nicomachean Ethics*, for instance, one can read (in another context): "a person of ambition, in regard to magnanimity, stands at the highest grade; but if one takes that he always does as one should, then one has to say that he stands at the middle" (1123b). Writing about the celestial firmament being spherical, Aristotle mentions "the center and the extremity" being one (*On the Heavens*, 8 = *Peri Uranu biblia*, 923b). Could not a melancholic be characterized as combining the center and the extremity in a single individual, one wonders? Not that this would mean peace and harmony; constant oscillation between the two ensures the balance that makes the creation of great works and the execution of great feats possible. But the same oscillation also makes inevitable the continuous transgression of borders without which great works and feats would be equally inconceivable. Thus, the melancholic perceives the order of the cosmos by constantly violating it. No melancholic, therefore, can on any account be an average individual—but rising above the average does not mean the person is sick; if anything, the person is capable of a healthier life than the average. That "outstanding health" (sickness, viewed from the viewpoint of sobriety), however, has other criteria than those of "average health."

Melancholics are extraordinary individuals; but how does their extraordinariness manifest? Aristotle gives no answer to that, though he does name a few persons whom he considers melancholic. The persons he lists are Ajax, Bellerophon, Heracles, Empedocles, Plato, Socrates, and Lysander. The first three are mythological heroes, the next three philosophers, and the last named was a politician. The common factor, at first sight, is the superhuman feats they accomplished. The labors of Heracles do not need to be rehearsed here, nor the world of thought inhabited by Empedocles, Plato, and Socrates; Lysander as commander of the Spartan fleet attained the greatest pinnacle of power that was available in his age; Bellerophon, a Corinthian, slew the Chimera, then defeated the ferocious Solymnes, and killed many of the Amazons; Ajax, son of Telamon, the king of Salamis, commander of the Achaeans' left wing in their camp at Troy, was one of the most powerful and most prominent of the besieging warriors. All these named have grandness, heroism, and extraordinariness in common, but not just that. The seamier side of their lives, if one may call it that, was likewise above the average.

Ajax was rendered invulnerable in childhood by none other than Heracles. He went mad after he was, in his view unlawfully, deprived of Achilles' armor, which then ended up in the hands of crafty Odysseus. He swore vengeance against the Greeks, but Athena dimmed his eyesight, and instead of his brothers in arms he slaughtered a flock of sheep grazing near the camp. When he recovered his wits, he was unable to bear the shame and committed suicide. Ajax, as Sophocles writes, was "a prisoner of his own unalterable destiny" (*Ajax*, 250): he bore a human nature inside himself, but he could not contain his desires within this natural boundary. As the strongest warrior, he surpassed everyone else; he rejected the assistance offered by Athena, trusting that he would succeed in battle on his own, unaided. His strength and splendid heroism, however, isolated him from others; hence, the mocking he is subjected to and the incomprehension by which he is surrounded. It was not his wits but his physical prowess that made Ajax famous; yet the predominance of his physical strength was enough to throw his mind off balance and off course, and so "devouring his lonely heart he sits" (613). He "lies whelmed by a storm / of turbid wildering fury" (206–7), his concubine, Tecmessa, says of the *delirious* Ajax, who, on regaining his senses, realized that his world had been irreparably shattered: the dignity of his physical excellence was coupled with a sense of pettiness (after all, was it not feebleness to go crazy over mere weapons?). That mental pettiness, however, was also a sign of immoderation: anyone flying into such a rage and wanting something badly enough to go mad must ignore the customary order of the world. He had lost his honor not only in the eyes of men but of the gods also, who had induced a fit of madness in him. Looking at it from Ajax's point of view, though, his condition could also be interpreted as meaning that for him people had ceased to exist, had lost their importance just as much as the gods had. Putting the words of Sophocles into his mouth: "Receive me now no more worthy to seek help of the gods, / Nor any more from fellow mortal men to claim kindness" (397–99). He had lost all connection with earthly beings and also with the celestial world, ending up outside the universe: "ἐκστατικὸς ἐγένετο," says Aristotle—he ended up in ecstasy, he remained stuck outside himself. The internal chaos, which had gone hand in hand with a breakdown of the order of the external world, drove him to suicide.

Much the same can be said of Bellerophon of Corinth. His heroic deeds entitled him to consider himself superior to everything, which led to his beginning to doubt the given order of life: anyone who surpasses the ordinary laws of the world will inevitably become curious about new limits and unfamiliar laws. For Bellerophon, the universal validity and meaning of existence had been lost, so he began to doubt the very existence of the gods: "Does anyone maintain that there are gods in heaven? No, they do not exist. They do not!" Euripides has him say in a fragment of the play *Bellerophon* (286, 1–2). On his horse, Pegasus, he takes to the heavens to look for traces of the gods, but fails to reach them: the gods thrust him back to Earth. Thus, for anything beyond the certitudes of simple faith, the gods are not only inaccessible but also cruel. Bellerophon plummets to Earth, and awareness of the absurdity of existence gains ascendancy over him:

> But when even Bellerophon came to be hated by all the gods,
> he wandered all desolate and dismayed upon the Aleian plain,
> devouring his own soul,[4] and shunning the paths of men,

(Homer, Iliad, bk. 6, 200–202)

Homer recounts, and that "even" is a signal that Bellerophon had fallen victim to some dreadful principle. "A thing which is sweet beyond measure is awaited by a most bitter end," Pindar writes by way of warning (*Isthmia*, 6). He was not driven by the depths of despair to suicide in the way Ajax was, but becoming an outcast was tantamount to death. "I too say," he declaims to the audience, "it's best for a man not to be born" (*Bellerophon*, 287, 1–2). Sophocles has the chorus of *Oedipus at Colonus* say the same thing, as Kierkegaard was fond of quoting: "It is best not to have been born at all: but, if born, as quickly as possible to return whence one came" (1388–91). Human life is condemned to failure from the very outset; indeed, it is not that failure will happen but that it is unceasingly present, it is continuous. Bellerophon speaks of those who suffer the fate of humans, who live a double life: a life of suffering and a life of awareness of such suffering. Human beings suffer not only from being human, but also from being fully conscious of their human predicament. Heroism and dejection emerge in the same individual, raising the suspicion that dejection and a sense of hopeless failure, of futility, seized hold

---

4. ὅν θυμὸν κατέδων. θυμός denotes mental power, will, demeanor, courage, passion, and soul.

of Bellerophon precisely because he was marked out from birth for superhuman feats, outstanding actions.

The suffering and death of Heracles seem to reinforce this hypothesis. Born of an earthly mother and a celestial father, he is one of the strangest figures in Greek mythology: so human and yet superhuman that his solitude appears to be virtually predestined. He has no partners or allies; his enemies are shrouded in obscurity, just as his wife and children also hide in the background. Heracles stands before us statue-like, without any frame of reference, to the point that by dominating everything wherever he makes an appearance, he discredits reality itself, the world, the places he visits where he accomplishes his deeds, and holds all existence virtually under a spell.[5] The twelve labors seem incredible even in the fairy-tale world of mythology: here the solid boundaries of existence melt away, and compared with the miraculous atmosphere of the labors, more than a few mythological stories seem downright prosaic. The very basis of Heracles' existence is boundlessness: for him, anything is possible, and he comes to the realization (and this is what mere mortals do not experience) that anything is also possible in the world surrounding him. It is for this reason that his figure, pellucidly delimited and statuesquely rounded off, awakens a sense of infinity: as if time and space, the whole universe, were organized to suit his pleasure, to comply with his wishes. His strength, though, was at the same time his weakness: he owed his strength (not just his physical but also his "world-creating" power) to the fact that he was not a mere human and also not a divinity, but rather *intermediate*, being at home in both worlds.[6] Yet that meant that he was truly at home nowhere: "I will unfold to

---

5. Perhaps that metaphysical solitude explains why Heracles plays a negligible role in Homeric epics, which designate people's place in society in a complex way.

6. Herodotus noticed that Heracles, on account of his dual nature, was worshipped equally as a hero and as a god, and Diodorus Siculus names the specific places: at Opus and Thebes he was revered as a hero, whereas in Athens as a god.

you why life now, as well as formerly, has been unbearable to me."
Heracles says these words unworthy of a hero in the tragedy of Euripides (1257), after which one reads the following: "He who is always unfortunate feels no such pain, for sorrow is his birthright" (1292–94). The metaphysical homelessness cannot be lifted (when Odysseus descends into the underworld, he encounters only the *body* of Heracles, for his *soul* ascended into the divine regions; that is, not even death can put an end to this homelessness, the condition of being ripped asunder), for there is no foothold to grasp in one's effort to render the world contained and snug: there is nowhere to set off from, and nowhere to arrive. At first, Heracles had no presentiment of all this; most likely his destiny became clear to him when, before his descent into the underworld, he had himself initiated into the Eleusinian mysteries. The mutually complementary concepts of life and death, a fateful preoccupation with boundlessness, and an anxiety over finitude made themselves felt in him there, and presumably that superior way of looking at things—one that he acquired there, a hair-raising overture for a finite mortal being—opened up the irrevocable split that he owed to his divine-human, eternal-mortal nature. After he returned from the underworld, people started worshipping him under the name Charops as well (an epithet kindred to "Charon," the name of the ferryman of Hades), which indicated the unexpectedly frightful nature of a transformed Heracles. And the madness that erupted in him following the initiation into the mysteries and the "excursion" to the underworld, and that, as an external force, made him exterminate his own children, did not differ from the madness of Ajax and Bellerophon. "O Zeus, why hast thou shown such savage hate against thine own son and plunged him in this sea of troubles?" the chorus asks, perplexed, in Euripides' drama *Heracles* (1086–87). The "troubles" signify more than simple melancholy in the present-day sense: κακός and τὸ κακόν also denote unsuitability, weakness, badness in a moral sense, unworthiness, poverty, suffering, and misfortune. τὸ κακόν stands for an unsuitability lacking any kind of comparison. The more

one is the victim of this, the less one is capable of seeing the context and measure of one's blunder. "(*Inside, we are*) a complex store-house and treasury of ills, with many possibilities of suffering," says Democritus (Kathleen Freeman, *Ancilla to the Pre-Socratic Philosophers*, 105, frag. 149). The treasury that he comes upon is the irremediable and increasingly certain condemnation of his life to failure. The sea into which Heracles plunged is, in the final analysis, a sea of deprivation of something, a *deficiency*; and the suffering caused by madness, horrifyingly, is increased by the fact that this deficiency, the sense of an all-enveloping negativity, is the reward for *perfect, unsurpassable* labors. Madness is the reward for all-surpassing extraordinariness, for supereminence[7] — this at least is the conclusion to which the fate of these three melancholic heroes points.

Identifying madness with melancholia, especially with the current preoccupation with psychology and clinical psychiatry, seems to give the problem short shrift. But madness in this case is also an ingredient of mythological tales, and just as the myth as a whole has a meaning, so too its separate parts have broader significance than it would appear at first sight from a rational point of view. A myth cannot be puzzled out — only, at best, endlessly unraveled — without flinching from relating it to our own situation, which itself is not much different from a maze and is in no way more solid than the soil of mythology. The same can be said about frenzy. Lyssa was the goddess, or *daimona*, responsible for raging madness — it was she who planted its seed in the mind of Heracles in Euripides' drama. Her mother was Nyx, the dark personification of Night, her father, Uranus, and that family tree places madness in a wider context. Uranus is the god of the sky, and so on the paternal side, madness can be traced back to the very beginnings of existence. On the maternal side, born of the night as she is, she stems from the realm of invisible entities; for

---

7. The word περιττότης as also used by Aristotle means "extraordinariness" as well as "unevenness."

the Greeks, however, night did not just conceal things but—like the dream world—could also make the invisible visible.[8] At night, a new world unfolds itself, and this new world is not merely some dreamland of the imagination: it is also related to the daytime world. In his short treatise *On Prophesying by Dreams*, Aristotle articulates a widespread Greek belief that in nocturnal dreams profound truths are revealed to the dreamer. The night allows us to catch a glimpse of invisible things and thus makes divination possible. *Prophecy* is therefore a sibling of *madness*, which is further confirmed by the spirit of the Greek language: the verbs *to prophesy* (μαντεύω) and *to rage* (μαίνομαι) go back to a common root. (At this point, it is enough to note in parentheses that Aristotle also saw a connection between melancholia and the night,[9] but this, in any case, was considered self-evident: the connection between raving mad and melancholic heroes, as well as that between melancholia and divinatory talent, to be discussed in more detail later on, automatically offered a kinship of night and melancholy.) The family tree of madness is therefore far-reaching: on the paternal side it can be traced back to the very beginnings of existence, and on the maternal side to the realm of the invisible. Plato could justifiably say: "The ancient inventors of names if they had thought madness (μανική) a disgrace or dishonor, would never have called prophecy (μαντική), which is . . . the noblest of arts, by the very same name" (*Phaedrus*, 244b–c). Madness is a divine gift, at least if it fits into the aforesaid context. Plato writes also about the kind of madness that is not a gift of the gods but afflicts the human mind as a darkening here on earth. Just as two kinds of love are distinguished, the heavenly, temperate, and the unrestrained, unbridled Eros, so too there is a distinction made

---

8. Orphics regarded the counsels of the dark, unlighted night as the most profound sources of wisdom.

9. In Nietzsche's *Thus Spake Zarathustra*, "The Song of Melancholy" (ch. 74) is likewise heard with the onset of night.

between two kinds of madness. At the same time—and this is worth noting—Plato regards one of the variants of earthly madness clouding the eye as melancholia. In the *Timaeus* (86b), he discusses sufferings of the soul, even to the point of defining melancholia, without actually naming it; while both in the *Phaedrus* (268e) and in the *Republic* (573c), he uses the words "melancholia" and "melancholic" in the mundane sense of "crazy." The notion of mania, of madness, however, leads off into the otherworldly realm; raving visited upon us by the gods allows a glimpse into higher spheres of being: "The fourth and last kind of madness . . . is imputed to him who, when he sees the beauty of earth, is transported with the recollection of the true beauty; he would like to fly away, but he cannot; he is like a bird fluttering and looking upward and careless of the world below; and he is therefore thought to be mad" (*Phaedrus*, 249d). The Platonic duality of a divine madness that tempts a person into the sky (mania) and more mundane madness, which shackles a person to earth (melancholia), was resolved by Aristotle: to mania with a metaphysical tint, he attached a scientific sense by making it medically explicable on the basis of bodily symptoms while broadening the notion of melancholia. He mixed the specific metaphysical characteristics of mania with the physical attributes of melancholia and thereby instigated a radically new conception of the latter. For Aristotle, melancholia of physical origin had its metaphysical associations to thank for being able to provide grounds for eminence and extraordinariness. (In the Middle Ages, one could witness a downgrading of those metaphysical characteristics, and only in the fifteenth century, in Ficino's notion of melancholia, did it regain the rights won with the Aristotelian theory.) What was characteristic of melancholia, as of madness, was the ecstasy, the stepping outside oneself, and re-creation of the laws of existence in a wider sense. Indeed, in Aristotle's time, *to rave* (μαίνομαι) was also used in connection with melancholia. The madness of the three heroes thus becomes the source of melancholia, but this madness—and their *whole* lives are proof of this—is not, in and of itself, its basis: also pertinent are the realization of great feats, the accomplishment of superhuman actions, and the vanquishing of the powers of darkness. The heroes are not melancholic because they are mad, nor even because of their extraordinary strength and talent, but because the two are inseparable in them: *madness is a consequence of their extraordinariness, while they owe their extraordinariness to their inherent possibility of going mad.* Since there is no earthly standard for measuring their extraordinariness, their madness is likewise not definitively curable by earthly medicines; indeed, medication would destroy them.[10] Their madness opened the gates of a new world, and passing through those gates would cause the earthly arrangements of this world to lose their significance, and the horizons that arose before them would put all existing things in a radically new light. "[Where] madness has entered with holy prayers and rites, and by inspired utterances found a way of deliverance for those who are in need; and he who has part in this gift, and is truly possessed and duly out of his mind," writes Plato, "is by the use of purifications and mysteries made whole and exempt from evil, future as well as present, and has a release from the calamity which was afflicting him" (*Phaedrus*, 244e). Melancholia, which in Aristotle (and also in Hippocrates) is inseparably intertwined with mania, enables those who come down with it to step beyond the usual boundaries of human existence and withdraw themselves from the demands of everyday life. In the words of Heraclitus: "Immortals are mortal, mortals immortal, living the others' death, dead in the others' life" (frag. XCII, in Kahn, *Art and*

---

10. This is a matter of melancholic *heroes*: the ancients prescribed numerous medicines for the melancholia of "ordinary" lunatics (the best known of those was the plant called hellebore, to which great curative power was attributed even in the nineteenth century). The mythological interpretation of melancholia and madness indicates the irresolvability, the "incurability," inherent in both, and it is to be incorporated into the stricter interpretation of melancholia and madness that is valid to the present day.

Thought of Heraclitus, 71). For them, a gradual breakup of the mundane world is under way (melancholic heroes are doubtful even of the divinities who vouch for existence), and they will be the beholders of, and passive parties to, "coming into being" (γένεσις εἰς οὐσίαν)—to use a Platonic expression—that is, to the continuous interchange of being and nonbeing (ὄν καὶ μὴ ὄν).

That explains melancholics' talent for surprisingly accurate prophesying, noted and commented on by the ancient Greeks. In the aforesaid short treatise, Aristotle draws attention to the ability of melancholics to foretell the future with great accuracy, and in his younger days, when he had still believed in the divine origin of dreams, he went so far as to connect this ability with sleep. Melancholics, he says, have transient dreams and are plagued by the same sorts of notions that visit febrile patients—and these notions reveal to them the deeper relationships of existence. Thus, a prophet should not be imagined in the present-day sense as someone *lodged in the present* who prophesies an event that will occur at some later date, but as a person who *stands outside time.* Thus, Homer writes of one such prophet: "Calchas son of Thestor, wisest of augurs, / who knew things past, present and to come, rose to speak" (*Iliad*, bk. 1, 68–70). For Calchas there was no decisive difference between the past, the present, and the future: for him who understands everything, sees and hears everything *simultaneously*,[11] time becomes of secondary importance. Time is part of the world of opinion (δόξα), proclaims Xenophanes; reason in search of truth, on the other hand, is not at the mercy of time: in comparison with something having existed, existing now, or coming into existence, it is incomparably more important that it is part of existence, which generates time. Because it is Being, namely, that which exists (ἔστιν), which in the view of Parmenides "has no

---

11. "For eyes, and ears, and feet, are mine," says the soothsayer Theoclymenus in the *Odyssey* (bk. 20, 365, trans. William Maginn); according to mystery religions, vision and audition are particular endowments of the initiated.

coming-into-being and no destruction, for it is whole of limb, without motion, and without end. And it never Was, nor Will Be, because it Is now, a Whole all together, One, continuous" (*Fragments*, 8). Soothsayers find themselves at home in a world of Being beyond time, in a place where they are not captive to any particular tense and where, with impunity, they can transgress the boundaries of things laid down by time. An oracle navigates freely in time and space; not detained by beliefs and opinions, his attention is always directed instead at the truth, which is not revealed in response to his glance but could not exist without that glance. That is why a soothsayer's words seem as though they emanate straight from the heart of things. Not for nothing did the ancient Greeks hold Delphi, seat of the oracle of Apollo, to be a central point of the world, its omphalos, or "navel," where any mortal could learn what is and what will be. But only a select few found their home in this navel, which could be known only to those whom the gods regarded as worthy. Epimenides denied that the Delphic omphalos was the central point of land or sea. "If any there be," he writes, "it is visible to the gods, not visible to mortals" (Freeman, *Ancilla*, 10, frag. 11). One would thus have to become divine in order to glimpse the omphalos; one has to be one of the elect of the gods to be capable of prophesying while seated on that navel. That is why soothsayers were so mysterious and frightening, like the sibyl, who, according to Heraclitus, "with raving mouth utters things mirthless and unadorned and unperfumed" (frag. XXXIV, in Kahn, *Art*, 45). The madness is the mania that raises the oracle up high, and in the course of that elevation the earthly truth that has been left behind is unraveled. The prophecies inspired by god take the form of "dark sayings and visions" (*Timaeus*, 72b), but the suspicion arises that this is because the truth that has been recognized is itself an insolvable mystery. Soothsayers transgress boundaries, and they become embodiments of a strange detachment. And because they are not gods, merely partaking of the divine, this strangeness within them will be a source of pain. For that reason, genuine prophets are equipped with double vision: they impart nonhuman truth with human words; they are possessed by gods[12] yet speak for themselves; they are less than gods, owing to their human fate, but because of their familiarity with the gods, they are more than human beings — just like melancholic Heracles. A soothsayer's destiny is to experience the destructive forces of intermediacy, homelessness, and elusiveness.

"Your life is one long night," Oedipus says to the prophet Teiresias (Sophocles, *Oedipus Rex*, 374), and by this he alludes not merely to his real blindness. The seer has partaken of enlightenment, but that radiance is the light of night. Plato held divine possession to be one of the sources of the power of augury: in that context, Philo was subsequently to write: "For when the divine light sets, this other rises and shines, and this very frequently happens to the race of prophets; for the mind ($\nu o \tilde{\nu}s$) that is in us is removed from its place at the arrival of the divine Spirit ($\pi \nu \epsilon \acute{\nu} \mu \alpha \tau os$), but is again restored to its previous habitation when that Spirit departs, for it is contrary to holy law for what is mortal to dwell with what is immortal. On this account the setting of our reason ($\lambda o \gamma \iota \sigma \mu \acute{os}$), and the darkness which surrounds it, causes a trance and a heaven-inflicted madness ($\check{\epsilon} \kappa \sigma \tau \alpha \sigma \iota \nu \ \kappa \alpha \grave{\iota} \ \vartheta \epsilon o \phi \acute{o} \rho \eta \tau o \nu \ \mu \alpha \nu \acute{\iota} \alpha \nu$)" (*Who Is the Heir of Divine Things*, 264–65). Philo brands melancholia an illness, even though he connects ecstasy not just with divine possession but also with melancholia (249), thereby bringing home the connection between divinatory powers and melancholia. On falling into an ecstasy, one steps out of oneself without having the faintest idea of the direction of the excursion or the place of "arrival." Nor could one, since it is a condensate of moment, of the *now*, in which space and time, which imply directions and positions, are shrunk to nothing. Melancholics experience their life as consisting of a series of such moments, and scanning the world from that point of view, they give proof positive of a gift for prophecy. By virtue of

---

12. $\vartheta \epsilon o \phi \acute{o} \rho \eta \tau os$, theophrast: a god conveyor. Aeschylus describes Cassandra thus in his play *Agamemnon*.

their singular position, they become immersed in the process of "becoming," and from there they speak to us who are purely observers of this process and, furthermore, are able to interpret it only after the event by freezing its individual moments. Prophets are immersed in the process of coming into being; for them, existence is constant change. The name of dark, mysterious Heraclitus appears before us, the Heraclitus who, according to Diogenes Laertius, left some of his works unfinished because of his melancholia and who held wise men (that is, prophets) in great esteem. Despondent at seeing the contingency of unambiguous things, taking note of the struggle of being and nonbeing, and suffering on that account, Heraclitus could himself be called a prophet in a profound sense of the word, because when he asserts, "It is not better for men to obtain all they wish" (Freeman, *Ancilla*, 32, frag. 110), he then testifies to a most profound talent for inverse prophecy. Anyone who participates in the process of coming into being will inevitably glimpse the doom of death—not the death that will befall us at some appointed hour, but that which is constantly threatening us and shapes our every moment. Heraclitus writes of mortal immortals, and immortal mortals—in other words, about the relativity of life and death. A true prophet is not a person with the ability to foretell what is going to happen *tomorrow*, but one who can tell what is happening *today*; a person who opens up our own inner self to our gaze, not someone who confronts us with an outer self that will be realized some day. "Know thyself," the ancient Greeks could read on the façade of the sanctuary of Apollo at Delphi. The future within us, not without: we make the future into the future, or in other words, we are not at the mercy of time but solely of ourselves. True prophets, St. Francis of Assisi would later teach Brother Leo, "if they . . . had the gift of prophecy . . . could reveal, not only all future things, but likewise the secrets of all consciences and all souls" (*The Little Flowers*, 8). That is why Empedocles names the prophets of all men dwelling on the earth as the first of the four most important vocations, followed by hymn writers, physicians, and chieftains—

those who, in their own manner, likewise see it as their business in life to spy out the formation and principles of our lives. That is why Plato uses the passive voice of the verb "to foretell" (μαντεύω) in the case of poetry and philosophy. By use of the participle μαντεύεσθαι, he refers to the inner exaltation and transfiguration with which the poet and the philosopher, in the last analysis, assist in revealing not so much future events as the truth lying concealed in the depths of the present. A prophet is present *within* what he speaks of and does not just experience it by maintaining a neutral relation to it, from the outside,[13] which is why he is better placed than anyone to perceive the mysteries of existence, which for ordinary people is a mere given, lacking any sort of mystery.[14] A *prophet* (μάντις) is kin not just etymologically but also by predestination to a *mad* person (μαντικός), who, from another point of view, is a twin of the *melancholic,* and that kinship shows that all three are parts of a connection that has been forgotten in our present-day culture: the fortune-teller has become a charlatan, a mad person mentally ill, and the melancholic just moody.

A melancholic stands on the borderline between being and nonbeing, which is how the prophet and the madman were characterized, and one might so characterize melancholic heroes as well. The case of Bellerophon, however, shows that this border position arms the melancholic with knowledge, insight, and wisdom. If that is compared with what has been said about prophecy and divine madness, that knowledge can be considered the deepest possible, and one can also trace the beginnings of philosophy itself to there. In one of Aristotle's early dialogues that is extant in fragmentary form (*On Philoso-*

---

13. Aristotle likewise indicates the inner feelings nourished by the gods with the verb "to foretell": μαντεία περὶ τὸν θεόν.

14. In his *Poetics,* Aristotle expounds that a dramatist must himself be sensible of the sufferings of his protagonists; the dramatist is a μαντικός, prophet; thus here, too, a prophet's chief task is not to divulge things that are to come, but to uncover the laws of existence.

phy), he traces the love of sagacity historically to ancient Greek theology, to the Orphic doctrines, and the magi of Persia, and claims that
the acquisition of philosophy is a process akin to initiation into the
mysteries (think of Heraclitus, who, after his own initiation, became
mad, melancholic, and penetrating in vision), and, like Plato, calls
those initiated in the mysteries true philosophers. We have seen that
Plato indicates the enthusiasm of poets and philosophers with the
passive voice of the verb "to prophesy," and the young Aristotle also
considers *passivity* to be a characteristic state of those who were to be
initiated into the Eleusinian rites (that is, predisposed to philosophy
and thus suited to being readied for a philosophical way of looking at
things): "Those who are being initiated into the mysteries are to be
expected not to learn anything ($\mu\alpha\vartheta\epsilon\tilde{\iota}\nu$) but to suffer some change,
to be put into a certain condition ($\pi\alpha\vartheta\epsilon\tilde{\iota}\nu$)" (Aristotle, *Aristotelis qui
ferebantur librorum fragmenta*, frag. 15). "Pathos" means at once pas-
sion, fate, suffering, and an intriguing experience — that is to say, an
inner identification with things, suffering them in the widest sense
of the word, as opposed to *mathesis*, mental discipline, the objective,
rational comprehension of things (though the adjective "rational" is
hardly appropriate for characterizing the process). Pathos, or its exer-
cise ($\pi\alpha\vartheta\epsilon\tilde{\iota}\nu$), leads to so-called illumination ($\check{\epsilon}\lambda\lambda\alpha\mu\psi\iota\varsigma$), which for
Plato was the key to seeing the Ideas, and for Aristotle, a more pro-
found understanding of Being. A true philosopher is thus also a soothsayer — in line with the expression taken from *Philebus*, he too examines the process of coming into being — but since, as a soothsayer, he
is strongly linked with madness, he is at the same time also melancholic. He too, like the *prophet* Heraclitus, stands on the boundary
between being and nonbeing, and is compelled as a result to return
constantly to where he started: to negativity, which, however, is not
the converse of a state of being regarded as positive but *being* itself,
totally positive reality. "I know I know nothing" — that statement by
melancholic Socrates (for Aristotle thought of him also as that) is no
mere play on words but irony engendered by his astonishment. And

his reply when asked whether it was worth his getting married or not, as recorded by Diogenes Laertius (bk. 2, 33), was: "Whatever you do you will regret it," once again testifying to a philosopher's profound sense of mission: he leads all who desire instruction to the boundary of being and nonbeing not in order to drive them to despair but to lead them to self-understanding. (The diabolical inference that this is precisely what will drive one to despair was the handiwork of the Baroque way of looking at things, more particularly of Kierkegaard, Socrates' most faithful latter-day disciple.) "What shall be done to the man who has never had the wit to be idle during his whole life," Socrates says, "but has been careless of what the many care about— wealth, and family interests, and military offices, and speaking in the assembly, and magistracies, and plots, and parties. Reflecting that I was really too honest a man to follow in this way and live, I did not go where I could do no good to you or to myself" (Plato, *Apology*, 36b–c). (It was likewise recorded of another melancholic philosopher, Empedocles, that he held freedom dear, disdained all power, and declined the royal post that he was offered.)

Melancholic Socrates was an obsessed (*manic*) seeker of truth, and his madness, the love of wisdom (he was a *philosopher*), as well as the deep melancholia stemming from that, gave him some insight into the most profound secret. The accusation leveled against him by the Athenians—Socrates was infringing the law "by speculating about the heaven above, and searching into the earth beneath" (*Apology*, 18b)—was true at a deeper level, since Socrates declared more than once that his daemon (δαίμων), or familiar spirit, would always tell him what was to come. Demons, who became evil spirits only much later, were not only responsible for the future but were also the source of possession, and perhaps the main cause of Socrates' melancholia was his connection, never fully clarified, with the other world. That was what drove Bellerophon mad, just as unapproachable destiny troubled Ajax, and homelessness between earthly and divine existence first landed Heracles in madness and later onto the bonfire he himself had built. The same irresolvability troubled Empedocles of Sicily, whose name likewise figures in Aristotle's list of melancholics: "It is not possible to draw near (to god) even with the eyes, or to take hold of him with our hands, which in truth is the best highway of persuasion into the mind of man; for he has no human head fitted to a body, nor do two shoots branch out from the trunk, nor has he feet, nor swift legs, nor hairy parts, but he is sacred and ineffable mind alone, darting through the whole world with swift thoughts" (*Fragments*, 344). It was this that clouded Bellerophon's mind, and Empedocles can be considered to have been possessed in his own way: he may not have had doubts about the gods, but as mystics are wont to do, he made their existence almost inconceivable. He declared himself to be a god who, because of sins committed in an earlier life, was obliged to remain far from the world of the gods for a long time, wandering along the weary pathway of life. "But why do I lay weight on these things, as though I were doing some great thing, if I be superior to mortal, perishing men?" (113): he was an immortal god (θεὸς ἄμβροτος) who was fully aware of every enigma of earthly life, and through that knowledge he was able to observe everything as if from outside. "For scant means of acquiring knowledge are scattered among the members of the body; and many are the evils that break in to blunt the edge of studious thought. And gazing on a little portion of life that is not life, swift to meet their fate, they rise and are borne away like smoke, persuaded only of that on which each one chances as he is driven this way and that, but the whole he vainly boasts he has found" (2). Human existence is eternal suffering ("O eternal mystery, what we are / And what we seek, we cannot find; and what / We find, that we are not"—this is Hölderlin in the opening scene of his play *The Death of Empedocles*), and like the melancholic heroes, Empedocles wanders in the region that lies beyond human existence but falls short of the divine. His knowledge gave him the right to form an opinion about everything, but that same knowledge also cast him out of all contexts of earthly existence: for he who sees through everything will find his home—or more precisely, his homelessness—in the infinite. Whether the historical person named Empedocles really did know everything is an open question (his contemporaries certainly thought so, and Lucretius was later to write: *Ut vix humana videatur stirpe creatus*—"He scarcely seems to be from the mortal race" [*De rerum natura*, bk. 1, 733]). More importantly, he himself was convinced of that. But that conviction was sufficient for his fate to be the same as that of the heroes: his superhuman, extraordinary achievement (he was the greatest physician of his day) and his inner state, that of an outcast (he was a philosopher and therefore mad, which is to say, ecstatic), were inseparable. "For me as well this life became a poem," Hölderlin puts in his mouth (act 1, scene 4), with a touch of Romantic bias toward apparent roundedness (for what appears from the outside as a poem is from the inside an aggregate of torn prose). There is no roundedness; in a portrait of Empedocles in Orvieto Cathedral, Luca Signorelli depicts the philosopher leaning out a window while examining the stars, and in so doing his figure virtually demolishes the fixed rules of Renaissance perspective. *That* is Empedocles, the person felt to be a kindred spirit by Hölderlin and Novalis, and the person about whom Nietzsche wanted to write a tragedy (in measureless prose!). His melancholia was multiply compound: his belief in his own divinity made him obsessed in the Platonic sense; his search for the secrets of death carried him beyond the boundaries of life: Empedocles instructed Pausanias, his pupil, on how a person in a state of suspended animation should be restored to life, and according to a story reported by Heraclides of Pontus, he had saved many people from Persephone's underworld empire. On reaching the border between being and nonbeing as an oracle, he had a glimpse into the secrets of life. Thus, his death was not an ordinary affair: for anyone able to make life and perishing relative, death is not death but a consummation. Not in a Christian sense, of course, but in accordance with the beliefs of antiquity: life and death become of secondary importance when compared with the exclusivity of being. Being lays a claim on us even beyond death: recognizing this is at once uplifting and depressing. Inevitably, two kinds of reports of Empedocles' death have remained extant. According to one of them, early one morning after a sacrificial feast, the philosopher could not be found by his companions. A servant recounted to them that he had been awakened at midnight by the sound of Empedocles' voice, and on rising from his bed, he had seen a light flickering like a flaming torch in the sky. Empedocles' pupil Pausanias unraveled the mystery of the celestial light: the gods had summoned to their presence the philosopher, who left the earth behind him, not as a human but as a god. According to the second version, he had not been summoned by the gods: he brought his life to an end voluntarily by jumping into the crater of Etna in order thereby to prove his divinity. This *salto mortale*, however, has a deeper meaning: it was looked on by ancient Greeks as one of the forms of ecstasy, hence (bear in mind the connection between ecstasy, melancholia, and divine furor) a fine death ($\epsilon\dot{v}\vartheta\acute{a}\nu\alpha\tau\sigma\varsigma$); and at the same time, death by fire brought about purification. A person committed to die in flames was purified ($\kappa\alpha\vartheta\acute{a}\rho\sigma\iota\sigma\nu\ \pi\tilde{v}\rho$) of earthly dross. For that reason, fire was a source of a higher order of life.[15] According to Greek religious beliefs, Heracles' death by fire, which was an inevitable consequence of his melancholia, guaranteed him immortality, just as it was to do for Empedocles.[16] That is how fire becomes a source of

---

15. In his *Geography*, Strabo describes the case of an Indian, a Brahmin, who *laughed* as he committed himself to the flames in Eleusis (!) and on whose tomb was this inscription: "Zarmonochegas, an Indian, a native of Bargos, having immortalized himself according to the custom of his country, here lies" (bk. 15, pt. 1, 73.). The same mode of self-immolation was chosen by Croesus, the last king of Lydia (who, incidentally, considered himself to be a descendant of Heracles), and the Phoenicians Hamilkar and Sardanapalus, who hoped for resurrection for themselves and their people by doing so.

16. Josephus Flavius in *Antiquities of the Jews* calls the rite of death by fire "the

higher life: it is itself logos (Heraclitus).[17] Empedocles' self-immolation went ahead under the spell of "resurrection," and it led him out of the world of earthly existence, which in Plato's view was a prison, and in Empedocles' view a cave. (As Schiller wrote about Heracles, who was translated to the other world after death by fire: "casting off his earthly frame" ["The Ideal and Life"]). Resurrection, however, does not necessarily follow the moment of death; just as a soothsayer, standing outside time, can obtain an overview of human time itself, resurrection is not simply an event that occurs in time: it proceeds outside time. It eclipses life just as it does death. Just as death does not imply resurrection for everybody, few partake of resurrection in their life as well. As the word itself suggests, resurrection is a physical as well as a spiritual phenomenon; its Greek equivalent (ἔγερσις) also means "awakening," that is, stepping out of the previous state. Since that stepping out (ἔκστασις) is connected with the moment, it is therefore absolutely *present tense* (not just in the sense of the verbal tense). From all this it follows that resurrection is granted to those who recognize not only the laws of our existence in time but also those of our existence prevailing over time itself, and who see its possibilities and its limits. These are the soothsayers, the mad, the extraordinary people, and the philosophers—those whom we can describe in one word as melancholics.

At every moment, the life of a melancholic partakes of resurrection—that is why he does not die, at least not in the physical sense. A life that encloses resurrection within itself is a complete life and is therefore threatened not by death but by ordinary life, which rejects the ever-present possibility of resurrection, that is, of ecstasy.

resurrection of Heracles"; moreover, in some places Heracles was worshipped as a sun god.

17. That notion was preserved by Christianity: in the New Testament, John the Baptist said that Jesus would "baptize [people] with the Holy Spirit" (Mark 1:8), and in some versions also with fire.

That is why melancholic heroes were misanthropes (as heroes, they differed from everybody else anyway), while melancholic philosophers, if not expressly misanthropic, looked down on those who were stuck in darkness and ignorance, for once the soul reaches the state of knowledge (in Plato's vocabulary, the invisible realm, which is akin to it), then it becomes perfect, and as the initiated say, their remaining time is spent in truth and among the gods (see *Phaedrus*, 249c–d). A person who partakes of resurrection rises out of the world of earthly beings toward *real beings* (εἰς τὸ ὂν ὄντως, 247e). Ascent, however, like the Platonic notion of anamnesis, should be interpreted as a metaphor and, over and above its literal meaning, should be related to earthly existence per se: to unfurling and understanding our life here, in this world. That, however, as we have seen, is given only to those blessed with certain abilities — to the elect who, because they see past everything, become isolated from others, and whose knowledge and vision make them outcasts. This outcast state is dual: not only are they excluded from the world of others, but they must also step out of themselves. On that account, their knowledge is not uplifting but disheartening, depressing; they are incapable of living like others — since they see everything, they also cannot forget.[18] Soothsayers, with their divine knowledge and earthly fate, maniacs well-versed in the realm of invisible things but threatened by illness, philosophers examining the turning of being and nonbeing into each other; in short, all those who are melancholic are solitary, and since they are partakers not just of human but also of superhuman existence, even death will fail to bring an end to their solitude.

That is not the solitude of the Romantics of the modern age. The workaday world of the Greeks did make attempts to break through the carapace of the solitude of melancholics and, in contrast with the modern age, strove to master, or at least grasp, their point of view.

---

18. The Greek word equivalent to "truth" is ἀλήθεια, meaning "not subjected to forgetting," that is, removed from the dominion of Lethe.

The possibility of this-worldly resurrection, offered by the mysteries, was inseparable from the melancholic interpretation of existence, and although these mysteries themselves had seemingly nothing in common with melancholia, the way of looking at things and knowledge that the mysteries sought to offer to initiates pointed in the direction of melancholia.[19] The mysteries were therefore among the most daring experiments of Greek culture: they allowed thousands to partake of knowledge that would render them melancholics (that is, prophets, madmen, and philosophers). But the most fundamental law of human coexistence does not permit everyone to become omniscient, all-seeing, and so in the final analysis, solitary and isolated. For melancholia to overwhelm a person, it is necessary that others be free of it; to live in truth, it is necessary to be surrounded by a world of untruth;[20] for a person to be deeply penetrating, something has to be deep lying, there have to be both shallows and depths. Truth and knowledge are not given to all, they are not distributed on a democratic basis, whereas the mysteries were "democratic" institutions in both their political and intellectual aims.[21] For precisely this reason, they were the most baffling formations of Greek culture: as if they had attempted to mix fire and water, but the two nevertheless did not extinguish each other. Only a negligible fraction of the initiates became melancholic (though anyone who was melancholic had almost invariably been initiated). In other words, the mysteries per se were not directed at melancholia, but they did carry the potential for initiates to become melancholic. And not just that: they also

---

19. According to Galen, the gall bladder was an *organum plenum mysterii*—an "organ full of mystery"—just like melancholia, which is the epitome of mystery.

20. Admittedly in another context, Heidegger in *Being and Time* noted the predatory nature of the notion of truth.

21. Schopenhauer was only partially correct in seeing the aim of the ancient mysteries in the elect being separated from the mass. He was striving to discern the elitist attitudes of his own age in antiquity.

mark out a system of relations in which any melancholic can get en-
tangled. In the case of heroes, as we have seen, there is no manifest
reason for their melancholia, for if there were, a cure might also be
possible. Yet there are certain situations that can burst latent melancholia open (Achilles' armor is confiscated from Ajax, Bellerophon
ascends to the heavens, Heracles visits the underworld, etc.). In this
sense, the mysteries are borderline situations. Initiation, at least in the
view of Dio Chrysostom, was in effect tantamount to contemplating
the universe;[22] that is, initiates partook of the most profound knowledge. According to Plato, before the beginning of life on Earth, we
had been participants in the happiest initiation, that is, earthly initiation is already an intermediate act of a colossal drama, an evocation of an otherworldly, prenatal, and postmortem existence. In the
course of that evocation, the soul recollects everything it had once
seen while it consorted with the divine spirit, and for that reason —
one thinks here of the original meaning of the word "philosophy" —
"the mind of the philosopher alone has wings; and this is just, for he
is always, according to the measure of his abilities, clinging in recollection to those things in which God abides, and in beholding which
He is what He is" (*Phaedrus*, 249c). Only a person who makes proper
use of his recollections can lay claim to true knowledge; *only that
person* can be a complete person and can *partake of true initiation*
(τελέουςἀεὶ τελετὰς τελούμενος). Initiation makes a person learned;
the greatest knowledge, however, does not recognize the limits of
earthly existence: it draws into its own sphere the world of unearthli-
ness, of prenatal and postmortem existence. In a certain sense, then,
initiation is akin to soothsaying and resurrection: it places the initiate outside time, draws birth and death together into a single moment, and, as it were, complying with the doctrine of Thales, according to which there is no fundamental difference between life

---

22. That is meant literally in the case of the Mithraic mysteries: initiates symbolically ascend through the planetary spheres to the sun god Mithras.

and death, makes the opposition of the two relative. That was why Sophocles held those initiated in the mysteries to be the happiest: not only do they discover death in life, but in death they also come across life. The very word used for "initiation" (ἡ τελευτή) refers to stepping out of customary frameworks: it is related to the verb "to complete" or "to die" (τελευτάω),[23] its root being formed by the word τὸ τέλος, which means equally "goal," "end," "boundary," "decision," and "fulfillment." The initiate dies in a certain sense, or at least becomes intimate with death. The fourth-century author Firmicus Maternus, who nurtured hostile feelings toward the mysteries, referred to would-be initiates as *Homo moriturus.* Since death transports the initiate into the world of "truly existing" things, he is reborn: he turns his back on his previous life. For those initiated at Eleusis in ancient Greece, a happy existence in the hereafter was guaranteed, but the symbolic-voluntary acceptance of death[24] was a precondition for gaining salvation (σωτηρία). Death itself was the supreme mystery: as reported by Plutarch, in a work entitled *On the Soul,* Themistios wrote, "The soul (at the point of death) has the same experience as those who are being initiated into the great mysteries; for that reason, a similarity subsists between the verbs 'to die' and 'to be initiated' and the actions they designate" (quoted by Edgar Wind, *Pagan Mysteries in the Renaissance,* 181). According to Socrates, sound philosophizing consists in the preparation for death, whereas Pindar writes as follows about the Eleusinian initiates: "Blessed is he who has seen these things before he goes beneath the earth; for he understands the end of mortal life, and the beginning (of a new life) given of Zeus" (frag. 102).

Time appears in a new light for initiates: fading away and coming into existence, life and death, do not follow each other in time but unite in the moment—time itself is merely a product of practical divi-

---

23. Premature death, for instance, is προτελευτή in Greek.

24. One might add that the Greeks did not have a doctrine of redemption that was of *general* validity.

sions. According to Empedocles, the two mainsprings of existence are love and strife (φιλία and νεῖκος), that is, union and separation, which permeate all natural phenomena. In the Eleusinian mysteries, the initiates venerated Demeter and her daughter Persephone, and the figures of those two divinities are themselves symbols of the interfusion of life and death. For one thing, Demeter was the goddess of cereals, which is to say, of fertility, but for another, she was also the personification of infinite sadness. After Hades had abducted her virgin daughter and taken her to the underworld, her thoughts were constantly straying to that region (the cultic name of the dead in Athens was δημήτριοι). In her lifestyle, too, Persephone was captive of that duality: she was compelled to spend part of the year in Hades, but by the permission of Zeus, she was allowed to spend the other part among the divinities on high. On the one hand, she was the queen of the underworld (that is one of the possible significations of her name; "destructive through killing," πέρθειν + φόνος);[25] on the other hand, like her mother, she is also related to flowers and crops. As a goddess of both death and fertility, she spans the universe; love and strife appear jointly in her figure.[26] As a member of the divine underworld, like the other chthonic deities (Demeter, Dionysius, Hades), she embodies and unites opposites in one person; as a goddess of the soil (χθών), she is nevertheless a representative of the darker side of existence. The path of initiates into the mysteries therefore called for sacrifices: death was not just a deliverance but also a *destruction*; birth was not just the creation but also the *demise* of something. The knowledge of prophets, madmen, and philosophers produced melancholia because it led them to a point of ultimate ignorance, to riddles undecipherable for mortals. They embody in themselves the irresolvability that is typical of the gods venerated in the mysteries—their

---

25. Hölderlin associates her name with light on the basis of the word περσέφοσσα.

26. Persephone's home was considered to be Akragas (modern Agrigento) in Sicily—the birthplace of Empedocles.

existence concentrates every aspect of human existence in *one* moment. (It was not by chance that the twelve labors of Heracles, who was honored along with the chthonic gods, were interpreted as the sun's passage through the zodiac. Heracles was just as much at home in the winter and in the night as in the summer and in the day: he rescued Theseus and Alcestis from Hades, but inflicted death on his closest blood relatives.)

The dual nature of initiation is nicely illustrated by Lucius, the narrator of Apuleius's *Golden Ass:* "I reached the very gates of death and, treading Proserpine's threshold, yet passed through all the elements and returned. I have seen the sun at midnight shining brightly. I have entered the presence of the gods below and the presence of the gods above, and I have paid due reverence before them" (ch. 9). Apuleius deliberately mentions the sun shining at midnight: he has in mind the mysteries of Egypt. According to their way of thinking, the glorified dead follow the sun god, who likewise steps into the realm of the dead (the initiates). This idea was not unfamiliar to the Greeks: according to Pindar, for example, the sun illuminates the realm of the dead at night. In the mystery of Mithras, Helios is evoked as an underworld god who — according to an extant text of the Mithras liturgy, resides in the realm of the dead, namely, in the Elysian Fields.[27] At the same time, Apuleius, being a skilled connoisseur of magic, was well aware that the Babylonians worshipped Saturn, the planet stationed firmly in the same place, as the nocturnal equivalent of the sun. Its light might be weak, but they still called it brilliant, shining, and other cultures adopted this tradition. According to Plutarch's record,

---

27. For the Mithras liturgy, see Wolfgang Schultz, *Dokumente der Gnosis,* 83. Nearer the present day, Antonin Artaud regarded the sun as the god of death, though the true manifestation of that was the total death of the sun (that is, the light), which leads to "the rite of the black night and of the *eternal* death of the sun," and from there to an ecstasy that enhances life to an unbearable intensity (see his poem "Tutuguri: The Rite of the Black Sun").

the Egyptians held it to be the Night Watch (νυκτοῦρος), the Greeks called it "the visible" (ὁ Φαίνων) and also "the sun star" (ὁ Ἡλίου ἄστηρ), and the Indians worshipped it as the son of the sun. The first-century CE Roman poet and astrologer Marcus Manilius placed the sun and Saturn at the opposite ends of the world's axis, and in his opinion, viewed from Saturn the world appeared from a converse parallactic angle. This gains its true meaning when we add that in the days of Hellenism in Rome of the first and second centuries CE, astrologers and philosophers discovered a profound correspondence between the planet Saturn and melancholy (everyone born under the sign of Saturn was melancholic). Consequently, when Lucius, in the course of his initiation into the mysteries experienced the spectacle of the midnight sun (rite of the black sun), by making that note in his *Apologia*, without lavishing any superfluous words on it, addressed those who understood what he was saying: alluding to a profound, never completely apprehensible affinity of saturnine melancholia and the mysteries, and in particular by mentioning Saturn, he made manifest what, for the Greeks, was a latent possibility contained in the mysteries.[28] And when festivities were held for the gods of the dead in Rome in December, the holy month of Saturn and the last month of the year, then the Saturn-mysteries-melancholia connection was made all the more unequivocal: the Romans believed that in that month, the inner essence of the world revealed itself, while on 17 December, the day of the Saturnalia festival, the souls of the dead, along with all the things resting in the soil, would rise up, and with that resurrection a demonic, lawless force would be liberated.[29]

---

28. In a work bearing the title *The Mysteries*, the Neoplatonist Iamblichus writes about casting spells with light or the awakening of light (φωταγωγία), which he regarded as a state of enlightenment and which modern theosophy identifies as glimpsing the light of the sun at midnight.

29. Some legends claim that the Temple of Saturn in the Forum in Rome was founded by none other than Heracles-Hercules.

The Greek equivalent of Saturn was Cronus (whom Plutarch classed as one of the chthonic divinities), and the Athenians likewise celebrated his day, the Kronia, as a time when everything broke loose. By Hellenic times, the notion had arisen that Cronus was the son not of Helios but of Uranus and thus, on the paternal side, was a half-brother to Lyssa, goddess of rage, fury, and madness. And to cast the net even wider, what could be more characteristic of the Greek belief system and its profound conception of existence than the fact that according to Orphic theology, melancholic Cronus possessed powers of prophecy: he was a *promantis*, that is, a foreseeing spirit or prophet who could foretell the secrets of being. (During the period of Hellenism, the view would gain ground that all who were able to foretell the future and were familiar with the esoteric rites of the mysteries were born under the sign of Saturn, the melancholy planet.) Thus emerges the logically almost incomprehensible and yet coherent and indestructible net that encircles melancholia, the nodes of which are soothsaying, madness, philosophy, initiation into the mysteries, the relativization of life and death, and resurrection, all in the sense that it had carried in antiquity.

A person who possesses knowledge is isolated from people who do not. A prophet speaks to those who see only dimly at best; to the sane minded, the thought processes of the mad cannot be followed; the path to the mysteries is common for everyone, but toward the end of the initiation, the crowd starts to break up, and in the course of the final acts, the would-be initiates make their own way alone. The mysteries are democratic, yet initiates could justifiably speak of election. The path is open for everyone, but not everyone reaches its end.[30] The end, as we know, is the beginning itself. A person who has wisdom has a synoptic view of everything; things uncover their hid-

---

30. The initial mysteries in Crete were public; it was from there that they spread out to other parts of Greece, where they became secret.

den face, and the initiate is transported into a new world that differs from any he had hitherto known. A consequence of the lethargy associated with Dionysian ecstasy is, in Nietzsche's view, that a Greek's "longing went higher, beyond the gods, he denied existence along with its colourful glistening mirror of gods" ("The Dionysian Worldview," 89). The denial of existence, however, is not an absolute denial: the world opened up by longing is a new, admittedly never fulfilled existence. It differs qualitatively from all those that had existed up to that point: everything closed and confined collapses within it, and since deep insight reigns here, there is nothing that could gird itself to an observer's gaze with the appearance of permanence. A person acquainted with wisdom, a prophet or madman, that is, a melancholic, is not lonely on account of longing for separation, but because he cannot live in any other way: it takes an extraordinary effort on the part of those who see through things to close their eyes and pretend there is nothing beyond that. Those who know something can play ignorant only at the expense of their own intellects. The very word itself, language, this objectified projection of the intellect, comes undone: it loses its definitiveness, and if language is a possibility for others, it will be an obstacle for the melancholic: "If you continue to be not too particular about names, you will be all the richer in wisdom when you are an old man," Plato writes (*Statesman*, 261e). For anyone who glances into the inner mysteries of existence, words lose their signification; they crack and reveal their own fallibility. The melancholic is compelled to silence. Aristotle noticed the outer mark of that: "Some maintain a complete silence, especially those atrabilious subjects [i.e., melancholics] who are out of their mind (ἐκστατικοί)" (*Problemata physica*, bk. 30, 953b). That external silence, conspicuous to a listening stranger, leads on to the essence of the mysteries: initiates have to keep quiet about all that they have seen (the very word "mystery" derives from the verb μύειν, "to shut up"). Homer writes of the ceremony for Demeter:

> She [Demeter] revealed to them the way to perform the sacred
>   rites, and she pointed out the ritual to all of them
> —the holy ritual, which it is not at all possible to ignore, to find
>   out about,
> or to speak out. The great awe of the gods holds back any
>   speaking out.
>
> .   .   .   .
>
> But whoever is uninitiated in the rites, whoever takes no part
>   in them, will never get a share of those sorts of things
>   [that the initiated get],
> once they die, down below in the dank realms of mist.

(Hymn to Demeter, 476–82)

Knowledge acquired in the mysteries was unutterable (ἄρρητος). Indeed, even the names of the priests were sacred: it was forbidden to speak their names, and even in official documents only their patronymic and birthplace were mentioned. The main teaching of the mysteries was likewise not related verbally but through suggestion (ἐποπτεία); the name for the priests literally means "holy presentation" (ἱεροφάντης).[31] The order to keep silent arrives from the outside, though anyone who had been initiated had no need to be ordered: he would fall silent not for fear of being overheard by eavesdroppers or the curious, but out of an inner need: "In speaking we have men as teachers, but in keeping silent we have gods" (Plutarch, *De moralia*, 6:417).[32] That inner silence, the need to keep quiet, strips down the

---

31. "Let us visit the dear land of Cecrops," Aristophanes writes in *The Clouds*, "where the secret rites are celebrated, where the mysterious sanctuary flies open to the initiate" (299–300).

32. The Egyptians venerated the crocodile as a symbol of divine silence on account of its remarkably short tongue. The Greeks had a separate god for mystic silence: Harpokrates, with the index finger held to his mouth.

world to such a degree that it almost vanishes into nothingness. We end up close to mysticism, the representatives of which, by no accident, have usually been recruited from among the melancholics of this world. "Accept my reason's offerings pure, from soul and heart for aye stretched up to Thee," one reads in a Hermetic dialogue from the *Corpus Hermeticum*—"O Thou unutterable, unspeakable, Whose Name naught but the Silence can express" (Hermes Trismegistus, "Pœmandres: The Shepherd of Men," sec. 31). An *infinite* knowledge of (or love for) God can guide one to the unspeakability of God—and that profound, sincere feeling of ineffability can *nullify* God himself. "God is all Nothingness, knoweth not here nor now; / The more we grope the more elusive he will grow," Angelus Silesius was later to write (*Alexandrines*, bk. 1, no. 25). It is this experience of ungraspability that runs at the bottom of the worldview of the Greek melancholics; if I am at one and the same time more and less than myself (at one and the same time a possibility and reality of myself), if being is burdened by nonbeing, the present by the future, life by death, resurrection by extinction, then one cannot speak about the world, because there is nothing to talk about. This is the greatest danger that the mysteries present to Greek public life: those who cannot bring themselves to a recognition of the relativity of life and death, the exclusiveness of desire, must be commanded to keep silent, but those who can reach that point do not need to be commanded: having sunk into perpetual silence, recognizing transience in becoming, deficiency in completeness, they are irretrievably lost for the rest of mankind.

The Greek physician Aretaeus of Cappadocia regarded the fear of gods and demons as one of the signs of melancholia. The lives of melancholic heroes and philosophers, however, prove that a loathing for the gods is sometimes stronger than fear: "Not even the gods fight against necessity" (a saying of the lyric poet Simonides of Ceos, quoted by Plato in *Protagoras*, 345d); an ambiguous relationship with divinity is possibly the most characteristic feature of Greek melancholics. On the one hand, man is an imperfect copy of god, but on the other hand, by virtue of his intellect, he is also divine. Put that way, this idea is very Christian in inspiration — just as the notion of an earthly vale of tears was also not alien to Greek culture. According to Empedocles, everything springs from *suffering* caused by the world, from *sadness* caused by human injustice. Ancient Thracians wept on greeting newborn babies and put on celebrations in honor of the dead — the melancholic view of life was hardly unknown to them. On seeing the human condition, melancholic Heraclitus wept, whereas the similarly melancholic Democritus burst into fits of laughter, though as Socrates hints in the final section of the *Symposium* (223d), it was most natural to the Greek spirit to see tragedy and comedy as closely related. After all, crying and laughter have their common wellspring in all-consuming despair. Man is mortal, although he knows what immortality is — for all their internal kinship, death and immortality cannot be confused. To Greek thinking, there was nothing new under the sun;[33] death and immortality were conceivable only within the borders of this closed world. The melancholia of heroes and philosophers was rooted in this: their intellect was drawn to infinity, indeterminacy, the lifting of constraints and borders, disorderliness in the widest sense, but the exclusivity of the world, the ultimate boundedness and orderliness of existence, made this impossible.[34] "[Ananke], necessity or fate personified ($\acute{\eta}$ $\mathring{\alpha}\nu\acute{\alpha}\gamma\kappa\eta$),

---

33. Aristotle, for instance, determined that imagining resembled sensing in that it was a movement brought into being as a result of the latter (*On the Soul*, 427).

34. Originally, "cosmos" denoted not only "the universe" but also "order" — Homer uses the word in the sense of "battle order" — and so it essentially alludes to closedness. Although the notion of infinity was not unknown to Greek thinking, Aristotle distinguished between actual and potential infinities and was willing to acknowledge only the latter. From the point of view of human reason, he said, infinity in the sense of indeterminacy was imperfection, and thus it was out of the question for thinking to arrive at indeterminacy through an infinite chain of cause and

binds together our existence," says Socrates in Plato's dialogue *Theaetetus* (160b): while everything closes concentrically into one, man experiences his uniqueness as exclusiveness just as much as helplessness. His inner boundlessness awakens him not just to his life's restrictedness but also to its attendant burden: the fact that the whim of an unknown force has, as it were, handed him over to existence. This force has entrusted him with existence, which he now cannot get rid of. This whim, this personified fate (Ananke), is standing guard over his existence like a Fury, and having received life from her, he can escape only at the cost of his life; and Ananke, the goddess of inevitability and necessity, behaves like one of the Furies according to Orphic notions as well.

> For powerful Necessity holds it in the bonds of a Limit, which constrains it round about, because it is decreed by divine law that Being shall not be without boundary. . . .
>
> But since there is a (*spatial*) Limit, it is complete on every side, like the mass of a well-rounded sphere, equally balanced from its centre in every direction; for it is not bound to be at all either greater or less in this direction or that. . . . For, in all directions equal to itself, it reaches its limits uniformly.
>
> (Parmenides, *Poem*, frag. 8, in Freeman, *Ancilla*, 44)

But if there is not, and will not be, anything beyond existence, then is it conceivable that the shackles of limits would coil around it? And does not anything that lies beyond the limits equally belong to the existing? And if the only thing abiding beyond the boundaries is Ananke, holding in her grasp the whole of existence, then does that not imply that existence is permeated by Ananke? For a melan-

---

effect. Needless to say, melancholics considered the chain of cause and effect to be one of the forms, albeit not the sole form, of explanation for being, and thus they did not see sheer imperfection in indeterminacy.

cholic, totality is condensed into Ananke; and it is then that he is overwhelmed by the desire to escape from her authority, to step outside existence, but it is also then that the realization dawns on him that he would flee in vain: Ananke is nestling there too. By being at the mercy of existence, he is also at the mercy of himself.

Such recognition drove melancholics to despair, but it also compelled them to accomplish breathtaking feats. Bellerophon wished to rise above everything, and he had to pay a price for his hubris.[35] "Strive not to become Zeus. . . . / Mortals must be content with mortality," Pindar remarks (*Isthmia*, 5). Bellerophon wanted to step outside life's circles of moderation, presumably for many of the same reasons that Antiphon the sophist held life to be deplorable: "The whole of life is wonderfully open to complaint, my friend; it has nothing remarkable (περιττός), great or noble, but all is feeble, brief-lasting, and mingled with sorrows" (Freeman, *Ancilla*, 150, frag. 51). Bellerophon wanted to *believe* in the nonexistence of the gods, and since they had flung him back to earth, his faith lived on as a sense of loss. What he sensed was not the absence of a definite existing entity; instead, earthly existence itself had become an absence. There is no way of knowing the absence of what, specifically; the all-embracing, enclosed world is capable of successfully concealing any absence. For Bellerophon, however, this absence became an exclusive attitude to life, though he was not the least comforted by this; indeed, if anything, it made him still more unfortunate. It was as if he were falling interminably into a bottomless chasm. The explanation for his sense of absence, as with other melancholics', we, the children of a no less depressing age, can only guess at: the finitude of their world depressed them and rendered them incapable of action. (The Spartan Lysander be-

---

35. Etymologically, "hubris" is derived from roots in Proto-Indo-European. It is cognate with *ud* = "up," "out," and with *guer-* = Latin *gravis* "heavy," "grave," "weighty," the combined meaning of which is approximately to set about something with all one's might, to stake *everything* on *one* item.

came melancholic because he had seized for himself every power that was attainable, from which point onward he was at a loss what to do.) Antiphon had good reason to feel that life lacked overabundance (περιττός), and melancholic Empedocles saw fit to write: "In the All there is nothing empty, and nothing too full (περισσόν)" (*Fragments*, 13). Melancholics are prominent (περιττοί) precisely because they are too full of life; because of them, existence overflows itself. That explains their unappeasable sense of absence: since they have left the world of moderation, overflowing is inconceivable without being emptied. The universe is damaged in their person; hence, melancholics' sense of being among the elect, but also their self-hatred to the point of self-annihilation. That makes them strong and outstanding, but also exceedingly frail. Their strength is infinite, because they have gained knowledge of the end, but they are unhappy, since having experienced the ephemeral nature of humans, they have lost their trust in existence. Their strength and frailty, their unhappiness and their heroism, cannot be detached from each other. This leads us back once again to the starting point of our argument, to the Aristotelian question "Why is it that all those who have become eminent in philosophy or politics or poetry or the arts are clearly melancholic?"

Chapter 2

IN THE PRISON OF THE HUMORS

The Aristotelian hypothesis concerning melancholia was omi-
nous in spite of its attempt to hold the extremes in check with the
moderating force of the middle. The example of melancholics shows
that they turn away from the world, and all the fixed achievements
of civilization become questionable for them, whereas their indisput-
able capacities for learning and astuteness make them solitary and
withdrawn. Not surprisingly, melancholia evoked in part envy and in
part contempt from ordinary people, and the Aristotelian hypothesis
itself ended up in the parentheses of that dual judgment. The sign
of that contempt was a scoffing that dismissed melancholia, whereas
that of envy was a striving to "tame" melancholia, to present it as a
condition typical of ordinary people as well. In the age of Hellenism,
some (Cicero, for instance) were either astonished by the assertion
that melancholics were extraordinary individuals or they mocked it.
The Stoics, for example, held melancholia to be a humdrum disease
that deprived its victims of their senses. In his biography of Lysander,
Plutarch used the word "melancholia" in the sense of "crazy," while
Empedocles was widely held to be half-witted.[1] Seneca characteristically misinterprets Aristotle and in so doing anticipates the spirit
of the Middle Ages (he credits Aristotle with the thought *Nullum
magnum ingenium sine mixtura dementiae fuit*—"There has been

---

1. In *Dialogues of the Dead* (20), he is given the following retort by Lucian:

MENIPPUS: Tell me, my brazen-slippered friend, what induced you to jump
   into the crater?
EMPEDOCLES: I did it in a fit of melancholy.

no great genius without some touch of madness," translating "melan-choly" as "dementia"). The late Roman age was in agreement with the early Christians in denying that melancholics had prophetic abilities, seeing divination as the ravings of people sick with fever. Such was the opinion of a self-confident age that placed too much trust in reason: the thirst for knowledge can be satisfied *within* the bonds of existence. Querying the conditions of perception was therefore an unhealthy, lamentably uncalled-for endeavor. But there was no denying the fact that intellectual abilities went hand in hand with melancholia. Those abilities, therefore, in line with the democratization always associated with practical notions of knowledge, had to be made attainable by *everyone*. Oddly enough, attempts at curing melancholia were in the service of this way of looking at things, for if melancholia were cur-able, then it could be drawn into the orbit of empirical science, so its symptoms (for example, extraordinary intellectual abilities) would thereby lose their extraordinariness, and consequently all could ac-quire them and could be prevailed upon to come under the spell of common sense. A typical example was Aristotle's comparing the substance of black bile to wine; Galen in the second century BCE, on the other hand, wrote that a heavy red wine could cause melan-cholia—and of course, drinking red wine requires no special skills. The physical signs of melancholia spring to the foreground, and they seem to lose the comprehensive cosmic-metaphysical grounding that had characterized the Hippocratic and Aristotelian notions of this condition. In the fourth century BCE, Diocles of Carystus, seeing a close connection between liver and bile, attributed melancholia to the swelling of the liver, and by the beginning of the Christian era, liver complaints were thought to be always connected with it. In Galen's view, however, melancholia stemmed from a disorder of the hypochondrium, the upper abdomen,[2] so it is easy to understand that

---

2. That was via Greco-Arabic intermediaries, who located melancholy in the epi-gastric region—a view that survived into more modern times. In 1652, the Munich-

he associated it with diseases of the gastric tract. (Kierkegaard was later to protest against this and to reject the suggestion that everyone who has a digestive disorder is suffering from melancholia.) The disorder of the hypochondrium affects the liver on the right-hand side as well as the spleen on the left,[3] and Galen linked it not just with digestive ailments but also with mental disorders. Those mental complaints were later cut free from digestive ailments, but physicians continued to label mental disturbances with unknown causes as hypochondria, which is why melancholy came to be imputed to hypochondria, or imagined bodily ailments.

The spread and propagation of the explanation that melancholia has a purely physical basis is inseparable from the notion that strove to represent its "mental" symptoms as "baseless" or "unwarranted." If a melancholic judged the world differently from a nonmelancholic, then there was not a question of some novel interpretation of existence; his thoughts were to be disregarded as mere side effects of some bodily change. The dual doctrine[4] of a "pure mental problem" and "unalloyed physical change" sundered the original, indivisible unity of body and mind that had characterized the classical Greek interpretation of melancholia. Hellenism's notion of melancholia presumed from the outset a duality of mind and praxis (body and soul)—hence, an expressly psychological or somatic explanation for melancholia (which, of course, is not to say that the two were diametrically opposed, as they have become in recent times). Duality, it seems, is the normal state of existence, and even the most compre-

based physician Malachias Geiger devoted an entire book to the topic: *Microcosmos hypochondriacus sive de melancholia hypochondriaca tractatus.*

3. Melancholia ascribed to the spleen was later to have an equivalent in the "spleen" (that is, melancholy) of the Romantics.

4. In the first century CE, Cornelis Celsus's book *De medicina libri octo* was the first to recommend a wholly psychiatric treatment for melancholics. Galen, by contrast, ascribed all mental abilities to the mixture of bodily humors.

hensive way of looking at things needs to behold its subject in that perspective. It is understandable that public opinion tried to make melancholia accessible, mundane. The most characteristic manifestation of that process was humorism as it evolved from the theory of humors, which, just by grouping people, took the edge off melancholia, for something that is classifiable in a group cannot be used to force that group apart. Humorism hypothesized closedness, which excludes the possibility of a person stepping outside his own bounds, precludes his self-transcendence, and shackles him from the outset. It is generally believed that the theory of humors can be tied to Hippocrates (before him, Alcmaeon of Croton, in the fifth century BCE, had sought the source of diseases in the body's humors), but in truth it was only a good deal later, in the Middle Ages, that it was articulated in its definitive form. Of course, the basis for the four temperaments—choleric, sanguine, phlegmatic, melancholic—stretched back into antiquity and stemmed from the cosmic outlook characteristic of that era. The teaching about the four humors, though, was empirical in origin (Alcmaeon, Hippocrates), though not as yet unequivocally connected with the temperaments. Each of the humors had its own season, which meant that anyone suffering from an overabundance of black bile would have no complaint on entering autumn, the atrabilious season, though they might take ill in the other three seasons. Much the same applied to those suffering from congestion (they would be healthy in spring). The season of yellow bile was summer, whereas that of phlegm was winter. One thing implicit in the theory is that a humor can signify disease as well as temperament—but never a normal state of existence: anyone who is healthy throughout the whole year is not suffering from an overabundance of any humor; therefore, he is not sick and has no temperament. But can one really be human without having any temperament? Deep at the bottom of humorism there is also another way of looking at things, related to the number four. The conferring of cosmic distinction on four, a sacred number of the Pythagoreans, goes back to Empedocles. He was the first to name the four elements of the world (earth, air, fire, water) and to make the number four a basic principle of the cosmos. This number determined everything, including humankind, both its body and its soul. Empedocles was also the first to write about the four kinds of mental disposition, which in his view were the product of a mixing of the four elements (not humors). There were two kinds of school of medicine: on the one hand, an empirical school based on humorism (Hippocrates), starting from the physical reality of the body and organism and arriving, via the concept of κρᾶσις, at a cosmic way of looking at things. On the other hand, the school of a cosmic outlook (Empedocles) arrived at man's physical reality from a background of examining the cosmos and the universe. The two schools differed in methodology, but they agreed in regarding human beings as part of the cosmos in both body and soul, and they considered treatment to be inconceivable without bringing the patient into harmony with the universe. That was how the empirically demonstrable four humors were given cosmic significance, and the immaterial number four, privileging the cosmos, became physical reality. The manifest connection of the two viewpoints was accomplished by the treatise *On the Nature of Man*, the author of which was presumed to be either Hippocrates or his son-in-law and disciple Polybus.

The cosmically based doctrine of the elements and the unity of the empirical humors comprised *everything* that could be said about humankind in classical antiquity. But in parallel with the cracking of the unity of the universe, mankind gradually slipped out of the tethers of this universe: the cosmos and the individual (body and spirit, mind and praxis) appeared as two poles. Instead of being concentric enclosures, they ended up at the opposite ends of a straight line. The connection was maintained; only its nature changed: in place of an organic interdependence, the universe became a system of correspondences: everything corresponded with something, but nothing contained everything within itself. Typical of the later classical, Hellenistic theory of melancholy was a growing overcomplication and the ever-more prolix, diffuse, meandering, and inconclusive literature devoted to the subject (numerous treatises were written, including a famous, partially extant two-volume work by Rufus of Ephesus in the time of Trajan). The Hippocratic concept of melancholia lost its cosmic background and continued to live as an empirical theory of humors. The Aristotelian concept, on the other hand, seemed to be forgotten: the idea that physical extraordinariness and intellectual excellence might be associated with despair was alarming, and the spirit of the age did all it could to hold melancholy at bay. Galen revived the Empedoclean theory of the four elements, supplementing it with Hippocratic humorism and adding ethical correspondences to the humors, and thus the outlines of a doctrine of the temperaments began to emerge. In the second half of the fourth century CE, Helvius Vindicianus, a physician friend of St. Augustine, devised a typology, a scheme of categorization totally alien to classical antiquity. The likes of it were again encountered in a sixth-century treatise entitled *On the Humors:* by that stage, the four temperaments indicated four normal states. The taming of melancholia was complete: on the one hand, if it was reminiscent of melancholia in the Aristotelian sense, then it was purely a matter of an illness, but on the other hand, *everyone* could be categorized as belonging to one type or another. The excrescences had to be lopped off to make the world snug for everyone. Having accomplished this, theorists could expand the domain of the individual temperaments with impunity and without affecting the typology: the basic principle, that is to say, the averageness or typicality, was left undisturbed. Thus, each humor corresponds with one element of the cosmos, one season, one age of life, a time of day, a metal, a mineral, a color—indeed, from the ninth century on, a planet as well. A fully crystallized doctrine of the temperaments saw the light of day in the first half of the twelfth century: the first time the four words "phlegmatic," "melancholic," "sanguine," and "choleric" make an appearance is in an encyclopedic work on natural philosophy with the title of *De philosophia mundi,* by William of Conches, and although the natural-historical foundations of humorism had been demolished by the discovery of the circulation of blood in 1628, the theory lives on in the mind of the public to the present day. The four kinds of temperament lock people into four castes, from which it is impossible to step out. In the classic notion of melancholia, one's freedom of temperament, interpretation of existence, and choice of fate did not exclude one another: in contradistinction, Hellenism saw persons as being subject to their own temperaments, incapable of surpassing themselves. (We characterize persons as melancholic or choleric, and often feel that with this adjective their whole existence can safely be placed in the parentheses: we are no longer curious about who they are or what kind of worldview or existential condition induced them to become melancholic. We are interested only in how melancholia as their defining feature can be shown in every facet of their behavior.) A person is no longer master of himself but a prisoner of his own being from birth, whether healthy or not (since antiquity, melancholia could mean both *average health* and *sickness that departs from the average*, but never *health that departs from the average*). A person locked into his own created nature is no master of either himself or his existence, but in every respect is of a lower order than his creator (or "merely" his destiny), and by becoming resigned to this necessity, he gives up, from the outset, trying to force open the limits of existence. William of Conches unwittingly and very astutely touched on the essence of humorism when he called the four temperaments defects ("quia corrumpitur natura"—"which are of corrupted nature," as quoted in Hellmut Flashar, *Melancholie und Melancholiker in den medizinischen Theorien der Antike*, 115). The humors of prelapsarian humankind became mixed after the Fall, or in other words, the four temperaments were four kinds of manifestation of original sin. No person is without a temperament; there is no temperament without sin. We are in the Middle Ages.

Chapter 3

THE EXCLUDED

How are Saturn's offspring, the melancholics, to be identified? A late-medieval manuscript gives the following response: melancholics have dark, possibly yellowish-green skin; they have small, deep-set eyes that rarely blink, they are constantly downcast, gazing at the ground; their beards are scanty; their shoulders are bowed; they are sexually weak; they are lazy, slow on the uptake, although a thing that once catches their attention is never forgotten; they bore other people and rarely laugh; they dress carelessly; they cheat, steal, are ungrateful, stingy, and generally misanthropic in character (see Klibansky, Panofsky, and Saxl, *Saturn and Melancholy*, 61). Another author has it that melancholics are brutish, vile persons, and melancholia (one can read in a fifteenth-century manuscript in Tübingen) is the vilest of the temperaments, the most fallible, and the sickest (see Schönfeldt, *Die Temperamentenlehre in deutschsprachigen Handschriften des 15. Jahrhunderts*, 61). In the seventh century, Isidore of Seville endeavored to derive the word *malus* (bad) from *melancholia*, the Greek name for black bile, and this perception anticipated a widespread belief several centuries later: melancholia had to be banished into the domain of the most damnable notions and phenomena.

Yet if we leave behind the society of robbers and killers (because in the Middle Ages they too were held to be melancholic) and turn our attention to men of letters, we encounter another interpretation of melancholia. This was hardly more favorable than the above, but telling nevertheless: "And all those will fall into melancholy," wrote Constantine the African of Carthage in *Libri duo de melancholia* in 1080, "who overexert themselves in reading philosophical books, or books on medicine and logic, or books which permit a view [theory] of all things; as well as books on the origin of numbers, on the science which the Greeks call arithmetic; on the origin of the heavenly spheres and the stars, that is, the science of the stars, which the Greeks call astronomy; on geometry, which bears the name of 'science of lines' among the Arabians, but which the Greeks call geometry" (quoted in Klibansky, Panofsky, and Saxl, *Saturn and Melancholy*, 84). The cause (not a symptom!) of melancholia is excessive intellectual effort (*studium vehemens*—passionate study), but this is concentrated in the singular purviews of scholarly research, being directed at "ultimate" matters, the origins, the beginnings, the kinds of things, by the unraveling of which everything can be cleared up. A melancholic's thinking leaps from the domain of earthly matters to the sphere of the imagination—a world of *equivocal, undemonstrable, dubious* ideas. "Great is the force of imagination," Arnald of Villanova wrote in the thirteenth century, "and much more ought the cause of melancholy to be ascribed to this alone, than to the distemperature of the body" (quoted in Robert Burton, *The Anatomy of Melancholy*, partition 1, sec. 2, member 3, subsec. 1, 253). The Stoics had already pointed to a connection between melancholia and falling ill (Sextus), and this idea was picked up unaltered by the early Christians (for example, Nemesius in the fourth century). Melancholia no longer led toward an understanding of the deepest problems of existence, but became a concomitant of vain and fruitless speculation. Instead of being an undecipherable secret, existence displayed a clearly arranged order guaranteed by God. Those unwilling to accept this and trust exclusively their own reason would get lost, step by step, in the gloom: the divine meaning of existence lost its validity for them, and they were left to themselves. Since St. Augustine, Christian theology has regarded a self that deliberately shuts itself up as the source of sin (*De civitate Dei*, bk. 16, 2), amounting to a willful separation from God. Neither the visible nor the invisible Church would accept a skeptic who put mercy at risk by calamitous argumentation.

Plummeting from the frames of the rational universe, he became a heretic, an easy prey for the devil. According to Constantine the African, a melancholic is "convinced of the fearfulness and horror of things that are not to be feared, thinks about the kinds of things it is unnecessary to reflect on, and perceives things that do not exist" (quoted in Winterstein, *Dürers "Melancholie" im Lichte der Psycho- analyse*, 12), though he also classifies as melancholic people who ob- sessively fix their eyes on God and care about nothing else. If we do not wish to expose ourselves to the temptation of melancholy, then we must accept not only the existence of God but also the unique- ness of the world that he has vouched for, and we must live with the fact that sin is shared, redemption is shared, and mercy is shared. A melancholic is physically the frailest, the least viable—yet more wretched than this physical debility is his mental state, and, arising from this, his loneliness and inclination to damnation. A melancholic racks his brain over *unnecessary* things, general opinion has claimed for a millennium or more. And anything that is an unnecessary, a dis- pensable part of the universe, and nevertheless manages to find its way into being has a disruptive effect. Excess corrodes existence and its closedness. Since existence is whole and, thanks to God's grace, extends to everything, an excess can only be imagined as a lack. The Middle Ages, living as it did under the spell of a *horror vacui*, was not inclined to tolerate either a gap or an excess. If, nevertheless, melan- cholics thought about the sorts of things that were unnecessary to think about, then in the final analysis they fantasized *about nothing*. They were vehicles of an unresolvable contradiction; they were an- tagonists of a world that did not recognize nothingness and was thus unable to accept lack as a "natural" part of existence. Brooding mel- ancholics render the universe itself problematic: even if unwittingly, they turn the unknown into an essential element, a final cause of the world. In other words, they set it in God's place. Although nihil- ism was not considered a characteristic feature of melancholia in the

Middle Ages, it lurked deep in the brooding restlessness of the soul. It explained the proneness to suicide among melancholics, which was noted by Avicenna (though he ascribed it to moral corruption), and suicide was far from common in those days.[1] A melancholic questions everything, and rejects everything; he is left to himself, having nothing to believe in, and therefore he does not know how to deal with divine mercy arriving from outside. But boundless despair and boundless loneliness do not preclude God's boundless love: the example of great mystics is evidence that despair spreading over everything may be coupled with an unequalled intensity of God worship. The fact that they turned nothingness into a god explains the mystics' melancholia, which in the Middle Ages was viewed as requiring not only a medical but also an "ideological" treatment: melancholia, like mysticism, has a disruptive effect in a culture of closed minds. In the eleventh century, Constantine the African wrote in his treatise about melancholia:

> Numerous goodly and born-good people fall victim to this disease due to their fear of God and terror of the Last Judgment, as well as their longing for the contemplation of the supreme good. . . . Increasingly they fret about how they can love and fear God, and in, so to speak, the intoxication of their grief and their sense of their own void, they become prey to illness. With such people, it is not just their spiritual activity that is damaged but their physical activity as well. . . . Those who continually occupy themselves with studying philosophical and similar books also cannot always avoid the disease.

> (quoted in Rainer Jehl, *Melancholie und Acedia*, 275)

---

1. Research on this question suggests that between 400 and 1400 CE, one cannot find even so much as a reference to suicide, since religious prescriptions served as internal prohibition and inhibited its spread.

A hundred years later Maimonides, as court physician to Sultan Saladin of Cairo, while trying to cure the ruler's son of his depression, wrote a treatise on regulation of diet, in which he mentions melancholia together with a mystic disposition. Presumably, the prescribed diets were unable to pull up the deeply intertwined roots of melancholia and mysticism—doubt about general grace and a destructive belief in the strength of solitude. Medieval melancholics shut themselves up: they constructed the world out of themselves, creating a god for themselves out of their own efforts, a god of the universe as well as of solitude, but this god could not be a god for other people. To the extent the world is mysterious to them, they are mysterious to the world.

Nothing characterizes the medieval judgment of melancholy better than the attitude of early Christians toward the mysteries of antiquity. The rejection of mysticism becomes truly comprehensible from the rejection of the mysteries. It has already been noted that the possibility of melancholia inhered in the mysteries of antiquity because they rendered growing and decaying, being and nonbeing, relative for initiates. A person who has been initiated has also partaken of a less than cheerful understanding of being and human existence. The mysteries were democratic institutions, but the knowledge they offered belonged to the elect: not everybody could become a melancholic, a prophet, a philosopher, and an initiate all at the same time. Those able to acquire knowledge and become seers set themselves apart from everyone else; the relaxation of the laws of existence excluded all possible connections with the world at large (from that point of view, social connections also lost their credence), and their fate became that of solitude wrapped up in silence. Roman Catholicism, true to its name (καθολικός, universal), strove to rescue the believers from solitude—in the final analysis, a sinful, God-denying state. During the third century, when the cult of the Church was evolving, Christianity took up the battle against the pagan mysteries. The main pretext was the salacious sensuality, the orgiastic practices, perceived as characteristic of the mysteries; the Church Fathers declined to see in these the cosmocentric way of looking at things, which sustained the mysteries and was radically alien to the spirit of Christianity. Moreover, the Fathers were not initiated, so their judgments were usually on the basis of external intelligence, or—as in the cases of Tertullian, Asterius of Petra, Eusebius of Vercelli, and Clement of Alexandria—they knew at best the Alexandrian mysteries, in which sensuality did, indeed, run wild at times. It is not hard, however, to discover the cause of the basic antagonism lying behind the repudiation of the outward features of the mysteries. The Christian convert Julius Firmicus Maternus, lashing out at the errors of pagan religions, addresses the followers of the mysteries as follows: "Tell me, you unfortunates, why have you mixed death into natural phenomena? Why do you infect God-created order with inhumanly cruel killings? What is the purpose of the idea of associating with God-ordained things a series of events ending with death? You muddle the earthly with the heavenly, the ephemeral with the eternal, the obscure with the clear when you make the pain and grief the subject of divine veneration" (*The Error of the Pagan Religions*, 7). Earlier, Clement of Alexandria had already drawn attention to the consequences of such "meddling." He objected, for example, that a priest of the mysteries ventured to behold and unite with God unaided. In his view, that was the reason for the priest's going astray in the night. The attempt at beholding God *unaided* was a sign of arrogance; an initiate sought to glimpse God in the hope of being deified. All who sought to become God, however, were lacking entirely in humility and forgot their created nature, and instead of becoming a creator, they fell victim to their createdness: they partook of eternal death. Clement correctly noticed that initiates set off on their path alone, unsupported. Initiates in the mysteries, the definitive seers, the melancholics, had *no community*, just as the Greek body of beliefs did not recognize the notion of a *universal* mercy that extended to everyone—that only came about with Jesus, and with his appearance the meaning of the mysteries also altered. Among the Greeks there was allegedly a shrine that was set up in honor of the Unknown God (Ἄγνωστος Θεός). According to St. Paul, it was the God of the Christians that the Greeks did not as yet recognize (Acts 17:23). The difference is decisive: in the shrine of an unknown god (can one find a more splendid equivalent of the way of looking at things that was intrinsic to Greek culture?), the god is indefinable because he is unnamable — everything leads to him, but the paths are nevertheless lost in obscurity. The search for the unknown god cannot be closed: his mercy is deferred into infinity, which entails that *endless ignorance will be the final characteristic of humankind.* Worshipping an unknown god is an admission of our own ultimate inscrutability, a resigned recognition of the unsolvability of the mystery and the secret. That resignation can only be the result of an enormous effort: the only person worthy of entering the shrine to the unknown god is the one who has settled all accounts with everything. That shrine is the shrine of the elect: of those who go to such an extent in acknowledging their own frailty, the certainty of their demise, and the fact that with every single death an irreplaceable life comes to nothing that they wish for no mercy coming from outside. The naming of the unknown god, however, alters everything at a stroke. God becomes *one, defined,* accessible: mercy becomes a function of a given time, and it can be attained by everyone. For the Greeks, there were plural mysteries — for Christianity, there is just one mystery.[2] That mystery was no less than human history, in the course of which God comes to the decision to redeem sinful humankind from its free will. Christianity usually employs the word "mystery" in the singular, because it is a matter of one story, because the essence of God's secret is "that in the dispensation of the fullness of times he might gather together in one all things in Christ, both which are in heaven, and which are on earth; even in him" (Ephesians 1:10). There is only one

---

2. For the Greeks, "mystery" in the singular meant just "secret," without any wider, ritual connotation.

true mystery religion, Clement of Alexandria said, and that is Christianity—and he cursed the founders of the pagan mysteries as Satan's tools. In the mysteries of antiquity, initiates are reborn; in the Christian mystery, they win forgiveness. Experiencing forgiveness means that in the Christian mystery, humankind does not take an active part (in the antique mysteries, the experiential state—$\pi\alpha\vartheta\epsilon\tilde{\iota}\nu$—does not imply passivity, as becomes clear from Aristotle's previously noted remark). The story from the Fall to the Resurrection is well known and, according to the eschatological view of things, is unidirectional and cannot be changed. Concerning God's mystery, men are ignorant to the same extent that they are small in proportion to God, St. Irenaeus declared in the second century. Man is completely at the mercy of God. Only faith will get us to salvation ("Christian truth is incomparably fairer than Helen of Troy," St. Augustine said much later); faith has a definite object, however. The Greek mysteries recur again and again; they are cyclical like the eternal cycles of nature—that is why initiation can never be brought to an end, just as there is no end to the understanding of existence. The path leading to the Christian God is finite, and it can be completed; since faith has an object, and that object can be named, the possibility of faith is given to everyone. An opening up on the part of the human being is absolutely decisive, but opening up, in a Christian sense, means entering the holy house of God, the church. The mystery that lasts from baptism to resurrection, that starts again with the birth of each person and is nevertheless identical with the sole true mystery, the story of Jesus Christ, is granted to everyone. Partaking of universal grace preserves believers for God, and for themselves it is a guarantee of the ultimate sense and purposefulness of existence.

As a consequence of the trust placed in divine omnipotence, the mysteries lost their earlier role: initiation was no longer accompanied by a solitude shrouded in mute silence but by an opening-up toward God. Christian initiation is collective in nature; the individual is lifted out of his or her individuality into the intellectual and political

domain of faith. Although Christianity does acknowledge the concept of individuality (indeed, in all probability it is the only religion
that genuinely does), the solitude that became the lot of Greek melancholics is unimaginable for Christians: persons are individuals, but
through their intellect they are also parts of the universal. Divine
judgment as well as grace create the arch that stretches between the
personal and impersonal, but the tension between those two poles,
which is natural in the context of a faith-based tradition, appears to
many as most unnatural; many representatives of Islamic mysticism
turned melancholic precisely because of this tension. To what extent
was a man a unique, unrepeatable individual and to what extent was
he a part, a mere "instance" of redeeming grace—that was one of
the fundamental problems for a person in the Middle Ages. But the
question was not posed in just this way, since that would have implied a ready answer. It was those already suffering from being abandoned to their fate who posed the question in that way—those for
whom their own being and the possibility of God's grace had become
questionable, who had to make certain things the object not just of
questioning but also of outright doubt. Belief in grace could margin-
alize the force of the feeling of abandonment, but it could not extinguish it—and despair was still present within those margins. Melancholy and a sense of growing isolation were just as inseparable in the
Middle Ages as they had been in antiquity. But whereas solitude, for
the Greeks, was a product of turning away from things that seemed
fixed and unequivocal (to make use of Christian terminology: loneliness was a result of "searching for God"; the search, however—as was
shown by the story of Bellerophon—found nothing and thus coiled
back on itself), in the Middle Ages solitude was considered to be a
phenomenon attendant on estrangement from grace. A melancholic
was usually a heretic, the devil's accomplice; but as Constantine the
African noted, someone who brooded too long over God could also
be a melancholic. Brooding, daydreaming, does not make the world
of inscrutable things comprehensible, and loneliness, which springs

from an insoluble contradiction between divine judgment and grace (and which, because of this insolubility, engenders dread), does not differ from the solitude of heretics and fanatics. St. Jerome writes about those who turn their backs on their previous lives, escape into solitude, and become monks, but since they are looking for solitude rather than for God, they usually relapse into their previous lifestyles. "Some too there are," St. Jerome writes in letter 125, "who, from the dampness of their cells and from the severity of their fasts, from their weariness of solitude and from excessive study, have a singing in their ears day and night, and turn melancholy mad so as to need the poultices of Hippocrates more than exhortations from me." An illustrious exemplar of such a melancholic is the monk Stagirius. This pious soul found the nightly vigils intolerable and began to be afflicted by nightmares and disturbed speech, with frequent spells of fainting getting the better of him, which his companions interpreted as tests of his character: he had to vanquish the temptations of the devil within himself. Constantine the African regarded the depression that often overcame monastics, the *morbus melancholicus*, as a deadly sin, and with every right from his point of view: a melancholic monk was left to himself not just physically but spiritually as well—he broke away from the house of God and became prey for the devil.

The expression "left to oneself" is metaphorical: the metaphysical solitude of the Romantics, which will be dealt with later, was as yet unknown. No one could be left to himself in the Middle Ages; at most, he might abandon God and thereby go over to another transcendental power: the devil. A person's sense of loneliness was broached by the Church paradoxically: not only did it have to wrestle with the issue of "projecting" an individual smoothly into the abstract infinity of the divine substance, but, in parallel, it also needed to define the individual's sensory individuality. Christianity was an intellectual and political empire in which the individual was bound by contingent, abstract threads to the totality of the "empire"—and the Church tried to take that contingency into account by working out the individuality of the soul and the personality. The question was asked in the following form: to what extent is a person an independent, finite, unique being and to what extent a part of God's infinite universe? St. Augustine, founder of the substantiality of the individual soul, expounded the idea that the self is not the sum total of its activities (that is, it is not an accessory of the everlastingly existing parts of the universe that can be assembled at any time) but a finite, independent reality. With that idea, he set the European concept of freedom and individuality on its future course; he thought through the conflict of the soul's individuality, its independence, and at the same time its repeatability, its "episodicity," in a way that is valid to the present day. "For what would I say, O Lord my God, but that I know not whence I came into this dying life (shall I call it?) or living death," he asks (*Confessions*, bk. 1, 6, trans. Pusey), and elsewhere declares, "I want to know God and the soul. Nothing else? Nothing whatever!" (*Soliloquies*, bk. 1, pt. 2). And who could ask for more? An individual in the mirror of God is nothing; in his own mirror, everything. And the reverse is also true: in God's presence, an individual is substantiality; in the mirror of his own soul, a void. There is no need to determine how big a distance or gap separates the single from the general, the individual from the universal. Though faith readily bridges that divide, the totally subjective character of an act of faith intensifies even further the dizzying maelstrom between the subject and object of faith, which can easily make melancholics of those who gaze into the deep. St. Gregory of Nyssa in the fourth century was the first in the history of Christian thinking to assert that God is infinite, thus breaking from the notion in Greek metaphysics that infinity is a negative, not a positive, predication. From then on, the idea of emptiness and infinity, creatureliness and noncreatureliness, would give European consciousness no rest. Surpassing even St. Augustine, St. Thomas Aquinas no longer saw the individuality of a person as a problem just of the "soul" but also of the "body"—and if the soul could become infinite despite its individuality, the body was exclusively a boundary, a restraint. Aquinas tied the question of singularity to materiality, and posed the problem of the individuality of the soul in relation to the body: "The body is not of the essence of the soul; but the soul by the nature of its essence can be united to the body" (*Summa Theologica*, I, q. 75, a. 7). People differ from one another by virtue of the individuality of their bodies; therefore, it is impossible for *one* intellect to belong to all men, he notes; otherwise, it would follow that Socrates and Plato were one man. Such a dispersal of souls, however, makes it impossible to have knowledge of *one* God. The mind by its very nature wants to know about *everything*, which is why it longs for God—thus, the existence of one God somehow defines the existence of all other souls. "If my intellect is distinct from your intellect, my intellect is an individual [*quiddam individuum*], and so is yours; for individuals are things which differ in number but agree in one species. Now whatever is received into anything must be received according to the condition of the receiver. Therefore the species of things would be received individually [*individualiter*] into my intellect, and also into yours: which is contrary to the nature of the intellect which knows universals" (I, q. 76, a. 3). Because of the generalizing capacity of the intellect, then, an absolute individuality cannot possibly be imagined, and this is guaranteed not only by the structure of the soul but also by the divine essence: "Everything participated [*participatum*] is compared to the participator [*ad participans*] as its act [*actus*]. But whatever created form be supposed to subsist 'per se,' must have existence by participation; for 'even life,' or anything of that sort, 'is a participator of existence,' as Dionysius says (*Div. Nom.* v). Now participated existence is limited by the capacity of the participator; so that God alone, who is His own existence, is pure act and infinite" (I, q. 75, a. 5). If, therefore, we assert of something that it exists, then it stands to reason that we are asserting the existence of God. *God is the ultimate guarantor of the existence of individual things*, yet he is not only the ultimate guarantor but a fundamental condition as well. *The independence of things is therefore relative*, and God, *because of his omnipotence* and his *ceaseless presence*, makes the world even more closed than the cosmos of antiquity. God is infinite, but since his existence automatically rules out emptiness and vacuum, his infinity is also *depressing*; there is no way of escaping him, no "secluded" nook where one might be left to oneself. This is why one's abandonment is metaphorical: only the desire to be left alone exists, but that desire has no specific target, and therefore it cannot be assuaged. The idea of individuality and the inevitably attendant sense of loneliness are as ineradicable a part of Christianity as the idea of the omnipotence of God and the notion of grace, which, by their extending to everyone, are pacifying to all. God's grace and omnipotence are the Church's legitimate, the former two its illegitimate, children; and when individuality and its loneliness start to demand the rights owed to them, they are dispossessed of everything and in the end swindled out of themselves. In the eyes of the Church, an insatiable desire leading to muteness is not a sign of the mysterious aimlessness of a limited, unrepeatable human life (that is, a fulfillment of the senselessness of existence) but a sin, sheer negativity, about which one should feel guilty, and which, following the disappearance of the Greek Empire, has burdened Western culture to such an extent that it has not been able to shake it off to the present day.

Grace presupposes faith—seen from the position of solitude, however, faith takes on the form of a command. For that reason, the flight of a recluse from grace is a flight from external commands, which can be regarded as insisting on one's freedom. That freedom consists of a denial of faith; but since for the Middle Ages, living under the spell of a *horror vacui* as it was, what was denied was just as much an emanation of God's existence as what was accepted (even sin exists only because God exists); therefore, denial on the part of an abandoned medieval melancholic was essentially directed at an affirmation of *nothing*. God cannot be denied, because God is present even in that denial; existence cannot be denied, because existence itself is a precondition for denying existence; one cannot deny oneself, because even the ultimate gesture of suicide is carried out by a "superego" in the Christian sense. There is no *ultimate* denial extending to everything—merely a desire to deny. Yet the *nothing* that this desire confronts is not nothing, since simply by asserting it one is asserting its existence. Thus, denial, seeking an object in its desire for freedom, is compelled to affirm—to affirm nothingness. Which means that deniers strive to assert the absolute validity of all the things that cause their sense of loneliness. The outcome is the deification not just of the *individuality* of the body but also of the soul, and consequently of the *uniqueness* of life.

In stepping outside the order created by reason, passions tend toward sin; within that order, they tend toward virtue, teaches St. Thomas. Sin implies a rejection of the Christian interpretation of existence conceivable by reason, and thus, in the final analysis, it goes hand in hand with a loss of grace. Since the time of St. Augustine, intentionally shutting oneself up and turning away from God (*aversio a Deo*) has been regarded by Christian theology as a major sin. A sinner rejects grace, slumps into loneliness, and, as has been seen, becomes a prisoner of melancholia. Anyone who is melancholic steps out of the rational order created by *reason* and therefore, as measured by medieval standards, can in no way be considered wise. (In writing about melancholia, scholars fall into a deep hush about the Aristotelian notion.) Since melancholics can only long for metaphysical solitude, they are prisoners of that longing. It has no object, and therefore it falls back on itself: the self begins to fantasize, to imagine things, and it takes an inward turn that can be seen only as pathological. True wisdom is not touched by sickness, the Middle Ages vow (first, St. Augustine in his work *De beata vita*), but the antique meaning of *apatheia* is altered, with less emphasis given to the stoical overcoming of the passions and more to the mind's self-control. Anyone who fails to observe that is sick in the eyes of the Middle Ages. "So pleasant their vain conceits are," the Robert Burton writes about melancholics, "that they hinder their ordinary tasks and necessary business, they cannot address themselves to them, or almost to any study or employment" (Burton, *Anatomy*, partition 1, sec. 2, member 2, subsec. 6, 246). The black bile rises to the opening of the liver, thence to the heart, and its final destination is the brain, Constantine the African writes; the black bile that makes its way to the brain dulls the powers of judgment. Melancholics are overcome by undue fright and imagine that "the sort of thing is occurring which will never occur in reality." The mind becomes deranged and incapable of getting its bearings in a familiar world. "As with the sun, which loses its light if clouds or vapors reach it, so too the mind of a sick person becomes deranged if the noxious vapors of black bile reach him; he is unable to shine any more, and he does not recognize things according to their inner reality" (quoted in Heinrich Schipperges, "Melancholie als ein mittelaltlicher Sammelbegriff für Wahnvorstellungen," 728). A melancholic is alienated from everything, said Constantine, who considered melancholy to be both a corporeal and a mental illness, since in his view, fantasizing too was an illness. The medieval world ejected from itself all imaginings, yet it is questionable whether everything that a system seeks to eject can be adequately characterized by the word "sickness." Naturally, the exaggerated fantasizing of a medieval melancholic was sick, since, after all, it was corroding the body of a healthy society, but—and this is where the melancholia of the Middle Ages was one step ahead—those who called melancholia an illness did not inquire into the question of health itself. Ulysses crossed the Strait of Gibraltar, the boundary laid down for mankind, and that was why, in Dante's opinion, not only was his flight wild (*folle volo—Inferno*, canto 26, l. 125), but so, too, was he himself (*Paradise*, canto 27, l. 83). The limits imposed are those of God, and we should know our limits. The boundlessness of a melancholic, his longing to be negative, was, according to the contemporary conception, sick, irrational, and contradictory to all the rules of reason. "In melancholy persons," writes Avicenna, "the vividness of the imagination (*imaginatio*) of depressing things itself causes them to appear, because the thing whose image is represented to the mind is already there in actuality. . . . We find that the understanding is drawn away from rational actions by the senses and by the phantasy" (quoted in E. R. Harvey, *The Inward Wits*, 26). Melancholics, he writes elsewhere, are "usually sad and solitary, and [they are] continually, and in excess, more than ordinarily suspicious, more fearful, and have long, sore, and most corrupt imaginations" (quoted in Burton, *Anatomy*, partition 1, sec. 3, member 1, subsec. 3, 402). Melancholia is a product of a sick fantasy—sick, because it does not recognize generally agreed boundaries. According to Avicenna's doctrine, *imaginatio* is the storehouse of sense perceptions, whereas the *vis imaginativa* is the faculty that mobilizes the collected sensory data. A healthy imagination is not free, but subordinate to the senses; perception itself, however, is of a lower order than thinking—*cogitatio*—which alone leads to God; and if imagination, in its attempt to break loose from this hierarchy, tries to acquire autonomy, it becomes sick (*morbus imaginationis* is the frequent accusation laid against melancholics).

The cause of fantasizing, of the roving imagination, was not merely noxious vapors of black bile rising to the brain; it also stemmed from an elemental human need. A person longs for solitude and at the same time is fearful of it. He can be rid of God's omnipotence only by elevating himself into an absolute. This, however, is just as depressing a state as God's solitude, which no crafty philosophy is capable of resolving. Seen from the outside, an individual who longs for freedom is daring and self-confident; naturally, in the eyes of the age his fantasizing is sickly, but there is determination and resoluteness behind this sickness. He of course sees the situation differently. Rebelling against divine omnipotence, he wishes to grant individual things, retrieved from under the authority of the general, their own ultimate justification, subject to no one's backing. This entails that he absolutize himself as ultimate certitude. The rejection of grace and the choice of freedom is *madness* in the eyes of the outside world, and the individual who chooses to act like that is truly mad: his desire to understand himself, the individuality and irreplaceability of the self, forces him to return to the question of being, which, in turn, lands him back with God. He is forced to realize that he does not have even himself at his own free disposal—and *experiencing* that can truly drive one mad. *He cannot change the fact that he was created*, and the fantasizing, which is essentially aimed at turning himself into a creator, comes to *nothing*: he becomes unintelligible, muddled, crazy. An *inner* derangement is inevitable for anyone wishing to cut himself free from God: the desire for freedom plunges the desirer into madness. He will be branded by others as a madman, and they have every reason for doing so: the culture around the melancholic—Christianity—produces the *possibility of endless freedom* (that is, sin) only to suppress it in madness and transform it into the *greatest possible servitude*, into self-slavery. "One cannot sufficiently condemn Christianity for having devaluated the value of such a great purifying nihilistic movement, which was perhaps already being formed . . . through continual deterrence from the *deed of nihilism*, which is suicide" (Nietzsche, *The Will to Power*, 143). This inseparable intertwining of the possibility of freedom and servitude brings about an inner breakdown (most people writing about melancholia in the Middle Ages list symptoms that are used to characterize schizophrenia nowadays), and in the case of melancholia, that condition is degraded into a mental illness. From the early Middle Ages, indeed from the early days of Christianity, physicians (Soranus of Ephesus and Caelius Aurelinus) and thinkers considered it to be a mental illness, which embraced everything from schizophrenia to manic depression or, to narrow the range, from rabies to lycanthropy. The interpretation of existence inherent in antiquity's notion of melancholia thereby lost its validity, but its medieval career had not yet come to an end. Melancholia was born originally out of a profound longing for freedom, a longing that was condemned to die from the start. The medieval interpretation of existence, however, in consequence of its totalitarian nature, not only bound the desire for freedom hand and foot but also, by declaring it to be a mental illness (or making effectively mentally ill those who had started to doubt), managed to exploit melancholia for its own glorification. Anyone who wanted to oppose the scheme of existence, to transgress the boundaries that had been laid down, would truly become sick—and what could serve as a better proof of the viability and vigor of a system? The Christian mystery was a unique event, the beginning and end of which are known, and for that reason, there is no scene in this world that does not have a prescribed place in that drama. The medieval view, like the teachings of Greek mythology, associates every type of mental illness, thus melancholia as well, with the night (the symbolic creatures of which include the owl and the bat). Night in the Christian sense—unlike the notion in antiquity—does not allow a glimpse of a new world that has never been seen before; instead, it is darkness taken in the strictest sense of the word. (Naturally, that does not apply to mystics, who were on intimate terms with melancholia.) To express this in the language of mystery: night was the era without Jesus Christ (Romans 13:12), which would pass soon so that the faithful might triumph; and in a figurative sense, the night is death (John 9:4). By becoming a mental illness, and by being connected with the night, melancholia achieved "world-historical" ranking: it was integrated, won its place on the stage, and melancholics became flailing actors whose fate was known by audiences in advance.[3]

The fact that melancholia was declared an illness indirectly contributed to the strengthening of faith. In illness, people no longer have command of themselves, and Christian theology discovered the ambiguous nature of a person's creaturely nature in illness: a person was simultaneously a passive and an active being. It is in a sick person that the double freedom—creaturely and individual—which charac-

---

3. That was why St. Augustine regarded Cain as the first melancholic—thereby anticipating Leopold Szondi, who called him a typical melancholic on the basis of the dialectic of instincts.

terizes healthy people as well, manifests most obviously. The conflict between these two kinds of freedom culminates in the melancholic patient, and thus melancholia is not just a specific disease but also an epitome: an embodiment of the duel that, in the Christian view of the world, characterizes world history and is fought between sin and redemption. The word "devil" (διάβολος) originally had connotations of throwing, vexing, strife; or in other words, the devil is present in the sick body or soul even if the illness seems to be derived from the most "natural" causes. In the Christian theological sense, the devil has existing substantiality, but he cannot be seen as God's opposite number: he is a finite creature, and divine authority sets limits to the evil he can do. Pursuant to the Fourth Lateran Council in 1215, nothing is evil by nature, but all evil is finite, temporal and stems from a creature's free decision (see Karl Rahner and Herbert Vorgrimler, *Concise Theological Dictionary*, s.v. "evil"). Evil is inconceivable in the absence of good, since it stems from the rejection of God, of the good. *True evil, therefore, is not manifested in destruction and ruination but in the rejection of divine goodness and grace.* In the case of the melancholic, this means that his illness is a scaled-down replica of the strife between God and the devil: a melancholic wants to be enough for himself, to acquire completeness in himself. According to St. Bonaventure, "every sin is a result of the inner chaos of the soul or will" (quoted in Jehl, *Melancholie und Acedia*, 175); and by making order (God's order) the ultimate basis, he invalidates from the outset the sense of existence of the melancholic, who discerns in everything disorder and instability, guaranteed by death. Melancholics are surrounded by such a high degree of incomprehension that in the Christian view, they are truly ill, and behind their sickness lurks the devil. According to Avicenna, the bile is painted black by the devil, which is why black bile was proverbially said to be the devil's bath (*balneum diaboli*). (Galgerandus of Mantua, a famous physician, allegedly tried to cure a demoniac woman "by purging black choler," that is, bile; see Burton, *Anatomy*, partition 1, sec. 2, member 1, subsec. 2, 200.) Melancholia is the result of the devil's machinations; this is the opinion of the Arabian Rhasis, of Michael Psellos, Gordonius, Paracelsus, Luther ("where melancholia raises its head, the Devil bathes"—quoted in Werner Leibbrand, *Heilkunde*, 201), and St. Teresa of Avila ("There are varieties of this temper [melancholia]. . . . I verily believe that Satan lays hold of it in some people as a means whereby to draw them to himself if he can"—quoted by Rudolf Wittkower and Margot Wittkower, *Born under Saturn*, 106). The devil makes his entrance and does everything possible to divert the melancholic from God. Burton cites Gentilis Fulgosus, who writes that he had a melancholy friend who had a black man "in the likeness of a soldier" following him wherever he was—this man was obviously the devil himself. Explanations connecting melancholia with a diabolical origin proliferated particularly from the twelfth through the thirteenth centuries—at the time when heresies also began to spread. Melancholics are inclined to heresy to begin with, and when this heresy appeared as an organized phenomenon, nothing could be more natural than to brand its followers as sick. "Anchorites, monks, and the rest of that superstitious rank," Guianerius writes, "through immoderate fasting, have been frequently mad" (quoted in Burton, *Anatomy*, partition 1, sec. 2, member 2, subsec. 2). Regarding the so-called religious melancholic (note the collocation!): "Some seem to be inspired of the Holy Ghost, some take upon them to be Prophets, some are addicted to new opinions, some foretell strange things," writes Gordonius. "Some will prophesy of the end of the World to a day almost, and the fall of the Antichrist" (partition 3, sec. 4, member 1, subsec. 1, 312). This is an unmistakable example of ideology at work (although the word "ideology" was coined only at the end of the eighteenth century), which became so far-reaching that in the early seventeenth century, in his massive work on melancholy the Anglican Robert Burton introduced two groups of religious melancholics: Enthusiasts (that is, Puritans and Catholics) and Atheists. Everyone who failed to find a place in the prevailing Anglican denomination was melancholic. Similar assertions are made by Melanchthon, who calls atheism now monstrous, now poisoned melancholy (*monstruosa melancholia* and *venenata melancholia*).

Melancholics are uneliminable figures in the world-historical drama of Christianity, obliged to play out the role of an all-rejecting desire for freedom. For the medieval melancholic, as for his Greek counterpart, the accustomed order of existence was overturned, leaving him with no foothold to grasp in order to create a habitable world. In the case of medieval melancholics, the complete turning away and denial are even more conspicuous: the surroundings from which they try to break out are much denser, more impenetrable than the heterogeneous culture of antiquity. There is just *one* mystery, *one* story, *one* basic principle, *one* God. The melancholic of antiquity could hunker down here and there among varied spheres of existence (as a soothsayer, madman, or philosopher; ever-newer worlds opened up for him, and even though these differed radically from the day-to-day, the customary, he could still consider them to be his own); this small degree of latitude, however, was not granted to medieval melancholics. In the Middle Ages, melancholia was an endangered state: a melancholic would smash up against a brick wall and get badly bruised. Or one could say that rather than hitting the wall, he was walled in from the outset. A melancholic wishes, first and foremost, to escape *from himself*, but he can find no crack in the homogeneous, overarching culture, and resignation grows in him, together with a sense of helplessness. In the end, he petrifies inwardly as well, feeling he has been robbed of his capacity for both wanting and not wanting. He has lost himself: he feels as if his body and soul had been replaced by a void, a yawning gap. (In the Middle Ages lead weights were placed on the head of some melancholics so they could feel that they had a head and body.) At the same time, he perceives his entire being as a dead weight, an immovable stone block. Aegidius Albertinus writes about melancholia in the following terms: "The grief, which otherwise moves the heart to meekness, only makes him more and more obstinate in his perverse thoughts, for his tears do not fall into his heart and soften its hardness, but he resembles a stone which, when the weather is damp, only sweats outwardly" (quoted in Walter Benjamin, *The Origin of German Tragic Drama*, 154).

"It is, therefore, no strange anomaly partly to will and partly to be unwilling. This is actually an infirmity of mind," writes Augustine (*Confessions*, bk. 8, 9), thinking of inertia, of melancholy, and of the unwillingness of the body to do what the mind commands. Medieval melancholics, unlike the ancient Greeks, did not walk but idled in one spot. They turned away from the world, withdrew into themselves, did nothing that might win them grace: they are inert. Inertness, or acedia[4] — the original Greek ἀκηδής means "without care, negligence" — is discouragement, absolute indifference to the good, spiteful indolence. Dante considered *acidia* (sullenness) one of the seven deadly sins, and those who were guilty of it were located in the Fifth Circle of Hell, in the foul water of the Styx. Sloth, in the Middle Ages, was called the devil's cushion or pillow, and those inclined to idleness were held to be melancholic. "I have often seen," said Rhasis, as cited by Burton (*Anatomy*, partition 1, sec. 2, member 2, subsec. 6, 242), "that idleness begets this humour [melancholia] more than any thing else." On account of its very slow speed of revolution around the sun, Saturn, the planet of melancholia, was called *Shani* (from the Sanskrit *Sanischana*, "the slow mover") or *Manda* ("slow") by the Indians. In a thirteenth-century manuscript, one may read the following about acedia: "On Sloth. The fourth principal sin is sloth in the service of God. That is if I should turn from a laborious and demanding good work to idle rest. If I turn from the good work when it

---

4. According to St. Thomas Aquinas, acedia is *tristitia de bono spirituali divino*, "sorrow is about spiritual good as much as it is about a divine good" (*Summa theologica*, II, q. 22, a. 35).

becomes heavy, this gives rise to bitterness of the heart" (quoted in Benjamin, *German Tragic Drama*, 155). Indolence or sloth (this we must certainly not judge from the viewpoint of today's work ethic) averts one's eyes from the good, and the consequence of doing so is eternal death, which fills the heart of the melancholic with infinite sorrow.[5] Acedia was the mother of "gloom," *tristitia* (in medieval Latin, *acedior* meant "languid, slothful," hence, "to be wearied of a thing"), the sadness that melancholics feel on account of their being destined for death, the extinction of their unrepeatable earthly existence, even though they feel that earthly existence to be unbearable. St. Paul distinguishes two kinds of sorrow: "For godly sorrow worketh repentance to salvation not to be repented of: but the sorrow of the world worketh death" (2 Corinthians 7:10). Sorrow of the world (ἡ τοῦ κόσμου λύπη) freezes one in one's own createdness—on the other hand, however, sorrow is not just a cause, but also an effect: the consequence of a state that was hopeless and doomed to damnation from the outset.

The condition of Egyptian monks in the region of Alexandria drew attention to acedia in the fourth century, with Evagrius Ponti-

---

5. Dante places melancholics in the muddy waters of the Styx, putting the following words in their mouths:

> Wedged in the slime, they say: "We had been sullen
> in the sweet air that's gladdened by the sun;
> we bore the mist of sluggishness in us:
> Now we are bitter in the blackened mud."

(*Inferno*, canto 7, 121–24)

The blackened mud refers to black bile; "sullen" in the original refers to *tristi fummo* (sorrowful soul) and, more particularly, to acedia (*accidioso fummo*—sluggish reek). Melancholia, sadness, and sloth all mutually presuppose one another. It should be noted that the automatic connection of acedia and melancholia was established only after the turn of the first millennium—until then, acedia had been virtually synonymous with *tristitia* and *desperatio*.

cus naming it as the most serious of the (then still) eight evil thoughts (*capita cognoscitiva*) from which all sinful behavior springs. A monk in a state of acedia did not wish to remain in his cell, found work repugnant to him, and felt forsaken and inconsolable. Since acedia is not just a devilish suggestion but an evil spirit, a demon as well, the soul is compelled to experience hell. Thus, acedia is more than simple idleness: it is a sign of turning away from God, and it can be manifested just as much in sleepiness and laziness as in restlessness and instability. It is not of work that *Homo accidiosus* is tired, but of God's oppressive almightiness; in vain he turns his gaze from God to the world, for instead of replenishment, from here too everything leads back to God. E. M. Cioran, a great melancholic of the twentieth century, writes about acedia as follows: "The dull sadness of monasteries wore an emptiness into the soul of the monks, known in the Middle Ages as *acedia*. . . . It is a loathing not *of* God but *in* him. Acedia gathers into itself the meaning of all those Sunday afternoons spent in the weighty silence of the monasteries" (Cioran, *Tears and Saints*, 86). According to Bonaventure, acedia has two roots: curiosity (*curiositas*) and disgust (*fastidium*). Disgust follows curiosity, and the initial question, "Is it worth living for God?," is quickly modified to "Is it worth living at all?" Aegidius Albertinus in the sixteenth century writes as follows in *Lucifers Königreich und Seelengejaidt: Oder Narrenhatz* (*Lucifer's Kingdom and His Hunt for Souls; or, The Hounding of Fools*):

> We legitimately compare acedia or sloth to a rabid dog's bite; because a person who is bitten by such a dog is soon overtaken by frightful dreams, they shiver in their sleep, and they become rabid, refusing all drinks, fearing water, barking like a dog, and trembling so hard that they swoon. People like that soon die unless given help. It is those haunted by the devil of sloth that are bitten by rabid dogs: people like that have dreadful dreams, they tremble without reason; things which for others are easy they

find difficult to do; they just gaze at the sight of others working and are themselves lazy; although they protest if they are called indolent.

(324–25)

St. Thomas Aquinas recommends numerous medications for the cure of acedia and *tristitia de bono spirituali divino*—searching for joy, crying to relieve spiritual tension, a sympathetic friend, sleep, baths, prayer—but these remedies by no means get at the roots of melancholy, the irresolvable conflicts attendant on being plunged into created existence. St. Thomas's suggestions are designed to *conceal* melancholia, to hide sadness, while aiming indirectly at preserving the existing world order. (In the Middle Ages the royal court was also intolerant of gloom: that was the privilege of the court jester. He was allowed to be melancholic, to unveil the transience beyond every joy, the sadness inherent in all things. He did not have to be taken seriously, but he was needed as a sort of "safety valve.")

It is *sin* that lurks at the very bottom of sloth and worldly sorrow: "This strife was against my will," writes St. Augustine of the above-mentioned sickness of the soul, "but the punishment of my own. Thus it was no more I who did it, but the sin that dwelt in me" (*Confessions*, bk. 8, 10). It was Adam who made humankind sinful, as a result of which, sin is a collective legacy of us all. St. Hildegard of Bingen (twelfth century), the "Sibyl of the Rhine," who acquired fame through her prophetic visions and unusual spiritual experiences, saw the origin of melancholia in this shared sin: "What is now gall in him sparkled like crystal, and bore the taste of good work, and what is now melancholy in man shone in him like the dawn and contained in itself the wisdom and perfection of good works; but when Adam broke the law, the sparkle of innocence was dulled in him, and his eyes, which had formerly beheld heaven, were blinded, and his gall was changed to bitterness, and his melancholy to blackness" (quoted in Klibansky, Panofsky, and Saxl, *Saturn and Melan-*

choly, 80). (Of course, "black bile" meant "melancholy.") In this view, then, melancholia was not an attribute of the individual, but of the genus humankind, and was born when the Tree of Knowledge was robbed. The consequences of melancholia are sorrow and despair, since humankind is incapable of forgetting paradise: in St. Hildegard's understanding, it automatically extends to everybody. (Her contemporary William of Conches called the four temperaments "deficient forms"—referring to the mixture of man's humors after the Fall, as opposed to the balanced mixture before.) But original sin as "deficiency" is not the same as the sin of a specific individual. In the case of melancholics, the sin is double, since in addition to the collective original sin, they are weighed down by individual sin; after all, they have rejected the good *of their own free will* as well, not only as a result of their being created. According to Roman Catholic theology, sin is a *mysterium iniquitatis*, a mystery of evil, as a result of which creaturely freedom may even set itself against God and choose evil. Choosing evil of one's free will, the rejection of God, produces melancholia, but *that melancholia only nominally resembles the melancholia springing from original sin.* Even before making a choice of good or evil, a person, as a descendent of Adam, is guilty of original sin, but thanks to Jesus Christ, can find redemption. Thus, the possibility for individual decision is restricted to the space between these two points, and by choosing individual sin, one cuts oneself off from Jesus. From a medieval medical point of view, a mentally ill person— including a melancholic—can be cured of his illness by looking at a portrait of Jesus or Mary for a long time. That was why for lunatics there was an almost proverbial chant: *Eamus ad videndum filium Mariae*—"Let us see the son of Mary." The tracing of the origin of melancholia to original sin and to the Christian anthropological interpretation of humankind provides nothing less than an *existential* explanation of human existence; melancholia stemming from individual choice, on the other hand, admits of a practical-ethical image of humankind—one that the Church persecuted vehemently, judging it an indication of sinners venturing a universal interpretation of existence. (At the beginning of the seventeenth century, yet still completely in the medieval spirit, Robert Burton too made a distinction between two kinds of melancholia: the universal sort, which is an inseparable aspect of being human, and a special melancholia, typical only of certain people.)

This dual conception of melancholia was far from clearly distinguishable to thinkers of the time; the two were intertwined, and in most cases "original" melancholia was also considered to be a mental illness. The interpretation of melancholia produced by St. Hildegard of Bingen or William of Conches went beyond other interpretations customary at the time: although they associated it with sin and with evil, in the last analysis they used it as a metaphor for humankind's originally conflicted, precarious condition. This melancholia did not have its own special manifestation: the sorrow referred to by Hildegard, who was supposedly a melancholic herself, was not the "sadness" of the mentally ill but a consequence of the inevitable fate of being cast into the world and being created. Humankind elected sin of its own free will, says Hildegard, thereby predating Kierkegaard, who likewise brought the notion of "fear and trembling" into the context of original sin: Adam tasted the fruits of the Tree of Knowledge, but along with freedom he also chose to sin. According to Hildegard also, sin and free will were deeply connected (the nonmelancholic Anselm of Canterbury argued that only God and the good angels were free, whereas humankind was totally predetermined), and by relating melancholia to freedom of choice (even if in a condemnatory tone), she threw open a perspective on the interpretation of melancholia that was to resonate well beyond her own times. As long as it operated as a closed system, Roman Catholic theology, as has been seen, was able to integrate melancholia to a good purpose: by declaring that opposition and reticence, discernible at the root of every case of melancholia, were tantamount to madness and mental illness, this theology ultimately glorified itself. In the eyes of the general public as well, melancholia was irrational degeneracy. Medieval melancholics were the victims of a paradox, and the contradiction was not permitted to unfold, whereby it could have self-destructed through its freedom, but instead was ignored. Hence, the manifold modes of treatment that were proposed for melancholics, none of them radical, since in the end one could hardly abolish by purely physical means a condition that had been branded theologically. Treatments included "medications" like the flesh of an old cock, a ram's head, a wolf's heart, the water of the Nile, goat's milk, whey, and also herbal remedies, such as "a simple potion of hellebore" (already in Strabo's time hellebore was recommended against madness), bugloss (which was used in Homer's *Odyssey* to bring forgetfulness to those suffering from the malady), melissa, borage, black salsify, cockscomb, marigold, lupin, artemisia, centaurea, pennyroyal, endive, wild chicory, dandelion, and fumitory.

The derivation of melancholia from original sin placed the illness in a new light. It extended to everyone; the sadness, the desperation, the thrownness (*Geworfenheit*), and the desire to be elsewhere were transformed into a normal state of being, a condition that has been impossible to rectify since man has existed. The state of being human is "incurable"; the deep chasm between a person's createdness and grace is unbridgeable. In parallel with the medieval notion of melancholia, following the turn of the first millennium the view became ever more common that if inner conflict and self-alienation were common states of existence, shared by all of us, then they ought to be "made use of." It did not matter whether this would be against God or to his glory; all that was important was that the torrent of doubt that estranges people both from God and from themselves should gain legitimacy. This judgment of melancholia in itself was medieval: the daring view had not yet been born that melancholia not only provided an opportunity for an alternative take on existence but was also just as autonomous, self-supporting, and therefore unassailable as the well-known "ordinary" way of looking at things. Although in relation to ecstasy St. Bonaventure writes of "a divine melancholy" and "a spiritual wing" (Burton, *Anatomy*, partition 3, sec. 4, member 1, subsec. 2, 343), which proves that he is far from regarding melancholia as just a mental sickness. But in general the era still spoke of melancholia disapprovingly, which is why he thought of ecstasy differently from the Greeks: he saw it not as a "stepping out of" but as a "stepping into" the Christian realm. The story of Jesus, no less, justifies this view. Jesus's disciples in Capernaum considered him deranged because he stepped out of (that is, neglected) a regular style of living.[6] In Jesus's case, stepping out of or standing beside himself (ecstasy) meant at one and the same time stepping out of the earthly realm, which is to say, stepping into God's kingdom. Bonaventure's "ecstatic melancholia" is good only insofar as it diverts attention from worldly vanities: if it encourages that, then it is a testimony to God's love.[7] If the Aristotelian scheme of melancholia ever cropped up, it was interpreted also in that spirit toward the end of the Middle Ages. It was first mentioned by Alexander Neckam around 1200 and not much later by Albertus Magnus, but both of them took the edge off the original concept. William of Auvergne, the thirteenth-century bishop of Paris, likewise made reference to Aristotle, but reinterpreted him in a Christian manner: melancholia liberated people from sins of the body and enlightened them: "This complexion withdraws men from bodily pleasures and worldly turmoil. Nevertheless, though nature affords these aids to illumination and revelation, they are achieved far more abundantly through the grace of the Creator, integrity of living, and holiness and purity" (quoted in Klibansky, Panofsky, and Saxl, *Saturn and Melancholy*, 73). Melancholy was a form of asceti-

---

6. ἔλεγον γὰρ ὅτι ἐξέστη (Mark 3:21). In the King James Version of the Bible, the phrase used is "beside himself."

7. Bonaventure remarks disapprovingly on a desire for annihilation as a consequence of nausea due to acedia, but he appraises it positively if the goal is union with God as soon as possible.

cism, and William saw it as a desirable state exclusively in that sense: he had heard about many pious men whose "most fervent wish was to be afflicted by melancholia, since that surely strengthened spiritual goods" (quoted in Günther Bandmann, *Melancholie und Musik. Ikonographische Studien*, 104).

This conception of melancholy remained within the bounds of the Christian interpretation of existence. That positive perception nevertheless represented a kind of countercurrent against the prevailing view. With the appearance of St. Francis in the thirteenth century, the rigid separation of nature from spirit came to an end; *all* phenomena of existence became equally important, and this was evident not only for ordinary all-embracing faith but also for the sensual take on the world. Sensual diversity (that is, the profusion of the world) did not preclude divine unity; and the focus on the individual, which had started to gain ground in Europe, signaled the cracking of a closed system of beliefs. Antiquity's interpretation of melancholia obviously found a breeding ground in between those cracks. If the Middle Ages began to regard melancholia as a disease of the mind, then in the last analysis it managed to hide the cracks, but when melancholia was analyzed as a positive state of being, the cracks were not hidden from posterity's gaze but were in fact made more visible. If melancholia is regarded as an illness, then it will be seen as dangerous by society, and for that reason—and there are plenty of examples of this in more recent history—it will be invested with collateral political significance. Melancholics themselves, however, do not in the least think of themselves as being either ill or subversive. Their mournfulness and despair relate not to one or another, possibly adjustable or rectifiable, form or manifestation of human contact or institution, but to existence in general, and therefore they are not pinning their hopes on any remedy. A judgment of melancholia hinges on whether one tries to put oneself in the shoes of a melancholic or treats him purely as an object. One has the impression that toward the close of the Middle Ages an ever-increasing number of people strove to recognize the legitimacy of the melancholic interpretation of existence — but for that to happen, the whole culture had to move. The revival of Hellenistic astrological explanations for melancholia laid the groundwork for that earthquake.

Notions formed about "children of the planets," indeed, the science of astrology in general, were revived from the eleventh to twelfth centuries onward. Through Arab stargazers (Abu Ma'shar and Ibn Ezra), a gradually spreading antique Hellenistic astrology aimed to find a correspondence between individual diversity and the unity of the world. The Greeks adopted from the Orient the idea that there was a parallel between the human body and the universe (the body of the cosmos); the two kinds of medical schools of thought — the Hippocratic and the Empedoclean — likewise grew out of these; indeed, in the sixth century BCE, Alcmaeon of Croton, often referred to as a pupil of Pythagoras, anticipated Plato in discerning a connection between the constant movement of the stars and the immortality of the soul. (Pythagoras is said to have called the planets the dogs of Proserpine; see Jaap Mansfeld, *Die Vorsokratiker: Auswahl der Fragmente*, 1:191.) The late Middle Ages revived that doctrine, and the astrological approach began to gain ground within the field of medical science. Paracelsus was of the opinion "that a physician without the knowledge of stars can neither understand the cause or cure of any disease, either of this [melancholia] or gout, not so much as toothache" (quoted in Burton, *Anatomy*, partition 1, sec. 2, member 1, subsec. 4, 206). According to Melanchthon "this variety of melancholy symptoms proceeds from the stars" (ibid.). In the sixteenth and seventeenth centuries, an *external* cause was always sought in relation to the mind, and mental illnesses (for example, melancholia) were attributed to supernatural forces, and above all to an influence of the stars.[8] The derivation of melancholia from the position of the stars

---

8. A famous example is the book entitled *Planetomachia*, published c. 1585 by Robert Greene.

set it in a new light in opposition to the theological interpretation of the Middle Ages. Anyone who was melancholic was under the sway of Saturn—his condition was therefore not a matter of *choice*, a consequence of rejecting grace or shutting himself down, but of fate, against which one could only fight, at best, with the help of other planets. The *closedness* of a cosmos made up of seven planets was not the same as the power of divine omnipotence to close up everything (which was why Christianity persecuted astrology at various points in history), so the Christian perception of the Hellenistic era had to provide the planets with a Christian-ethical interpretation in order to fit astrology into its worldview.[9] In the Christian view, the planets, too, were moved by God and were thereby deprived of their omnipotence: "This Mind . . . was fashioned by the seven Governors [that is, the spirits of the planets], who encompass within their orbits the world perceived by the senses. Their government is called destiny," one reads in "Pœmandres," an early Christian Hermetic dialogue. Boethius, in the *Consolation of Philosophy*, wrote: "Providence embraces all things, however different, however infinite; fate sets in motion separately individual things, and assigns to them severally their position, form, and time. . . . So the unfolding of this temporal order unified into the foreview of the Divine mind is providence, while the same unity broken up and unfolded in time is fate" (bk. 4, 6). According to the Gnostics, a soul, on descending to Earth, comes ever closer to the material world and, resting every now and then in the circles of the seven planets (that is, the seven low-lying spirits), acquires ever-newer material (that is, bad) attributes (the way the seven Christian cardinal sins appear in "Pœmandres" is that in the soul's fight with the spheres, the higher she rises, the more she sheds her sins). For Christian Neoplatonists, by contrast, the higher the planets raised a soul

---

9. It adopted the astrology of the Roman imperial age, which had toned down and expanded Ptolemaic-Julianic astrology with an admixture of science and mythology.

toward God, the more good properties (the seven virtues) they could bestow on her. For both approaches, the seven planets were tools with which God renders earthly souls *material*. Their role is nevertheless ambiguous: they are characterized by polarity and ambivalence. This manifests itself most spectacularly in the case of the seventh and most distant planet: according to the author of "Pœmandres," the soul in the seventh zone divests herself of "the malicious lie" (25) or, according to other Gnostics, the sin of dolefulness, idleness, and stupidity. According to Plotinus, however, the seventh planet ensures a person's intellect ($\nu o\tilde{v}s$) (see Klibansky, Panofsky, and Saxl, *Saturn and Melancholy*, 153); in his commentary to *Somnium Scipionis*, on the other hand, Macrobius endowed the seventh planet with the capabilities of logic and theory ($\lambda o\gamma\iota\sigma\tau\iota\kappa\acute{o}s$ and $\vartheta\epsilon\omega\rho\eta\tau\iota\kappa\acute{o}s$, ibid.).

The seventh planet is Saturn, and it seems fateful that this planet—which according to astrology and its related body of beliefs is endowed with the most extreme properties (for Neoplatonists, Saturn exerts the greatest influence on earthly affairs)—was allied to melancholia during the Hellenistic era. Melancholics were seen as persons of extremes ($\pi\epsilon\rho\iota\tau\tau o\acute{\iota}$), exposed to risk from all directions. Their capabilities extended to the limits of human life, and like the planet Saturn, melancholics could rightly claim that beyond them there was either *nothingness* or *God*. It mattered not whether one gave a name to that void and held it to be God; it was more important that on reaching that utmost point, the melancholic would no longer be faced with any human being. Standing there, he was no longer surrounded by people; anyone hitherto familiar would become unfamiliar, and anything that appeared before him would arouse feelings of homelessness. As a result of his extreme position, he felt himself to be an outcast, an elect, sinful and saintly. And like souls that reach Saturn after voyaging among the other planets, where they have to leave their earthliness behind and become incorporeal (according to Neoplatonists) as well as to *step into* earthliness and assume a definite form (Gnostics), the melancholic is subjected to multiple trials: in one and the same person, the most excellent and most unfortunate, like Heracles; the wisest and most ignorant, like Socrates; the most blasphemous and holiest, like Empedocles. The Neoplatonist and the Gnostic explanations of Saturn seem, at first sight, to contradict each other. Plotinus explained the name of Cronus, the Greek counterpart of Saturn, as being a compound of *koros* (a boy or plenty) and *nus* (spirit), seeing Cronus as a symbol of fulfillment (other suppositions derived the name from the verb κραίνω, "to carry out, accomplish"): "Kronos, as the wisest, exists before Zeus; he must absorb his offspring that, full within himself, he may be also an Intellectual-Principle manifest in some product of his plenty" (*Enneads*, V. 1. 7.). According to the Gnostics, however, the seven planetary gods guaranteed the materiality of a world that had broken away from the Creator; their leader was Jaldabaoth—also known as Moloch, Cronus (that is, Saturn)—about whom the Perates (a Gnostic sect) said: "For Cronus is a cause to every generation, in regard of succumbing under destruction, and there could not exist (an instance of) generation in which Cronus does not interfere" (Hippolytus, *The Refutation of All Heresies*, bk. 5, ch. 11). But the two different views agreed on the matter of Saturn's extreme position—as was authenticated by the condition of melancholia, which united the most extreme human states (without their extinguishing each other), and its planet became Saturn, which the Arabic astrologers called the "Star of Great Misfortune." In both the Gnostic and the Neoplatonist interpretations, Saturn was a boundary. Melancholics would reach that boundary: despite being humans, they stepped beyond the limits of human existence to a place where worldly notions lost their meaning and were set in a new light; a place not only where excellence and misfortune, wisdom and ignorance, presupposed each other, but also where the most profound search for God and the most highly consistent rejection of God could equally become a source of the most unfortunate lunacy. Souls under Saturn's influence were opposed both to the earthly world and to God, and turned their back equally on both.

That, too, applied to melancholics, although they understood this in a figurative sense because they were not "confronting" God but carrying God within them, and instead of "confronting" the earthly world, they were themselves part of it. Consequently, if they "turned their back on" God and the world, then they were coming into conflict with themselves; they denied God, even as they were carrying him within themselves, and their existence would be inconceivable without him; they denied the earthly world, even though they were dust—and thereby they made the void the fundamental principle, the God of the world. Nothingness, however (being nothing), was elusive: it resided in the heart. It was inseparable from the melancholic interpretation of existence: it presupposed Something, without which Nothingness would be inconceivable—but the shadow of Nothingness was also cast onto Something, which for that reason was cloaked in obscurity for melancholics. They would fain escape from Nothingness, and throw themselves fanatically into the tangible earthly world; but the Something onto which they wished to cling was unknown and therefore did not offer a home, and wherever they might have turned, everything led back to Nothingness. They discovered the ephemeral in the finite, whereas they missed the finite in the infinite. They were Saturn's children, and like Socrates, who according to the medieval conception had a "*Daemonium Saturninum et ignium*" ("saturnine and fiery daimon"; Burton, *Anatomy*, partition 1, sec. 2, member 1, subsec. 2, 191), whichever way they turned, they were faced with absence. That made them refined, sensitive, and ironic, but also downcast, despondent, and inconsolable.

Polarity and ambivalence—those were what marked out Saturn and melancholia. The Babylonians worshipped the planet Saturn as the deity Ninib, the nighttime counterpart of the sun, and that belief was augmented by Marcus Manilius, a Roman astrologer, to the effect that since Saturn faced the sun but was located at the other end of the world's axis, the world viewed from there was seen from a fundamentally *opposing* perspective. In this case, opposition implied ambiguity; since the world was inconceivable without the sun, people and things that were under Saturn's influence enjoyed both the light of the sun and Saturn's nighttime glimmer—they could simultaneously see the face of the world and its reverse side. Cronus, the Greek counterpart of Saturn, like most Greek deities, was himself of ambiguous character. On the one hand, he was lord of the Saturnian age, the master of annual fertility and renewal, the founder of city building and agriculture; on the other hand, deposed from his throne, he was a solitary god who, according to some notions, resides "at the outer gates of [Olympus's] many valleys" (*Iliad*, bk. 8, 479), "in the depths that are under earth and sea" (bk. 14, 204), and "who rules the world below" (bk. 15, 225), a prisoner; in some cases, he is even represented as the god of death and the dead. Saturn was a father of gods and humankind, but he devoured his own children: with the sickle used for reaping, he castrated and deposed Uranus, making his own father infertile. The sickle is thus a symbol of both fertility and infertility. Those who are born under the influence of Saturn-Cronus inherit his characteristics, in the view of Hellenism, prone as it was to link mythology with astrology, making Saturn (its symbol: ♄) the planet of melancholics. Anyone born under Saturn's sign will be torn apart by contradictions, the astrologers taught, long before the planet was associated with melancholia, and their interpretation determined views on Saturn's earthly influence that are held to the present day. According to early Greek astrology (Dorotheus), which was concerned with general planetary effects, the influence of Saturn assured a person of sturdy character, intellect, and talent; during the period when scientific astrology was evolving, Ptolemy held the view that Saturn's offspring were fond of solitude, were deep thinkers, and were prone to mysticism, but at the same time were down-to-earth: stingy, dirty, and decrepit. In the opinion of Roman imperial astrologers (Valeus, Firmicus), in line with the conjunction of the planet, Saturn's children were famous, high-born personages, but they might also be completely unknown, extremely low-ranking people who had to endure much pain. Saturn's children might be under the threat of being exiled, shipwrecked, or imprisoned (they might become robbers and killers, the Middle Ages vowed), but they were just as likely to possess a lofty intellect and a profound soul. (Saturn was a patron of learning; in Dante's *Divine Comedy*, the representatives of the *vita contemplativa* appear in the "Seventh Heaven, the sphere of Saturn"—*Paradise*, canto 21.) Those born under the sign of Saturn were characterized by the most contradictory attributes (rich–poor, slave–master, stay-at-home–traveler, dry–damp, clever–stupid, etc.), including cases where just one of these attributes was present in them, but even so — as with true melancholics — the opposites might appear simultaneously in the same person. "Saturn," writes Ficino, "seldom denotes ordinary characters and destinies, but rather men who are set apart from the others, divine or animal, joyous or bowed down by the deepest grief" (quoted in Klibansky, Panofsky, and Saxl, *Saturn and Melancholy*, 253). The four attributes that Aristotle associated with the four elements (cold, warm, dry, wet) were transferred to the planets, with Saturn being characterized by coldness and dryness. (Since the time of Hippocrates, melancholics have been regarded as dry by nature.) John Scotus Eriugena explained this as follows: the rays of the sun,

> when they rise upwards into the uppermost regions of the world which are closest to the most rarefied and spiritual nature, not finding any matter for kindling, they produce no heat, and display only the operation of illumination, and therefore the ethereal and pure and spiritual heavenly bodies which are established in those regions are always shining, but are without heat. And hence they are believed to be both cold and pale. Therefore the planet which is called by the name of Saturn, since it is in the neighbourhood of the harmonious motions of the stars, is said to be cold and pale.

(Periphyseon, bk. 3, 27, 205–7)

Since among the elements earth is the one that is dry and cold, those born of Saturn are attracted to earth. (Cronus is, in part, a chthonian—earthly, or rather subterranean—deity, like the gods of the mysteries of antiquity.) Melancholics, being attracted to earth, seek their home in the world of perceptible things, which is why they remain down-to-earth (they become handicraftsmen and peasants; they are stupid, dull, and evil-minded). Long after the toppling of the theory of humors, Jakob Böhme considered melancholics, like the earth, to be cold, stiff, dark, disconsolate, lacking in light, and constantly afraid of God's wrath. That earthiness and cleaving to palpable things is not a natural state, however, but a flight in the literal sense: the melancholic is incapable of breaking away from the world of opposites and always perceives absence everywhere. His desire for safety turns his gaze to the ground, but earthly matters draw his attention to transitoriness and otherwordliness. Saturn's child, Agrippa von Nettesheim wrote in 1510, "constantly brooding, as it were drills through the ground" (quoted in Benjamin, *German Tragic Drama*, ch. 5, 350). That is so in a double sense. Agrippa interpreted the drilling through the ground literally, taking the view that melancholics were able to discover treasure hidden below the ground. In a broader sense, however, it was not just treasures that were hidden underground; the deep itself was also the antithesis of the surface, a denial of life, the domain of death (or "otherworldliness"). In a work published in 1727, Martin of Cochem propounded that if benignant God did not ward off the noxious influence of Saturn with his own power, or through the resistance of other stars, few people on Earth would remain alive. Melancholics hold on to the world more tightly than anyone else; or to be more accurate, they value it more highly, but a true accounting warns them of its transience (not of its vanity!). The correlation of melancholia with talent in soothsaying, as antiquity saw it, has already been noted. A person who is truly able to prophesy is *inside* things and is not approaching them from the outside; he is someone who does not warn one of an event that will happen sometime in the future, but who tells the truth about *today*, the *current* state of matters. A down-to-earth melancholic is a soothsayer in this sense.[10] Saturn invested him with the capability of adopting an ambivalent attitude, and that was why he was well aware that the earthly world itself provided no ultimate foothold: the only one truly able to assess the earthly realm was someone who saw its transience, but the only people who have any notion of its transience are those who have thrown themselves into the petty annoyances of this world. Saturn was the lord of the earth as well as the underworld, in body and soul; to quote Schiller's Wallenstein, "Lord of the secret birth of things is he; / Within the lap of earth, and in the depths / Of the imagination dominates" (*The Death of Wallenstein*, act 4, scene 1). The offspring of Saturn cannot find his home anywhere; he is unable to find a hold and sees himself as an outcast. In a letter to Andrea Dandolo, the doge of Venice, melancholic Petrarch writes: "Thus am I tossed about in the knowledge that there is no resting place here, and that I must long for such rest through many difficulties: here indeed I must perpetually toil and groan and—what is perhaps worst of all—amidst so many trials and fires of life" (Petrarch, *Letters on Familiar Matters*, vol. 2, bk. 15, letter 4, 260—a justification for his frequent moves). Saturn's children are doomed to long journeys, so says Agrippa von Nettesheim; and like his previous comment, this, too, is ambiguous: a long journey signifies adventures on sea and land (which is what Agrippa is thinking of), but it can also denote homelessness, a never-achieved arrival. And what could better characterize the deep kinship of the mythological-astrological notion with melancholia than the well-known ball of *Melencolia I*, Albrecht Dürer's copperplate etching of 1514—since antiquity, a symbol of death and good luck. Death and luck are poised, sleeping, on a ball, and it is just

---

10. According to a Babylonian notion, the highest spheres of the planets "scatter prophetic thunderbolts"; a Greek text specifically mentions Saturn in that context (see Karl Kerényi, "Asterobléta Keraunos," 86).

a matter of luck which way it will set off with them. The ball possesses uncontrollable power: it can roll this way or that, make a mockery of expectations; and while it possesses the most perfect, closed, and unopenable body, its movements represent the extreme uncertainty and homelessness visited on Saturn's children, the melancholics.

The ball signals Saturn's power, and what could be more natural than that astrology, professing cosmic closedness, should extend that power to everything. In keeping with the increasingly complex vision of the passing Middle Ages, melancholia thus extended to the whole of nature. According to Tycho Brahe, every part of the body had its own planet, and corresponding to Saturn is the spleen,[11] which was regarded as a cold and dry part of the body. The seven planets also denoted the seven ages of man;[12] advanced old age, in which life's forces and juices gradually cool and stiffen, belonged to Saturn. They could also denote the seven sciences.[13] But Saturn influenced even the direction of the wind: Hippocrates connected the pathological influence of black bile with a northerly wind—an idea revived by Dürer in his woodcut *Philosophia*, in the four corners of which are the four cardinal wind directions personified. The saturnine Boreas (north wind) appears grouped with earth (*terra*), winter, and melancholia. Saturn's power to bring on melancholia made its influence felt everywhere in nature. "Melancholy," writes Robert Burton, "extends itself not to men only, but even to vegetals and sensibles. I speak not of those creatures which are saturnine, melancholy by nature, as lead, and such like minerals, or those plants, rue,[14] cypress, &c.

---

11. From the Latin *splen*, which in turn derives from Greek. Thence "spleen"—the modern equivalent of saturnine melancholia.

12. See the monologue of the melancholy Jaques in Shakespeare's *As You Like It* (II.7).

13. In *Convivio* (II. 14), Dante associates astrology with Saturn.

14. Now somewhat archaic, the word still denotes sorrow, pity, or regret and repentance.

and hellebore itself; of which Agrippa treats, fishes, birds, and beasts, hares, conies, dormice, &c., owls, bats, nightbirds, but that artificial, which is perceived in them all" (Burton, *Anatomy*, "Democritus to the Reader," 179). In accordance with medieval so-called natural magic (Roger Bacon), owing to the unity of the cosmos, earthly materials also possessed some of the properties of the stars and planets, and for that reason these materials could have a therapeutic effect in the form of amulets. If certain materials, such as lead or turquoise, or (according to Niccolò Cabeo of Ferrara, a Jesuit-schooled philosopher) a magnet, are saturnian and melancholic, then other materials, whose effects oppose Saturn, may have the opposite qualities and thus be able to dispel melancholia. According to Albertus Magnus, in the gizzard of a swallow there was a stone called chelidonius, which, if folded in a piece of cloth and tied to the right arm, could cure melancholics. As late as the fourteenth century, Konrad of Megenberg still recommended chelidonius to counter melancholia, and Robert Burton, a granatus (or alternatively, hyacinth and topaz) to be hung from the neck. An influence of Saturn can extend to animals, as has been seen: certain animals, or parts of their bodies, are able to abolish melancholia (an old cock, a ram's head, and a wolf's heart, even goat's milk), whereas other animals embody melancholia. According to Agrippa von Nettesheim, melancholics were "all creeping animals, living apart, and solitary, nightly, sad, contemplative, dull, covetous, fearful, melancholy, that take much pains, slow, that feed grossly, and such as eat their young. Of these kinds therefore are the mole, the wolf, the ass, the toad, the cat, the hog, the bear, the camel, the basilisk, the hare, the ape, the dragon, the mule, all serpents, and creeping things, scorpions, ants, and such things as proceed from putrefaction in the earth, in water, or in the ruins of houses, as mice, and many sorts of vermin" (*Three Books of Occult Philosophy or Magic*, ch. 25, 99–100). Dogs, for example, are prone to melancholia, but according to William of Conches, oxen and donkeys are typically melancholic animals, or according to Thomas Nash, the owl, "that customary messenger of death"—but above all bats, which not only embodied nocturnal darkness and uncleanness (in the seventeenth century they were a symbol of the Antichrist), but also, in the view of Ficino, symbolized the futility and noxious effect of studying during the night. (In medieval miniatures, melancholics were often depicted sleeping.) Bats, the hearts of which, according to Agrippa, can serve as a talisman against somnolence,[15] were the very symbol of irregularity and extraordinariness: neither birds nor mice, but intermediates between those species. Opposing the bat is the eagle, which drives away melancholia, it being not only a bird of *light*, but also Jupiter's creature, and just as Jupiter defeated Cronus-Saturn, so too will the eagle vanquish melancholy. Jupiter's influence is displayed in another way too: the Jupiterian magic square (*mensula Iovis*), the numbers of which add up to the same total in each direction, as shown prominently in Dürer's engraving *Melencolia I*, is also capable of curing melancholia. According to Paracelsus, "this symbol makes its bearer fortunate in all his dealings and drives away all cares and fears" (quoted in Klibansky, Panofsky, and Saxl, *Saturn and Melancholy*, 326). The influence of the planet Jupiter can also stand in the way of melancholia: "For when Venus is located as we have described, and if Saturn is in any aspect," writes Firmicus Maternus at the beginning of the fourth century, "this produces minds involved in perverse vices, not successful in any normal human activities. . . . But if Venus in this house is aspected to Jupiter, the native is freed from the evil described above" (*Ancient Astrology*, bk. 3, 6). Bassardus Visontinus commends hypericum, or St.-John's-wort, gathered on a Friday in the hour of *Jupiter* (that is, during a full moon in July); whereas according to Melanchthon, "melancholy is much more generous if it is tempered by the conjunction of Saturn and Jupiter in Libra" (quoted in Benjamin, *German Tragic Drama*, 151). The horo-

---

15. On the other hand, in the opinion of Pliny the Elder, it is a bat's heart that acts against sleep (*Natural History*, bk. 29, 48).

scopes of Kleist and Nietzsche attest to the same: the strength of their dominant Saturn was moderated by Jupiter being in Libra, and that was why their melancholia was "nobler" than common depression.

We have now reached the late Middle Ages. Jupiter either abolishes melancholia or ennobles it. The influence the planets exert *may* be fateful, but is not necessarily so: a person, as natural magic declares, is not merely at the mercy of destiny, but can also meet it halfway, and even fight against it. *One may choose one's fate.* Melancholia is a result not just of rejecting divine grace but also of a singular interplay of natural forces. In the late Middle Ages, the astrological explanation refined the earlier monolithic way of looking at things, according to which melancholia was a mental illness. However paradoxical it may seem, the astrological conception smoothed the ground for the assessment of melancholia in modern times. Like the derivation of it from original sin, astrological explanations generalized melancholia: it could befall *anyone.* Something that could befall anyone and settle on a person like destiny or fate was in no way just an illness, at least not in the sense that illness was understood at the time; for in that sense, illness indicated a lack of divine grace. If anyone could lose grace, a sinless person just as much as a sinner, then the meaning of melancholia needed to be modified. Defiance of God was not a sin by definition, but an experiment, the goal of which was self-deification. Astrology and the associated concept of melancholia prepared the way for the dethronement of God.

Chapter 4

THE CHALLENGE OF FATE

Destiny challenged—nothing could be further from the scholastic picture of the universe. Haughtiness, closing in on oneself, rejecting grace, indeed tacitly disavowing God—those were still demonstrable characteristics of medieval melancholics, who were rightly and justifiably considered mentally ill by those around them: melancholics truly did go mad in a solitary way of life and did so literally, not merely symbolically. They were prisoners of destiny, helpless sufferers of their fate, however alive to it they may have been. The moment, however, that the ideological seal was broken by astrological explanations, those ties started to loosen. The condition of Saturn's children became ambiguous, as did Saturn himself. "Saturn cannot easily signify the common quality and lot of the human race, but he signifies an individual set apart from others, divine or brutish, blessed or bowed down with the extreme of misery," Marsilio Ficino writes in *De vita triplici* (*Three Books on Life*, bk. 3, ch. 2), composed between 1480 and 1489, which, alongside Burton's massive tome, is the other most important work on melancholia. Saturn's dual power did not only result in two human types but could also turn someone into a two-faced person. On one occasion, Ficino complained to Giovanni Cavalcanti about the bad influence of Saturn on him, whereupon Cavalcanti reproached his friend for having no cause for complaint, since it was exclusively through Saturn's assistance that he had become such an excellent and clever person; Ficino agreed with him—"I shall, in agreement with Aristotle, say that this nature itself is a unique and divine gift" (*Epistolae*, vol. 2, no. 24)—and moreover added that maybe he could also thank Saturn for his talent, since

Saturn's detrimental effect could be mitigated by the other planets. In his response, he writes: "Saturn seems to have impressed the seal of melancholy on me from the beginning; set, as he is, almost in the midst of my ascendant Aquarius, he is influenced by Mars, also in Aquarius, and the Moon in Capricorn. He is in square aspect to the Sun and Mercury in Scorpio, which occupy the ninth house. But Venus in Libra and Jupiter in Cancer have, perhaps, offered some resistance to this melancholy nature" (ibid.). Saturn was just as responsible for depression as for intellectual excellence, for ill humor as for enlightenment. This duality is the starting point of the chapter on melancholia in his *Three Books on Life*. The ambivalence typical of the melancholic was at one and the same time the basis of a dynamic personality. In book 1, chapter 2, of *De vita triplici* he writes: "Therefore black bile continually incites the soul both to collect itself together into one and to dwell on itself and to contemplate itself." Because of the dynamic character of the mind, however, black bile influences the mind, and conversely, mental exertion is responsible for the ill effects of black bile. Melancholics can blame themselves just as much as Saturn; indeed, with sufficient exertion, the mind alone is capable of inducing melancholia, without any help from Saturn.[1] Ficino's innovation was the idea that not only were Saturn's children capable of intellectual achievements, but through appropriate intellectual activity, *anyone* might fall under the influence of Saturn. With intellectual effort, a person could transcend his or her customary circles and expand the dimensions of the existing world. "Hence

---

1. The title of a chapter in *Three Books on Life* is "How Many Things Cause Learned People Either to Be Melancholy or *to Eventually Become So*" (emphasis added). Helvétius was later to write in similar vein: "The most spiritual and most thoughtful people are, I know, sometimes melancholic; but they are not spiritual or thoughtful because they are melancholic, but melancholic because they are thoughtful" ("Les plus spirituels et les plus méditatifs sont quelquefois mélancoliques, je le sais: mail ils ne sont pas spirituels et méditatifs parcequ'ils sont mélancoliques, mais mélancoliques parcequ'ils sont méditatifs"; *De l'Homme*, 138–39).

by withdrawal from human affairs, by leisure, solitude, constancy, by theology, the more esoteric philosophy, superstition, magic, agriculture, and by sorrow, we come under the influence of Saturn" (ibid., bk. 3, ch. 3). Saturn is the most human and equally the most mysterious planet;[2] the way leading to the unknown, as in the case of the mysteries of antiquity, was open to all.

In Ficino's eyes, the melancholic personality was ambivalent and dynamic, simultaneously crazy and sane, enthusiastic and depressed. The most striking characteristic of melancholics was that they were responsible for their own fate—they could challenge and influence it. The notion of people being responsible *for their own fate*, however, had far-reaching consequences: it not only removed the individual from God's authority, but also invested him with an arbitrary power that made his solitude much more palpable and tormenting than in earlier centuries. Medieval melancholics were also solitary, but since their solitude was coupled with mental illness, because of their situation, they were incapable of assessing their own state: the culture around them was so closed that they were obliged to believe whatever others said about them. They were captives of their culture; if they were regarded as crazy, then they believed it—and that was enough to drive them truly crazy. Ficino's melancholics were responsible for their own fate; they withdrew themselves from the control of any authority. The cause of their solitude was not necessarily inertia but very often intellectual exertion; that was why they were fully aware of their position—in contrast with medieval melancholics, who were never able to emancipate themselves to this extent from their cultural surroundings. Melancholics realized their solitude, and their position became unbearable as a result, but this intolerableness, at the same time, became the basis of their sense of being chosen. They clashed with everything (since they made choices), and *that*

---

2. At the Platonic Academy in Florence, Saturn was venerated as the supreme deity, and Plato was considered to be one of his offspring.

was why they were regarded as *abnormal*, because others generally satisfied common expectations. They regarded themselves, however, as the *most normal* of all (they behaved according to their own will, after all, and they set their own rules for themselves). They knew and saw that the world was a system of expectations, but that ambiguous situation made them incapable of satisfying expectations of any kind. Either they had to accept that they were abnormal, sick personalities, for, after all, a normal personality accepted that the world was the way it was, but their sense of being chosen did not permit any such acceptance; or else they had to accept that they were chosen, extraordinarily talented, healthy people, but that, too, was beyond them because they sincerely experienced the abnormal nature of their situation. These mutually conflicting demands paralyzed them and, to use a modern expression, made them *neurotic*. Ignoring the ego's orders—as Freud would put it—was not neurotic (in this sense, neither a total masochist nor a mentally ill patient should be considered neurotic), yet living in the midst of conflicts and being caught between conflicting commands, without finding a way out (compensation, sublimation, foregoing certain desires, conscious avoidance of conflicts, etc.) would eventually turn one into a neurotic. Neurotics are not insane, but they are not healthy either; caught between conflicting commands, they drift this way and that, so in their situation they are as familiar with despair as with irony. (Melancholics in the Middle Ages could "decide" between a closed world and nothing— hence their madness; melancholics in the Renaissance, however, could not "choose": the world was open, riven from the outset.)

In Ficino's view, melancholia was not an illness, nor was it health, but some intermediate state that should not be called neurotic, because that would be forcing the melancholic state into a schema of modern notions. Naturally, melancholia preserved marks of the medieval outlook: even into the sixteenth century, physicians (see, for example, Tomaso Garzoni and Girolamo Fracastoro) considered it a mental disease, and Petrarch, that characteristically melancholic writer of the modern age, speaks with alarm about his own condition: "What prevents us from believing that I am suffering from a fever of mind?" he wrote to Andrea Dandolo, referring to his own shaky condition, which he considered unfortunate (Petrarch, *Letters on Familiar Matters*, bk. 15, letter 4, 261). Lurking behind that ambivalent pronouncement is fear: Petrarch feared the medieval conception, according to which a melancholic was mentally ill; he *feared* madness. That fear, however, was a signal that he was caught between two mutually opposing expectations; he was melancholic, but he was not mad. Of course, he did not yet possess the self-awareness of the great melancholics of the Renaissance era; he looked on his own melancholia as unequivocally reprehensible and damaging. Admittedly, in a section of his work *Secretum* subtitled "De contemptu mundi" ("On Scorn of Worldly Things"), melancholia is mentioned not as a form of insanity but as a normal state of mind, but his imagined interlocutor, St. Augustine, attempts to dispel his modern-style inner uncertainty with arguments that still evoke the Middle Ages. Petrarch was unable to decide which viewpoint to represent: he dared not admit to the new way of looking on melancholia, but he also feared medieval condemnation. The genre of dialogue was a product of this hesitation. (It was only with Ficino that it became possible to admit uncertainty *with confidence*.) And what could be more revealing than the fact that in the course of the third dialogue, Petrarch as St. Augustine mentions the name of Aristotle, whose notion of melancholia was radically different from that of the Middle Ages, but (on the basis of Latin-language sources, primarily Seneca) he misquotes the philosopher: instead of saying that in Aristotle's opinion every eminent person is melancholic, he declares that great talent is inconceivable without an admixture of madness (*Nullum magnum ingenium sine mixtura dementiae*). Thus, he changed "melancholia" to "madness," even though the way melancholia is handled in the dialogue shows that it is clearly no longer seen as madness.

Petrarch was ashamed of his melancholia, and he suffered not only from that melancholia but also from the shame itself.[3] He was solitary, and tormented not only by being solitary, but also by the recognition that to be solitary was not proper. Petrarch was the first conscious melancholic—that was why his melancholia was not madness, but at the same time it made it impossible to put an end to his own melancholia. The more he was aware of his own situation, the deeper he became submerged in it. The wish to escape evolved into desperation, but since he found no remedy for it, this desperation spread to everything: it became weltschmerz. Melancholia presenting itself as world-weariness was not a defect, however; not a distorted version of a theological explanation of being, but a sovereign, self-standing attitude to existence, a positive state, however fraught with pain it might have been. Weltschmerz does not judge any particular aspect of the existing world; it is not critical but, however contradictory it may seem, affirmative, furnishing evidence of a new world that does not supplement the existing one but supplants it. Weltschmerz has no tangible cause—or to be precise, anything might be the cause, but one cannot abolish one's pain by eliminating it. Medieval melancholics went mad over the world's closed nature; in Petrarch, by contrast, the world called forth a sense of infinite dissatisfaction, and it was not the world but a universal deficiency that became the source of his melancholia. That deficiency was intangible and interminable. There is no explanation for weltschmerz—there is only one single point that it can hold onto: death, which is the same as nothingness. For modern melancholics, unlike their fellow sufferers in antiquity, did not regard death as rebirth but as ultimate annihilation. Modern melancholics were among the first to discern themselves in the figure of Christ in Jacopo Bellini's *Crucifixion*, displayed in the Castelvec-

---

3. Likewise, melancholic Byron was later to write deprecatingly of Petrarch: "I detest the Petrarch [sonnets] so much, that I would not be the man even to have obtained his Laura, which the metaphysical, whining dotard never could" (journal entry, 17–18 December 1813).

chio Museum in Verona. This Christ no longer believes in anything. Protruding from an endless dark-blue background is the cross alone, which no longer serves for the acceptance of death in faith but is simply a gallows tree. Nothing at all counterbalances torment, pain, and death: in this picture of metaphysical homelessness, the world is represented solely by this tool of execution. In the aforesaid dialogue, Petrarch confesses to Augustine that he is incapable of diverting his thoughts away from death. For him, death is not an abstract idea but a physical process that may occur at any moment. Speaking about death, he warns his interlocutor, "Nonetheless, we should not allow either the syllables of the word or the memory of the thing itself to pass quickly from our minds," and lashes out with almost Heideggerian pathos at those who turn a deaf ear to the reality of death: "This, then, is what I call 'penetrated deeply enough,' not when you say the word death out of habit or when you repeat, 'Nothing is more certain than the fact of death, nothing less certain than its hours,' and other truisms of this kind that we hear every day. Such words just fly away; they don't sink down deeply and stay with you." Death should not be merely a matter of the imagination, but the *whole truth*, Petrarch admonishes: "And so I think about these dreadful events not as if they were far in the future, but as if they were to happen soon, indeed as if they were to happen now" (Petrarch, *Secret*, 1st dialogue, 63–67). According to earlier views, melancholics were sinful for, among other reasons, cutting themselves off from God in opening up to death (one should bear in mind the condemnation of suicide); melancholics of the modern age, on the other hand, did not fortify themselves against death with any kind of hope, and rather than being defensive, they were on the attack: they considered public opinion guilty. The real sin, in their opinion, was to cut oneself off from death rather than from God. An openness to death distinguished them from others, the nonmelancholics; that was what made them chosen, solitary, and, at the same time, the unhappiest of souls. If one is helpless in the face of a world-eroding void, then one has to turn against the Creator himself, and there is no way of getting over one's contempt for the world. "Do you think yourself bad?" Augustine asks Francesco, his interlocutor. "The worst," the latter responds. "Why?" "Lots of reasons," Francesco answers. "You are like those who at the slightest offense relive every grudge they have ever felt." "No wound on me now is so old that forgetting has erased it," retorts Francesco. "The injuries that torture me now are all recent. And if any of them were able to be alleviated by time, Fortune struck the same place again so quickly that no wound has ever completely scarred over. And when this is added to my hatred and contempt for the human condition generally, I am not strong enough to overcome my intense anguish. It doesn't matter to me whether you call this aegritudo or accidia or some other name. We agree about what it is" (Petrarch, *Secret*, 2nd dialogue).

World-weariness, Petrarch says, or at least so the expression can be translated into modern languages. The original Latin word was *accidia*, and what in the Middle Ages meant spiritual or mental sloth, apathy, was redefined in the writings of Petrarch and took on the connotations of weltschmerz, melancholia. Petrarch was sad, but that was not sadness in the eyes of God, nor even of the world, although that is how Augustine still interprets Francesco's ill humor in the dialogues. This ill humor was entirely novel: it derived not from a rejection of God but from an (unspoken) vain search for him. The wish that determines the attitude of modern melancholics could not find its goal; and even though Petrarch might still have kept reiterating that God was the goal, his boundless moroseness was a good deal more revealing. Melancholics of the modern age were left to themselves, and as in Ficino's case, that solitude was at once uplifting and crushing. The dejection that characterized him was previously unknown: nothing held him back, he knew no bounds. It was not a matter of madness, of mental illness; the melancholic was by then in despair, in the broadest sense of the word. A symptom of that is ill humor, the most characteristic feature of melancholia down to the present day.[4] This ill humor, as has already been mentioned, was incurable; it had no cause, otherwise it could readily be checked. (The death of loved ones, one could object, is a "tangible" yet irrevocable cause, but it does not make everyone melancholic; anyone who becomes melancholic does not do so because of that, but because of a deeper despair that was latent even before that death.) The ill humor that sets the melancholic apart is not the same as fleeting, day-to-day ill humor: one not only stands it but goes to meet it; this ill humor is not only triggered by something, but "precedes" any conceivable cause. The ill humor, or despondency, that characterizes a melancholic is not merely an endurance, a lethargic toleration, of existence, but an *active re-creation* of it: melancholics live in the same world as other people, yet they do not see the same world. They build for themselves a new world into which they alone can enter. They are Saturn's children, and for that reason stupid, stuck in the mud, and dull-witted — that, at least, is how the world in general thinks of them, since melancholics are incapable of seeing the simplest of facts "normally," in conformity with public opinion. But being Saturn's children, they are also clever, outstanding, magnificent, and wise — the same world asserts those things, too, for after all, a melancholic can discover shades and perspectives of existence that remain invisible to an ordinary person. They are, at one and the same time, abnormal and the most normal, and although either possibility in itself would be sufficient reason for the ill humor of a melancholic, it is nourished simultaneously by both.

---

4. In the Renaissance era, merriness was considered one of the most effective treatments against melancholia: Democritus, the Laughing Philosopher, was considered the chief antidote (though Hippocrates was of the view that he too suffered from melancholia), and many called on him as a support. In 1607 there appeared a book in England, penned by Samuel Roland, with the title *Democritus, or Doctor Merry Man: His Medicine against Melancholy Humours.*

Melancholics united in themselves extremes; they were at once divine maniacs—a feature that St. Bernard earlier had been inclined to recognize only in the lives of saints—and dragged down by the lead weight of despair. Ficino and other Renaissance humanists based their judgments of melancholia on that duality. The metaphysical point of view of Plato's interpretation of mania and the "natural-historical" point of view of Aristotle's interpretation of melancholia came together for the first time: in Ficino's opinion, the melancholia of great people corresponded to Plato's mania. (Half a century before Ficino, Antonio Guainerio, a professor at Padua, had accepted the superiority of melancholics and the divine nature of the melancholic state as a matter of fact.) In his *Of Occult Philosophy* (1510), Agrippa von Nettesheim writes about the superior inspiration with whose help the soul is able to ascend to the celestial truth, and he distinguishes three forms: dreams (*somnia*); rapture (*raptus*), brought about as a result of continuous contemplation of sublime things; and frenzy (*furor*). The last can be produced by—alongside such noble associates as the Muses, Dionysius, Apollo, or Venus—melancholia, the black choler: "For this, when it is stirred up, burns, and stirs up a madness conducing to knowledge and divination, especially if it be helped by any celestial influx, especially of Saturn, who . . . seeing he is the author of secret contemplation, and estranged from all public affairs, and the highest of all the planets, he doth as he withcalls his mind from outward business, so also make it ascend higher, and bestows upon men the knowledge and presages of future things" (*Three Books of Occult Philosophy or Magic*, ch. 60, 186).

The *humor melancholicus*, Agrippa writes, endows humans with marvelous attainments, and depending on whether it lodges in the imagination (*imaginatio*), in the intellect (*ratio*) or in the mind (*mens*), the person in question will become an artist, sculptor, or notable physician, politician, natural scientist, or divine prophet. According to Ficino, melancholia was the precondition of philosophy;

according to Dürer, a precondition of art and science; and according to the painter Giovanni Benedetto Castiglione, a precondition of virtue. In light of such judgments, it was hard to consider melancholia a disease (Paracelsus was sharply incensed by the idea that every disease might be derived from melancholia); nonetheless, its peril was undeniable: melancholics struggled in a network of irreconcilable conflicts and labored under a dual threat. On the one hand, so limitless was their solitude that they had a sense of constantly falling, and were attracted by death;[5] on the other hand, their awareness of their divine rapture, excellence, and superiority, and the endless contemplation and preoccupation with secrets, which inherently characterized melancholics, were perilous in themselves: melancholics could "slip over" in a trice, losing the ground under their feet, and once more find themselves hurtling into the aforesaid abyss. According to Aristotle, the extremes and the middle were united in melancholia; in a letter written to Jacopo Bracciolini, the Platonist Ficino follows Aristotle:

> The reasonable soul is set on a horizon, that is the line dividing the eternal and temporal, because it has a nature midway between the two. Being in the middle, this nature is not only capable of rational power and action, which lead up to the eternal, but also of energies and activities which descend to the temporal. Since these divergent tendencies spring from opposing natures, we see the soul turning at one moment to the eternal and at another to the temporal and so we understand rightly that it partakes of the nature of both. Our Plato *placed the higher part*

---

5. In the fifteenth to sixteenth centuries, the number of suicides grew markedly, and so too did the number of writings about them: between 1551 and 1585, some four discourses about suicide are known about, whereas in the seventeenth century, at least fifteen. The military laws drawn up for Fredrick the Great of Prussia give the cause of suicide as "melancholia or despondency."

of the soul under the authority of Saturn, that is, in the realm of mind and divine providence, and the lower part under Jupiter, in the realm of life and fate.

> (*Meditations on the Soul: Selected Letters of
> Marsilio Ficino*, letter 23; emphasis added)

A melancholic's path leads *upward*; however, not only is this path dangerous, but the goal is invisible as well. Instead of a futile tussling with God, attention is focused on the individual, left to himself. From the individual's point of view, however, fitting in is not the issue, whether in the transcendentally determined universe of the Middle Ages or in the intervention-fraught world as institutionalized by bourgeois society; rather, the issue is *absolute autonomy*.[6] Autonomy from both society and God—that was what innumerable people succeeded in achieving and that was where those who became melancholic failed. That dual determination of melancholia is most striking in Italian portraiture of the Renaissance: the profound sorrow of the portraits is thus comprehensible even if inexplicable. The earlier golden background behind the figures, which lifted them out of space and time, is lost; the landscape that now pops into view in almost every case is not a realistic one, however; it is a convention signaling that the model is sitting in front of the painter in time and space, but even as a mere convention, it makes time and space extrinsic and negligible. There is no all-embracing golden background, but neither is there a realistic earthly background; all we see is a solitary sitter, to whom neither divine timelessness nor earthly temporality is granted. We know nothing of the whereabouts of these sitters: if we sought to extend their location (which can readily be done with portraits of burghers or group pictures), we would be frustrated, because

---

6. This is obvious not just in books like Machiavelli's *The Prince*, but also in writings like Baldassare Castiglione's *The Book of the Courtier*, which sought to regulate matters of fine manners and dress.

they lack an external world.[7] The riddle, which without exception envelops all the portraits, follows from the situation of the figures: they have nothing to do with the world even though they are perceptibly offspring of the world. They have frozen into their own selves. They are stuck outside time of any sort, the divine just as much as the earthly, but they are incapable of creating time by their own power, since all of them are children, creatures, of this world. The shadow of death falls on them, and although they are living, they look straight in the eye of nothingness alone. The line at the corner of their lips indicates that they have overcome death, but their eyes indicate that they are the deadest of all people, if such a state can be graded at all. They too can recite Michelangelo's lines along with Cecchino dei Bracci, who died young, at sixteen:

> From clutch of clock and calendar now fled,
> my bondage once, I dread going back again
> more than I shrank from death, not knowing then
> die meant being born, meant death itself lay dead.

(The Complete Poems of Michelangelo)

It is precisely the Platonism of melancholic Michelangelo that brings one closer to the riddle of the portraits (though Michelangelo himself, out of some unaccountable fear, never painted any portraits): one must rise toward the otherworldly essence in such a way that one remains master of oneself; one's *this-worldly* persona has to blend in with the *otherworldly* essence. Naturally, there can

---

7. In certain Renaissance-era portraits, the subject points at a representation of a maze carved into a tree or a book cover (for example, Dosso Dossi, *Portrait of an Unknown Subject*, 1520; Girolamo Mazzola Bedoli, *Portrait of a Scholar*, first third of sixteenth century) or, as in the unsettling *Portrait of a Man* by Bartolomeo Veneto in the Fitzwilliam Museum, Cambridge, UK, the labyrinth that he points at is woven into the front of his garment. The center of the unsolvable riddle, the destructive monster, the seat of the Minotaur, is the heart itself.

be no room for peace here: teetering between earthly existence and otherworldliness, one becomes a homeless outcast. It is due to this homelessness that the people in theses portraits, who can rightly be regarded as the first and most typical representatives of modern melancholia, appear so sad and distant. What they go through is alarming for them, but what they long for is unattainable. Those who walk into this trap will become melancholics; they will be equally nostalgic for tangible reality and utopia.[8] They will not find their place anywhere, and therefore they crave, more than anyone else, simplicity and stability. In the thirteenth century, the Platonist Henry of Ghent distinguished two types of people: those of a metaphysical cast of mind and those who, captives of their sense perception, sought to see everything located spatially. Henry called the latter melancholics: they were unable to take wing, incapable of contemplating nonphysical entities (for example, angels), and melancholia was their principal punishment for their hankering for unequivocality. Henry, however, like all Platonists, was fond of one-sidedness, because just as there are no people endowed only with a metaphysical cast of mind or only an earthly view of things, so too melancholia cannot be associated merely with the latter. Keeping the portraits in mind, it seems more likely that those who are incapable of taking root for good in either metaphysics or the world of practice are the ones who become melancholics. Indeed, melancholics of the Renaissance era, thinking of themselves as the beginning and the ultimate goal of being, did not acknowledge this distinction; unaided, they create a world condemned to death from the very first, in which both the metaphysical and the earthly outlook will have to miss their goals. In 1608, Johannes Kepler, the most illustrious astrologer of the age, in draw-

---

8. It is no accident that this age was also an age of utopias, and without digressing into the deep-lying melancholia of utopias, let us simply refer to the fact that in ancient comedies, Kronos (Saturn) was called the "king of Utopia": the supreme lord of melancholia set up his throne in unknown places that never existed.

ing up a horoscope for Count Albrecht von Wallenstein, considered the following to be consequences of Saturn: "Saturn in ascendency makes deep, melancholic, always wakeful thoughts, brings inclination for alchemy, magic, sorcery, communion with spirits, scorn and lack of respect of human law and custom, also of all religions, makes everything suspect and to be distrusted which God or humans do" (quoted in Jean-Pierre Lasota, ed., *Astronomy at the Frontiers of Science*, 299). Melancholics are citizens of a brand-new world that differs from the present one, but that is situated outside space and time (utopia). But melancholics live here, on Earth, and therefore they are also citizens of this earthly world. On the one hand, they are linked to the spirit world (magic spells); on the other, they are slaves of the material world (alchemy); they disdain earthly laws and are constantly brooding on a new existence rooted in nothing. They are typically Faustian figures (it speaks volumes that German Romantics, while revering Dürer as a balanced individual, regarded the female figure in his etching *Melencolia I* as a Faustian figure racked by doubts); they do not sense anything as being alien, yet on account of their unappeasability, they are characterized by complete homelessness.

Melancholics would gladly be attached to anything, but they do not find their place anywhere. They are solitary in the widest sense of the word; like the figures in the portraits, they stand in the finite world and yet are outside all space. Their situation is undeterminable; their situation and their own conception of it differ so markedly that one cannot even venture a guess about which should be regarded as definitive. Writing about the mind, Marsilio Ficino says the following:

> It is a wonderful power that restores infinites to something one and something one to infinites. No one degree in nature belongs to the mind exactly in that it penetrates every level from top to bottom. It has no place of its own in that nowhere does it come to rest. It has no power that is, one might say, specific and determined in that it acts on everything alike.

> Demonstrating above all, it seems to me, that the mind's power is as it were undetermined is also its discovery that infinity itself exists, and what it is and of what kind. But since knowledge is perfected through some sort of equating of the mind with the objects known, the mind is equated in a way with the infinity it knows. But what is equated to infinity has to be infinite.

> (Ficino, *Platonic Theology*, vol. 2, bk. 8, 365)

Those words were dictated by Platonic faith, but melancholic Ficino must have been well aware that this faith did not conform to reality. Although it is true that seemingly nothing is able to check the human mind, those who possess the most boundless minds are, sad to say, Saturn's children — in other words, it is precisely the melancholics who see most clearly that this apparent infinity is very limited or, if you prefer, bound to man. Human infinity — can there be a greater obstacle, a mightier self-contradiction? Infinity of the spirit or, to be more accurate, a desire for infinity can be sensed truly only by those who are clear about its ultimate impossibility — and those are the melancholics, who are unapproachable because they are standing at the "crossroads" of the finite and the infinite, attracted, on the one hand, by the earth and, on the other hand, by the sky, and discovering nothingness in the existing world, smuggling transience into every beginning, the intangible into everything tangible. According to rationalist scholastic thinking, there lay a logical path from the finite into the infinite, and the transition between the two was smooth and unbroken. That transition came to an end with the separation of theological-metaphysical speculation and the "natural" intellect: Aristotelian logic was now valid only for the finite world, and Nicholas of Cusa (Nicolaus Cusanus) was already disputing that from the finite one could reach the infinite rationally, on a logical path:

> It is self-evident that there is no comparative relation between the infinite and the finite. Therefore, it is most clear that where

we find comparative degrees of greatness, we do not arrive at
the unqualifiedly Maximum; for things which are comparatively
greater and lesser are finite; but, necessarily, such a Maximum is
infinite. . . . For the intellect is to truth as [an inscribed] polygon
is to [the inscribing]. . . . Hence, regarding truth, it is evident that
we do not know anything other than the following: viz., that we
know truth not to be precisely comprehensible as it is. For truth
may be likened unto the most absolute necessity (which cannot
be either something more or something less than it is), and our
intellect may be likened unto possibility.

(Nicolaus Cusanus, *On Learned Ignorance*, bk. 1, 3)

Adequate knowledge is not the same as perfect knowledge, Cusanus
claims, contrary to the scholastics. Many individuals of the Renaissance era became melancholic because of the human mind wavering
between the finite and the infinite; nothing in the world was so exact
that it could not be more exact, Cusanus propounded; nothing was
so straight that it could not be straighter; nothing was so true that it
could not be truer. God was infinite and hidden (*Deus absconditus*),
and man had lost sight of him. He therefore had to be looked for,
even though it was obvious that a finite intellect was never going to
reach him. Cusanus did offer a solution: with the aid of intellectual
vision, a created being was capable of reaching God—that solution,
however, was not granted to the melancholic; at the point where Cusanus moves on, the melancholic gets stuck and sees his life as ultimately aimless.

The "crossroads" of the finite and the infinite is not accessible
to all viewpoints; at best, it can be understood only metaphorically.
Nevertheless, better light cannot be thrown on the situation of the
melancholic than by that metaphor. Since every existing being is
unique and unrepeatable, Cusanus asserts, and since the universe
is infinite, the Earth can in no way be the center of the world—
indeed, the world cannot have a center; any point could be consid-

ered that (this would become the favorite notion of Giordano Bruno), not just because any point can be selected arbitrarily, but also because the whole universe is reflected in every point. Every person regards himself or herself as elect (not on account of his or her knowledge so much as on account of his or her existence), and since only humans have knowledge of the world—this latter is stated by Pico della Mirandola in his discourse *De hominis dignitate*—man is the favored center of the universe. But since he is the center, he cannot relate his own being to anything; therefore, he is left alone. He is surrounded by the infinite, so he has to choose from among an infinite number of possibilities, has to build his life while facing an immeasurable set of possibilities. The never-ending, never-halting choices, however, are attended by infinitely many dangers: truly accepted individual freedom, choice, and danger are inconceivable without one another. (A melancholic Hercules at the crossroads is a favorite trope of Renaissance art.) Freedom for good thus becomes inseparable from freedom for evil, says Pico; one who is set at the absolute middle of the world—this is *our* conclusion—has just as much right to choose good as evil. Indeed, it is questionable whether *the idea and the possibility of good and evil does not emerge subsequently, after the act of choosing, and even then not in the person who chooses but rather in those who despise him or, for that matter, adulate him.* That is why the heroes of the so-called revenge tragedies of the Elizabethan and Jacobean stage choose evil uninhibitedly, and in so doing they are so consistent that, in the last analysis, they make the notions of evil and good themselves relative. How else can one explain why these scoundrels are such captivating fellows, for all their wickedness? Naturally, one feels sorry for the people whom they ruin; but that sorrow in all likelihood carries more than a dash of self-pity: we fear that the protagonists would probably treat us the same. Our sympathy is obscured, however, by our admiration: John Webster, Cyril Tourneur, and John Ford—who wrote a piece entitled *The Lover's Melancholy*, and every one of whose plays is about melancholia—set the kind of villains on the stage who, after all, do what is granted to everyone as a possibility: whatever the price may be, they test how far a person's abilities and power will go. These figures are not primarily villains, but people who have been left perfectly alone and are desperate, who are prepared to perpetrate anything to prove to themselves that life must have some solid basis after all. They strive for the infinite, like Marlowe's heroes, but they know quite well that man is born weak to start with and is ruled by uncertainty.[9] It is not bloodthirstiness, vengeance, or wickedness that lurks at the bottom of the souls of these villains, but *sorrow* mingled with fear—and the only reason we are not afraid to write that word is because that is how contemporaries characterized the heroes of these tragedies: *ecstatic melancholics.*[10] Sorrow clouds the trinity of *individual freedom, choice,* and *danger*; if one strives for complete autonomy, total freedom from both the world and the heavens, then one's hours are numbered.

That is how bloodthirsty despots and cowardly melancholics go hand in hand. The strong and the weak were sustained by the same insight, and their state was due to the same—frequently unformulated—interpretation of being, which to an external observer appeared very different.[11] The cowardice of a melancholic is not the

---

9. A similar fear would be felt by Kepler, who shuddered at the mere thought that he was drifting in this immeasurable universe, boundless and therefore centerless, where position could not be determined, since in infinity "whatever point might be taken at random, it is identically—to wit infinitely—distant from the infinitely remote outermost points" (quoted in Dietrich Mahnke, *Unendliche Sphäre und Allmittelpunkt,* 131–32).

10. This ecstasy, unlike the aforesaid ecstasy of Jesus, denotes exclusively stepping outside, making one's way outside oneself; despots do not step into anywhere, but step out into a void.

11. Constantine the African had talked about *melancholia leonina* and *canina* (that is, lion- and dog-hearted melancholia), and Petrus Hispanus later referred to the difference between *mania canina* and *mania lupina* (that is, dog- and wolf-hearted melancholia). The hare was considered to be a mournful animal in the Elizabethan era and later; Dr. Johnson says of the hare, "She is upon her form always solitary,

same as cowardice in its everyday sense. It would be more to the point to call it powerlessness, since it is not purely out of cowardice that melancholics fail to act, but out of their inability to commit themselves to taking a step. Others simply call them cowards, but because of a deep-lying kinship, they are no more cowardly than a bloodthirsty despot; *they simply attend to other things.* (Richard III's true partner is not so much Claudius as the other melancholic, Hamlet.) Of course, a melancholic's weakness cannot be denied, but it is a consequence of the fact that melancholics, who crave absolute autonomy and who, having completely lost their bearings, are the center of the world (God is intangible—*inattingibilis*—Cusanus says), are *solitary* and can count on themselves only. They would like to be almighty, but their solitude makes them fragile; they feel that wherever they tread, the invisible vault of the void will fall down on them. "It is, therefore, no strange anomaly partly to will and partly to be unwilling. This is actually an infirmity of mind," says St. Augustine (*Confessions*, bk. 8, 9); the other St. Augustine, this time the one invoked by Petrarch, says to his interlocutor about the latter's permanent fear of death and contempt for the world:

> You never commit your full attention to anything. And so whenever your mind, which is by nature noble, has arrived at the thought of death and at other thoughts that might direct it toward life, and is through its natural acumen delving into the most profound things, it isn't strong enough to stand there, and as the turmoil of various problems assault it, the mind turns back. And

and, according to the physic of the times, the flesh of it was supposed to generate melancholy." In Shakespeare's *King Henry IV*, Prince Henry says to Falstaff: "What sayest thou to a hare, or the melancholy of Moor-ditch?" (I.i.2). Moor-ditch was originally part of the great moat that formerly surrounded the City of London, extending from Moorgate to Bishopsgate. Its dull filthy stream, with marshes on one side and wretched houses on the other, allegedly gave rise to melancholy in the same way that the consumption of rabbit meat did.

so the healthy resolve shatters to pieces from excessive mobility, and there arises that internal discord about which we have already spoken at length, and the anxiety of a soul angry with itself.

(Petrarch, *Secret*, 1st dialogue, 69–70)

Ficino wrote in a similar strain in an undated letter to his good friend Cavalcanti: "At present I do not really know what I want; it may be that I do not really want what I know and want that which I do not know. The malicious influence of my Saturn retrogressing in Leo has denied me the security granted to you by the salutary effect of your Jupiter progressing in Pisces" (Ficino, *Epistolae*, vol. 2, letter 22).

Solitude results in weakness, and that weakness in turn leads to indecision and permanent hesitation. Whatever such a person does, the consequences of his acts spiral off in an unknown direction, depriving him of innumerable further possibilities. Acedia, or apathy, did not correspond in the Renaissance with what it denoted in the Middle Ages: back then, it meant the *rejection* of the self's possibilities in the eyes of others, nonmelancholics, whereas later it was more the *consideration* of possibilities. In medieval miniatures and in the illustrations of almanacs, the melancholic is usually asleep; the soul as well as the eyes are closed. From the fifteenth century onward, the melancholic is no longer sleeping but *ruminating:* brooding, straining his attention. According to astrology, Saturn acts as an aid to contemplation. In the Middle Ages, the *vita contemplativa* was held in great esteem (especially in Dominican circles) because it was directed, first and foremost, at God. Medieval contemplation was an intense, protracted inspection of the world proclaiming the glory of God. The *vita contemplativa* was, in fact, a *contemplatio Dei,* a contemplation of God—and the recognition of divine rationality was nothing other than dedicating oneself, body and soul, to the service of an ostensively superior being. Contemplation promoted the acceptance of existence, so from the outset, a man of contemplation took cognizance of given boundaries and limits, conformed to tradition, and stood far away from all kinds of independent action or creativity as it is understood nowadays.[12] Medieval contemplation (or at least its proper measure and scale) excluded melancholia: anyone who became melancholic had gone mad in the contemplation not of God but of his own sinful ambition. By contrast, the trap of melancholia was inherent in modern contemplation. Contemplation was no longer a matter of observing but of reflecting. If I am at the center of the universe, then I relate everything to myself: the world is, indeed, the way I see it. Existence is not inherently rational, but is given meaning by humans: it has not been justified but awaits justification, even re-creation, in much the same way that Dürer's brooding St. Jerome tries, not in the least self-confidently, to think everything through anew. In the sketches for the etching, *experimental* devices can be seen over Jerome's head: alongside the pensive scholar's books are chemical retorts and flasks.[13] Contemplation does not preclude practical activity; indeed, brooding and action presuppose each other, like the weak, cowardly melancholic and the tyrant with blood on his hands.[14] The *vita activa* and the *vita contemplativa* are interconnected, since by an active life one does not understand hustling, bustling, and fussing around. An individual left to himself broods because he has to make a choice; a foundation for his life (and not just in the financial sense) can be produced only by deciding and acting. The conditions of self-realization include contemplation as much as readiness to act. Consequently, people who on occasion shrink back from action are not really cowardly: they are reserving themselves for

12. That explains why the cult of Martha was never as big as that of Mary in the Middle Ages.

13. Their number is reduced in the final draft, but the dog sleeping next to a lion, a symbol of despair and sorrow, of the melancholic condition, is missing from the earlier sketches.

14. In his *Purgatory*, Dante places Leah and Rachel beside each other, with the former commenting: "She is content with seeing, I with labor" (canto 27, l. 107).

something else. As has been seen, however, the attempt to realize perfect autonomy, as it presents itself naturally to everyone, is doomed to failure; vacillating between heaven and earth, one will be obliged either to throw oneself into the arms of religion or to reconcile oneself to worldly existence. One is compelled by one's own weakness, which demands either *belief* or *justification*—and people wishing to realize themselves as God, for all their audacity, are weak and lacking in support. Melancholics of the Renaissance era—the figures in the portraits, the heroes of vengeful tragedies, the brooders—are incapable of believing in God, however much they might want to, but they are also unable to form an alliance with the world. They want to realize themselves and to accept their uniqueness, their unrepeatability, the fact that it does not lie in their power to relive their lives—yet that self-evident pretension expels them not only from the heavens but also from the world below. That is hell. They banish themselves into the void, where they cannot hope for anything, where life becomes an eternal *now*, a single enduring moment. *It was granted for melancholics of the Renaissance era to be perfectly sovereign, but the price they had to pay for that was inner destruction, which, in the last analysis, made sovereignty impossible.*

In a nearly forgotten, strange discourse, Charles de Bovelles wrote at length on nothing (*Libellus de nihilo*, 1510). Experiencing nothingness had become more excruciating for him than anything, and on that account it had to be differentiated from nonexistence, which at least can cause no pain: "Every existing thing is an existing something. Everything is full of being. The void is empty, indifferent, soulless. Void is outside complete being. Consequently, the assertion 'Nothing is not nothing' has two interpretations: one of those is negative, the other is declarative and affirmative. Both reveal the same truth and are equivalent. In other words, if we state that Nothing is not nothing, or that Nothing is not nonexistence, then we are saying that Nothingness is not nonexistence, or if you prefer; the existing nothing is not nonexistence" (*Libellus de nihilo*, bk. 1). Only that "existing nothing" can be looked on as the basis of "existing being," the foundation of material: "Material is an unfinished and imperfect existing, potential being. . . . Material is the beginning and end of existing beings. . . . And the substrate of the material is nothing. Material is the basis of everything, but itself it dissolves into, rests on, nothing" (ibid.). It follows from this, Bovelles could assert, that material is not being and not not-being, but "empty and free of every distinction" (ibid.). But because material, as Bovelles himself recognized, is not only the beginning but also the end of everything, the nothing that is "embodied" in material can permeate everything that there is. "Nothing is the receptacle of every creature, which is always present and in which they are. . . . Everything is therefore based on nothing: the full is in the void, being rests on nonbeing" (bk. 6). Nothing, therefore, does not surround existence, says Bovelles, anticipating Heidegger; it is not beyond it but homogeneous, though not identical, with it: "Nothing does not disappear in front of creatures but coexists with them" (ibid.).

Being is man's fundamental experience, but at the thought of annihilation, even nothing can turn into an experience. And the more it does, the less capable he is of distinguishing the two experiences. For melancholics, fulfillment is connected with being dispossessed. They see themselves equally as the chosen ones, standing at the center of existence, and as outcasts, a point hovering in nothingness. *For them, the preponderant experience of nothingness is nothing other than an experience of the fragmentariness of existence.* Wherever they tread, they end up in the same situation. What they reach is not life but total paralysis: the eerie immobility of the subjects of the portraits signals that the recognition of nothingness has fateful consequences: nothingness starts to expand in the melancholics themselves.[15] Richard III

---

15. "We are merely the stars' tennis balls, struck and banded / Which way please them," says Bosola, one of the protagonists in Webster's play *The Duchess of Malfi* (1613–14).

was a good deal more active than Hamlet, of course, but both of them realized that mockery was being made of them: the hope of becoming autonomous persons was dangled before them, and since they took it seriously, they had to die in the effort. They went to meet their destinies with the greatest helplessness, and nothing could alter that: once a person has gained a taste of knowledge, nothing will protect him any longer. At the beginning of the fifteenth century, in a work entitled *Observations on Death and Judgment Day*, Jacques Legrand wrote: "The more knowledge increases, the greater does the concern grow, and a person becomes more melancholic the truer and more perfect the knowledge he possesses about his own situation"[16] (quoted in Klibansky, Panofsky, and Saxl, *Saturn and Melancholy*, 232). We are unable to be reconciled to our own fate—whether we close our eyes (becoming believers, blending in with the earthly world) or accept our fate, we will equally lose ourselves. We do not know who whispered the fateful injunction "Be yourself!" into the ears of Renaissance melancholics, but it could not have been either the heavens or earth because then the injunction would not have been addressed to a few but to everyone. Melancholics are chosen (or rather preferred) people whose existence proves that between the celestial and earthly worlds there is another world, which is shrouded in secrecy. This is the realm of nothingness. It is ultimately due to the insolubility of this riddle that God and earthly existence are mysterious. Melancholics of the Renaissance era were the first to point out that nothing is natural and self-evident: neither the existence of God nor earthly, human existence. A melancholic may be seen as a huge question mark preceded by the questions "Who am I?" and "Why am I?"

The growing concern about which Legrand complains is caused by knowledge; that knowledge, in turn, is not merely the accumula-

---

16. The epigraph of Agrippa von Nettesheim's *Declamation Attacking the Uncertainty and Vanity of the Sciences and the Arts* reads: "Ignorance is bliss" (*Nihil scire felicissima vita*).

tion of acquired knowledge but is identical with rumination itself. True knowledge is that which offers the hope of becoming autonomous, but since that hope gives rise to disappointment, hope and the deprivation of hope are simultaneously present in knowledge. In that way, knowledge is a wonderment at existence; it does not *conceal* in itself an accumulated body of knowledge, but is constantly *revealing* itself: in possession of true knowledge, one feels one's way into the unknown, opens up to obscurity, and lets it stream in. True knowledge is not just being aware that I do not—and cannot—know anything, but is also a way of life: the acceptance of a precarious position even at the cost of destruction. True knowledge is not granted to those who simply collect the body of knowledge regarded as given and unalterable, but to those who, by smuggling sense into the world, try to create a new world by their own efforts. A scholar does not collect but radiates; his position is similar to that of the sun: he is the middle of the universe. Those, however, who try seriously to make use of knowledge become forlorn of hope; true knowledge does not create a world but drives one to despair, adds trouble to trouble. True scholars have to realize that if they believe their position to be like that of the sun, then that sun will hide behind clouds and eventually turn black. The way that melancholics of the Renaissance interpreted life was determined by this duality. The subjects of the portraits stand at once in and outside space; the murderous despots are caught in the yoke of time, but they are entranced by timelessness. What could be more typical of their situation than that modern melancholia spread at the same time that experimentation with perspective did. The universe of Uccello is truly just as a lonely person sees it; it is inconceivable that the perspectival world would be any other than eyes lingering at the vanishing point of lines perceive it. The world is not the work of God but of man musing as he looks around, of the individual armed with knowledge; if one makes a step to the right or the left, not only will one see the world differently, but it also really will be different. The structure of perspectival paintings necessarily gives the impression of being "natural"; the creator is not God, however, but a mortal who came into the world by chance. "A spatial object must lie in infinite space," says Ludwig Wittgenstein, adding in parentheses: "A point in space is an argument place" (*Tractatus logico-philosophicus*, 2.0131). The perennial problem of point of view derives from the fact that a central perspective is not "objective" (in the sense that God would be an objective creator compared with an earthly artist), but a random way of looking at things. The main limitation here is precisely that it is never possible to see and perceive the infinite multiplicity of things at one and the same time — a person cannot look from outside at what he is inside; thus one cannot be in command of totality. What we do have command over is one solid point (our own self), and we feel capable of re-creating the world. One's situation becomes unstable; there is nothing to hang onto in the surrounding nothingness. If the world is the way *I* see it, then what is *the* world like? As painting in perspective evolved, the standards of collective experience started to disappear. Everything becomes open to question — including the exclusivity of the perspectival way of looking at things. That is what melancholics of the time started to realize. Since no perspectival relationship is conceivable between the indeterminate position of the melancholic subjects of the portraits and the landscape behind their backs, those paintings of the time that best convey melancholia also make the contradiction inherent in the perspectival view of their objects. These paintings question the solidity of the universe.[17] The fate of Dürer is widely known: he sought to determine perfect beauty geometrically, but had to admit that the attempt was unsuccessful. In 1508 he declared, "What beauty is I know not," and "No single man can be taken as a model of a perfect figure, for there is not a man alive on earth who is endowed with the whole of beauty. . . . There is

---

17. "According to this view the representing relation which makes it a picture, also belongs to the picture," writes Wittgenstein (*Tractatus logico-philosophicus*, 2.0131).

also no man alive upon earth who could give a final judgment upon
what the perfect figure of a man is; God alone knows that" (Dürer,
The Painter's Manual). Twenty years later: "Without the certainty of
knowledge who would be able to tell us that [that is, how to make a
beautiful human form]? I do not believe there is any man alive who
could say about the tiniest living creature, let alone a human, what
is the greatest beauty in it. . . . The lie is in our understanding, and
darkness is so firmly entrenched in our mind that even our groping
will fail" (Dürer, *De Symmetria partium in rectis formis humanorum
corporum*, trans. Silvio Levy). Dürer's *Melencolia I,* his etching on
the theme of melancholy and all its appurtenances, which became
the most popular representation of the condition not just in the Renaissance era but generally, is well known. Yet melancholy is first
and foremost the theme of the picture; the perspective, the formal
principle, is not governed by the customary Düreresque skepticism.
The picture tackles the theme of melancholy but is not itself melancholic; the structure, the composition, the approach, all demonstrate
that in this case Dürer, who was prone to melancholia, did not relate
melancholically to his theme but viewed it (like a true theme) as an
outside observer—one with insider knowledge, we may add. Dürer's
picture attests to such a self-confident way of looking at things that,
despite presenting many of the distinguishing marks of melancholia,
at one point it comes to a sudden stop. It was probably the technical
limits of the etching genre that forced him to halt, since his paintings display a much deeper familiarity with melancholia. One has to
look elsewhere for an appropriate pictorial mode of representation of
melancholia. Dürer treated melancholia as an object, but we know
at least one painting in which melancholia is simultaneously subject
and form, in which melancholia, the melancholic state, is both represented and—on account of doubts regarding the perspectival, self-
confident way of looking at things—descriptive of the very mode of
representation. That is Jan van Eyck's *Portrait of Giovanni Arnolfini
and His Wife,* or *The Arnolfini Wedding.*

Above the prominently positioned mirror, there is an inscription minutely worked, yet free of any pedantry. The handwriting visibly lacks individuality, or to be more accurate, it seems as if the hand holding the quill were guided by a solid world creating similar expectations and effects in everyone. When people write like that, the writing has a singular task: the world about which something is being communicated means exactly the same to everyone, and therefore it is hard for anything at all to be written down that, potentially, could not become anyone's experience or message. The mode of writing relates to a closed, confined culture that represents the universe for its bearers and so seems definitive. To cross its borders can seem a worthwhile idea only in the eyes of posterity. The sentence written there nevertheless creates uncertainty: "Johannes de Eyck fuit hic 1434," it says — "Jan van Eyck was here in 1434." But if the painter really did pass by there, where did he set down his mark? On the wall? Or on the painting depicting the wall? With the stroke of his pen, the painter hit on an insoluble dilemma, one highly reminiscent of the paradoxical situation of melancholics of the Renaissance. To what specifically does the writing refer? To the actual situation of the Arnolfinis' espousal, or to the painting made to mark it? In all likelihood, to both: van Eyck was concerned both with the objective content and with the picture as an independent creation. If he had painted an allegory, the "role" of the writing would have been unambiguous, but the picture is quite obviously not allegorical, so this gesture reveals that the painter stumbled, even if unwittingly, onto one of the paradoxes of painting in the modern age: the nature of the relationship between the reality of the painting and so-called external reality. The handwriting, with its reference to a closed culture, confronts a way of looking at things that is fraught with tensions. Of course, glancing at the picture would almost certainly spot the handwriting only later on. The most prominent subjects in the picture are the married couple; one starts to discover their surroundings — the room and its objects — only after the two people have become familiar to us: the objects become important primarily through their relationship to the couple. In the picture, of course, there are no primary or secondary factors: everything is equally important.

The painter has caught the moment of betrothal, placing it in a strictly secular, domestic environment. On the other hand, the intimate ardor has not been transformed into a worldly one, but—primarily by showing the faces and the gestures—he has preserved the inner enigma, which was always mediated by religiosity even if later it lost its religious aspect. The glances, the complexions, the hands, the covered-over hair: all are etherealized, and the painter chose the points that, like "sensory" bridges, always lead one to the personal in other persons, to their individuality. The persons of Giovanni Arnolfini and Giovanna Cenani have not lost their sensuality but, in retaining it, have been transfigured; the features continue to belong to flesh-and-blood persons, but their refinement lifts them out of the tangible world, like the figures of contemporary Italian portraits. One can see that they live in this world, but one also senses that it leaves them untouched. They are solitary people—inwardly, they have so little to do with the world that is home to them that their attachment to each other is also external. They do not exchange glances; indeed, their glances have no object: they both turn melancholically inward. Their refinement and selectness, however, do not prevent them from regarding the world as their own. What was inconceivable for refinement from the nineteenth century onward was still obvious for them: they were able to live in harmony with the surrounding world. Van Eyck accomplished that primarily by attuning various shades of sensuality to one another—and one may exceptionally disregard the iconographic significations of the individual elements. The path leads from the ethereal-unsensual sensuality of the two people through the chandelier, which is provided with just a single candle, to the red slippers, almost erotically red compared with the looks of the figures. Apart from the individual objects, the mass of colors, the refined interplay of red and green as well as brown, makes the created world almost sultry without becoming excessive. Everything in their surroundings evokes the atmosphere of a decent burgher home, and that tames the concentrated sensuality (aroused notably by the red furniture and the green and blue of the woman's dress), which is transfigured, without losing any of its strength, in the persons of the two individuals. By creating a harmony of a refinement at home in a prosaic and ordinary setting that lends itself to being transfigured, van Eyck created a homogeneous world. This, however, forms a fragile unity and is prone to fall to pieces at any moment. The multiplicity of the world on display and the relatively large number of objects point to an arbitrariness that lurks in everything and to the fact that this world is not definitive: the fruits placed on the table and the windowsill will not stay like that for long; the scattered slippers were still on the feet a little while ago and will soon be worn again; the folds of the green dress will come down before long; more candles will be lit in the chandelier; the hands will touch things again, and the object of the glances will be more practical than inwardly felt. We only know all this because the painter has recorded an exceptional moment for our viewing. But he could not do away with the contradiction inherent in his subject: just as the window is cunningly opened so that we can both see out of it and yet cannot, and we are forced to notice that the room is not the sole existing space, so the objects in the room are not detachable from day-to-day experience. This painting, characteristically modern in its mode of portrayal, can no longer claim to create an all-exclusive and per se definitive universe of the type characteristic of medieval or early Renaissance paintings. Indeed, perspectival representation itself makes its appearance differently here than earlier: in the intimate space, the arbitrary position of the viewer (and the painter) becomes more obvious. They hardly need to move for everything to appear in another projection; the facial features and hands would be different, the pieces of furniture would be located in different places, the slippers would end up farther away. This problem was also present in the perspectival representations of the Uccello style, but it had not as yet emerged as a *possibility*: neither the subject matter of the pictures nor the relationship of a work of art to the "outside world" afforded the opportunity. Retreating ever further from God, man became both more careless and more exposed than he was in earlier times, falling into the trap (often not spotted even in retrospect) and making numerous Renaissance individuals melancholic. There arose a possibility for the insight that this world made distrustful all who wished to avail themselves of the autonomy on offer. In consequence of this melancholic bewilderment, the exclusivity of the given perspective becomes questionable in Jan van Eyck's painting. At the same time, however, the balance created within the picture also becomes problematic. A duality too can be detected in this picture: on the one hand, a harmony of the sensual and the intellectual, of the prosaic and the refined has been realized, which is possible only in exceptional moments; on the other hand, the environment, the space in which this has come to pass, suggests the *momentariness* of this moment, its time-boundedness. Medieval painting, which was unaware of the paradox of spatial representation, had unlimited power over time; in exchange for the acquisition of space, however, it had to submit itself to time. And that imperceptibly corroded faith in the reliability of space.

As a result of that duality, the role of the mirror placed on the wall of the room grows. In the present context, we are not particularly interested in the fact that in the system of Christian symbols, the mirror—like other objects and colors—had its own signification (cleanness, clarity of vision, wisdom—but also vanity). More important than the meaning of this object is the contradiction of which the mirror forms only a part, all the more so because its allegorical function is not primary. Nor is its ornamental function, as, for example, it is in the picture of St. Eligius that Petrus Christus painted at around the same time. The world portrayed in the latter picture is so bustling, with van Eyck's detachedness and simplicity so lacking, that the image of passersby in the street, reflected in a mirror placed on the table, merely completes and neatly expands the interior of the gold-smith's workshop. In the Arnolfini picture, the mirror does not complete the room but hints at the instability of a world assumed to be reliable. The painter captured an exceptional moment, and while the work was in progress, he came to realize that the idea of *exceptionality* as a situation in life was inconceivable without its own melancholic limits. Van Eyck wished to make artistically obvious something that at the time was no longer obvious: the medieval concept of universality and permanence was also aesthetic, and the world was also an aesthetic universe, whereas in the fifteenth century aesthetics had to give up the claim of comprehensiveness. *The Arnolfini Wedding* refers to this changed situation: aesthetics retreated into the world of private rooms, leaving behind the prosaic world outside. The use of the mirror is thus part of an experiment, making us aware, from the very start, of resignation and melancholia, by means of which the painter includes a world invisible to the viewer in a milieu that suggests transient harmony. The position occupied by the painter is just one of innumerable possible positions, the harmonious world looks the way it does from just one single perspective—and van Eyck called on the mirror's aid in order to point out the contradictory nature of that uniqueness in time and space.[18] The mirror creates what one would nowadays call with some justice a "distancing" or "alienation" effect, since the painter is deliberately bringing to our attention the point that his viewpoint is accidental, one-off, and he therefore forces the viewer into keeping an intellectual distance while also identifying with it. Parallel to identification with the observed world, the mirror paves the way for reflection: an aesthetic gesture that gives way to thinking about the world.

---

18. In all likelihood, it was due to a similar necessity that van Eyck "unfolded" the perspective of the left wing of his picture of *The Last Judgment* into several dimensions—thereby anticipating Leonardo's experiments in representing spherical space.

A curious trap: for a second, van Eyck achieved harmony in a modern world that accepted the prosaic world into itself, but by virtue of the mirror, he warned viewers of the uniqueness and exceptionality of the spectacle and the harmony, putting a question mark next to the world. The question mark (the mirror), however, is placed within the aesthetic sphere and thus tacitly presumes a receptive community with common expectations. The hope that there is someone to whom one can appeal on account of the contingency of harmony points beyond the world that is depicted. Van Eyck called perspective into question and thereby discovered the basic paradox of bourgeois panel painting, tied up with perspectival representation, which was akin to the problematic character of those life situations that provoked melancholia in modern times. The painting not only depicts the perceived world, but also renders perceiving per se problematic. Instead of a given, ready-made object, it regards the world as a living formation displaying, microcosmos-like, the basic questions of the whole world in every phenomenon. At one and the same time, melancholia becomes the picture's subject matter and its mode of portrayal, and for that reason this painting can be considered one of the most typical pictorial evocations of Renaissance melancholia. The world is a system of constantly unstable relations—and looking at van Eyck's picture, one becomes convinced that painting is a kind of interpretation of life: it doesn't merely mirror the world but has a life of its own. Painting is reality, and the world *also* goes on, takes shape, and changes in painting. Painting is a practical act, and our relation to painting, its reception, is the same sort of life technique—one attained on the aesthetic level—as any other activity. The process of painting, the completed painting, and its reception are re-creations of the world, each occurring at a different level. As the Arnolfini picture justifies it: reflection about painting (through the mirror) is at one and the same time an interpretation of the world; melancholic cogitation upon the world, on the other hand, if faced with art, will make that, too, problematic. If one goes back to what was said at the beginning about the Arnolfini picture and once again asks to what the sentence "Johannes de Eyck fuit hic 1434" refers, then perhaps the explanation will not seem forced. With the inserted text, van Eyck showed his relation, for one thing, to an unstably harmonious world created within the picture, signaling with the gesture of disappearing that at one moment he had been there and was part of that exceptional state. For another thing, though, this is an external reaction to the picture as a work of art: Jan van Eyck was there, and while painting a picture he mused about uniqueness, about exceptionality, about the melancholic instability of these, and about art. But maybe it is superfluous to analyze the two meanings of the inscription separately: the unity of the two is what elevates the Arnolfini wedding into an unparalleled masterpiece and exemplar of both art and melancholia.

We have seen the ambiguity of the position of melancholics of the Renaissance, their striving for absolute autonomy against both the heavenly and the earthly realm. Their melancholia was rooted in this situation, extraordinarily limited in both space and time, as well as in recognition of the situation's exceptionality and its being bound to the moment. The Renaissance personality endeavored to create a world out of his own resources, whereas melancholics of the Renaissance realized the fallibility of that world, its condemnation to failure. They knew they were damned to a *solitary* creation of the world, and they knew that failure would be unbearable: even if they remained alive, neither heaven nor earth would appreciate their experiment. Renaissance melancholics set a trap for existence, but they were the ones who fell into it: being alone as they were, they had to make the world habitable and bearable by their own effort—but the world so created differed from everyone else's world. There were as many brand-new worlds as there were personalities; since those were not in touch with one another, not only was it difficult to speak of a world that was shared by everyone (Jan van Eyck's mirror suggests as much), but each individual world became "worldless," point-like:

rather than being universal, they were shackled by each individual's point of view and sense experience (αἴσθησις). If God is in hiding, then the world will appear differently to everyone by day, not just in their dreams, as Heraclitus thought.[19] Although it is the same world in its materiality, everyone is linked with it in a different manner, and in the case of each individual, the construction of its intellectual dimensions results in a new world of his own, differing from every previous one. *Nihil novum dicere*—"There is nothing new to say," says Petrarch, still in the medieval spirit. The new human image, however, was attended by a new interpretation of being. "Of all writers under the Sun, the poet is the least liar," says Sir Philip Sidney in his apology for poetry (*The Defence of Poesy*, 1583). That assertion was based on the recognition that there is room for *all things* in reality, and the richness of reality depends on one's creative capabilities and imagination (which is no liar!). We encounter an extreme expression of the notion of the medieval personality in Averroës, according to whom the true subject of thinking is not the individual, the "self," but rather a nonpersonal, substantial being whose connection with the individual ego is external and accidental (see Ernst Cassirer, *The Individual and the Cosmos in Renaissance Philosophy*, 127). This idea was considered extreme also in that age, but even those who attempted to defend the rights of the ego (St. Thomas Aquinas) denied that individual souls differed from one another, because of their distinct *principia essentialis*. An individual was part of a deeper context, body and soul, and could lay no claim to either originality or creativity. And what does the Renaissance approach, with its insistence on the autonomy of the personality, have to say about this? Nicolaus Cusanus defended just as extreme a standpoint:

---

19. "The world of the waking is one and shared, but the sleeping turn aside each into his private world" (Heraclitus, frag. 89, quoted in Charles H. Kahn, *The Art and Thought of Heraclitus*, 31).

Just as an identity of proportion is not replicable, neither is an identity of mind. Without a corresponding proportion the mind cannot enliven a body. For example, your eye's seeing could not be anyone else's seeing (even if it were separated from your eye and were joined to another's eye), because it could not find in another's eye the proper proportion that it finds in your eye. Similarly, the discriminating that is present in your seeing could not be the discriminating in another's seeing. Likewise, your understanding of that discrimination could not be someone else's understanding of it. Hence, I deem the following not at all to be possible: that a single intellect be present in all men.

> (*Idiota de mente*, bk. 12, in *Complete Philosophical and Theological Treatises of Nicholas of Cusa*, 1:579)

There is no *common* intellect, no *common* judgment of the world, and therefore no commonly shared world can exist. The world breaks up into worlds with separate entrances that are fragile and fallible to begin with and serve as a trap for those who wish seriously to take them into account.

In the view of Pico della Mirandola, people should follow their own genius and natural attraction; in other words, they should trust and believe in their own powers of creation. If Renaissance personalities had obeyed the diabolical injunction to "be yourself," they would have had to turn into creators; the world was not "natural" and not given from the outset, but had to be created like a work of art or a piece of work. If they stepped onto the life-giving and yet ultimately fatal path of perfect autonomy, they had to turn into *artists*, in the broadest sense of the word. Departing from the analyses of melancholia in antiquity and the Middle Ages, anyone investigating the defining features of melancholia in the Renaissance and the modern era can remarkably often take examples from art. The literature of art criticism and theory, which awakened and then proliferated in the Renaissance, and the birth of a philosophy of art (later to be called aesthetics), indicate the changed position of art—the individual genres were not derivable from an existing, given culture, and the creations of individuals became arbitrary, *art*istic. (One sign of this was that, from the twelfth and thirteenth centuries onward, artists started to sign their paintings.) The religious and metaphysical ties that guaranteed the confinement of culture gradually started to loosen, and a work of art sought to represent, to depict, to reflect (those were the basic categories of Renaissance art theory), that is, it attempted to create out of itself ties able to bind culture together as a whole, creating a new world.[20] However, *individual* effort directed at creating a world of *general* validity indicates the contradiction that not only characterizes the Renaissance mentality but is also the source of melancholia in the modern age. Art previously had reflected on universality and all things in a fraction of the life, feelings, and adventures of an individual, but this could not be said at all about the art of the modern age. In cultures defined by religion and metaphysics there was no break between the individual phenomenon and the general worldview: the foliation winding endlessly above the gateway of a Gothic church is inseparable from the saints surrounding the gate, from which there is a similarly unbroken transition to the barely visible grotesque figures of the gargoyles placed high up—the Gothic church does not just represent and symbolize Christian culture but is identical with it. Christian art is a natural unfolding of an already-existing world—that is why the criteria of present-day art criticism can be applied to it only with difficulty. It is so far from being the

---

20. Reflection, representation, and depiction are not naturalistic but Platonic categories in Renaissance art theory. In his aforementioned treatise, Sidney talks a great deal about imitation, but he never lets it be known what a poet imitates. He does not say that the poet represents nature or humans, let alone assert that he reflects reality, but proclaims both laconically and eloquently that the root of poetry is the "idea or fore-conceit."

product of *individual* endeavor that one discovers the same pathos and faith in every work of art, irrespective of the quality of technical execution. One would look in vain for traces of melancholia in the art of the Middle Ages. *Separation* made melancholics so, whereas the art of the period stands for precisely the opposite of separation and introduces people into a world common for *everyone*. In the Middle Ages, melancholia was madness; art was sober and pious faith. The positions of the art of the Renaissance and modern times are contrary to this; we might even venture to say that from then on the boundaries of art have been demarcated by melancholia. Those boundaries are a claim to complete autonomy, a concomitant individual creativity, and a realization of the contradictoriness of the notion of individual omnipotence, which, as the Arnolfini picture demonstrates, is latent in every major work. (In the art of the Renaissance, of course, awareness of that contradiction was present only in embryonic form; however, it "blossomed" from the seventeenth and eighteenth centuries onward, when the *fracture* between individual endeavor and "objective" validity was the most determining mark of art.) The dilemma of art in modern times is identical with the dilemma of melancholia in modern times: is the work of art a closed formation that can be decoded exclusively on its own terms, not being determined by outside forces but much rather dictating rules to the "outside" world—or a mirror image that is supposed to depict and represent "external" conditions and, for that reason, can be explained by factors external to it? This is a typically modern problem, and whether one emphasizes the *transition* between world and artwork, or the *chasm* that yawns between the two, one divides the culture into poles between which, for all the subtlest dialectic, a connection can be created only externally. The formal problem of art in modern times is rooted in this. The world is reduced to what the work of art maintains about it (which accords with the notion of the autonomy of the work), or the work can be examined from the viewpoint of what it communicates about the world (this corresponds to the modern, empirical notion).

The formal problem of art reflects the paradoxical situation of Renaissance melancholics. The individual strove for infinite autonomy, but his reward was resignation, the insight that attaining the sole desirable human state would prove to be impossible. They wished to be omnipotent, but despair got the better of them: no one sees the limitations of human existence as well as those who wish to step over these limits. Renaissance melancholics were characterized at once by heroic effort and resignation, will and insight, an all-destructive denial and an all-accepting acquiescence. Melancholics were characterized by a Socratic *all-or-nothing* basic position — as is the art of the modern age, which creates an autonomous world, only to press it into form and, while asserting its right to be regarded as the exclusive reality, proclaim with masochistic pleasure its own illusory artistic being.[21] Presumably, a similar consideration prompted Thomas Mann to make the following observation: "Irony is always aimed in two directions: at life and at the spirit alike: that determines its behavior, making one melancholic and modest. Art, too, is melancholic and modest, insofar as it is ironic — or rather, the artist is that" (*Essays*, 2:45). The hallmarks of Renaissance melancholia may be discerned in art; for the first time in history, melancholia was the subject and predicate, the content and formal principle of art. On the one hand, there are works that deal with melancholia, either thematically (Dürer, Lucas Cranach, Jacob de Gheyn, etc.) or in their outlook (portraits, van Eyck), and on the other hand, melancholia lurks in the background of modern art as a whole, though it does not necessarily burst to the surface. The aim of art in the modern age is

---

21. According to a Christian interpretation, this artistic-melancholic inner conflict is sin itself; it is in that sense that Kierkegaard too regarded poetry as a sin: "From a Christian standpoint, such an existence . . . is sin, it is the sin of poeticizing instead of being, of standing in relation to the Good and the True through imagination instead of being that, or rather existentially striving to be it" (*The Sickness unto Death*, bk. 2, 1).

individual world creation—that is why artworks are utopian, in the original sense of the word. Instead of being led to a place existing *somewhere*, the viewer is instructed that the world created by an artwork exists *nowhere* (οὐτόπος). The world-creating intention of the work of art draws attention to failure and futility, to the nothing that entrenches itself in existence. Every significant piece of art is utopian because it lays out the nothing latent in the *here* and *now*, hence the sorrow and inconsolability that emerges from every major work of the modern age.[22] A *closed* work points at *nothing*, and it thereby opens. We are free to enter. Yet the dazzling wealth and diversity begin to disintegrate somewhere, at the most unexpected moment, and all the things that had seemed so captivating are gradually swathed in indissoluble grief.

The intimate link between modern art and Renaissance melancholia explains not only why, following the Middle Ages, the concept of melancholia had a fundamentally favorable ring to it, but also why *representative* melancholic figures appeared, mostly and understandably artists. The melancholics of the Middle Ages were anonymous, mentally sick people who were stuck outside the kingdom of God, who had ceased to exist, and therefore were remembered by nobody. During the Renaissance, however, melancholics showed the way; they were the ones most zealously obeying the command of the age, to build one's own world—and artists were the first in submitting themselves to the divine and destructive might of melancholia. It was during the process of artistic composition that the endless creative power and boundless capacities of the personality became truly obvious, but this was also when its limitations, vulnerability, and unreliability came to light. Works of art with capricious claims came into being; behind finished works, however, stood the torsos of unfinished compositions, which often, and by no accident, emerged from the

---

22. The noblest and most sublime calling of art, says the protagonist of Unamuno's novel *Mist*, is to prevail on a person to doubt his own existence.

workshops of the greatest artists. The more powerful the demand, the stronger the imperilment; the apparent assurance and solidity of the greatest works were the product of the most precarious balancing: perfect works were always haunted by the possibility of annihilation. Indeed, it may be that it is precisely in creations of the greatest reputation and fame that one perceives death, which simultaneously threatens the work, the creator, and us. That annihilation is not symbolic; it is an evocation of death, in the strict sense of that word, that has to be confronted by every solitary person. And since we are mortal, loneliness, whether bashfully or defiantly, threatens everybody. The person at the center of the universe—and with the loss, or even just the dimming, of religious belief who doesn't consider himself a center?—has to reckon solely with death; and anyone who fails to give up being the lord of creation is condemned to irresolvable solitude.[23] Creative genius-melancholics are famed for their solitariness, and the silence that surrounds them is also well known: if I cannot exchange my own world, my view of the world, with anyone else, then it is even less conceivable in the case of someone who, even at the price of his own perdition, wishes to create a world of his own, one that differs fundamentally from anyone else's. The aristocratic nature of art is a manifestation not of pride but of searching. Those who long for absolute autonomy are surrounded by solitude and silence (not chosen by themselves), and it is the price of creativity that they cannot take notice of anything else. The work of art is an offspring of the aforementioned imperilment—and what would be more irrational than to make that imperiled state and its result, the work, accessible to everyone. Art, from the Renaissance onward, was aristocratic, and it preserved that shield right down to the mid-twentieth century: it is just as difficult for the uninitiated to step into the world of Renais-

---

23. Leonardo da Vinci recommended that painters withdraw into complete solitude; the biographies in Vasari's *Lives of the Most Excellent Painters, Sculptors, and Architects* include numerous misanthropic, solitary artists.

sance portraits as into the world of twentieth-century artworks that are supposedly hard to comprehend. No one should be permitted to confront death and annihilation—and the danger of such a confrontation makes a work great; to put this more sharply: *the less a society occupies itself with art, the more viable it will be.* Melancholia relates to the art of the modern age as it did to the mysteries in antiquity. As it was with the mysteries, art is ambiguous: it is democratic because anyone can enter, but it is aristocratic all the same because only a few can make use of that possibility, and even fewer can pass to the very end, where, like the protagonist of Schiller's poem "The Veiled Image at Sais," drawing aside the veil concealing the truth inherent in poetry, they glimpse the nothingness that threatens them. It is these few who open up to melancholia—and just as a society cannot be, on the whole, melancholic, not everyone can be equally receptive to art. Art is "dangerous," at least in the modern age, when one of its main tasks is to smuggle solitude and the ultimate silence summoned by Hamlet's last words into the world of others. Great works disconcert one almost as much as does love: they abduct one from one's everyday life only to confuse everything for one. They are promising and yet offer nothing. One would most gladly identify with them, one would love to gobble them up, but instead they spurn us, and they provoke a nostalgia that, because of its aimlessness, cannot be assuaged. One might call art immoral, yet on coming face-to-face with the works, it turns out that "morality" and "immorality" are ridiculously puffed-up words that lose their ordinary meaning in art. We are helpless against art; we feel that we should not expose ourselves to the works; we know beforehand that we will fall short and go astray; we fear the incomprehension that will burst on us; yet we stubbornly go ahead, just as we stubbornly scratch open our wounds again and again.

Let us stay with art. "The greater part of the craftsmen who had lived up to that time [the time of Michelangelo]," Vasari writes in the "Life of Raphael," "had received from nature a certain element of savagery and madness, which, besides making them strange and eccentric, had brought it about that very often there was revealed in them rather the obscure darkness of vice than the brightness and splendour of those virtues that make men immortal" (*Lives of the Most Excellent Painters, Sculptors, and Architects,* 4:209). A sixteenth-century writer encouraged Michelangelo's apprentice Raffaele da Montelupo as follows: "Since you are a sculptor, you have the privilege of any extravagance." Paulucci, an envoy of Ferrara, wrote about the great Raphael: "He is inclined to melancholy like all men of such exceptional talent" (quoted in Wittkower and Wittkower, *Born under Saturn,* 104). But melancholia did not just lie dormant; not a few artists were regarded as patently melancholic. According to Boccaccio, Dante was melancholic, and so were, according to Vasari, Michelangelo,[24] Parri Spinelli, and Lorenzo Vecchietta; also melancholic were Raphael, Annibale Caracci, Guido Reni, and Carlo Dolci; among northern Europeans, Dürer, Hugo van der Goes, and Adam Elsheimer, who was active in Rome. The names proliferate, and it is not long before the average person comes to recognize artists primarily through their eccentricity.[25] One might add that the more the civil polity of Europe is consolidated, the more condemnable eccentricity will be perceived. Eccentricity (which, like antique ecstasy, denotes stepping out of oneself) is a sign of the frequent melancholia among Renaissance artists, a concomitant of loneliness and creativity—of an introversion without which it was impossible not only to create a new world but also to become an autonomous person. (That "turning inward" was for

---

24. In Raphael's fresco *School of Athens,* Michelangelo, representing Heraclitus, sits in the foreground of the picture in a characteristically melancholic pose.

25. "An awful habit has developed among common folk and even among the educated," the academician Giovanni Battista Armenini wrote in 1587, "to whom it seems natural that a painter of the highest distinction must show signs of some ugly and nefarious vice allied with a capricious and eccentric temperament, springing from his abstruse mind. And the worst is that many ignorant artists believe themselves to be very exceptional by affecting melancholy and eccentricity" (quoted in Wittkower and Wittkower, *Born under Saturn,* 92).

a long time a symbolic gesture, of course: the heroic determination with which Renaissance intellectuals realized themselves made them turn *toward* the world, but since that was tantamount to ignoring the given framework and rules of the existing world, the use of the phrase "turning inward" is justified.) In 1585, Romano Alberti explained the frequent melancholia of painters in the following manner: "Painters become melancholic because, wanting to imitate, they must retain visions fixed in their minds so that later they may reproduce them as they have seen them in reality. And this not only once but continuously, such being their task in life. In this way they keep their minds so abstracted and detached from reality, that in consequence they become melancholic" (quoted in Wittkower and Wittkower, *Born under Saturn*, 105). Alberti obviously saw this paradox as the most natural thing in the world, which sounds astonishing only to the empirically minded public opinion of our day: to copy reality, artists have to disregard it. This was a matter not just of the Platonism so much alive in the Renaissance, but also of the world-generating function of art in general. An artist has to create a new world—not from nothing, but from a set of things awaiting composition and arrangement. Material has to be taken from the sensory world, but earthly sensuality has to be left behind, in the manner of a god, in order to be able to create a new sensuality. Mimesis, as mentioned in speaking about Sidney, is not the mechanical reproduction of what exists but the representation of ideas or, as Shakespeare avows, the imitation of the divine act of creation. That makes it absolute, unique, and unparalleled, and its product, the work of art, incomparable and absolutely self-referential. Leon Battista Alberti, in the mid-fifteenth century, called the artist an *alter deus*, an alternative god, and although this echoed the belief of the Middle Ages according to which God was the supreme artist, it was not hard to spot the profanation of God as artist.[26] In Alberti's

---

26. According to Ruskin, starting in the fifteenth century God's hand vanished from art.

opinion, painting was not a handicraft but "a divine force." In a letter addressed to Peregrino Agli (*De divino furore*, 1 December 1457), Ficino links art to divine frenzy, and the holy madness that, according to St. Bernard, characterizes saints, pertains in Renaissance public opinion to artists—those who try to become God in God's stead and who do not hark back to a distant center but are themselves the centers of the universe. In the Middle Ages, *ecstasy* was an *entrance* into God's innermost circle. From the Renaissance onward, it regained its original meaning: ecstatic artists *step out* of the constraints of the world to create new worlds from their own resources, and ecstatic melancholics, who were identified with bloodthirsty despots on the Elizabethan and Jacobean stage, annihilate everything in order to step out of themselves, thereby preparing their own downfall.

Melancholics thus gradually became creators, and melancholia became a source of imagination (already in the fourteenth century, the French poet Eustache Deschamps declared in speaking about a repugnant matter: no single artist was sufficiently melancholic to be able to paint it, that is, it surpassed all the powers of imagination), and a manifestation of *genius*. This was an age of a rebirth of Aristotle's concept of melancholia: once again it became the distinguishing mark of outstanding people. In the Middle Ages there existed just one creator, God, and the notion of *a genius who is a creature* was unknown. The word "genius," which originally denoted begetting, bringing into being ($\gamma\epsilon\nu\nu\acute{\alpha}\omega$), is connected with God's manifestation in the New Testament, relating to the start of Jesus's functions on Earth (Hebrews 1:5),[27] his connection with God (Luke 3:22),[28] and

---

27. *Τίνι γὰρ εἶπέν ποτε τῶν ἀγγέλων,Υίός μου εἶ σύ, ἐγὼ σήμερον γεγέννηκά σε* ("For unto which of the angels said he at any time, Thou art my Son, this day have I begotten thee?").

28. *καὶ φωνὴν ἐξ οὐρανοῦγενέσθαι, Σὺ εἶ ὁ υἱός μου ὁ ἀγαπητός, ἐν σοὶ εὐδόκησα* ("And a voice came from heaven, which said, Thou art my beloved Son; in thee I am well pleased.").

his resurrection (Acts 13:33).[29] The original "genius" was the due of God alone, and, since his will is omnipotent, genius (that is, begetting and creation) in the final analysis was not the bringing of something *new* into being, but was always a *fulfillment* of the existing order, an honoring of the divine will, as the Gospel of Matthew preaches ("Thy will be done," using the passive voice of the verb γίγνομαι, "to give birth, to come into being": γενηθήτω τὸ θέλημά σου (Matthew 6:10). There is no room for individual genius in this context—it will acquire a role only when divine omnipotence starts to crumble and the cracks have to be filled by the creative force of the *individual* creature. People are left to themselves (they are microcosms, as Cusanus puts it) and become creative forces in the manner of god. The genius of melancholics was of divine origin, Ficino taught—but the genius here was the escorting angel of individual and antimetaphysical exertions. Genius, which initially adopted the form of an independent being and thus assisted (or thwarted) humans in creating a great work, during the sixteenth century lost its independence and became identical with a person's creative power; it lost its autonomous, metaphysical reference, which was independent of humans, and began to transform itself into a secular figure. Humans became endowed with genius but were incapable of avoiding the obstacles to the act of creation: as has been seen, *the desire for absolute autonomy leads directly to the recognition of the inability to fulfill that desire*—one has a simultaneous perception of self-mastery and utter vulnerability. The source of the melancholia of genius is helplessness: melancholics do not know who is putting their life and work at risk, but since they see that no one is lording it over them, *they can conclude only that the danger, their ultimate inability to move, origi-*

---

29. ὅτι ταύτην ὁ θεὸς ἐκπεπλήρωκεν τοῖς τέκνοις ἡμῖν ἀναστήσας Ἰησοῦν, ὡς καὶ ἐν τῷ ψαλμῷ γέγραπται τῷ δευτέρῳ, Υἱός μου εἶ σύ, ἐγὼ σήμερον γεγέννηκά σε ("God has fulfilled the same unto us their children, in that he hath raised up Jesus again: as it is also written in the second psalm, Thou art my Son, this day have I begotten thee.").

nates in themselves: they are their own worst enemies. Writing about the spirit working in humans, Joseph Scaliger took the view: "There are certain divine geniuses that we can neither see nor hear, but they manifest and settle in a person in such a manner that they illuminate with their light the secret things about which we write. That is why it is that when this heavenly incandescence cools in us often we are astonished at our own words and do not recognize them. Often we don't even understand them in the sense in which the genius dictated them" (quoted in Edgar Zilsel, *Die Entstehung der Geniebegriffs*, 284). Scaliger calls these geniuses benevolent, but it is questionable whether they are harmful from the creator's point of view. Because genius foists irresolvable contradictions on those who accept their own abilities and wish to exploit their own opportunities: they are forced to recognize both that everything they do bears their own imprint, yet they have only partially to do with the whole thing. *A genius is at the mercy of himself*—if he submits to that vulnerability, he has to give up on himself; if not, then he must still give up on being himself. He constantly, at every moment, endangers himself and keeps falling, spiraling down to ever-greater depths. He is not threatened by an external enemy, which is why he is unable even to defend himself. And what to an outsider appears to be creativity is in fact an internal rumination. True genius destroys itself—it is obliged to league with death. Genius leads man to the very brink of death, and vice versa: he who arrives at the brink of death is separated only by a hair's breadth from genius. "It's hard to die," Ernst Jünger wrote in the twentieth century, "yet one succeeds all the same. In this everyone still proved to be a genius" (Jünger, "Drugs and Ecstasy," in *Myth and Symbols*, ed. Joseph M. Kitagawa and Charles H. Long). Death is the better part of genius. The strong inclination of melancholics to suicide is a struggle between life and death in the most profound sense (the outcome, of course, is decided from the start). Genius is a manifestation of the tension between creativity and death—without that tension, however, there would be no "poles" either. The supplanting of the genius of God by individual genius is inconceivable without a not necessarily consciously felt sympathy for death;[30] yet facing up to death, the nonrecurrence and irreplaceability of existence, likewise makes geniuses of those who are willing to relate this to their own fate and conduct of life. That would become entirely true only during the period of Romanticism, but one can recognize the forerunners of the Romantics in the portrait figures of the Italian Renaissance, in the Arnolfini couple, in the protagonists of Elizabethan and Jacobean tragedies, and, not least, in the eccentric, melancholic artists of the Renaissance.

---

30. "Sympathy with death"—that was the expression Thomas Mann felt was most characteristic of himself.

Chapter 5
THE BRIBED

Notions formed in the Renaissance have affected our picture of
melancholia down to the present day. Sadness and deep thinking are
its most characteristic manifestations: melancholia is both an explanation of being that lays a claim to general validity and an individual
disposition, an ultimate source of our judging the world and a sheer
mood.[1] After the Renaissance, the individual related the world exclusively to himself, and he fell irretrievably into a trap not known to
either the Middle Ages or antiquity: the pitfall of the contradiction
of *indefinable infinity and concrete individuality.* Antiquity did not
concern itself with infinity from the point of view of the individual
(infinity was undeterminable and therefore not a positive quantity;
in his *Metaphysics,* Aristotle holds it to be inconceivable that human
thinking would be able to reach, via causes and effects, as far as in-
determinability, which was therefore considered an imperfection
from the viewpoint of human understanding [*Metaphysics,* bk. 2,

---

1. At the opening of his poem *Il Penseroso,* Milton wards off good humor:

Hence vain deluding joyes,
The brood of folly without father bred,
How little you bested,
Or fill the fixed mind with all your toyes.

In the twentieth century, in a formulation appropriate to the times, Walter Benjamin
wrote: "For whereas in the realm of the emotions it is not unusual for the relation
between an intention and its object to alternate between attraction and repulsion,
mourning is capable of a special intensification, a progressive deepening of its intention" (*German Tragic Drama,* 139).

2, 994b]. In the *Physics*, by contrast, he compares the infinite with the whole: "A quantity is infinite if it is such that we can always take a part outside what has been already taken. . . . The whole is that of which nothing is outside. On the other hand that from which something is absent and outside, however small that may be, is not 'all'" [*Physics*, bk. 3, ch. 6, 207a]). Christianity, on the other hand, while relating infinity to the individual, did not regard it as undetermined. (St. Gregory of Nyssa was the first to look on the infinity of God as a positive quantity, considering it possible that a creature's existence could become adjacent to God.) Concrete individuality and infinity regarded as positive first appeared as a paradox in the Renaissance era; it was to the credit of melancholics of the age that by *consistently thinking and living through it*, they came to realize its irresolvability. Individuals, as a result of their uniqueness and unrepeatability, are closed, one-time, limited beings, but precisely because of their complete isolation and point-like enclosure, they come to realize with astonishment their own inner infinitude. Their life is unrepeatable; no external standard is to be found against which to measure themselves, and therefore they will be standards for the world. Closedness and openness, finitude and infinitude, are characteristic of one and the same personality, and although the emphases may have changed, this remains true to the present day.

Renaissance melancholia was an extreme state: it was characterized equally by ruthless consistency and concomitant impatience. Renaissance melancholics availed themselves equally of the possibilities offered by a onetime existence and an indeterminable infinitude, and they thereby condemned themselves to death: melancholics of those times really had no life, just a continuous death, as despots had, or a petrified life, like that of the portrait figures. The melancholia of that age was also a symbolic suicide: it proved that total self-realization was the "most natural" and the "most human" state, but it showed also that this leads to death. Obviously, society cannot regard death as the sole natural state — but it also cannot conceal those dilemmas that are inseparable from the individuals of the modern age. Renaissance melancholia was still an all-consuming flame; the subsequent time period, right down to the present day, has been characterized by a desperate effort to transform this flame into ashes, to make sadness fit for polite society—to tame melancholia. Although there is no way of repressing melancholia, it is nevertheless possible to ensure that it does not burn down everything around it. It has to be rendered socially "acceptable": the melancholic has to be convinced that it is futile to dream about absolute autonomy; that trying to be omnipotent is doomed from the outset. Melancholics of the Renaissance admitted as much, too, but only after going through a number of dead ends of aiming for omnipotence. Following the Renaissance, the world dissuaded melancholics from pursuing that pointless quest, and they in turn reconciled themselves to the futility of those desires without even testing whether everything really was useless. By then, melancholics were, above all, *sorrowful* and not unviable; they too may have looked death in the eye, but they did not hurry to meet it. Everyone considered it natural that melancholics were gloomy; they were not asked about the reason for their sadness, but classed as self-evidently belonging to the rest of mankind—after all, they were like anyone else, just sad. Renaissance melancholics condemned to death both themselves and the world, while the modern world had no objection to melancholics being sorrowful—that was the price that had to be paid for having free disposal of their personalities. Society made it possible for melancholics to stay alive: it allowed them to be sad, but it did not let them die prematurely or condemn the world to death. *Sadness was bribery*, though of course melancholics did not notice: they did not see that sadness was the world's reward to them for giving up their muddling of the world.[2] In the Renaissance, sadness was a corollary of the most despondent condition; later on, sadness was de-

---

2. Walter Benjamin, admittedly with some exaggeration, explained Baudelairean spleen and melancholia as being due to intellectuals becoming commodities.

clared to be a passing mood that came and went "of its own accord" (the fact that bribery was involved had to be covered up), and therefore it was unnecessary to extend it to everything. On an etching by Battista Castiglione entitled *Melancholia,* made in the middle of the seventeenth century, stands the inscription *Ubi inletabilitas ibi virtus* ("Where there is despondency, there is virtue"). A century before, melancholia had been an acknowledgment of the ultimate hopelessness of being, but then it became a source of virtue. Of a virtue that in civil society is, first and foremost, *conformism*—a virtuous person accepts that the world is basically fine and respects the rules of the game established by others.[3] Melancholia was one of the preconditions of bourgeois morality, and was no longer personified as Saturn sitting in state over everything (as in the print *The Melancholic Temperament* by Jacob de Gheyn at the end of the sixteenth century), but, in the pictures of Rubens or Domenico Fetti, as Mary Magdalene adopting a virtuous pose that was in no way exciting or subversive.

The problem of infinity remained topical. In the modern world, however, it turned into an *earthly* infinity: it troubled doubters as a practical, not a metaphysical, concept—people had so much work to do that they were never able to get to the end. *Omnis cognitio fit per aliquam similitudinem* ("All knowledge is caused by means of a likeness"), said St. Thomas Aquinas (*Summa theologica,* I, q. 75, a. 2). The modern age employed his doctrine in its own way: since man is a transient, mortal being and can have no idea of infinity, there can be no autonomous existing thing independent of him. Nonetheless, since he does have some knowledge (presentiment) of infinity, it is obvious to suppose that the infinite per se is rooted in the his way of looking at things itself: that finite existing thing that he calls infinite is that which he cannot comprehend, that which is beyond his grasp. "Whatsoever we imagine, is Finite," argues Thomas

---

3. Milton expressed a similar opinion, characterizing melancholia as a "pensive Nun, devout and pure" (*Il Penseroso,* l. 31).

Hobbes. "Therefore there is no idea or conception of anything we call infinite. No man can have in his mind an image of infinite magnitude; nor conceive infinite swiftness, infinite time, or infinite force, or infinite power. When we say anything is infinite, we signify only that we are not able to conceive the ends and bounds of the thing named, having no conception of the thing, but of our own inability. . . . A man can have no thought representing anything not subject to sense" (*Leviathan*, bk. 1, ch. 3). Everything infinite is traceable to finite existing things, which of course is no obstacle to their being regarded as infinite. Infinity no longer relates to man's position, as in the Renaissance; it does not mean that he is the center of the world, and therefore he does not possess a point of reference outside himself; it relates to the position he occupies in the world. It is not that his abilities and possibilities are infinite, but rather that there is no end to finite things. In the civil world since the Renaissance, he has not been the *center* of the universe, but a *bit actor* in an institutionalized world that has settled on everything; *he lost himself without ever having possessed himself.* It was not himself but the hovering that was a consequence of his exclusion, which was felt to be infinite or, to be more accurate, never ending: he was tossed back and forth between the world's innumerable orders, and whatever he might try to comply with, he always found himself faced with fresher expectations. An individual in the modern age is a perpetual lawbreaker—there is always something left unsatisfied, and losing his bearings in a maze of institutions and mediators, he also loses himself. One might suppose there is a solution for everything, but man cannot meet all demands. The world of things is always one step ahead of him, and even though he talks about infinity, he sees only a finite world of objects around him. Infinity makes its appearance in the *relationship* of man to the objective world. Whether in the form of his having infinite opportunities in the world (seventeenth to eighteenth centuries) or in his being endlessly at the mercy of the world of objects and institutions (nineteenth to twentieth centuries), it is always finitude that lies in the depth. Forgoing absolute autonomy and conforming to the given world, he could regard his own existence as sensible or senseless only on the basis of existing standards.

Infinity was objectified and became sensory—that paradox altered the position of Renaissance melancholia in the modern era, creating tensions that are discharged not between man and heaven (Middle Ages) or between man and nothingness (Renaissance), but between man and the sensory world. "'Tis all in pieces, all coherence gone; / All just supply, and all Relation," writes John Donne, whose finest portrait, which can be viewed in Newbattle Abbey, depicts him, characteristically, in the pose of a melancholy lover. Everything is merely a matter of comparison—the heavens are not an ultimate standard for judging man, nor is man able to mold the world in his own image. Not only is he not born into a home, but he is also unable to create a home for himself in his homelessness. "Humans are not here for themselves," Nicolas Malebranche writes, "nor is their law or their illumination. Their substance is sheer profundity; they cannot see anything as they are contemplating themselves, and since they depend on God, they are not the master of their actions either" (*Méditations chrétiennes et métaphysiques*, meditation 5, in *Œuvres complètes*, vol. 10). Their homelessness is not just metaphysical in origin but also a consequence of their earthly vulnerability: the spectacle of the tangible, sensory world is a cause of pain and sadness:

> . . . Oh, it can no more be questioned,
> That beauties best, proportion, is dead,
> Since even griefe it selfe, which now alone
> Is left us, is without proportion.

> ("The first Anniversary," ll. 305–8)

Those lines are also by John Donne. But what could be more natural than that the human gaze should try, despite everything, to condense an alien world into a unity, devoid of all human scale. The eternal human desire to create a home challenges the world, which renders such an attempt hopeless from the outset. The more peremptory and desperate the desire, however, the more conspicuously fractured the world appears. Man becomes immersed in sensuality; this, however, is not mere dissipation but also a futile endeavor to create harmony—how else can one explain the deep sadness that lurks behind Baroque proliferation and stiffens every movement into numb immobility? It is as if by stuffy pageantry and a breathtaking cavalcade of bodies, those artists sought at any cost to hide something from us—the riddle of Baroque tension was not *compositional* but *existential* in origin (even though habit transposed all that to a technical level). Renaissance melancholics, like a light source, exuded a sadness that in portraits emanates toward us only from the human face. From the seventeenth century onward, gloominess no longer arose (at least not primarily) from man—he was the captive of an all-engulfing and all-pervading mournfulness: in the pictures of Ruisdael, Poussin, or Lorrain, the world itself is secretive, sad, and melancholic. The background becomes truly important; indeed, in more than a few of Lorrain's pictures (for example, *Landscape with the Nymph Egeria*), even the foreground paradoxically gives an impression of being background. Melancholia imbues everything,[4] and even though it was Caspar David Friedrich who made the assertion, nevertheless it was true from the seventeenth century on that melancholia was not the action of an external force, demon, or star, but a state of the soul, and since the soul interacts closely with nature, it can be discovered first of all in nature.[5] The mystery and the gloom that radiates toward us from those pictures reminds us of our homelessness like a distant light

---

4. The sonnet "Einsamkeit" ("Loneliness") by Andreas Gryphius (1616–1664) is a characteristic work of melancholia over a landscape.

5. In Germany in the sixteenth century, bare, dead trees were being called Saturn's trees—*Saturnbäume*—complicating further the connections between astrology, theories of humor, and melancholic notions of nature.

in a dark forest. What the most sensual and exuberant Baroque works of art tried to conceal tenaciously, Lorrain or Poussin attempted to reveal. Everything exudes sadness; after all, resigned mournfulness was the only weapon that remained for the onlooker to make bearable a world that had fallen to pieces and had lost all its proportions.

There is no tension that, in the final analysis, does not involve the questioning of the sense and appropriateness of existence. The most humdrum embarrassment, one that does not even come with a faint blush, makes existence—which is not unambiguous in any way and ostensively natural at most—just as mysterious as does the doubt veiled in the so-called ultimate questions. The tension that from the seventeenth century onward animates the petrified representatives of Renaissance melancholia stems from the aforementioned contradiction: man lost himself without ever having possessed himself. From Renaissance melancholia, the path leads unbroken down to the present day—if it gained new features, those were hidden in embryonic form in Renaissance melancholia. The individual seated at the center of the universe was soon toppled from his throne, and while being inhibited from creating his own world, he was forced into one that he had not created and was unable to feel comfortably at home in. That world has visibly nothing to do with either man or God—it lacks moderation and proportion. The most characteristic symptoms of this modern melancholia were resigned dolefulness and dread: there is no way of knowing who stipulated those provisions, or who is feared. In Claude Lorrain's pictures, even the foreground looks like a background: everything is mysterious, and he can barely be bothered to paint human faces, so little do the features give anything away. God still existed, of course, but that certitude was not the same as knowing the divine essence and will. The *Deus absconditus* was responsible for the despondency—God had left man to his own devices—and that was the reason for the dread as well: earthly solitude makes not just God but also the sense of human existence doubtful. "The first thing with which God inspires the soul that he designs to touch truly," writes Pascal, "is a knowledge and most extraordinary insight, by which the soul considers things and herself in a manner wholly new. This new light gives her fear" ("On the Conversion of the Sinner," in *Minor Works*, 388). The extraordinary knowledge and sight is a realization of the unfathomable mysteriousness of existence. How little is given away by the very word "mysteriousness." "If God discovered himself continually to men," Pascal writes elsewhere in a letter, "there would be no merit in believing him. . . . He remained concealed under the veil of the nature that covers him till the Incarnation" (*Letters*, 2nd letter to Mlle. Roannez, 354). Faith and melancholia are not mutually exclusive; in that respect, the melancholia of the Middle Ages and that of modern times adopt vastly different stances. Faith in a hidden God is permeated by despondency; without that, it would be pointless to hide. The true breeding ground of exasperation and despondency is not God's withdrawal into the background, but—it comes to the same thing—man's concealment from God. Faith and sin are intertwined.

The world is sinful from inception, so profess melancholics; sin, however, does not correspond to original sin as it was thought of in the Middle Ages. The discernment of the absurdity of existence plunges the world into sin; that discernment, however, is not a factor independent of man, like evil or original sin, which, in the judgment of the Middle Ages, extends to everyone, singling out no one. Sin derives from attitude and judgment; if melancholics call sin a state of the world, then that is not passing judgment on the world, but on their own existence. It is not the world that interprets the sin; the world is interpreted through the sinner's mindset—sin springs from the innermost part of the soul. The soul's tension, naturally, is identical with the tension of a creature that has been left to itself; the individual, like the world, has been shaken, its mainsprings lost sight of, and everything is veiled in mystery. God has hidden himself away, therefore he is the true sinner, according to melancholics, the ultimate reason for that pronouncement being that they themselves have become unintelligible: they have donned the mask of mysterious sorrow. One of the most melancholy figures of the seventeenth century, the physician Sir Thomas Browne,[6] writes as follows in his vexed treatise *Religio Medici*: "No man can justly censure or condemn another, because indeed no man truly knows another. This I perceive in my self; for I am in the dark to all the world, and my nearest friends beheld me but in a cloud. Those that know me but superficially, think less of me than I do of my self; those of my neer acquaintance think more; God, Who truly knows me, knows that I am nothing; for He only beholds me and all the world, Who . . . beholds the substance without the helps of accidents" (*Religio Medici*, pt. 2, sec. 4). Man is left to himself; he will be his own companion, and he judges the world also as his fellow companion: "There is no man alone, because every man is a *Microcosm*, and carries the whole World about him. . . . There is no such thing as solitude, nor any thing that can be said to be alone and by itself, but God" (pt. 2, sec. 10). The notion of a rounded world is a characteristic Baroque trope; melancholics, however, have dismantled precisely that roundedness. We see the same here as in the case of the Renaissance melancholics, who felt, more than others, that man was condemned to failure, precisely because he believed, more than others, in his omnipotence. The melancholic of the modern age (and here one has difficulty distinguishing Baroque, Romantic, or modern melancholia) like Thomas Browne believes more than anyone that a person is a microcosm and is not alone, yet it is exactly on that account that he also experiences most painfully the opposite. If he draws the sinful world into his own microcosm-like ego, then he will be the chief sinner, that is, the most solitary, since he tries most desperately to hide away from everything and would like to avoid everything. He sees himself as a microcosm, which means at one and the same time happiness and fateful futility: he revels in the rapture

---

6. "I was born in the Planetary hour of Saturn, and I think I have a piece of that Leaden Planet in me" (Thomas Browne, *Religio Medici*, pt. 2, sec. 11).

with which the spectacle of the depth of his own soul fills him, though he also shrinks back from this depth. Of course, there is nowhere to step back; he cannot get rid of himself, and is obliged to put up with the duality, even if he is unable to acquiesce in it. Robert Burton, who bequeathed us the most voluminous monograph on melancholy not just of the seventeenth century but of all time, describes at some length, in the versified abstract of the opening of his work, the double flavor that melancholia offers. The refrain of stanzas evoking the happier moments end with the couplet:

> All my joys to this are folly,
> Naught so sweet as melancholy.

Whereas stanzas evoking the sad and dark times end:

> All my griefs to this are jolly,
> Naught so sad as melancholy.[7]

(Burton, *Anatomy*, "The Author's Abstract of Melancholy," 79)

Melancholia cloaks everything, or rather, anything can be a pretext for melancholia. If a person is a microcosm, then melancholia can typify not just an individual but also the whole world: "Kingdoms and provinces are melancholy, cities and families, all creatures, vegetal, sensible, and rational, that all sorts, sects, ages, conditions, are out of tune . . . from the highest to the lowest have need of physic," the same Burton wrote in 1621, claiming that the bad distribution of humors and the collapse of states were akin to each other, indeed, might be regarded as identical symptoms, which was a typically Baroque notion: "What's the market? A place, according to Anacharsis, wherein they cozen one another, a trap; nay, what's the world itself?

---

7. In the last two stanzas, the final couplets are modified to: "All my joys to this are folly, / None so divine as melancholy," and "All my griefs to this are jolly, / Naught so damn'd as melancholy" — this melancholia extends equally to heaven and hell.

A vast chaos, a confusion of manners, as fickle as the air, *domicilium insanorum* [a madhouse], a turbulent troop full of impurities, a mart of walking spirits, goblins, the theatre of hypocrisy, a shop of knavery, flattery, a nursery of villainy, the scene of babbling, the school of giddiness, the academy of vice; a warfare, . . . wherein every man is for himself" (ibid., "Democritus to the Reader," 64). The world itself is sin incarnate; sin is the emanation of a deranged, unbalanced soul; derangement, however, is the consequence of a bad distribution of humors. If the *individual* was melancholic, then *the whole world* was melancholic as well, the Baroque understanding of melancholia declared, but the reverse was also true: if the world was melancholic, then every single person had to be melancholic. The great English melancholics of the seventeenth century—Thomas Browne, Robert Burton, and John Donne—were predisposed by their own interpretation of melancholic existence, whence the sly, devious endeavor to prove melancholia applied to everyone. Corresponding to the mixing of the four humors, four kinds of melancholia could arise, Burton informed his extraordinarily quick-learning contemporaries.[8] If *phlegm* was responsible for melancholia (that is, if it was the humor that was in excess) then the person in question was stupid, impassive,

---

8. The popularity of books about melancholia in the sixteenth and seventeenth centuries is striking. Timothie Bright's *A Treatise of Melancholie* was printed in two separate editions when it was first published in 1586, and was republished in 1613. An English translation of Juan Huarte de San Juan's *Examen de ingenios para las sciencias* of 1575 reached four editions between 1594 and 1616; Thomas Wright's *The Passions of Minde in generall* first appeared in 1601, reappeared in 1604 "corrected, enlarged, and with sundry new discources augmented," and was reissued in 1621 and 1630; André du Laurens's *Discours de la conservation de la vene: des maladies mélancholiques, des catarrhes et de la vieillesse* was first published in Paris and reached ten editions between 1597 and 1626, being also translated into Latin and Italian as well as into English in 1599 by Richard Surphlet (*A Discourse of the Preservation of the Sight: of Melancholike diseases; of Rheumes, and of Old age*). Robert Burton's colossal *Anatomy of Melancholy* saw as many as seven reprints between 1621 and 1676 before vanishing (it reappeared 124 years later, at the start of the Romantic era).

sleepy, foolish, pallid, prone to headaches, plump, and rheumatic; if
they were plethoric (that is, had an excess of *blood*), then they were
merry and witty, loved music, dancing, and women—could think
of nothing else—and knew nothing of sorrow, not even by hearsay;
if it was an excess of *bile*, then they were cantankerous, impatient,
bloodthirsty, and if they had a fit, they would speak in tongues;[9] and if
black bile was responsible for the melancholia, then they were timid,
solitary, sorrowful, and constantly preoccupied with death. There was
no one who was not melancholic, since melancholia was no longer
linked with a particular humor.

> . . . this worlds generall sicknesse doth not lie
> In any humour, or one certaine part.

> (Donne, "The first Anniversary," ll. 239–40)

Although Donne does not explicitly name melancholia, he was un-
mistakably thinking of it. Anyone born under the sign of Saturn (or
Mercury), who lived in a climate that was too cold or too hot, whose
parents had been melancholic, whose head was small, who had a
warm heart or liver, or a moist brain, or a cold stomach, who had been
ill for a long time, who was partial to loneliness, who was a scholar,
who filled his life with contemplation, was melancholic, as was every
aged person in principle. "The four and twenty letters make no more
variety of words in diverse languages, than melancholy conceits produce diversity of symptoms in several persons. They are irregular, obscure, various, so infinite, Proteus himself is not so diverse, you may
as well make the moon a new coat, as a true character of a melancholy
man; as soon find the motion of a bird in the air, as the heart of man,
a melancholy man" (Burton, *Anatomy*, partition 1, sec. 3, member 1,
subsec. 4, 408).

---

9. In this, Burton was endorsing a medieval notion: according to Avicenna,
speaking in tongues indicated the presence of Satan.

Humans are melancholic from the very start, says Burton: the causes of melancholia are numberless, which is why the illness is incurable. Yet if everyone is sick, then health must be an unknown concept; health is a utopian standard that, like every utopia itself, becomes a source of fresh melancholia. John Donne asks:

> There is no health; Physitians say that wee,
> At best, enjoy but a neutralitie.
> And can there bee worse sicknesse, than to know
> That we are never well, nor can be so?

> (Donne, "The first Anniversary," ll. 92–95)

All-embracing melancholia was a harbinger of omnipotent death. *Illness* became the normal condition, and there was nothing that was not a reminder of death. Every age was cognizant of the close relationship between melancholia and death, but whereas in antiquity the death of melancholics meant an assurance of a new, more highly refined form of life, and in the Middle Ages it went hand in hand with a denial of divine grace and a bowing to evil, in modern times it did not point to anything beyond itself; it meant bodily and spiritual annihilation and nothing else. Death became "down to earth," with nothing to do any longer with heaven or the afterlife. "Whosoever would grace this frail cottage, in which poverty adorns every corner, with a rational epitome," wrote Christoph Männling in seventeenth-century Germany, "would be making no inapt statement nor overstepping the mark of well-founded truth if he called the world a general store, a custom-house of death, in which man is the merchandise, death the wondrous merchant, God is most conscientious book-keeper, but the grave the bonded draper's hall and ware house" (quoted in Benjamin, *German Tragic Drama*, 159). Death lost its metaphysical connotations: it became a *this-worldly* death. It no longer stood outside life, it was no longer an independently existing entity but, despite every Baroque allegorization, an organic appurte-

nance of life, inseparable from man. In the sense not just that everyone must die, but also that death does not exist outside man: man
belongs to death, and death belongs to man. Man alone has cognizance of death because, strictly speaking, only *he* dies; there is no
other creature at whose demise the irreproducible unity of body and
soul comes to an end. Animals do not die, since they have no cognizance of their death; they just "pass away," become *past* in relation
to themselves, that is, disappear without a trace, as if they had never
existed. Angels do not die either, because they do not possess a transient body. Death is reserved for humans—it belongs *only* to humans,
and to *all* humans. Seen from life's perspective, naturally, every death
is different;[10] from the perspective of *death* (if such a thing exists),
however, there is no difference, there is only death, and even life is
settled in those terms. Death is the chief lord and master of earthly
life: "For the World," writes Thomas Browne, "I count it not an Inn,
but an Hospital; and a place not to live, but to dye in" (*Religio Medici*,
pt. 2, sec. 11). Life, in Browne's opinion, is a continuous death, but
because death makes man the most distinguished living thing in the
universe, death is also a special ability: a *negative possibility* that, if
man seizes the opportunity, puts life in a new light. Mortal man may
even be filled with pride on account of his own death. There are innumerable ways of destroying him, says Sir Thomas Browne again,
and then goes on to say: "There is therefore but one comfort left,
that, though it be in the power of the weakest arm to take away life,
it is not in the strongest to deprive us of death" (*Religio Medici*, pt. 1,
sec. 44). Death fills melancholic Browne with negative pride: he is
not proud of one thing or another (after all, he is aware that death
reigns supreme over everything), but rather, like the protagonist of
Dostoevsky's *Notes from Underground*, he is proud there is nothing

10. In Spain, physicians tried to cure Charles II's melancholia by prescribing
that he watch as many autos-da-fé as possible. For the melancholic king, death presumably had a different meaning than it did for those who were bound to the stake.

that would fill him with pride. The *death-irony* that is inherent in Socratic *knowledge-irony* unfolds in the melancholia of the modern age: knowledge means coming to terms with death, and death is a definitive obliteration not just of the body but also of the spirit. The seventeenth-century poet William Davenant writes as follows in his poem "To a Mistress Dying":

> But ask not bodies doom'd to die
> To what abode they go;
> Since Knowledge is but Sorrow's spy,
> It is not safe to know.

Knowledge is a harbinger of mortality: the greater the knowledge, the stronger the constant feeling of extinction. We know from astrological explanations of melancholia, however, that great knowledge, profound contemplation, and fear of obliteration are especially characteristic of melancholia. And melancholia, so antiquity teaches, is no stranger to irony, for knowledge that death is omnipresent yields the most diabolical irony. "The hour of dying," writes Rainer Maria Rilke in a letter, "is only one of our hours and not exceptional. Our being is continually undergoing and entering upon changes that are perhaps of no less intensity than the new, the next, and the next again, that death brings with it" (11 November 1909, in *Letters of Rainer Maria Rilke, 1892–1910,* 353). And another opinion, one that sets off the irony even more, from the pen of Miguel de Unamuno: "True life nourishes itself on death and renews itself second by second, in continuous creation. A life without any death in it, without any unpiling in its continual piling up, would be a perpetual death, the repose of a stone. Those who do not die do not live; those who do not die at every instant, to rise from the dead on the instant, do not live" (*Our Lord Don Quixote,* 174–75).

Irony refers to the aforesaid negative pride, and that, in turn, stems from recognition of the possibility of death as a negative possibility. But just as melancholics both relish and despise the world, death also has two faces: it is at once attractive and frightening. Fear of death and a wish for it arise from the same base: a desire for conquest of the universe and for infinity is unwilling to take account of death, but perpetual futility and failure cause so much pain that only death can bring relief. It is not a matter of two states alternating with each other. Melancholics do not typically shake with fear one minute only to long for it the next, but simultaneously feel both one way and the other. Galen wrote that melancholics doubt death yet also long for it. And Sir Thomas Browne wrote: "I can with patience embrace this life, yet in my best meditations do often defie death" (*Religio Medici*, pt. 1, sec. 38; manuscript versions and the first printing [1642] have "desire" for "defie"). What sets off melancholia from all other bodily and mental states is precisely that it makes a person capable of this ambivalent way of looking at things, which, in the modern age, leaving words and brushstrokes behind, freezes melancholics among the notes of *music*.

It is hard to separate the creation of a world from the creation of a work of art in the case of the Renaissance melancholic: in its own way, shaping a life is just as much an art as painting a picture or writing a poem. Completing a work of art is just as much an elemental world creation as an attempt at world conquest. Since this experiment is, ultimately, doomed to failure, it is not surprising that creating a work of art must also end in failure. Such failure was technical in only a few cases (including those in which the work remained unfinished); the true failure could be discerned much more in the profound sorrow that lies behind many outstanding works of art of the modern era. The greater the technical perfection, the more prominent the sadness. One has a feeling not only that (even in works on religious subjects) God has been squeezed out of creation, having been changed into a compositional element, but also that the creator was unable to take over God's "role" in a satisfactory way. He made a start on creation, but proved unable to create *everything*, to satisfy every point of view—what distinguishes a work of art of the modern era from a medieval work is, above all, the lack of a multidimensional perspective. (Think of the apparent illogic that characterizes epic literary works of the Middle Ages. In the plots of those works, linearity, the logic that presents individual arbitrariness as a world principle, falls flat; one might also call to mind the lack of perspective in medieval painting, which, in fact, amounts to taking all points of view.) Works of art in the modern era take a single point of view (perspective), and the resignation that has defined art from paintings of the Renaissance era onward springs from the impossible undertaking of a solitary creative artist, possessing one point of view, manifestly trying to produce a work that satisfies every viewpoint. A work of art would like to be a universe; however, a creative artist is not God but a mortal man; creating a universe on Earth is rather like pulling oneself up by one's bootstraps. And even if he were, like God, capable of viewing the human world from the outside, what would he see? Little different from what Robert Burton saw: "In a word, the world itself is a maze, a labyrinth of errors, a desert, a wilderness, a den of thieves, cheaters, &c., full of filthy puddles, horrid rocks, precipitiums, an ocean of adversity, an heavy yoke, wherein infirmities and calamities overtake, and follow one another, as the sea waves" (Burton, *Anatomy*, partition 1, sec. 2, member 3, subsec. 10, 274) A creative artist feels perpetual dissatisfaction—however great the work that is brought into being, there is a feeling that he was unable fully to cast it into the form that he conceived in himself—and the viewers, if they lose themselves in the work, find themselves face-to-face with infinite sorrow, which is either omnipresent (as in *Don Quixote*, for instance) or is the endpoint toward which everything heads (the movingly resigned final scene of *War and Peace* is like that).

Following the Renaissance, with the growing "refinement" of melancholia, the *music of the modern age* evolved as *the* branch of melancholic art, permeated through and through by melancholia.

("Is there really such a thing as cheerful music?" Schubert asks.)
Music has had a privileged position from the moment when the
frozen melancholic of the Renaissance was resuscitated by *earthly*
tensions (the tensions were already exceedingly this-worldly in the
religious art of the Baroque as well), and he was overcome by an ambivalent attitude toward life. It was equally significant that it was a
matter of ambivalence *and* feeling, or affect. It has been seen that the
melancholic of the modern age was, before all else, sad (and less desperate than his fellows of the Renaissance); we have seen that the sadness was no obstacle to him living his life and being freely at the disposal of the world, and we have also seen that sadness, mingled with
resignation, was regarded as a *transient mood* (it was not noticed that
the melancholic was sad *because* he had been deprived of the possibility of autonomously creating a world; the order was inverted — his
sadness was explained by his inertia). At the same time, the sadness
of the modern melancholic resulted in his having an ambivalent way
of looking at the world: since anything might evoke sadness, it had no
palpable cause. Not a single cause could be pointed to, because by
doing so the explanation of melancholia would be diverted onto the
wrong track. By naming any cause, we would merely force an arbitrary scheme on melancholia instead of getting nearer to it. Nothing
disturbs a melancholic more than if we try to console him, or even
just define his condition, with words. In his previously cited work
The Secret, Petrarch, in the second of his dialogues with St. Augustine, says:

> After all, how many things are there in nature for which we have
> no appropriate words? How many other things are there which
> have names yet whose full merit cannot be expressed by human
> eloquence before we actually experience them? How many
> times have I heard you complain, how many times have I seen
> your silent indignation, when neither tongue nor pen could ex-
> press thoughts that existed easily and with the greatest clarity in

your mind? Of what use, therefore, is this eloquence of yours, so narrow and fragile that it cannot embrace all things and cannot hold together what it has embraced?

(73)

The modern melancholic has a positive aversion for language: for one thing, language, talking, attempts to objectify melancholia, even though there is no special object to which melancholia could be tied; for another, by giving things a name, language forces melancholia into existing patterns of the world, although it is precisely due to that world that he suffers. To rid himself of his own melancholia, Thomas Browne preferred to put on the blinkers implied by words when he wrote: "I thank the goodness of God, I have no sins that want a name; I am not singular in offences; my transgressions are Epidemical" (*Religio Medici*, pt. 2, sec. 7). Community in sin allays a guilty conscience, and if a name is found for the transgression, then the transgressor is also a member of a society that we know will, sooner or later, albeit not reassuringly, smooth everything over. The true melancholic, however, can find no words for his condition: it is not possible to speak satisfactorily about death, and therefore not about the fear of, or wish for, death either. Language reassures us, while there is nothing less reassuring than death. The fine arts have a better chance than language, though even they are too strongly bound to the objective world; they had a major role in evoking melancholia in the Renaissance, when the objective world was not yet alien but considered to be conquerable. But when the world did not offer the melancholic the possibility of establishing a home, and he was surrounded ever more threateningly by objects, the role of music grew, and—lacking in all objective reference as it does—it became the most melancholic of all the genres of art.

The connection between music and melancholia was known in all ages (it speaks volumes that in ancient times, music and augury, which was related to melancholia, were thought to share the same origin; to the mythological mind, music was the basis of life, and without it nothing at all could be perfect), but earlier that connection was external: music per se was not melancholic but a remedy (or poison) for melancholia. "And it came to pass, when the evil spirit from God was upon Saul," the Bible recounts about Saul's melancholia, "that David took an harp, and played with his hand: so Saul was refreshed, and was well, and the evil spirit departed from him" (1 Samuel 16:23). According to Asclepiades of Bithynia, a famous Greek physician, a therapy for melancholia had to include tunes in the Phrygian mode; Galen explicitly recommended that melancholics listen to music — and that was also avowed throughout the Middle Ages.[11] A medicine, however, was supposed to act on the body by being akin to — indeed, to some extent identical with — it; music was a cure for melancholia, which implied that a melancholic nature was also characteristic of it. Receiving more than the prescribed dose of this medicine was poisonous; if, on the one hand, music was a medicine, because it represented cosmic order (*musica mundana*—music of the spheres), on the other hand, it was potentially poisonous and a harbinger of death (siren song); it could ennoble, but it could also corrupt, because, as Plutarch professed, it could be more intoxicating than wine. "Truly," Jean Starobinski quotes Soranus from the beginning of the second century CE, "music causes plethora in the head, which may be experienced even in the case of healthy people: in certain cases it is thought it may evoke madness; when those who are inspired sing their prophesies, it may seem as if a god had taken possession

---

11. According to Constantine the African as well, music was the most effective remedy. In the early 1300s, and for some four centuries thereafter, in the southern Italian region of Apulia, a slothfulness that was called melancholia, allegedly due to the bites of poisonous spiders, spread epidemically through the town of Taranto. Patients were impelled to dance to the music of fife and drums (hence the derivation of the dance—"tarantella" meaning "little spider"), and this remedy was still being recommended in the seventeenth century, with flute and drum being given preference, because string instruments were supposedly unable to drive melancholia away.

of them" (Starobinski, *Histoire du traitement de la mélancolie des origines*, 73). Linking music with madness and augury shows that music too was connected with understanding existence: when it is a medicine, it aids the understanding of existence, but when it is a poison, it inhibits such understanding and spreads gloom around. Music can embrace everything, and on hearing it one sees the world from a different angle from before: music not only sets the mood of its listener, but makes him reinterpret existence itself. Starobinski cites the Spaniard Ramos de Pareja, who in 1482, in a book entitled *Musica practica*, matched four primary pitches to the four humors and their planets: the *tonus protus*: phlegm, the moon; the *tonus deuteros*: the bile, Mars; the *tonus tritus*: blood, Jupiter; the *tonus tetartus*: melancholia, Saturn. Music was ubiquitous, extending its influence over everything; if, in the Middle Ages, God accepted responsibility for existence, then music could not be melancholic. With the decline of the Middle Ages, however, when everything depended on man, now abandoned to himself, music was also left to itself; instead of divine harmony, the voices of temperament were intoned. Following the Renaissance, music became *intimately* melancholic, and from then on it was regarded less and less as a medicine. A medicine can be recommended only if one can differentiate between sickness and health, if there is a standard for comparing the two kinds of condition. For melancholics of the Renaissance and the modern era, this absolute standard was lost, starting with God taking a step back and handing the mortal joy of self-determination to humans, and ending with sickness and health becoming — just as seventeenth-century thinkers proclaimed they would — relative concepts — in fact, with everything being determined by illness. But if the whole world is sick, then it is vain to hope to find a remedy — and the melancholic, while fearing and wishing for death simultaneously, does not even seek to be cured, since that would push him back into the old routine of an earlier state, shove him into the arms of the world, render his position unequivocal (albeit just as hopeless as in his melancholic days). Now music is no longer a medicine;[12] it is useless for restoring an upset balance, but since everything has been shaken, it acts disruptively: it does not mediate a single external order for the benefit of the listener, but instead becomes hopelessly subjective, representing a mental state but not the world. A melancholic can have no hope of a remedy; he cannot trust anything, can count on only himself and compare music, the equivalent of wordless melancholia, to himself. Music no longer changes but preserves the existing condition. "I damn the melancholic inclination," Ficino writes in a letter to Cavalcanti, "for me it is exceedingly bitter unless it is mellowed and sweetened through frequent use of the lute" (*Epistolae*, vol. 3, no. 24).[13] Music sweetens melancholia, that is, the melancholic genuinely finds himself in music.

In 1737, the queen of Spain invited Farinelli, the celebrated singer, to sing for Philip V, who suffered from deep melancholy. Farinelli, himself a melancholic, cured the king with his singing the first time he performed for the monarchs; as a result, "it was determined that he should be taken into the service of the court," and "for the first ten years of his residence at the court of Spain, during the life of

---

12. Jean Starobinski mentions some counterexamples as well: in the seventeenth century, at the time so-called affectology was born, the idea that music was therapeutic was revived in works such as Anne-Charles Lorry, *De melancholia et morbis melancholicis* (1765), and Pierre-Joseph Buchoz, *Mémoire sur la manière de guérir la mélancolie par la musique* (1761).

13. One may add that Ficino, despite all his complaining, considered melancholia to be the most splendid state; music, which sweetens melancholia, thereby took possession of the *whole* person: "The sound of music," he writes, "assails the body through air movement; through the cleansed air it excites the aerial spirit, which is a link between the body and the soul; through the emotions it acts on the senses and at the same time on the soul; through interpretation it touches the intellect; finally, by means of that same easy air movement, it softly caresses us, the pleasantness of its material overwhelming us with marvelous delight; through its intellectual and material nature it simultaneously captivates and totally takes possession of the whole person" (quoted in Starobinski, *Histoire du traitement de la mélancolie*, 78).

Philip the Vth, he sung every night to that monarch" (Charles Burney, *The Present State of Music in France and Italy*, 218). In the modern age, melancholia was not a *subject* of music, but rather *permeated* it. From the Baroque onward, musical compositions *about* melancholia—which have an external and "rhetorical" rather than fateful relationship to it—are perhaps less melancholic than works in which melancholia is not brought out at all as a subject.[14] Melancholia does not tolerate objective definition (that is why its true medium is music), and if music is "about" anything at all, it is about there being no point in the world in relation to which one might define, or make, one's position unequivocally. The modern melancholic, fraught with tensions and, at the same time, infinitely resigned, makes his appearance in the company of music: John Dowland's collection *Lachrimae, or Seaven Teares*, Gesualdo's madrigals, Monteverdi's music for the stage, and Purcell's operas and choral works alike articulate melancholia—and one does not need to strain too much to hear in these works the later tones of Schubert or Schumann, Mahler or Wagner, Satie or Webern, Giacinto Scelsi or John Cage or even Klaus Nomi. There is no sense in assembling a list of names: *the music of the modern age is not melancholic because it spreads a doleful mood, but because it was created in the form of music.* Whether sorrowful or cheerful in mood (how meaningless that distinction is, as if profound cheerfulness and inconsolable sorrow did not spring from the same stock!), music, from the Baroque onward, has had only a single true topic: the homelessness and the fateful-seeming abandonment of the modern melancholic. "Music," writes Bruno Walter, "is no daytime art; it does not yield its secret roots or its ultimate depths to the un-

---

14. For an example of the thematic, programmatic deployment of melancholia, see the Trio Sonata in C Minor for two violins and continuo of Carl Philipp Emanuel Bach, in which Melancholia and Sanguineus argue, only to be reconciled in the last movement, or the adagio introduction (entitled "La Malincolia") to the Finale of Beethoven's String Quartet no. 6 in B-flat Major, op. 18, no. 6.

shadowed soul. It comes out of the dark, and must be understood and felt in the dark; it is akin to the somber heave of the ocean, not to the clear blue of the Mediterranean" (Walter, *Gustav Mahler,* 121). Or turning for help to Céline, who experienced the melancholic's fear of and desire for death more than anyone, and therefore was truly sensitive to music as well: "Nobody can really resist music. You don't know what to do with your heart, you're glad to give it away. At the bottom of all music you have to hear the tune without notes more just for us, us all, the tune of Death" (Louis-Ferdinand Céline, *Journey to the End of the Night,* 264).

The melancholic of the modern age is, above all else, sad, the heroic endeavor and universal desperation of the Renaissance having been supplanted by mere despondency. He has been denied the possibility of creating a new world, but also prevented from dodging a world that is alien to him. Turning away from the world takes place inside the soul—the world torments and crushes as it pleases anyone who, by creating an inner world, tries in vain to escape from external pain. The sadness of the modern melancholic springs from helplessness; whatever he does, he feels that all efforts are futile—no one is capable of cracking the world's armor. Sadness, however paradoxical it may sound, is at one and the same time a visor and armor—a visor because the melancholic, by turning into himself, refuses to take cognizance of the fact that the despondency deriving from helplessness was actually imposed on him; a weapon because it gives an opportunity to create a new, inner world in opposition to the outside one. The melancholic would give himself over to despondency with masochistic pleasure: the soul always has a realm into which no one else is permitted entry. That dominion extends "inwardly"; the stronger the external pressure, the more the inner boundaries expand. The world is unacquainted with this dual nature of sorrow: it fails to notice both that a person can take cover in sorrowfulness, and that sadness is capable of denying everything. All that is seen is that sorrow always renders a melancholic weak, and his weakness is explained by his own superior strength: "Whatever excuse we may find for our sorrows, often it is only self-interest and vanity that cause them," La Rochefoucauld opines (*Collected Maxims and Other Reflections*, V: 232), offering a novel interpretation of sadness: instead of connecting it with an all-embracing despair, he tries to ensure a place for it in the preordained framework of an unchangeable world. If sorrow depends only on interest or vanity, then this rules out making the world itself questionable: a person's sadness is caused by this or that not being to his liking in this world, but that sadness would not extend to the whole world itself. The world always tries to console the sad and convince them that sooner or later everything will work out. And indeed, in the modern age, the biggest offence against decorum is to thrust someone who is despairing and sad into even greater depths of despair by telling him that he does have a reason to be sad and, what is more, not just because some trouble has befallen him, but because the world is deliberately constructed to be a fount of woes. One is just as much expected to console a sad man as to deceive a terminally ill one about his true condition — consolation, however, conceals deception: it does not abolish despondency but defers it, makes it invisible. And sadness that has been made invisible proliferates like cancer: the less the consoled person takes note of it, the more violently will it well up at an unexpected moment.

La Rochefoucauld tried to make despondency presentable in good society. The melancholic is not fleeing the world but trying to find himself a quiet nook within it; he does not make immoderate demands; he is not enraged and raving, as in antiquity; he is not mentally ill, as in the Middle Ages; he is not desperately calling anything to account, as in the Renaissance; but he is, above all, depressed: quiet, withdrawn into himself, feeble, and inert. According to Pascal, the aim of the French court at the time was to stifle the sadness and melancholia that was breaking out on all sides:

> Put it to the test; leave a king entirely alone quite at leisure, with
> nothing to satisfy his senses, no care to occupy the mind, with
> complete leisure to think about himself, and you will see that a
> king without diversion is a very wretched man. Therefore such
> a thing is carefully avoided, and the persons of kings are invari-
> ably attended by a great number of people concerned to see that
> diversion comes after affairs of state, watching over their leisure
> hours to provide pleasures and sport so that there should never
> be an empty moment. In other words they are surrounded by
> people who are incredibly careful to see that the king should
> never be alone and able to think about himself, because they
> know that, king though he is, he will be miserable if he does
> think about it.
>
> (*Pensées*, no. 142)

Sorrow does not spare even a king ("Mournful melancholia usually
dwells in palaces," writes François-André Philidor, a French com-
poser of the Baroque era), but that sadness can be explained also by
the world turning gray: if everything is alike, then there is no place
to withdraw from boredom and despondency. Court etiquette, with
its Baroque pomp, was unable to lift the insidious monotony, even as
the dazzlement of each stroke of inspiration outdid the previous one;
indeed, it seems that it was precisely grayness, an ever-intensifying
sense of helplessness, that necessitated pomp and splendor. Although
the seventeenth and eighteenth centuries presented great opportunities, compared with the heroes of the Renaissance and the great
adventurers of the sixteenth century it is impossible to fail to notice
the graying: the organized, constitutional, or absolutist form of government narrowed individual opportunities to a great extent, in both
a metaphysical and a practical sense. During the seventeenth century, typically, interest in so-called character sketches grew throughout Europe—*species* and *types* came to the fore at the time when
the place of the great man was taken by the *average* person. That was

a characteristically modern phenomenon.[15] Until the seventeenth century, only those in power possessed "individuality"; however, as power started to become depersonalized, the common man came to power. "A middle-class manner is sometimes shed in the army, but never at court," La Rochefoucauld writes (*Collected Maxims*, V: 393).

Courts created sham occupations—the refined and proliferating rules of etiquette, however, although making those affected forget that they had lost their true power and individuality, could not eliminate *tedium*. Next to sadness, that is the other distinguishing mark of melancholia in the modern age. Boredom is elicited by order, or to be more accurate, by *foreordained order*: if people are deprived of the possibility to act, boredom takes over everything. Tedium becomes a way of life forced on all. In the course of the seventeenth century, the great representatives of boredom emerged from the ranks of the nobility, from a nobility whose way of life began increasingly to lose its raison d'être. La Rochefoucauld mentions his own melancholia as an almost compulsory fashion item for the nobility: "To speak first of my temperament, I am melancholy—to such a degree that, in the last three or four years, I have hardly been seen to laugh three or four times," he says, before continuing, "Most of the time I am either daydreaming without uttering a word or else giving very little attention to what I am saying" (*Collected Maxims*, 277). Melancholia was not just a matter of temperament and nature: the reference to a specified time frame (three to four years) signals that it was a consequence of something—presumably of boredom and inertia. Whiling away his time at a salon, on one occasion the duc de Saint-Simon noticed that a bored La Rochefoucauld was breaking the rules of etiquette by playing chess with his valet: "Monsieur de Chevreuse and I could not even say a word. Spotting this, La Rochefoucauld was himself embarrassed . . . tried to explain the situation, saying that the valet played

---

15. It was not entirely without precedent: the Hellenistic typology of humors came into existence under similar circumstances.

very well, and one could not play chess with everyone. De Chevreuse did not contradict him, and neither did I; we behaved courteously and sat down but then soon got to our feet so as not to disturb the game, and we slipped away as speedily as we could" (quoted in Wolf Lepenies, *Melancholie und Gesellschaft*, 172). La Rochefoucauld himself had the following to say about the relationship between duty and boredom: "If we carefully consider the various results of heartache (*l'ennui*), we shall find that it causes more failures of duty than self-interest does" (*Collected Maxims*, V: 172). *Duty* is the be-all and end-all of life, and it is not good manners to challenge life; it bespeaks bad form to deliberately flout it. Boredom, hand in hand with sadness and inertia, puts up with everything; bored people allow the world to direct their footsteps. What really bores people is being condemned to inaction. Their personalities urge them to make the best of their rights and realize everything inherent in their individuality, but they have to endure being clapped in irons: order, or more precisely, the world that is held together like a net by proliferating institutions and precepts, allows one only *faith* and *illusion*. Tedium is not simply the enduring of something but also a *negative realization* of the personality; for the person who is bored, it is not purely a matter of time passing but, as time passes, of recognizing the innumerable opportunities that are not being put to use. The fulfillment of time betokens one's own emptying. The more extremely one is bored, the more stultifying one's own ego becomes to oneself. One is horrified to observe oneself. Pierre Drieu La Rochelle appositely pointed out in the middle of the last century that "terror is the grimacing face of boredom" (Drieu La Rochelle, *Geheimer Bericht und andere biographische Aufzeichnungen*, 205): terror and tedium share a common root. Bored people see everything as empty, nothing, condemned to annihilation, and while they involuntarily also see that boredom is hastening the path toward death, they realize with horror that it has already taken up abode in them: from birth on, nothingness, space, death, has been building a nest in them. Those who are truly bored experience their own personality as a negative imprint, an intaglio—and the greater the tedium, the more plastic and tangible the negative relief that their personality forms. "Extreme heartache rids us of heartache," La Rochefoucauld writes (*Collected Maxims*, PV158: 3), no doubt thinking of the negative pleasure that, as a result of tedium, offers a new and independent personality to those who are bored because they suffer from an ordered, regimented life, even if that new personality accentuates a feeling of loss. There are two kinds of tedium: the sort that is on *this side* of orderliness and accepts the world for what it is—that kind of tedium does not call itself by its rightful name and indeed strenuously objects when it is accused of boredom;[16] the other kind of boredom is *beyond* order: it is desperate boredom, which, by accepting itself, turns the world upside down and claims that its orderliness is unnatural and dreadful. Self-imposed boredom that is taken upon oneself is a silent *protest*, an exchange of the existing order and world for a negative order and world (Kierkegaard calls boredom the daemonic side of pantheism). Consciously accepted boredom lifts its subjects out of the world, making them capable of regarding *nothingness* and *negativity*, which the world forces them to suffer, as the supreme characteristics not just of their own being but of the world as well. The bored person senses that his burgeoning opportunities are being squandered, his personality is realized as negativity—though he can sense that only because the innermost essence of the world, which reproves him, is itself negative; it is an inverse world that fritters his opportunities away, and in it the passage of time brings inevitable ruination. Boredom would not exist if man were immortal; what is gradually exposed in boredom is precisely that man is just as condemned to perdition as any lifeless ob-

---

16. "Those who do not bore themselves," writes Kierkegaard, "are generally people who, in one way or another, keep themselves extremely busy; these people are precisely on this account the most tiresome, the most utterly unendurable" (*Either/Or*, 237).

ject. "Boredom," writes Georges Bataille, "makes it possible for us to keep watch on the universe with the hopeless and uncomprehending eyes of a dying wasp. . . . At times like this, we keep watch with impotent rage on the world of illusions. Observing a deep silence, and with a pleasure that frightens us, we step in bare feet onto damp ground in order to feel how we sink into the nature that will destroy us" (*Oeuvres complètes*, 1:522). Boredom is inseparable from man's existence; it is telling, though, that it was only from the seventeenth and eighteenth centuries onward that people began to occupy themselves with it more thoroughly: at just the time when faith placed in the magnificence of civil development was trying, with previously unknown fervor, to cover up the withering and decay lying at the bottom of all existence. Although it was only in the nineteenth century that the view spread that vulgar plebeians were unacquainted with boredom (Leopardi, Schopenhauer, Nietzsche), in civil society tedium lurked *from the very start* as a negative impress of the world and a negative protest against the world's setup. The notion of boredom, as historical linguistics testifies, was born in the modern age. In German, *Langeweile*, literally, "long while" or "long duration," makes its appearance at the end of the fourteenth century, but in the seventeenth century it was still being used as a substantive in the sense of "long-lasting" to characterize an illness, time, a journey, or a road. After a scattering of precedents, it was only in the eighteenth century that it spread in the modern sense of "tedium." In French, *ennui* or *ennuyer* was initially, as in German, connected with the notions of weariness and pain,[17] and only in the seventeenth century did it gain the modern sense of "tedium." *L'ennui naquit un jour de l'uniformité* ("One day boredom was born of uniformity"), wrote Antoine Houdar de la Motte. In the English of the fourteenth century, the word "spleen," synonymous with boredom, still denoted only the organ

---

17. In *La Chanson de Roland*, it meant worry, pain, but in the twelfth century it denoted weariness.

situated near the stomach, but by the end of the seventeenth century Sir William Temple was using the word in a "sociological" rather than anatomical sense when he described England as a "region of spleen," and Swift in *Gulliver's Travels* likewise uses the word in the sense of ennui, or a feeling of listlessness, weariness of life, a general dissatisfaction resulting from lack of activity or excitement: "Spleen . . . only seizes on the lazy, the luxurious, and the rich." The history of the Hungarian language attests the same: *unalom* did not originally mean "tedium" in the sense it has nowadays, but described a person being "fed up" (even in the physical sense) with someone: "The champions of the mother church did not have enough (*nem unták*) suffering," Péter Pázmány[18] wrote in one of his sermons, and elsewhere, "great God never gets fed up (*unatkozik*) with the many supplicants." The primary original meaning of *unalmas* was "heavy with," "burdened," "arduous." Thus, in a sermon written in 1696, András Illyés[19] says: "Paying taxes is burdensome (*unalmas*)," and just a few years later, in 1702, in the first Hungarian bestiary Gáspár Miskolczi[20] wrote: "The fly is an impudent and burdensome (*unalmas*) animal." It was only later, in the eighteenth century, that the word acquired the connotations of "misery, care, vacillation, world-weariness, dejection, melancholy."

Boredom permeates the modern world;[21] it is born in the bourgeois world, but that same world condemns it and disowns it like a stepchild. Boredom results in idleness (though the person who is bored, as in the case of seventeenth-century nobility, has nothing to

---

18. Péter Pázmány (1570–1637), a Hungarian philosopher, theologian, Catholic cardinal, pulpit orator, and statesman, was an important figure in the Counter-Reformation in Royal Hungary.

19. Transylvanian-born András Illyés (1637–1712) was a Catholic bishop.

20. A Calvinist preacher (1628–1696).

21. "Society is now one polish'd horde, / Form'd of two mighty tribes, the *Bores* and *Bored*," Byron writes in *Don Juan* (canto 13, 95).

do in the first place), and idleness is branded by the world at large as *laziness*, which, next to sorrow and boredom, is the third main trait of melancholia in the modern age. In the Middle Ages, sloth, or acedia, likewise denoted neglect of earthly business, but it was condemned first and foremost as a sin against God; in the modern age, however, it was not so much a sin against God as against the world.[22] The world can offer a million arguments and charges against lazy people — those reasons, however, become self-defeating at some point. Bored people are fed up with the world, and that is a sign of the tediousness of the world itself. "Why, then, is action more justified than inaction?" a bored person might ask, and since boredom is intertwined with dire melancholia, drawing attention to the transience and dissolution that lie in wait in everything, he receives no satisfactory answer. Others, of course, list numerous reasons, from the practical aspects of making money to the metaphysical notion of self-creation, yet none of that moves a bored, lazy person, and to borrow some words from Friedrich Schlegel: "What's the point, then, of this unremitting aspiration and progress without rest and purpose? Can this storm and stress provide nourishing sap or beautiful form to the infinite plant of humanity, growing unnoticed by itself and cultivating itself? This empty, restless activity is nothing but a Nordic barbarity and so leads to nothing but boredom — our own and others!" (*Lucinde and the Fragments*, 65).

Of course, not every lazy person is melancholic; but the possibility of turning melancholic is implied in laziness, as much as in boredom.[23] There is no great diversity in the expression of indolence,

---

22. Protestantism, especially Puritanism, smuggled God into its concept of laziness, but it was the neglect of earthly matters that was regarded as the fundamental lapse.

23. The German word *Faulheit* (laziness, indolence) derives from Middle High German *vulheit*, which has the primary meaning of rottenness (*Fäulnis*). In laziness, the inexorable decay of existence manifests as being at the mercy of destruction; that was why Friedrich Schlegel could call it "the godlike art of idleness" (*Lucinde and*

yet on the other hand, it can be experienced in many ways: those who become melancholic (or those melancholics who become lazy) are characterized by the aforesaid desperate boredom. The laziness of those who are beyond the daily arrangements of this world, and whose boredom is boundless, is not laziness in the ordinary sense of the word: *their inaction is a kind of negative occupation.* Petrarch contrasted the *miser occupatus*—the wretched workaholic—with the *felix solitarius*—the happy loner; people who immerse themselves in philosophical preoccupations are, from a certain viewpoint, happy—happy because, presumably, they experience the world differently from people who hustle and bustle. Meditation has always been one of the distinguishing marks of melancholia; in its own fashion, it facilitates the creation of a new world in much the same way as regular work does. In the eyes of a bored and "idle" melancholic, there is in any case no essential difference between contemplation and practical occupation—it was a distinction dreamed up by a bustling world, among other reasons, precisely so that it might brand melancholics, stigmatize them as outlaws, detrimental to the cause of civil society. Robert Burton, who in many respects was still a child of the Middle Ages, explained how a conscientious citizen saw the general melancholia of the nobility of his days as a function of their laziness and idleness: "For idleness is an appendix to nobility; they count it a disgrace to work, and spend all their days in sports, recreations, and pastimes, and will therefore take no pains; be of no vocation; they feed liberally; fare well, want exercise, action, employment . . . and company to their desires" (Burton, *Anatomy*, partition 1, sec. 2, member 2, subsec. 6, 244). Such nobles were not simply idle, however: they were different from ordinary civilians. Even if a growing bourgeoisie managed to "break them in" (that is, either persuade them to adjust to a civil mentality or destroy them), it was unable to prevent indolence

the Fragments, 63): decay and deterioration are states of existence as elemental as formation and unfolding.

and inactivity, hitherto considered the preserve solely of the nobility, from raising their heads within the civil world as well: it has already been seen how Sir William Temple in 1690, a full generation after the Civil War, considered England to be the region of spleen, and the mercantile-spirited island nation did not lose that prerogative in the eighteenth and nineteenth centuries.[24] (The French, with similar pride, considered tedium a characteristically French malady.) Boredom has kept company with the civil world right up to the present day. It is not even necessary to be melancholic to conclude from this that boredom is an essential part of that world and that a utilitarian civil order primed for practical action would be inconceivable without idleness. It is one and the same world that "sweats" indolence out of itself while also sweating profusely in frenzied activity.

Sorrow, boredom, and indolence associated with melancholia were ideologically branded much as they were in the Middle Ages, which had regarded melancholia as an obstacle to its own equally monolithic endeavors. Modern melancholia is, at one and the same time, inactivity and passivity, but also a tacit *protest* against the extant world. The stiff protest of the Renaissance melancholic and his attempt to create a positive existence proved futile, but the *protest* and the *nothingness* with which he confronted the world were left to his distant posterity. And just as the Christ of Renaissance interpretation was still involved in *self-redemption*, while the Christ of the civil world (especially of Romanticism) awaited *grace*, melancholics also gave up on self-realization and sank into a waiting passivity that was mistaken for idleness. There are two ways of judging the melancholic: either he is a dangerous pest who—with his laziness, bore-

---

24. In 1672 there appeared a work by Gideon Harvey entitled *Morbus Anglicus, or a Theoretick and Practical Discourse of Consumptions, and Hypochondriak Melancholy*, and in 1733 from the pen of a physician by the name of George Cheyne appeared *The English Malady; or, A Treatise of Nervous Diseases of All Kinds, as Spleen, Vapours, Lowness of Spirits, Hypochondriacal and Hysterical Distempers.*

dom, passionate interest in death, and flirtation with nothing—is an adversary of the existing world (he points out the pitfalls of the civil world's interpretation of itself), and therefore in the eyes of others he is an enemy and rebel, in the worst case a sick, psychiatric problem; or else he is a *bel esprit* who, on account of his passivity and inaction, wouldn't hurt a fly, and is concerned solely with building up his own soul (which is, of course, the declared goal of the civil world as well). He can be subversive but also sentimental, a hero—and this does not depend on his comportment, but only on the angle from which one views *the same* person.

The cultural reinterpretation of melancholia was not congruent with the melancholic's interpretation of himself. The two were never fully in line with each other: the notions professed about melancholics in antiquity, in the Middle Ages, and in the Renaissance diverged similarly from the way the melancholic interpreted his own state, but the schism did not lead to such a degree of social schizophrenia as it did in the modern world. The modern melancholic was condemned to passivity and sufferance, and since he remained within the range of what he rejected through his melancholia, the world ignored him as someone not to be taken seriously. (Melancholics can never be accused of being revolutionary!) Ideological labeling always implies disdain ("Come on, what does he want now!"), while the pat-on-the-shoulder gesture exudes self-satisfaction ("What a decent chap he is after all!"). The more that liberalism and democracy gained ground, the more obvious it became that these ideologies were intolerant of anything that threatened the frontiers of their world. The rejection, complete by the twentieth century, of myth and transcendence—pancriticism—was itself a kind of myth, a substitute for religion; and because such criticism was unwilling to notice that valid norms in society owe their strength to notions that society cannot come to terms with (for example, sin, holiness—Georges Bataille), it started to self-destruct. Never in the course of history has melancholia (and also schizophrenia and neurosis) had such fertile ground as in the modern era: the more people put their trust in tolerance, democracy, enlightenment, and progress, the more readily they fall victim *voluntarily* to all forms of repression and self-deception. Modern societies flow over everything, gobble up everything, to such an extent that in their extreme manifestations they identify themselves as the goal of history. Human existence is ever less mysterious, more solvable and expressible; Christian culture reduced the mysteries of antiquity to *one* mystery, but the bourgeois world drove even that remaining mystery from the world. It is not the enigmatic rhythm of life and death that is fundamental to existence, but as Friedrich Schiller writes in the "The Eleusinian Festival"—the title of which is promising, but the poem offers disappointingly little—from "rough spirits" a new civil nation will arise that will be intertwined by "moral bonds."[25] Everything that was sacred about the sanctuary marches out to the front of the sanctuary, into profane space, excluded from the temple, as the Greek for *profanum* (προφανής) indicates—that which is visible, demonstrable. The more obvious a thing is, the less it is worthy of respect; the more unambiguous it is, the more disenchanting and the more disappointing. The world tries ever harder to define and give a name to everything, but where everything is clear and comprehensible, boredom grows more intense. Boredom signals the dilemma that lies at the bottom of melancholia in the modern age: things seem to become ever clearer (enlightenment) and ever more accessible to everybody (democracy), but people are nonetheless unable to conceal their growing sense of lack, which accompanies each naming of a thing by its proper name, each definition. The melancholic is sensitive to precisely that sense of lack; behind the seemingly ultimate definitions, he senses the mystery that towers over the world of existing things like an unnameable *deficiency*. The antimelancholic bourgeois mentality has no understanding of boredom—for it, therefore, there is no entry

---

25. It speaks volumes that the first version of the title was "Das Bürgerlied" ("Song of the Citizen").

from the profane into the sanctuary, from the world of visible things into the realm of secrets, and for that reason it tries, by means of naming and pointing things out, to render melancholia harmless and tameable. In his treatise on occupational diseases, *De morbis artificum diatriba* (Diseases of Workers, 1713), the Italian physician Bernardino Ramazzini did not explain the high incidence of melancholia in painters in a metaphysical context, as colleagues had done in the Renaissance era, nor did he relate it to issues directed at, and faltering over, being, but explained it as a physiological effect of the paints used. And since the modern world promises that it can overcome all problems in practice, melancholia likewise becomes a subject of sociopolitical opinion: the all-consuming bourgeois mentality considers it a political problem, one that can be put down to social class and tidied up as such—with weapons if it comes to that, or just by pointing out its roots. Many modern thinkers condemned melancholia—among others, Thomas Hobbes, Julien La Mettrie, Baron d'Holbach, John Locke, Lord Shaftesbury, and Jonathan Swift. Anything that offended certain class interests was counted as melancholia: the Anglican Robert Burton accused atheism, Catholicism, and Puritanism of melancholia, and Catholics in Germany considered Lutherans to be melancholic; in eighteenth-century France, the leading figures of the Enlightenment proclaimed that Christianity was the cause of melancholia, whereas in 1789 the ancien régime accused the revolutionaries of melancholia; Georg Lukács reproached modernist writers like Franz Kafka, James Joyce, and Samuel Beckett for "the melancholic disdain for reality" (Adorno, on the other hand, praised them for their melancholia), and alluded to Walter Benjamin's melancholia with mild sarcasm; and the melancholic Benjamin rejected the poems of Erich Kästner, who came to terms with the German *haute bourgeoisie,* on account of "left-wing melancholia." In writing about melancholia, it is striking that one cannot form an opinion about it without some presupposition: however hard one might strive to treat the subject as a neutral point of discussion, sooner or later it will turn out that the subject has automatically imbedded itself in one's thinking. The less an author takes this into account, the greater the tension that will arise between the subject and the discussion of it. That is adduced by one of the important, comprehensive analytical books of recent times, Wolf Lepenies's work, the purview of which is denoted by its title: *Melancholie und Gesellschaft* (*Melancholy and Society*). The optimistic spirit of 1968 flickers tacitly over the book, which appeared in German in 1969—the belief that melancholia, along with the other distresses of life, was finally eliminable, and could be described wholly by sociological analysis. His book is, therefore—above and beyond its valuable analyses—also a document of the period in which it was written. Since, sooner or later, every work intended to be definitive and produced with pretensions to objectivity is gradually infused by melancholia, so the tone of this book about melancholia was also imperceptibly colored by mournfulness. The author becomes interesting against his own intention, as it were: the very thing from which he sought, albeit tacitly, to wean his readers becomes fascinating; if he were to make a fresh start on writing the book today, he would most probably not only work into it newer data he would have learned about the history of melancholia, but also the experience of writing about melancholia, which in itself nourishes melancholia.

The modern melancholic was not in any way the perfect human that Ficino and the Renaissance interpretation took him for. He was a mundane, earthly creature who was melancholic not because of a *yearning* for perfection but because of the *reality* of the imperfection that exists. "One of the most effective reflections for hardening ourselves against our misfortunes," writes Montesquieu, "is reflection on the immensity of things and the pettiness of the sphere we inhabit" (Montesquieu, *My Thoughts*, 22). Existence may be imperfect, but not in the medieval sense: the emphasis is not on the distance from divine perfection but on the limitations of man. The world seems intolerable because his capabilities are finite, professes the modern melancholic. It is not hard to spot the change in emphasis: Renaissance melancholia was prompted by the attempt to create a new world, whereas its modern counterpart was based on the melancholic's being shut up in himself. Man is hamstrung by extant things, and this is what makes him melancholic: he is aware of perfection but is unable to extricate himself from a state of imperfection. In his article under the heading "Mélancolie" in *L'Encyclopédie*, Denis Diderot wrote, among other things, the following: "The cause of melancholia is a habitual feeling of our imperfection. . . . It is most often a consequence of weakness of the soul and the organs. It can also be a product of ideas about a certain perfection that is not found either in ourselves or in others, in the objects of our pleasure or in nature" (*Encyclopédie ou Dictionnaire raisonné des sciences, des arts et des métiers*, 10:307). Melancholia "swoops down" on man; it is not a matter of him going out to meet it. The melancholic is resigned to his imperfection from the outset; and since that imperfection is not just in his mind but deadly real, melancholia cannot be prevailed upon to cease by sheer force of insight or arguments. Ideological judges of melancholia (can a nonmelancholic be anything else?) ignore precisely that reality; the melancholic is the way he is not through his own will but because of the starkest reality of his life. There is a conspicuously great lack of understanding between bourgeois ideologues who censure melancholia, and melancholics themselves: there is no contact between the mostly trite, generalizing judgments of the former group and the uncommunicative, taciturn *personalities* of the latter. In a work entitled *Historia critica philosophiae* (1742–44), Jakob Brucker condemned melancholics and made not the slightest effort to understand melancholia, the *furor fanaticus*. In a book that appeared in 1777 with the title *Versuch über die Temperamente*, Heinrich Wilhelm Lawätz likewise interpreted the condition in a typically absolutist fashion: "Usually the people who are victims of the most dreadful horrors of melancholia are those who view all human deeds gloomily, ungraciously, and with inherent malice against the world and people, each and every one to the root, and they go astray in this truly dreadful maze to the point that no human wisdom is able to guide them out of there any longer" (67). The melancholic, who, in Lawätz's view, was inherently *rebellious*, would most likely have been baffled by reading these words, which were not applicable to him but to an imaginary phantom constructed by public opinion in order to offer an easy proof of its unviability. The "ideological parenthesis" is the most convenient procedure imaginable: it makes it superfluous to understand psychological states (even mental disturbances) that deviate from the average and the ordinary in relation to their own internal interpretation of existence, and it implicitly denies that melancholics and nonmelancholics live in a shared world. These ideologues, instead of acknowledging that the reason a melancholic sees the world of other people the way he does is because this world really does lend itself to such a different viewing, deny that the world is contradictory and paradoxical, and by making reference to Hegel, they assert that whoever looks upon the world irrationally is also presenting an irrational aspect to the world. But those who behave that way fail to pose a simple question: how is it possible to look irrationally upon the world? And instead of admitting that irrationality is an essential part of the world, they maintain that whoever looks upon the world irrationally has only himself to blame because the fault lies exclusively in him. That presupposes that whoever looks irrationally upon a rational world is actually *not even part of that world*, and his irrational way of looking at things—given that he has nothing in common with the world (with existence)—is not really genuine; it is nonexisting. The ideological parenthesis on this occasion, as ever, not only destroys thoughts but also sees even solid, flesh-and-blood individuals as nonexistent. Whenever public opinion encounters any unusual, extraordinary behavior or interpretation of existence, nothing seems simpler than to dismiss them with a wave of the hand. Montesquieu, referring to an earlier train of thought, wrote in one of his letters: "Day after day I think again of this profound silence, of solitude, in which I converse merely with my pains and my deep melancholy" (quoted in Fritz Schalk, "Diderots Artikel 'Mélancolie' in der Enzyklopädie," 180).

The world is not on speaking terms with the melancholic, which immerses the latter even more deeply in his melancholia. "A melancholic flees from society and only feels all right alone," Diderot wrote in 1765—good-naturedly, it is true, but simplifying the problem (quoted in Schalk, "Diderots Artikel 'Mélancolie' in der Enzyklopädie," 182). The melancholic does indeed flee, but he does so because he is persecuted. Being ignored, he becomes isolated and solitary (he can count on himself only—ἰδιωτικός, as the Greek has it, a private person); yet in following the command of the most elementary vital instinct, he tries to prove that he most certainly does exist, and his feelings and thoughts are not illusions but are real and solidly grounded. From the eighteenth century onward, the melancholic has been singled out by *loneliness* and a *compulsion for self-justification.* The sentimentality that the modern era associates with melancholia is not pure affectation, but a *self-indulgence* of the melancholic personality, an inward-looking self-justification derived from isolation. The word "sentimental" began to spread in England from the 1740s: Thomas Warton published in 1747 what is still his most famous poem, "The Pleasures of Melancholy," following the success of Edward Young's *The Complaint; or, Night Thoughts on Life, Death, and Immortality* (1742–45), in which he observed links between *loneliness, pleasure,* and *suffering.* In France, the Jesuit *Dictionnaire de Trévoux,* which first appeared in 1734 (that is, well before Diderot's article in *L'Encyclopédie*) coupled melancholia not just with sadness but also with pleasure (*un certain triste plaisir*) and called it a satisfying form of daydreaming (*une rêverie agréable*). The usual place of the verb *songer* had by then been taken over in the context of melancholia by *rêver,* with its more personal connotations, to the point that in the eighteenth century "daydreamer" and "melancholic" had virtually become synonyms.[26] In spite of all its negative side effects, Diderot called melancholia a "sweet feeling" (*sentiment doux*) that had the merit of allowing one to enjoy oneself when in that state, and to be *aware* of oneself. Sweet, sentimental melancholia became a platitude, even a pose, in the eighteenth century[27] — nevertheless, sentiment and sentimentality, while becoming a fashionable norm to be observed, did not conceal from the inward gaze the by-no-means-painless gesture of self-justification. Of course, that in itself became a kind of trap, and things that were painful to contemplate inwardly appeared to the outside world as pleasant sentimentality. If one shuts one's eyes to the attempts at self-justification, then all that remains is what one can relate to oneself: a feeling that in itself is harmless and puts one under no obligation. But if one genuinely enters the world of the melancholic, then one will discover something beyond feelings — the sort of thing about which the Hungarian poet Dániel Berzsenyi could write in 1820: "My soul died long ago, and its place was occupied by a new, unknown soul, which is dark and cold, like the sky, and tranquil as a grave" (Berzsenyi, *Összes művei*, 430).

---

26. *Rêverie* would become a key word for Jean-Jacques Rousseau in *Julie, or the New Heloise* and *Reveries of the Solitary Walker*.

27. It was promulgated by the novels of Pierre de Marivaux and Abbé Antoine Prévost, and by a statue titled *Sweet Melancholy* (1763) by Étienne Maurice Falconet.

Chapter 6

PREMATURE DEATH OF THE ROMANTICS

Compulsive self-justification and self-absorption are in a way also an expression of political impotence. As an anthropological "factor," melancholia has always been sensitive to given social relations. The inadequacy of these relations — an ideal society is conceivable only in a utopia, that is, nonexistence — cannot be explained sociologically; it seems that the sociopolitical fact that man is incapable of establishing an ideal society points to a more basic phenomenon that, like melancholia, is an anthropological characteristic. That explains the dual sensitivity of melancholia: a sensitivity to politics as much as to the preconditions of the prevailing politics. It not only pays attention to sociologically demonstrable negatives but also offers a sociologically illimitable existential raison d'être. It relates to positive endeavors of human communities as death does to life: it is always menacingly present, and although one may forget about it, it is insurmountable. Sociopolitical arrangements always conceal within themselves the threat of disintegration, even in the absence of an outside enemy, that sooner or later they will start wilting like a plant. The circumstances and manifestations of this can be described politically and socially, but its cause, the why of it, can be approached only existentially, without the hope of receiving a satisfactory answer. An existential raison d'être is necessarily destructive: an insight into the fragility manifested in decay is unlikely to inspire hope in anyone. Nor is there any need for philosophical-historical perspectives: a frustrated encounter, a momentary irritation, or a recoiling at the beauty of a child is sufficient to expose how unstable the ground is on which one tries to organize one's life as if it were eternal. Melancholia may even be regarded as a negative imprint of everyday life: everything that one suppresses there becomes articulated here, and what is mere possibility there is let loose as "negative" reality here. Melancholia views the world from the reverse perspective, and the more perceptible the lines of force of modern development, the more obvious is the rectitude of the melancholic way of looking at things. The melancholic openly accepts solitude, which the bourgeois world would like to gloss over by reference to the community, society, humanity, etc., even though it keeps reproducing the foundations for that solitude; the melancholic sees the world as senseless and evil, and although everyone senses that, no one admits it; he says out loud that the emperor has no clothes on. In modernity, this had all become clear by the time of the Romantic era—modern development had been sketched out sufficiently to permit everything to be turned into its opposite. Negative standpoints began to lose their negativity; indeed, it looked as if that was the only normal attitude that a self-respecting person could adopt, and it was the world's judgments and opinions that were upside down. The compulsive self-justification connected with solitude, as well as the pleasure in the self that a person derived from it, was constructed on a tacit insight that for man, he himself is the ultimate reality. However enticing it may be to place one's trust in the community, in others, one can never be free of oneself and can never dissolve definitively into anyone or anything else. The Middle Ages traced all souls back to one substance, giving it a theological explanation; melancholia had to be denounced precisely because the melancholic trusted exclusively in himself. In modern times—after numerous failed attempts had made it obvious that the self could not be traced back to a single substance but, notwithstanding its independence, was not omnipotent either—Kant raised the possibility that ultimate powerlessness, with its attendant loneliness and isolation, should be regarded as the *normal* human condition. By tracing everything back to the apperception of the self, and by being the first to declare that everyone constructs the world for himself, he posited individual autonomy as the most important criterion of human existence. Since one's constitution could be based only on itself, it could not be traced back to anything; it was not explicable theologically, only aesthetically and ethically.[1] What earlier had been seen as negativity (namely, that individuals regarded themselves as the ultimate basis), with Kant, whom one might therefore count as one of the great Romantics, became man's positive possibility. Melancholia—which in the final analysis was metaphysical solitude, self-justification, and relish of the self—also won a positive note,[2] and since it was ethically tinged, that was a sign of *ethical self-consciousness*. Ideal freedom made an appearance in melancholia, and a mournful withdrawal from the bustling world became a noble gesture. "Melancholics," Kant writes,

> have a sense for the sublime. Beauty itself, for which they also have a feeling, does not merely excite and lure them, but while it fills them with wonder, it moves them. . . . They care little about the opinions of others; they are not interested in what others hold to be good or true, resting purely on their own insight. . . . They are indifferent to changes of fashion, disdaining their glitter. . . . They will not tolerate any kind of vicious subjection, breathing in freedom with noble breast. For them chains of any kind are loathsome; the gilded chains that people wear at court just as much as the heavy iron shackles of galley slaves.
>
> (*Observations on the Feeling of the Beautiful and Sublime, and Other Writings*, 24–26)

Even those kinds of notions of melancholia, however, could not obscure the sense of insufficiency lying behind it. This sense of insuf-

---

1. The title of one of Kant's books, containing his characteristic anthropological analyses, is *Observations on the Feeling of the Beautiful and Sublime* (1764).

2. Kant, however, did not dispute that melancholia had negative overtones of rapture and fanaticism.

ficiency might have been by then a positive, normal condition, but it still did not quench the dissatisfaction, the sense of lack, and the concomitant pain that a melancholic felt. It was precisely the striving for autonomy that exposed the world's attempt to do away, at all costs, with such autonomy—and this was a matter not just of politics but of the most basic contradiction inseparable from human existence. Writing about concepts of pure reason, Kant showed that a sensory object and the conceptions formed about it never coincide, and that it is not the object that serves as basis of those conceptions, but rather a schema of the object: "The conception of a dog indicates a rule, according to which my imagination can delineate the figure of a four-footed animal in general, without being limited to any particular individual form which experience presents to me, or indeed to any possible image that I can represent to myself *in concreto*" (Kant, *Critique of Pure Reason*, bk. 2, pt. 1). The formation of concepts refers to an absurd situation: man is a concrete, sensory, individual being but at the same time, through the intellect, is also a subject of the realm of "generalities," and it is not possible to construct a genuine passage or correspondence between the two spheres. The requirements of generality infringe on a person's individuality, whereas the concrete, sensory individual cannot become of general validity, which in Kant's opinion is an indispensable precondition of autonomy. The *schematism* that links the general and the unique, the intellectual and the sensory, as far as a melancholic is concerned, does not conceal but reveals the never-reconcilable antithesis between the two and bares the crevasse that reminds people of their mortality, at the bottom of which death can be glimpsed. A person is a person precisely through being a member of two worlds without being a citizen with full rights in either. Kant goes on to characterize this (inevitable) schematism as follows: "This schematism of our understanding in regard to phenomena and their mere form is an art, hidden in the depths of the human soul, whose true modes of action we shall only with difficulty discover and unveil" (ibid.).

Kant was unable to solve the ultimate riddle of the human soul. *Autonomy*, toward which a morally minded human should be striving, is not able to become *omnipotence*—and the inevitable schematism, which is a necessary concomitant of the human mind, is also a source of a melancholic's despondency. On the one hand, everyone is a unique, irreplaceable, autonomous personality, but on the other hand, everyone is subject to the same destiny, a fate that pushes the personality toward a *common* death—do we need another reason for sorrow? In a treatise entitled *Observations on the Nature, Causes, and Cure of Melancholy* (1780), Benjamin Fawcett wrote: "It is impossible for any one to ascertain his perpetual freedom from it; whether he be high or low, rich or poor, virtuous or vicious; no, not the most gay and cheerful. . . . As is the good, so is the sinner; and he that sweareth, as he that sweareth an oath. This is an evil among all things that are done under the sun, that there is one event unto all" (7). From the viewpoint of the modern conception of melancholia, the late eighteenth century brought a decisive change: a fateful drive for individuality and a growing uniformity, which were not just sociopolitical but also anthropological factors (for example, the fact that man dies and his individuality is irrevocably wiped out), confronted people who were sensitive to it with such an insoluble and distressing dilemma that they literally died of it. "I am an unspeakable person," Heinrich von Kleist averred—an admission that directs attention to the most sensitive spot in the culture of the modern age. The development of individuality as it is now understood has meant freedom from metaphysical constraints, supposed liberation from powers "behind" man. The price of that freedom, however, has been "unspeakability"—after all, just as it is impossible to utter or imagine infinity without rendering it finite (people who speak with God are either gods themselves or about to die), so the personal freedom of the individual grows in direct proportion to the "invisible" representation of external constraints. The modern individual becomes increasingly free and infinite, yet he is bound more and more by obligations, by external constraints that make their appearance in the form of words designed to define his freedom. For the modern individual, complete freedom lies beyond words: in death, which no longer needs to be concerned with the antinomy of speakability and unspeakability. Kleist "realized" himself in death: he freed himself from the polarized contradiction of *personal infinitude* and *social finitude*, of indescribability and communicability.

It was no accident that it was in classical German philosophy, which, for all its antagonism, supported Romanticism most vigorously, that questions about individuality that had been posed in previous centuries were resuscitated. Faith in the magnificence of the evolving modern world perforce accentuated the faith in a harmonious relationship of the individual and the community (the singular and the general). Reviving a thought of St. Thomas Aquinas, Kant applied his own conceptual apparatus to sketch out the aforesaid question of autonomy, and he concluded that only a totally self-legislating will could be free. (Kleist's heroes would later give full voice to Kant's conviction; and if one takes those figures—together with Kleist himself—to be pathological, then one would also be obliged to discern pathological shades in a civilization that produced these kinds of excruciating conflicts.) Kant, however—although he never articulated this to himself—was led by his methodology to an antinomy and its unforeseeable attendant consequences. Proclaiming absolute freedom, and trusting in the boundlessness and unconditionality of the individual will, he hoped that a harmonious community of man could be established, but in the prosaic modern world, fraught with constraints, he was able to deliver only negative, indefinable, and unworkable proposals for the self-realization of the individual. When consistently thought through, the injunction of the categorical imperative and absolute autonomy leads to the conclusion that *any earthly realization for an individual goes hand in hand with the acceptance of constraints, burdens, and self-mutilations.* In proclaiming the freedom of the individual, Kant admittedly did try to resolve his aspirations for the individual in culture, that unspoken human community, but his methodology involved debunking the reality of the modern world and the inverted critique of all manner of this-worldly communities. As far as that goes, Kant was the most consistent critic of the modern bourgeois world; his epistemology, based as it was on *als ob*—on skepticism—contains a great deal more than that. The skepticism relates to the modern world, but the doubts about knowability and absolute certainty served, at the same time, as recognitions that life does not permit there to be *definitive* judgments about anything. With this postulation of the inconclusiveness of cognition, Kant raised the idea of man's self-creation and eternal striving for perfection (to that extent, he prefigures Hegel's philosophy and aims to lay the theoretical foundation of a fundamentally antimelancholic disposition);[3] with his ethics, however, he questioned self-creation (despite having apparently reached the opposite conclusion on more than one occasion previously): the endlessness and unconditionality of individual freedom on the one hand, and associations (communities) brought into being by free individuals on the other, logically exclude each other (to that extent, he prepared the ground for Romanticism and recognized the legitimacy of the melancholic way of looking at the world).

Kant himself was to fall victim to the antinomy, or perhaps the insoluble contradiction of his theory was the manifestation of the inner conflict of his own life. For Kant rejected the "rapture" and "fanaticism" that were also responsible for melancholia, but he was so fanatical in doing so,[4] and he displayed such a rapture for a rational lifestyle, that he himself was overcome with melancholia. From the

---

3. Which explains why Kant sometimes wrote disapprovingly about melancholia.

4. One of the most dogged undertakings in his life was to study Swedenborg, whom he wished to refute at all costs and under all circumstances. But can passion really draw a line between attraction and denial, one wonders.

pages of three surviving contemporary biographies of him (by Ernst von Borowski, Reinhold Bernhard Jachmann, and Ehrgott Andreas Christoph Wasianski), one gains the impression of a man who compressed his life into a system of rigorous rules, but whose facial features were touched by a severe melancholia. "Everyone who knew him can testify that Kant's most characteristic quality was the persistent endeavor to proceed in everything according to well-reasoned and, at least in accordance with his own convictions, well-based principles," von Borowski wrote. "An endeavor to set himself certain maxims in large things or small, important or insignificant alike, maxims from which it was possible to start and to which it was possible to return. Over time, those maxims became so interlaced within his innermost ego that he still acted on that basis even when he was not thinking of them" (quoted in Felix Groß, ed., *Immanuel Kant*, 51–52).[5] But for all the positive features of that life, it did have one drawback, of which Kant himself was also aware: "Once," von Borowski writes, "in my presence he expounded to a lady, who enquired after his health, that in point of fact he was never healthy and never sick either" (52). To feel neither healthy nor sick is an indication of a severe personality imbalance. When a sense of the elusiveness of existence takes

---

5. In writing about Kant, the French writer and philosopher Albert Caraco noted appositely that "Kant was consumed by being thought highly of, and like others of a similar background (that is, middle-class people) he needed to have moral fiber, simply moral fiber. . . . That might explain the bad temper of that ugly, virtuous and sickly man, who dreamed of subjugating the ruling classes by spontaneity that they favored much more than the exertion flaunted by the bourgeoisie (Caraco, *Bréviaire du chaos*, 134). In a work entitled *Nachrichten an das Publikum in Absicht der Hypochondrie* (Information for the public on the intent of hypochondria), which appeared in 1767, the Berlin physician and surgeon Johann Ulrich Bilguer listed the causes of spleen, to which all burghers of his day would have given an approving nod: early marriage (but also celibacy), prolonged sitting, luxury, bad upbringing, consumption of sweets, enjoyment of tobacco, mimicry of the upper classes, urban life, disdain of religion, freethinking, philosophical indifference, naturalism, and hypersexuality.

possession of man, terror will overcome him. Nothing could be more natural than to try to escape — to flee one's fate. The goal, however, is unfathomable: in seeking sanctuary from a threatening existence, one is bound to realize that one can count only on oneself, yet even before one can take a rest in oneself, that threatening existence falls in like a vaulted ceiling. One becomes unreliable even to oneself, and no section of one's being is left in which one might hide for relief: the soul becomes just as unpredictable as the body. Let us not forget that the eighteenth century was a century not just of the Enlightenment but also of hypochondria, or as it was called at the time, "melancholia hypochondriaca." Even a lifestyle regimented from top to toe was unable to protect Kant from that: "Perhaps no person has ever paid more attention than Kant did to his body and everything connected with it," noted Jachmann (quoted in ibid., 194); while von Borowski adds: "As long as I was acquainted with him, he paid constant attention to his own body, and he willingly conversed with others about all methods by which he might preserve his health; although he never had recourse to medical assistance for himself, he nevertheless had a predilection for studying medicine, paying lively attention to its innovations and results" (53). One dismisses the complaints and perennial anxieties of hypochondriacs as imaginary physical illnesses, but an imbalance of the imagination can induce genuine ailments. One should not think only of organic diseases that hurry to meet hypochondriacs, but rather focus on disturbances of the imagination — on the reasons behind those "groundless" complaints. Such disturbances are not merely a harbinger of an imaginary, and maybe later a genuine, physical complaint, but also a sign that the hypochondriac senses that all existence has become disordered for him. Reality condenses around hypochondriacs, but as with every vortex, here, too, everything turns to nothingness beyond a certain point. Kant was not spared terror at the thought of dying: "He concerned himself with reaching a ripe old age," Jachmann wrote. "In his mind he compiled a whole list of people who had lived to see an advanced age, he liked to invite people in Königsberg who were older and of higher rank than him, and he was happy to push ever nearer to the front and to have ever fewer older people ahead of him; *for many a long year he had the Königsberg police inspectorate send him the monthly mortality list so that he could calculate his life expectancy based on that"* (quoted in ibid., 194; emphasis added). Was that a happy life? Did all that calculation make for a balanced existence? Was it able to drive the fear from him? By way of an answer, let us quote Kant himself as reported by von Borowski: "Is there anyone who has not read in his writings, or any friend who had not heard more than once from his own lips, that there were no conditions under which he would live his life again if he had to live it the same way all over again from the beginning?" (53).

Modern thinking marks its start from Kant, and the two paths that took him as their starting points so exclude each other that when their followers seek to refute one another, they are usually reduced to stumbling in the dark. Since the evolution of modern reality substantiated Kant's "pessimistic" thinking and rendered it doubtful that human self-creation would lead to a harmonious community of free individuals, theoretical disputes in philosophy, after Hegel's appearance, were characterized by the fact that whereas Romantics (melancholics) had based their arguments on the practical experience and cognition of reality, ideologues[6] called them to account for promoting some kind of utopian idea of society (ignoring the fact that a utopia would be, just as much as reality was, a breeding ground for melancholia). Hitherto it had been perceptible, but from that point on it became obvious that there was no point of contact between the reality of melancholia and the ideology that condemned it: words just kept passing by one another, and the charges leveled

---

6. By then the term "ideology" had been minted: Destutt de Tracy devised the term for the title of his work *Éléments d'idéologie,* the four volumes of which were published between 1801 and 1815.

against melancholia were subjected to the laws of the schematism denoted by Kant—they did violence to the object in order to be able to
pronounce judgment on it. Disputing melancholic subjectivism and
finding fault with it, Hegel attempted to show Kant's tenets in a positive light. He tried to create a harmony between the individual conscience and absolute, general knowledge in which the individual's
finite and *unique* spirit could dissolve completely in the realm of
the *infinite* spirit. But Hegel did not so much as attempt seriously to
differentiate the finite and infinite spirit, and therefore he was also
unable to express appropriately the value of uniqueness: that was the
price he had to pay for eliminating the melancholic "subjectivism"
of Kantian ethics. For that reason, the Romanticism that he rejected
could have no role within his system: Hegel shaped reality into a
monumental arch (pleasing and aesthetically entrancing though it
may be in its own way, of course) in which only the transitions form
"solid" footholds, but those autonomous (matchless, irreplaceable,
unique) phenomena out of which one's own life largely consists could
not have any independent, absolute value. Kant believed in the absolute value of individual lives even though their realization—and the
lives of numerous Romantics are proof of this—could be consum-
mated only beyond the bounds of this earthly life, in death. Hegel
had no such ambitious pretensions. Admittedly, he declared that free
persons would regain their senses in one another's freedom, and for
an imaginary society, nothing could be more desirable than that. But
autonomy, the possibility of which was developed by that same European culture that also provided the means for the Hegelian abolition
of autonomy, dissolved irrevocably and became uninteresting in the
Hegelian system. Hegel reproached the Romantic and melancholic
Novalis for lacking a firm "bearing," but actually, the main negative
feature of his system was that the individual had no need of bearing
in the Hegelian world structure: the individual was supported by the
system, by the bridge of mediations. If Novalis jumped into the dark

from that bridge of individual lack of bearing, then that was exactly a proof of bearing—a bearing that, entertaining no hope of the system, of its alleged totality, tried to be exclusively master of itself.

One has the impression that *philosophy* and *life* were conducting a debate; and looking at it from the viewpoint of ordinary life, Hegel's polemic with the Romantics genuinely seemed to prove the rift of theory and practice. The role of philosophy, however, was much more a matter of life and death and cut much more to the quick than one might think today from the indigestible mass of textbook extracts. In its own way, classical German philosophy was as much an attitude toward fate as was the individual life and death of melancholic, prematurely deceased Romantics. "The mind is forever seeking to justify itself," said Novalis, sensitive as he was to philosophy (Novalis, *Ausgewählte Werke*, 3:5). True philosophy is not a specialist branch of learning but an existential inquiry, or to use the words of Socrates, it is a preparation for death. Nowadays, the shock effect that contemporary philosophy had on the Romantics is almost incomprehensible. After reading Kant, Heinrich von Kleist suffered a breakdown, and melancholia overcame him; he drifted into such a creative crisis that he almost regarded his own existence as senseless. "Not long ago I made my acquaintance with the new, so-called Kantian philosophy," he wrote to his fiancée, Wilhelmine von Zenge, on 22 March 1801. Then he resorted to the example of a pair of green eyeglasses to explain his despair: "If everyone saw the world through green glasses then they would be forced to judge that everything they saw *was* green, and we could never be sure whether our eyes see things as they really are, or whether they add something which pertains to the eyes not the objects. The same goes for the intellect" (Kleist, *Werke und Briefe*, 4:202).

Kleist asserted nothing less than that the only one capable of seeing things in their true reality was he who has no need of eyes as a means of seeing. To see, but without the contingency of earthly eyes—only a god could be capable of that. Or a melancholic, who saw through the surface of things, the way melancholic Kleist saw through everything. "Ah, there exists a sorry state of clarity," he wrote to his half sister Ulrike on 5 February 1801, "from which nature has luckily spared people who see merely the surface of things. It shows me the thought behind every facial expression, the true meaning of words, and the motive behind action—everything around me, including myself, in its entire bareness, and my heart is starting to grow disgusted with that nakedness." He wrote the following lines to Ulrike too: "The thought shook the sanctum of my soul, that we know nothing, absolutely nothing, about reality; that after death what we call truth here we shall call something else entirely, and consequently it is totally futile and fruitless to strive to acquire something that will follow us into the grave" (Kleist, *Werke und Briefe*, 4:202–3). Kleist thought his way carefully and consistently through Kant's doubt about the knowability of reality; he hit upon a basic paradox of human existence: human cognition and the object that is to be recognized are inseparable from each other; we do not simply relate to an "external" reality, but are responsible for that reality.

By advising the Romantics that an individual is in reality whatever he makes himself out to be in reality, in practice, Hegel offered us sturdy footholds, but since he dissolved unique, irreplaceable individuality in totality, the reality he offered was one without man, one that would grow over man as a reality to which the individual could assimilate but essentially be unable to influence. Hegel disputed the absolute sovereignty of the individual, but in his hands the apparently solid category of "reality" was no more than the most characteristic feature of the modern world, which stifled individuality and had been placed in parentheses by the Romantics. What had bewitched and paralyzed the Romantics was the fact that there was no solid foothold beyond the ego. Prejudices, thoughts that had been digested or chewed over by others, became nullities for them just as uninteresting as the boundaries of existence "beyond" man. Novalis, by his own admission, was "enchanted" by Fichte's philosophy, and with an

almost Hegelian sensibility, called the philosopher the most dangerous of thinkers. Fichte considered being (*Sein*) and activity (*Tätig-
keit*) to be identical, and thus for him reality was not a neutral object
to be conquered but something created by man. Hegel said man was
whatever he made himself in "reality," but according to Fichte, man
was what he made of himself—and along with the term "reality," any
accommodation or adjustment to reality was dropped from the sentence. Man was identical with his own *possibilities*, said Fichte by
way of an answer to the Hegelian thought that man had to realize
himself within reality. Actually, the Hegelian way of thinking was not
"true to reality," "real," or even a "normal" way of thinking, but much
more a system of prejudices that, having accepted and acquiesced in
the structure of the existing world, presumed that the essence of man
lay in complying with his circumstances. Although Hegel and philosophers who followed in his footsteps tried to differentiate between
real and abstract possibilities, for the Romantics (primarily those of
German background), who regarded the world not as finite but as
contingent and transitory, drawing that distinction was no more than
devious long-windedness; when Fichte and the Romantics (or later,
Kierkegaard) held possibility to be more important than reality, it was
not a matter of lack of basis, feverish daydreaming, or schizophrenia,
but of the perception imbedded in melancholia that man was not
born to accept the world but to create it.

It was never as obvious as in the Romantic era that individual
freedom and the unsparing regularity of the existing world could be
congruent. Inevitably, one of them had to prevail: if (as was usually
the case) objective regularity won out, then the schematism adum-
brated by Kant was asserted and the individual submitted to the
world, obeyed the rules, satisfied the expectations, renounced his
own definitive freedom and the possibilities inherent in his personality. If, on the other hand (as with modern genius), subjective freedom won out over objective regularity, then the world looked at this
with suspicion: people tended to talk about madness or, with greater

restraint, about abnormality, even in the case of manifest genius. It is always those who transgress the bounds of any given society that are regarded as insane, but only Romanticism suggested the idea that brilliance verged on madness. Aristotle's theory of the golden mean seems to hold to this day. With Aristotle, melancholics were outstanding and endangered personalities threatened, on the one hand, by mania and, on the other, by depression. In modern societies, geniuses are likewise outstanding and endangered personalities, and they are threatened, on the one hand, by facelessness and a gray monotony and, on the other, by insanity. Aristotle's perception seems pertinent to the present day: men of genius and melancholics are likewise people on whom fate has imposed greatness fraught with sadness. Greatness intimates the proximity of the threat of insanity. Beyond a certain point, greatness breaks through all frameworks when the person in question is no longer great but insane. (Which, of course, does not mean that every madman started as a great man.) Sadness, however, signals a risk of becoming jaded, of falling in line: not only does a great man die in just the same way as anyone else, but life also does all it can to divest him of his greatness and rank him among the mediocre—and not always without success. A genius is not insane, but not healthy either (at least not in the quotidian sense; for that reason, people who would like to label a genius as ill or healthy are mistaken).[7] Geniuses are not sick, just not well. They vitiate this exclusionary way of looking at things because they are characterized by a state that implies a fundamentally different lifestyle and outlook. "Genius," writes August Wilhelm Schlegel, "spans a person's whole interior, and it consists of nothing less than the energy and innermost harmony of all that is autonomous and boundless ability in human sensitivity and intellectuality" (*Kritische Schriften und*

---

7. Genius is an illness, avowed the likes of Cesare Lombroso, Moreau de Tours, Alphonse de Lamartine, and, in the twentieth century, Lionel Trilling; genius is an embodiment of health, stated Charles Lamb in the essay "Sanity of True Genius."

Briefe, 2:76). The genius and the melancholic are inseparable from each other: both stand at the *boundary* of human possibilities. They belong together. A melancholy genius dwells on the boundary: he is absolutely lonely, and this metaphysical solitude sets him apart from everyone. His loneliness is not the same as that of the mentally ill, who are closed and unapproachable, nor is it the occasional sense of loneliness of the healthy, which stems rather from a lack of company than from fate. "Nothing is sadder or more oppressive in the world than this situation: he [the solitary figure] is the sole spark of life in death's broad dominion, the lonely center of a lonely circle" (Kleist, *Werke und Briefe*, 3:502). Kleist's words do not relate to melancholics of genius in general, but to the solitary human figure in an oil painting by Caspar David Friedrich titled *Monk by the Sea*. The large painting depicts the tiny figure of a monk standing with his back to the viewer, in front of a vast sea and under an overcast sky. The solitary figure is the melancholic genius himself, born at the time of Romanticism. Friedrich, who according to reports from friends[8] was characterized by the deepest melancholia and painted the most melancholy pictures of all time, had an infallible sense of all the touchstones of modern melancholia: metaphysical solitude, a compulsion for self-justification, suffering in self-enjoyment, a death wish merging into a fear of death, and a condition bordering on that of a genius.

The autonomy won from the world gradually crumbles; geniuses will become mad: either they become drab and monotonous, or they die from their own brilliance. Genius lasting over a long life is given to no one (except Goethe, who—with some justice—was prone to count himself among the immortals). Melancholic geniuses are well aware of their own fateful claims to individuality, their fated genius, as well as the trap the world sets for them—and the consternation,

---

8. These included Carl Gustav Carus, a significant person in the history of German medicine, who concerned himself intensively with psychiatry and was not negligible as a painter either.

not yet assuaged by custom, as in the twentieth century, results in the voluntary acceptance of death and, together with that, the free indulgence in melancholia. Many Romantics died young; to elucidate the cause of their death, we need to turn to one of Friedrich's paintings again: *Chalk Cliffs on Rügen*, possibly one of the most mysterious of all his pictures. He painted one of the chasms formed by chalk rocks on the Baltic Sea. The sea is a long way down below, bearing two ships. There is sunlight all around, and the white cliffs reflect the light. Near the edge are three people gazing down at the sea. On the left, a squatting woman is clutching at a bush; in the middle, a man is lying prone and peering down; and on the right is a second man, arms folded, standing on the root of a tree, the crown of which is dangling above the chasm. An undisturbed idyll. Yet as anyone knows who has passed by the rim of the chalk cliffs of Rügen, the scene depicted is probably augmented by dreamlike elements; the painter, who spent a prolonged period on the island, was well aware of the difficulty of venturing to the rim of those fragile cliffs: they begin to crumble and collapse on taking the slightest weight, carrying with them anyone who peers into the deep. Anyone standing on that cliff edge would no longer be standing there. The picture's melancholy is derived from this. Maybe smoldering passion led the three figures to the unapproachable edge of the cliffs; Friedrich knew full well that the relationship of two men and one woman (even just their being together) was the most stirring, most passion arousing of all everyday social relations. The foolhardy or negligent figures are obviously not interested in the danger, or at least not the danger that threatens them directly. They are not afraid of death. They are gazing into the deep, but there is little doubt that they find the depths attractive — attractive because they recognize their own fate in the eddies down below. Indifference, foolhardiness, a passionate love of the deep, drew them here — and in the depth of the chasm, perceptible to us as well, they recognize the depths of their own inaccessible interiors. The interior and exterior depths merge — and the melancholic demeanor of the three figures is a signal to us, the viewers, that they are participants in an irreversible process: the outer and the inner, subject and object, have not separated in them, and the surrounding nature, interwoven with their own human nature, pours through their bodies, so to speak—bodies that are truly just a mortal coil; therefore, they should not worry about falling and destruction. "'Twixt fate and us there is but little space," wrote Thomas Chatterton ("Ælla"), who killed himself at the age of seventeen.

Friedrich's three figures are poised on the brink of death, but they are so casual in the face of perdition that they seem almost bored. Everything is enveloped in boredom, a basic characteristic of melancholia in the modern age and one of the key notions of the beginning of the nineteenth century, the period in which the picture originated. It is not a matter of being bored with this thing or that but of unending boredom with existence itself. The Don Juan of Nikolaus Lenau's poem is so bored that he grants the gift of his life to his enemies and is even bored with the thought of dying. According to more than one entry in his diary, Byron was so bored that he did not feel strong enough even to commit evil or to blow his brains out. It was also he who wrote bitterly about Napoleon that rather than dragging the whole world down with him, the man was gradually sinking into insignificance. He preceded that with a comment: "Past events have unnerved me; and all I can now do is to make life an amusement, and look on, while others play" (18 November 1813; *Letters and Journals*, 2:339). On studying the French Revolution, Georg Büchner felt that the dreadful fatalism of history had all but crushed the individual, and the futility of glorious events led him to a realization: "I find an appalling uniformity in human nature, an inevitable violence in human relations. . . . The individual is just foam on the crest of a wave, stature a sheer accident, the reign of genius a puppet show, a ridiculous struggle against an iron law over which it is impossible to gain the upper hand" (Büchner, *Werke und Briefe*, 395). And in *Danton's Death*, the cry goes up: "The world is chaos. Nothingness is the yet-to-be-born god of the world" (act 4, scene 5, trans. Gerhard P. Knapp). Büchner, who loathed life yet at the same time took "wild delight" in it, sensed that he would die early, and his fatal illness did not catch him unexpectedly. At thirty-two, Lenau went mad in his futile searching, in hopeless love, and in vainly waiting for the "song of the nightingale." Byron did not blow his brains out, but he lived with such indifference that it is a sheer miracle that death waited until he was thirty-six to get him.

It is fairly easy to list the motifs: the defining features of Romanticism, which have been rehearsed to the point of boredom, play the leading role—disappointment in the French Revolution; nausea felt over Classicism, disenchantment with values, etc. The causes are of no concern here; the consequences, more so. The stimuli for the "political" English and the "apolitical" German Romanticism were divergent, at least when looked at from a strictly sociohistorical point of view, yet the consequences were similar in many respects. We are looking for similarity, the reasons behind the strikingly similar individual lives. A horror of this similarity guided every single one of them. "I am an unspeakable person," Kleist wrote to his sister, but all the same, the similarity of fates seems, mysteriously, a more powerful force and law than the desire of individual persons to be different. Was Hegel right, after all? Hegel, who was simply an interpreter of a truth that hounded so many Romantic melancholics to death? "We seek the unconditional and always find ourselves facing conditions and limits," said Novalis, formulating the Romantics' basic paradox. Byron averred the same as the chorus in *Oedipus at Colonus:* "Not to be born is best / when all is reckoned in." Being is a *constraint*, the Romanticist acknowledged, but immediately added: it was precisely the recognition of this that guaranteed the desire for *infinity*. Unlike melancholics of antiquity, the Romantics experienced both constraint and infinity in their own completeness, and for them the recognition of finitude was just as tragic as the yearning for infinity was attended by happiness. This melancholy paradox had been pointed out earlier: John Donne's poetry, Sir Thomas Browne's miscellaneous tracts, and Pascal's *pensées* were concerned with that duality. Nevertheless, Romanticism was the first to consider this paradox a task for the *technique for living*, not just a theoretical-artistic task and challenge. And although one may agree with Paul Valéry that he who attempts to define Romanticism must have lost his senses, the similarity and consistent reappearance (that continues to the present day) of certain ways of living are strong indications that individual fates have general legitimacy. They can be placed in a historico-philosophical context—although it was precisely from all-revealing and all-resolving (that is, blurring) histories of philosophy and universal explanations that those people fled into death, insanity, or (voluntarily donning eyeshades) back into the bustle that knows nothing of paradoxes.

In Friedrich's painting there are three people peering into death or maybe looking toward us from death. But other faces loom up from the abyss. Hovering eternally young are twenty-eight-year-old Novalis, twenty-five-year-old Wackenroder, twenty-two-year-old Körner, twenty-five-year-old Hauff, twenty-four-year-old Büchner, seventeen-year-old Chatterton, twenty-one-year-old White, thirty-four-year-old Kleist, thirty-three-year-old Wilhelm Müller, thirty-five-year-old Grabbe, twenty-six-year-old Wilhelm Waiblinger, twenty-one-year-old Maria Mnioch, thirty-one-year-old Charles Wolfe, thirty-three-year-old Froude, thirty-three-year-old Shelley, twenty-seven-year-old Burns, thirty-six-year-old Byron, twenty-nine-year-old Anne and thirty-year-old Emily Brontë, twenty-six-year-old Karoline von Günderrode, and, somewhat further away, having died a bit older, thirty-nine-year-old Platen. And behind them are those who went mad: Bürger, Hölderlin, Lenau, Robert Schumann, and, further back, thirty-one-year-old Franz Schubert, surrounded by painters, in which group one can spot twenty-two-year-old Karl Philipp Fohr, twenty-four-year-old Franz Pforr, twenty-seven-year-old Johann Erhard, twenty-six-year-old Oldach, and, at the edge,

thirty-three-year-old Philipp Otto Runge, who was at least as familiar with the cliffs on Rügen as Friedrich. The crowd is of course much
bigger, but out of the mass of indiscernible faces, let us mention just
a few who pushed to the foreground around 1800. On this side of the
chasm, standing on secure ground, is Friedrich Schlegel, making the
following remark: "We call many of them artists, though in reality
they are nature's works of art" (quoted in Krimmel, "Naturgestalt
und Kunstfigur," xxxvi). Of course, it was easy for him to talk: he did
not venture to the brink of the abyss, and apart from the Romantic straying of his younger days, up until the age of fifty-seven he
had a sure touch in telling the difference between self and nature,
life and death, health and sickness. He was caught up by the specter
that threatens melancholic geniuses: he did not go mad, just dull.
He had nothing but knowledge of what others experienced: that an
individual has not only boundaries but boundlessness as well—and
for the modern mind, that contradiction is the most decisive experience. Those who died prematurely young did not die of the sheer
existence of this duality but of its irreconcilability. But the destruction of human lives, the irrevocable disappearance of personalities,
is a warning to us, successors and contemporaries, that precisely because of its irreplaceability, the single person, the individual and his
unique life, has its own exclusive, definitive, and irrefutable truth,
just the same as history or "progress" that has outgrown man or some
historical perspective that ignores melancholia entirely. It is in their
own defense, as it were, that those who stayed alive claimed that those
who died were sick, feeble sleepwalkers, or that the great number of
coincidental deaths was pure chance. In claiming this, they essentially said nothing about melancholic Romantics. They treated this
problem as a cause-and-effect matter, a problem reminding us that
life is of an inexplicable, inscrutable character beyond rational logic.
Rational argumentation connected to the death of others (he or she
died because . . . ; he or she died, but I am still living; he or she died,
although . . .) is always a manifestation of the reasoner's healthy and

primitive vital instinct, and it serves only to distance us from facing up to death and our own uniqueness.

Man's place in the universe—hardly any notion was more distressing to the Romantics. Under no circumstances could they accept that the goal should be to accommodate, to comply with given conditions, and European culture in 1800 was maybe the first turning point in its history that made questionable every value that had been thought secure. "God is dead," the young Hegel declared well before Nietzsche, and it was the Romantics who drew the lesson. Hegel was not alone: a similar thought is expressed by Jean Paul in his novel *Siebenkäs* (1796–97) and by August Klingemann in the novel *Nightwatches*, published in 1804. William Blake writes in a poem titled *The French Revolution*: "God, so long worshipp'd, departs as a lamp / Without oil." If the values that human beings had developed were not eternal truths, then it was ludicrous to regard adjusting to them as the ultimate goal in life. The Romantics sloughed off their prejudices like a snake its skin, leaving just their bare, denuded epidermis, which gave no protection and felt painful for no particular reason. Emily Brontë writes in "The Prisoner":

> O dreadful is the check—intense the agony—
> When the ear begins to hear, and the eye begins to see.

Pain was incarnated in them, and since the pain was a consequence of human culture and civilization, it could not be alleviated. "My soul is so wounded," Kleist wrote in a letter to his sister,

> that it almost hurts when I stick my head out the window and the sun shines on it. Some people consider this to be illness and overstress,[9] but you, who are capable of not looking at the world only from your own point of view, will not see it as such. Since the beginnings of my youth, I have been irresistibly preoccupied

---

9. As it would also be considered nowadays, and called neurasthenia.

with beauty and morality in my thoughts and writings, and for that reason I have become so sensitive that even the tiniest of touches to which every person's senses are exposed in the course of worldly matters hurts me two or three times as hard.

(*Werke und Briefe*, 4:411)

This pain is pain in the literal sense of the word: suffering is still suffering when it is induced by psychological factors—indeed, it is all the more that. And it is perhaps in a state of pain that a person is least able to judge the world objectively, in abstraction. That was doubly true for the Romantics, who already suffered from the knowledge that there was no objective point of view—that "truth" did not exist—and immersion in the interior world did not even hold out the promise that from there an escape to somewhere was possible. At such times, one is like a hedgehog turned inside out: on the outside is raw flesh, all nerves, and on the inside the spines. The descent into an internal realm of thought is a *flight* from the world, from a lack of goals, and, of course, from poets and critics. In Schlegal's words, "The dull person judges all other people like people but treats them like things, and is absolutely incapable of understanding that they are human beings distinct from himself" (*Lucinde and the Fragments*, 225). The descent into the interior is a *relinquishing* of the world, which fails to give answers to the most personal, ultimate questions. August von Platen notes in his diary about love and fondness: "Why do I have to be so deeply alive to it, if I cannot partake of it?" Although Goethe, with extraordinary sensitivity, found precisely love missing from Platen's works, his attention did not extend to noticing that the "inner" repression and pain were negative imprints of an "external" world lacking in love and faith. (Two generations later, Theodor Storm, old but far from devoid of torments and "irresponsible" passions, noted in a letter: "I have a need of external limits and of scarcity so that inner perspectives open up to me" [*Briefe*, 2:227]). Descent into the interior was a *compulsion*, not an end in itself or an aesthetic pleasure, as Hegel saw it: "This is a longing which will not let itself go in actual action and production, because it is frightened of being polluted by contact with finitude, although all the same it has a sense of deficiency of this abstraction" (*Lectures on Fine Art*, I. 3. A. 1. c). He was wrong. He argued on behalf of a reality that glorified activity and proclaimed finitude, failing to notice that action had long since hit back at the doer, that finitude was a constraint, and that the bourgeois world showed an entirely different face to the single individual than to the impenetrable armor of the absolute spirit. Descent into the interior was an unbearable compulsion, since one must experience day by day one's continuous destruction. Novalis was prompted to inquire about the place of man in the universe by the death of Sophie von Kühn, his fifteen-year-old fiancée: "She alone tied me to life, to the Earth, to my activity. Due to her I broke with everything because now I no longer have even myself at my disposal," he writes in one letter (*Ausgewählte Werke*, 1:xxxiii), and, a few months later: "The evening never passes, and soon it will be night" (1:xxxiv). It was no accident that his creative genius was practically liberated from the moment the girl died, and incandescent works marked the remaining traces of his short life. Depth and interiority: a release from the external world, which therefore allows its mysterious and otherworldly face to be glimpsed. Observing this is not granted to ordinary mortals. "Unutter'd harmony," writes Emily Brontë in "The Prisoner," "that I could never dream, till Earth was lost to me."

Depth and interiority result in suffering (putting up with the "outside" world), but the works born out of this, the partial *communicability* of experiences that are approachable to some degree, remind us that we should notice not only the suffering in the lives and melancholic moods of the Romantics. One can suffer only *from* something, yet the object of the suffering, or more properly, its cause, is itself manifold. Since objects have more than one face and possess more than just one layer, *suffering guarantees, for one thing, that ever more faces of the object may be seen and, for another thing, draws attention to the multifaceted nature of existence.* (It is not at all an accident that ever since Romanticism, which made suffering a "state of the world," a significant proportion of artworks owe their existence precisely to sensitivity, a discriminating sensibility derived from suffering.) One should relate in many diverse ways to something multifaceted. The much-talked-of irony of the Romantics, the ironic approach to the world, was a result of this duality. (Nothing seems more natural than the interweaving of irony and melancholia: it is a kinship that has been unbroken from antiquity to our day.) For on the one hand, the world *hurts,* but on the other hand, it is the *world* that hurts (those who are drowned in negativity and deny the world are also obliged to resign themselves to the world's existence). This makes it possible for us to notice life even in death, pleasure in sin, enjoyment in suffering, health in sickness. Thinkers who apprehend the world in its prosaic one-sidedness naturally reject the possibility of identifying life with death, suffering with enjoyment. Nor can they do otherwise, since they see the world as a multiplicity of incomprehensible and senseless things in which they cannot discover the inner kinship of contradictory phenomena, only their mutually excluding antagonism.

Melancholic suffering caused by life becomes the basis of a new life. "We dream about travelling in space," writes Novalis, "but is not the universe present inside us? We are unacquainted with the depths of our soul. The secret path leads inward. Nowhere else, just inside us, is eternity with its own worlds, past and present. The outside world is a mere shadow world which throws its shadows into the realm of light" (Novalis, *Ausgewählte Werke,* 3:7). The outlines of an internal landscape loom before the eyes of the melancholic, who becomes ever more remote from worldly matters, from tangible facts. This new world is not to be compared with anything—*it seems that it is only through the creation of an internal world that man can become incomparable and unique, not through external action, which simply dissolves individual acts in an anonymous crowd.* Kleist, whose torments were hardly commensurable with anyone else's, wrote to his sister: "It is only within the world that it is painful; not outside of it" (Kleist, *Werke und Briefe*, 4:163). And it was also he who, winding up outside the world early on, lifted the pain of this exclusion up to the daylight of his consciousness and wrote as follows: "The future before me never looked so dark as now, though I never looked ahead more cheerfully than now" (ibid.). The forehead of this new outlook is marked by *serenity:* a serenity that is not a joke, not a jest, not at all a creation of will and decision, but a mental state. The serenity with which he looked ahead to a voluntarily accepted death manifested inner liberation, delight coupled with suffering, and a new way of looking at the world. In the farewell from life, which lasted up to the crack of the pistol, there was no trace of forcedness; after all, it was precisely such forcedness that he presumably was taking leave of. The same went for the rest. Tieck, a friend, described Novalis in the following way: "Just as in the course of conversation he most willingly disclosed the depths of his frame of mind and conversed enthusiastically about the regions of invisible worlds, so, at one and the same time, he was happy as a child, jested in an easy manner, and had his share in the high spirits of a gathering" (quoted in Novalis, *Ausgewählte Werke*, 1:xlii). He had an unclouded, serene death, or at least that was how it was seen by one eyewitness, Friedrich Schlegel, and it seemed that for him, his twenty-eight years meant just as full a life as eighty-three years did for Goethe. Wackenroder was fond of revelry; Körner went into battle happily and optimistically; Büchner was partial to farce; Burns, Shelley, and Byron were greedy for life; unrestrained good humor was a feature of Fohr until death claimed him at twenty-two years of age. Posterity, kitsch-creating memory, is fond of highlighting only the suffering in melancholia—a basis for that is given also by the contemporaneous remarks of Goethe and Hegel. The suffering of the Romantics was not affectation, however; rather, it derived from the sadness that (as Byron was fond of citing in his journal) generally characterized great geniuses, according to Aristotle's observation. Melancholia, springing from the impossibility of imagined and craved happiness, was attended by pain as a matter of course ("All deep feelings are melancholic to some degree," Thomas Mann noted), but since the suffering was caused by neither this nor that specific object, and gloom had its foundation in the temperament, the suffering therefore appeared in the melancholic's relationship to things. This explained why happiness and good humor were not obstacles, for (perhaps under the influence of the daimon residing within us) who among us has not noticed the ludicrous futility of one's own good humor; who, like the biblical King Solomon, has not looked at one's own jollity from the outside? Naturally, not in the ordinary and superficial sense of self-criticism, but as a result of a kind of deeper amazement. In his journal, Byron records the following case: "People have wondered at the Melancholy which runs through my writings. Others have wondered at my personal gaiety; but I recollect once, after an hour, in which I had been sincerely and particularly gay, and rather brilliant, in company, my wife replying to me when I said (upon her remarking my high spirits) 'and yet, Bell, I have been called and miscalled Melancholy you must have seen how falsely, frequently.' 'No, B.,' (she answered) 'it is not so: at heart you are the most melancholy of mankind, and often when apparently gayest'" (quoted in *Letters and Journals*, 4:73n1).

To make even good humor a target of gloom—that was one of the oddest features of these Romantics who died young. It was a recognition of uniqueness, finitude, inevitable demise; and when the Romantics attempted to protect their individuality against an all-leveling totality, they had to realize that if they did not give full vent to their character, then their individuality would degenerate into a foppish eccentricity. The world itself was the main barrier to a true life, so they created a new world within the boundaries of the soul. Not that they were so naïve as to imagine that the inner world was completely independent of the external world. As Novalis put it: "Inside us we also have an external world, which relates to our inner world as the outer world beyond us does to our outer world. . . . We can gain closer access to nature's inside and soul only with our thoughts, in just the same way as we can only get acquainted with the outside and the physical essence of nature with our senses" (Novalis, *Ausgewählte Werke*, 3:27). Hence the gloom: freedom cannot be thought of without constraints. The Romantics were perfectly aware of their impossible position, and this awareness dictated their steps—not the sheer yearning that Hegel tried to attribute to them. The fundamental paradoxes of the Romantics can be seen to derive from this: from the *suffering* that at one and the same time offered the possibility of a liberated enjoyment of a new world; from a new *world* formed by an internal region of the soul and therefore more destructive than the outside world; from the *recognition* that the internal being is just as much a restraint as the external one; and from the *astonishment* that if God has in fact died, then it is vain hoping to conjure an absolute out of anything (even the self).[10] Existence had not simply become senseless—one could easily see that—but one could not do anything with it because it kept slipping out of one's hands. And that was no longer a hypothetical matter but a problem of how to live, which started with astonishment at one's own existence and, after every conceivable detour, found its way back again to that starting point.

"As I grow older," Byron wrote to Shelley, "the indifference—not to life, for we love it by instinct—but to the stimuli of life, increases" (26 April 1821; *Letters and Journals*, 5:268–69). Mention has already been made of boredom, which, inasmuch as it relates to existence itself, can also be called indifference. Indifference engulfs everything with a loss of faith and interest; it is ever harder for anything to awaken one's interest. "There is no freedom in Europe—that's certain," Byron wrote, but his own apathy was divulged in the second part of the sentence: "it is besides a worn-out portion of the globe" (3 October 1819; ibid., 4:358). The Romantics withdrew into their

---

10. Novalis's or Schleiermacher's subjective religiosity did little to change this: that was "merely" a special variety of nihilism.

own "internal," unapproachable world, in contrast with the classicists, who strove to acquire eternity by self-realization in the "outside" world. Indifference toward the external world is inevitably attended by the muddling up of that external world. In characterizing Romantic poetry, August Wilhelm Schlegel apprehended the difference in the following way: "Ancient poetry and art is a rhythmical *nomos*, a harmonious promulgation of the eternal legislation of a beautifully ordered world mirroring the eternal Ideas of things. Romantic poetry, on the other hand, is the expression of a secret longing for the chaos which is perpetually striving for new and marvellous births, which lies hidden in the very womb of orderly creation" (quoted in René Wellek, *A History of Modern Criticism, 1750–1950*, 2:59). The two types of poetry rest on two different interpretations of human nature. The origin of the word "classic" alludes to this: in Rome, the listing of citizens for taxation purposes was called classification. So Classicism refers not so much to the perfect, many-sided development of something (that definition is based on a preliminary, tacit acceptance of the notion of Classicism) as to an *image of man*. In Classicism, labeling, subordination, classification, respect for measure are asserted — even when there is seemingly no question of it (for example, in the case of individual works of art), this notion still lurks in the background (Horace's *Ars poetica* or the architecture of Palladio are extreme examples). Classical sculpture, classical poetry, the classical conception of man equally have a liking for and lay stress on the *typical*. But what is considered typical at a certain time is always relative. At the bottom of classical notions there usually lies a trust in history, a faith in progress, identification with the goals of a country or politics, etc. For that reason, Classicism always favors the whole over the part, the general over the singular. (True, the great creative works of Classicism usually reek of melancholia, but that is a sign of the ultimate failure of the aspiration of classicist art; Palladio's interiors are "melancholic" spaces because the architect palpably did not wish to be melancholic.) "It is only the whole which properly has reality," Hegel pronounced in *The Phenomenology of Mind* (2:690), and at the bottom of that statement is a solid picture of man: man is heart and soul, root and branch, part of a larger whole, can "use" his body and soul only as part of that larger whole. Classicism is a belief in there being a goal for life, for existence, for the universe or anything else. Classicists mostly grew old—they preserved both body and soul, that is, they unconsciously stood (set themselves) in the service of something.[11] A chasm yawned before the Romantics, and at most they could serve only that—even at the price of their own lives. Romanticism was indifference in the strictest sense of the word—and because it was interested in man rather than people, it was indifferent to politics as well. (Goethe, who in many respects was more Romantic than the Romantics, and Nietzsche were both indifferent to politics, which from the eighteenth century on became ever more formal and became subject to reasoning instead of action. And Byron, who started his career as a parliamentary speaker, noted: "As for me, by the blessing of indifference, I have simplified my politics into an utter detestation of all existing governments; . . . I don't think politics *worth an opinion. Conduct* is another thing:—if you begin with a party, go on with them. I have no consistency, except in politics; and *that* probably arises from my indifference on the subject altogether" (journal entry for 16 January 1814; *Letters and Journals*, 2:381). The measure was lost, or, more precisely, the earlier measure had come to be regarded chiefly as one that served for the destruction of the individual. Romanticism did not see any all-embracing whole into which the individual could have been incorporated body and soul.[12] Unlike the

---

11. A book by the German physician Christoph Wilhelm Hufeland entitled *Macrobiotik, oder die Kunst das menschliche Leben zu verlängern* (*Macrobiotics, or The Art of Prolonging Human Life*, 1796) greatly influenced Immanuel Kant, according to whom advanced years could be considered a great moral credit.

12. The failure of Romanticism's attempts at mythopoeia (Schelling, Friedrich Schlegel) was likewise proof of that.

classicists, the Romantics were incarnates of "passionate fragments" (Musil)—they were wastrels, at least from the point of view of the classicist or the everyday world, which in losing sees only the loss, in winning, the gain, and is unable to notice the gain deriving from loss, and the loss or narrowing associated with gains.

Being left alone can also become a source of strength. Unlike their meditating successors, the Romantics were just as energetic and ready to act as the classicists—it was not their fault that none of their plans worked out. The dramatist Christian Dietrich Grabbe wrote: "God creates out of nothing, man out of ruins. We must break ourselves to pieces before we know what we are, what we can be and do! Horrible Fate! Yet, so it is! It is my lot, too, and I follow my stars" (*Don Juan and Faust*, act 1, scene 2). Many of the Romantics did literally destroy themselves; they were so unconcerned about themselves that, sooner or later, earthly destruction was bound to ensue. "I was never a good arithmetician of chances, and shall not commence now," Byron recorded (journal entry for 9 January 1821; *Letters and Journals*, 5:164), and a lot of his contemporaries could have said much the same. Not only did they not believe in redemption in the next world (though more than a few Germans believed in the transmigration of souls), but they even doubted the viability of this-worldly communities: being aware of the uniqueness and irreproducibility of an individual being, they found it ludicrous to refer to human communities. Without batting an eye, they accepted that they could count only on themselves, and therefore they seemed reckless—assuming that one perceives recklessness not just in a physical sense (for example, leaping across a crevasse) but also in an intellectual sense (for example, thinking fully through a hitherto-inconceivable thought for the first time). Yet there was no marked difference between the two, since physical recklessness indicated the presence of intellectual recklessness, and the presence of intellectual recklessness very often had to face physically manifested effects.

Recklessness projects the shadow of irrevocability onto everything. Those who are reckless are well aware that their actions are irrevocable; indeed, since any revocation would pull them back into a world of deliberation and premeditation, that is not even posed as an option. With a nonchalant wave of the hand, Kleist burned his manuscripts, among them two plays and a two-volume novel; after burning one of his works, Byron wrote that it caused him as much pleasure to burn it as to print it. More than one work of the Romantics was produced as though no other person existed on earth apart from the creator; these works were not produced for others, but were the overflows of souls closed in on themselves, which is why it is hard to consider them works at all. Of course, posterity, its tactless curiosity knowing no bounds, regrets the incinerated works, though not the lives that were put into them, since it thinks in terms of art and aesthetics rather than matters of fate and existence. What lies behind recklessness is never an aesthetic point of view; the perpetrators of reckless deeds do not behave as they do to set an example, with some sort of purpose (education, warning, craving for the limelight, rivalry), but for its own sake: *the point of recklessness is to experiment with our own latent possibilities, to make sure of their existence.* Death hovers over it as a matter of course — but just as the shadow of mortality and of unrepeatability is cast on every single human gesture, word, and deed (things can be repeated, of course, but that is done by another person, another experience, another potentiality), so the transition between the passing of moments and death is also unbroken. "Life is the start of death," Novalis writes. "The aim of life is dying. Death is at one and the same time closure and beginning. Simultaneous separation and tighter connection" (Novalis, *Ausgewählte Werke,* 3:7). Well known is Goethe's dictum that classic is what is healthy, and Romantic is what is sick: "I call the classic healthy, the romantic sickly. In this sense, the *Nibelungenlied* is as classic as the *Iliad,* for both are vigorous and healthy. Most modern productions are romantic, not because they are new, but because they are weak, morbid, and sickly; and the antique is classic, not because it is old, but because it is strong, fresh, joyous, and healthy. If we distinguish 'classic' and 'romantic' by these qualities, it will be easy to see our way clearly" (Johann Peter Ecker-mann and Johann Wolfgang von Goethe, *Conversations of Goethe with Eckermann and Soret,* 2 April 1829). Friends of Romanticism usually reject Goethe's view, though Goethe himself was very rea-sonable in his dealings with Romanticism. He did not cloak what he had to say in philosophical categories; he did not throw into play against them the absolute spirit, totality, truth, etc., but, very sensi-tively, relied on biological notions in his arguments. He was right, too: after all, biological reasoning does not judge; it merely states things. Romanticism was sick, Classicism healthy, he asserted but, with customary caution, did not add that anything sick is bad, to be rejected, negative; indeed, on one occasion he pronounced that when possessed of intelligence, both a Classicist and a Romantic could create great works. Romantics would more than likely sub-scribe to that dictum, and although Goethe abhorred a great many things in which he suspected sickness, he must also have surmised that it *was unhealthy to have such a horror of disease.* The concepts of sickness and health are subject to the all-embracing fact and reality of life; their significance is therefore secondary. The borderline between sickness and health is far from being as sharply defined as mundane life would like—especially not when one gets to the borderline of an era like Romanticism, which began to doubt not just all comprehen-sive human communities or solutions, but also the human body itself. Johann David Passavant, a painter-cum-historian of Romantic art, wrote as follows in the early eighteenth century: "The start of my days, just like many valuable hours of my life, is filled with daydreaming. This affliction is based on intellectual weakness. It indicates dimin-ished vitality and increased irritability. I hope that I shall be cured of the disease if my mind is engaged by a well-defined occupation and will or necessity forces me to choose some sort of career" (quoted in Krimmel, "Naturgestalt und Kunstfigur," xvi). Passavant did pick a vocation, and it may have been thanks to that that he lived to the ripe age of seventy-four. Many others, however, chose no occupation—not for lack of will or necessity, but because their minds were absorbed by something else more imperatively than anything that one might choose resolutely. Novalis was struck down by tuberculosis, but he had expected to die many years before; Büchner likewise readied himself for death at a young age, and it may have been his will that brought on his illness; Bürger, Hölderlin, Lenau, and Schumann owed their madness to their frazzled nerves and a series of deeply felt disappointments; Grabbe and Burns became victims of alcoholism; they drank—to use a line from Chekhov—so that the "world may look like the world." Just days before his death, Schubert spoke to a friend of the "absolutely new harmonies" running through his head, and he did not flinch from dying. Wackenroder stated, "In the case of less strong souls, everything that a person uses to create runs through the blood and transforms the insides without the person being aware of it" (Wilhelm Heinrich Wackenroder, *Dichtungen, Schriften, Briefe*, 230). Accordingly, soon after Wackenroder's fictitious musician, Joseph Berglinger, created the greatest work in his life, he contracted a nervous debility and quickly died, to be followed to the grave shortly afterward by twenty-five-year-old Wackenroder himself. Lenau mentioned the "streak of unluckiness" in himself several times, and the painter Philipp Otto Runge blamed his internal dissolution for his artist's block and precipitous decline in health. On hearing of Runge's early death, Goethe is said to have noted, "He did not last long, poor devil, it's already the end for him, and it could not have happened any other way; anyone who is so flimsy either has to die or go mad—there is no mercy in such cases" (quoted in Richard Friedenthal, *Goethe: His Life and Times*, 558). What he had to say about Kleist is also noteworthy: "with horror and shuddering, as if an incurable disease had assailed a body that nature had intended to be so fair" (557). Byron was dispatched by malaria—which was just as fateful as Hölderlin's insanity, for Byron deliberately courted death, and it eventually took this form to finish him. (He could go no further because "he reached the summit of his creative power"—that is Goethe again [Eckermann and Goethe, *Conversations*, 18 May 1824].)

The prematurely dying Romantics did not simply die—they, so to speak, threw down the gauntlet to fate and did violence to death. Life slipped out of their hands ("It is truly odd that nowadays everything to which I set my hand miscarries; every time I decide to take a certain step, the ground slips from under my feet," Kleist wrote in the year of his death [*Werke und Briefe*, 4:485]), and they sought refuge from life in death. "Death is life's main prize," said Novalis (*Ausgewählte Werke*, 3:6), who possibly experienced the relativity of life and death more deeply than anyone. Since the world is fraught with disappointments, failures, and limitations, it does not permit even death to unfold its full nature. Heidegger came to the following view on the notion of death held by everyday consciousness, surmising as it does a rigid contrast between life and death and thinking on a mutually exclusive basis in all things:

The analysis of the phrase "one dies" reveals unambiguously the kind of Being which belongs to Being-towards-Death. In such a way of talking, death is understood as an indefinite something which, above all, must duly arrive from somewhere or other, but which is proximally not yet present-at-hand for oneself, and is therefore no threat. . . . Dying is leveled off to an occurrence which reaches *Dasein*, to be sure, but belongs to nobody in particular. . . . In the way of talking which we have characterized, death is spoken of as a "case" which is constantly occurring. Death gets passed off as always something "actual"; its character as a possibility gets concealed, and so are the other two items that belong to it—the fact that it is non-relational and that it is not to be outstripped. . . . This evasive concealment in the face of death dominates everydayness so stubbornly that, in being with another, the "neighbors" often still keep talking the "dying person" into the belief that he will escape death and soon return to the tranquillized everydayness of the world of his concern.

(Martin Heidegger, *Being and Time*, §51).

For Romantics who died early, death itself was life come to fruition; it was not something that would ensue sometime in the future but that threatened one day by day. Confronting death was by no means a flight from life: for Romantic melancholics, there was nothing to escape from. Death thereby became a possibility, an experiment in which the individual was finally able to find himself; only in death was he able to become absolute, since life is full of failures and dispersions. "No more let Life divide what Death can join together," Shelley wrote on the death of Keats ("Adonais," 53). We successors are of the opinion that an ebbing of the vital force is responsible for premature death. But anyone who, even if only fleetingly, has instinctively felt his own ephemerality and irreplaceability, and has come to realize that there are boundaries beyond which solitude is the sole possible state, is well aware that at such moments the "life force" does not ebb but springs forth. For the Romantics, the whole of life was one such moment; the explosion of the vital force destroyed degenerated life on behalf of Life, as it were, under the spell of another state that was, on all counts, more promising than the one at hand. They acquired superhuman strength merely in order to die like that; they bore witness not only to the freest death but also to the bewilderment and seclusion in which they, too, could recount, along with no less melancholic Job, the words he addressed to God: "My face is foul with weeping, and on my eyelids is the shadow of death" (Job 16:16).

Chapter 7

LOVE AND MELANCHOLIA

Romantic creative genius consisted in the melancholic acceptance of death, the recognition that the individual, yearning for self-
determination, was unable to achieve that goal in this world. Creative
genius rejects any compromise; melancholia, however, warns that
this rejection is not just the result of careful deliberation, a conscious
decision, but also a matter of fate: melancholic geniuses cannot do
other than choose death. The attraction of melancholics to suicide
was always conspicuous; during the period of Romanticism, this attraction, by the force of circumstances, entered into an alliance with
creative genius. Originally, "genius" meant a guardian spirit—it is
an irony of history that in the modern era it was *death*, of all things,
that sat as a guardian spirit on man's shoulders. Nothing was more
typical of the Romantic era, however, than that public opinion held
love, next to death, to be the other genius. If love was a genius, and
it, along with death, nurtured melancholia, then it stood to reason
that love and melancholia were also bound to meet. The correlation
of love and death peaked with Romanticism (*Liebestod*), though for
the ancient Greeks Eros and Thanatos had predicated each other.

The signs of melancholia started to appear well before Romanticism—in point of fact, at the time when Christianity was being consolidated, when love "broke away" from the net of human relations
and inevitably became solitary. Not just in the sense that the lover
and the object of love definitively broke away from each other, but
also in that love itself became homeless—it could not find its place
in this world because it did not wish to acknowledge finalities, definitive restrictions, and, being an earthly phenomenon, it had no

business in the other world. It was Christian philosophy, born in the Roman Empire, that first posed questions about the individual, as well as those about individuality and uniqueness, and the role of love and affection became problematical around the same time: the lover was left to himself, yet because his love was nevertheless directed at something, this solitude was not just loneliness but also *deprivation*. If a melancholic's most tormenting problem, from the Middle Ages on, has been that of self-determination, of sovereignty, then this difficulty has applied with double force to a lover.

There are two concepts of love in the history of European culture, and they radically, though not conspicuously, differ from each other. One was that of the Greeks, which thinkers like Spinoza and Hegel wanted to revive. According to this school of thought, love does not result in a radical break in the system of human relationships but fits in seamlessly among the other social relations of everyday life. The lover's desire is associated with remembering, says Empedocles (see *Fragments*, §64), and the act of remembering vouches for the recognition of the unity of being. Of the two forces that move the world, anger and strife (νεῖκος) separates everything, whereas fondness (φιλία) ties everything together. The basis of love (ἔρως) is liking: its essence is binding, unity, and perfection. Love and affection are not separated from the other spheres of life; indeed, they are, rather, the precondition for their unity. A lover does not just experience his own love: it is through love that the underlying harmony and enclosure of existence is realized for him. The object of love guides the lover toward deeper cognition—nothing is more natural than that Plato, in *Phaedrus*, should connect the initiate, the philosopher, the madman, the obsessed, and the seer, and designate them all with the single word "lover" (ἐραστής). But as we have seen, precisely those people whom Plato collectively calls lovers were susceptible to melancholia; it was through them that melancholia appeared in its completeness. Thus, love in antiquity was not untouched by melancholia. After all, if love and affection facilitate a deeper understanding of being and existence, then ultimately they bring the lover to a recognition of the state of cosmic closure (enclosure). Therefore love, though it strikes one as a happy and comforting state, since it brings a lover closer to the beloved object, is actually endangered at every moment. Eros is an *intermediary*, creating a connection between heaven and earth, and if lovers do not watch out, they can easily come to grief; Eros will enslave them and carry them off into an unknown domain, toward fateful insights. One is at the mercy of Eros, and that is not only a joyful state but also a suffering. The Greeks regarded passionate love as burdensome, something one suffered almost like an illness; hence the name used for passionate love was νόσος, which also meant illness, misfortune, and suffering. (In Euripides' *Hippolytus*, for example, the notions of ἔρως and νόσος are presented together in every case.) Eros, unruly and uncurbed, can push one into perpetual homelessness: with due prudence and circumspection, however, lovers can avoid that fate and partake of (mutual) happiness:

> Joy will come to those who share their marriage bed
> with the calm of Aphrodite's love and
> not with the frenzy of Eros' stinging arrows!
> This god, this god with the golden hair,
> lifts his bow and shoots two arrows of passion,
> one to bring us life's greatest joy,
> the other to send us into a whirlwind of confusion,

(Euripides, *Iphigenia in Aulis*, 543–49)

Love fulfilled makes the lover outstanding and offers the possibility of a harmonious life. Plato writes as follows: "For the principle which ought to be the guide of men who would nobly live — that principle, I say, neither kindred, nor honor, nor wealth, nor any other motive is able to implant as surely as love. Of what am I speaking? Of the sense of honor and dishonor without which neither city nor private person ever does any good or great work" (*Symposium*, 178c–d).

With Plato, love is mediation: a link between heaven and earth, body and spirit, and thereby it promotes the harmony of the individual and the state; indeed, according to Plato, only love promotes it. We are at our best when in love; according to this notion, love helps us realize our abilities and possibilities in relation to others, to society as a whole; it makes us able to find our place in the world. In antiquity, love was not automatically melancholic, though, as has been mentioned, it bordered on melancholia. If love is reciprocated, then arm in arm with Empedoclean love, it makes the cosmos closed and unitary from the *inside*. The intertwining of two bodies guarantees the unity of the world and makes it even more perfect, just like two souls recognizing each other.

This interpretation of love was revived in the philosophy of Spinoza and, especially, Hegel, but in such a manner as to deny it the possibility of definitively turning melancholic. The antique notion of love was taken over by modern thinkers who made it a war banner, since it was revived in an era when a harmonious relationship between the individual and the world seemed possible again. Hegel, who saw the fulfillment of history in civil society and who considered America suitable for the creation of a new epic, would have liked to see every human capability as uniform, commonly shared, and in harmony with the world. He perceived love as such an ability: "If love is the *one* point of union, and does not also draw into itself the remaining scope of what a man has to experience in accordance with his spiritual education and the circumstances of his class, it remains empty and abstract, and touches only the sensuous side of life. To be full and entire, it would have to be connected with the entirety of the rest of the mind, with the full nobility of disposition and interests" (*Lectures on Fine Art*, I. 3. B. II. 2. c). One may look at Hegel's definition as echoing that of the Greeks, but one cannot help noticing a decisive difference: he adopted the Greek concept of love, but attempted to apply it to a radically different situation. The Greeks would never have spoken about empty and abstract sensuality: not only because such a thing did not exist (after all, either love was love, and to that extent definite, or it was not love—and "sheer" sensuality was not empty either, but very much a concrete reality), but also because they never set sensuality and intellectualism as antitheses. The decisive difference lay in the way that Hegel was unable, even at the level of terminology, to obliterate the existence of Christianity—the culture that completed the work of pitting the sensual against the spiritual, and the conceptual against the worldly. After the birth of Christianity, it was no longer possible to think about love in the same way as before, and if anyone, like Hegel, tried to do so, then he was obliged to ignore the special character of love and the fact that the relations between the individual and the community had also changed radically since antiquity. Hegel's definition of love was empty: the sensual and the spiritual had a different character, a different relationship to each other, than they did in antiquity. Evoking the Greek way of looking at things in the modern era was not a way of articulating the concept of love (if that was possible at all); instead, it was a subjective pathos that concealed Hegel's faith in the magnificence of the civil world. It was typical that elsewhere, to make sure that love did not slip out of his grasp and that he would not be obliged to cede it to the Romantics—that is, to the melancholics who alloyed death and genius— Hegel was forced to institutionalize love, sensing that if he were to make it the symbol of earthly harmony, then he would somehow have to make that harmony palpable. In the modern world, reserving love in this way could only happen on an institutional level, in the form of marriage: "On the relations between man and woman, it should be noted that a girl loses her honour in [the act of] physical surrender, which is not so much the case with a man, who has another field of ethical activity apart from the family. A girl's vocation [*Bestimmung*] consists essentially only in the marital relationship; what is therefore required is that love should assume the shape of marriage, and that the different moments which are present in love should attain their truly rational relation to each other" (*Elements of the Philosophy of*

Right, 204–5). In Hegelian philosophy, what is lost is precisely the difference that separates the modern spirit from the Greek. Faith in earthly harmony deprives love of its reality, but the notion of love cannot be eliminated (out of prudery?); some reality has to be secured for it, but that reality is not the reality of love. Love melds into other human relationships. The reality of civil society, however, raises a doubt whether multifarious human capabilities and relationships fit so seamlessly into one another. The Hegelian notion of love identifies love with liking, blurring their fundamental difference. One can respond to Hegel by taking the words of Amfortas to speak for the reality of love in the modern age: "Oh! May no man, no man, undergo this torture / wakened in me by the sight which transports you!" (Wagner, *Parsifal,* act 1).

The other kind of notion, that of fulfilled melancholic love (insofar as one can speak at all of fulfillment), was evolved by Christianity. In this case, one should not speak of a *notion* of love, as in the Hegelian concept, so much as the actual *reality* of love, because Christian-Romantic love permeates the culture of the modern era as a matter of practice. Christian-Romantic love is a coming to terms with a changed world; after antiquity, the possibility of Greek love ceased, and a world split into the sensual and the spiritual modified love as well. It did not split love in two, since love continued to be markedly unitary and independent; it "merely" altered its place. That "relocation," however, did not leave love untouched. Christian love, which is directed not at lovers entering into an alliance with earthly powers but rather at a betrothal with heaven through the object of love, lies closer to reality, paradoxically, than does love as sketched out by Hegel. For Hegel does not describe love but calls it to account for something—a utopia, a certain view of society. Christian love, entering into an alliance with heaven, does not call it to account for anything but acquiesces in the way things are; it is fully aware that the era of Greek love has passed, and that in the changed world love too has been modified.

The reality of heaven was no metaphor: for the Middle Ages, the duplication of the world into heavenly and earthly domains, spirituality and sensuality turned against each other, was a manifest reality. This was the biggest legacy of the Middle Ages to modern culture. Heaven was no longer heaven, but the possibility of being able to step beyond the given reality toward another world that, if not real and manifest, was at least as existent as the other; heaven was a spiritualization of everyday life. In the modern world, that legacy was necessarily connected with the concept of alienation: with the spiritual and sensual doubling of the world, the possibility of a harmonious relationship between individual and society ceased. Love evaded that: only the place it occupied in the world changed; it did not become divided against itself. Such things as spiritual love and sensual love do not exist; love is not divisible into "empty and abstract" love and sheer sensuality. Sheer sensuality and physicality do not lack "spirituality," and vice versa; yet "physicality" or "sensuality" does not necessarily mean love, just as platonic love cannot be considered love in every case. Love continues to be unitary—it does not differ from the love of antiquity in that respect. The decisive difference appears in the fact that whereas then the world seemed unitary (for want of a better word), and for that reason love linked up organically and seamlessly with the system of human contacts, in the modern age, because of the "alienation" of the world, love became detached from other connections and separated from all other human relationships by a chasm. Greek love, with its simultaneous striving for the beautiful and the good, truly beautified and improved the whole of existence, and thus appeared as a special contact, the relationship between two people. Modern love has no say in the course of the world as it is given; by its existence, it does not contribute to the formation of that world. It condemns the lover to solitude; love cannot be objectified—it can exist only as a desire. This is a unidirectional movement, in contrast to the longing that was characteristic of the Greeks; it lacks the reciprocity of Greek love, and this difference determines other relationships in the modern age (affection, friendship, marriage). Modern love is not a bilateral relationship but an absolutely private affair—and every attempt to judge love as a reciprocal affair truly misunderstands the place and specific characteristics of love.

Christian culture did not recognize private affairs: everything was a part of the worldly empire, and even the most personal-seeming gesture evoked God, whether dissentingly or affirmatively. Christianity sought to confirm the sensual and spiritual division of the world within love as well, and modern love became melancholic, or rather became one of the typical manifestations of melancholia, precisely because it resisted that division. The roots of a distinction between heavenly and earthly love had appeared with Plato, who made a distinction between two Aphrodites. One of these was heavenly (Aphrodite Urania) and had no parents, whereas the other, the younger (Aphrodite Pandemos), had parents (Zeus and Dione), and was the one usually called the goddess of love. There was no doubt, however, that both goddesses of love were *celestial* beings, that is, spiritual and physical love were far from being strangers to each other, as Plato's Christian disciples later insisted. At the time of Hellenism and early Christianity, the two goddesses became estranged, and physical love had less and less to do with spiritual love, which was essentially directed at God. Love is in part divine, in part a harmful daimon and passion, Plotinus proclaimed; according to St. Augustine, Jerusalem called upon the love of God, and Babylon upon that of earthly life, the former being the source of all good things, the latter of all evil. "Beloved, let us love one another: for love is of God; and every one that loveth is born of God, and knoweth God. . . . Beloved, if God so loved us, we ought also to love one another," John wrote in his first epistle (1 John 4:7, 11), though with him that love, like the love in Paul's "Hymn to Love" (1 Corinthians 13), was a special capability: *agape* was manifested through the intervention of God; love on the part of humans, on the other hand, was for helping them stay in communion with God. Physical, erotic love was a sign of turning away from God: it was during the period of early Christianity that theologians developed the view that the original, collective sin was passed down from descendant to descendant by *physical* contact. Love was fulfilled in virginity, as promulgated by the Gospels—virginity was supposed to express love toward God. The doctrines of Jesus's virgin birth and Mary's Immaculate Conception were connected at the deepest level with the assessment of love in the Middle Ages and the modern era.[1] Perpetual virginity (*semper virgo*) freed one from the earthly world, from creatureliness, and from sin, and therefore Christian-Catholic ideology had to judge physical love in a diametrically opposed way, denying any sublimity to it, because of its sinfulness. (St. Thomas Aquinas's principal argument against physical love was that it deprived people of their minds.) A couplet noted in the Middle Ages faithfully reflects this point of view:

Femina corpus opes animam vim lumina vocem,
Polluit adnihilat necat eripit orbat acerbat.

[Woman defiles, annihilates, kills, snatches away, robs, and
    aggravates
body, riches, the soul, strength, the light of the eye, the voice.]

(quoted in Wayland Hilton Young, *Eros Denied*, 173)

Love is submergence in creatureliness, refusal of the summons from God. Man in love is overcome by the same selfishness that characterizes melancholia, according to medieval perception: man himself steps into God's place, regarding himself as the basis and goal of existence. Since lovers did not accept the Christian division of the

---

1. The dictate regarding the celibacy of the priesthood was a result not so much of theological as of political deliberation: in the eleventh century, Pope Gregory VII sought by this means to guard against the development of a feudal priestly caste for which (because of the inheritance of wealth and rank) the election of the pope would lose its validity.

world, they had to be branded ideologically, and what could be more appropriate than melancholia: every feature of melancholia was demonstrable in love too; indeed, love was capable of inducing melancholia. The following simile, which stems from the quill of the medieval scholastic St. Bonaventure, is instructive and speaks volumes: "For just as putrid and melancholic humors, if they come to have preponderance, cause scabies, eruptions, and leprosy . . . so impure thoughts, disordered tempers, and detrimental images of desire directed at women, if they overwhelm the heart, yield putrid fluids and disordered carnal desires" (quoted in Jehl, *Melancholie und Acedia*, 86). Lovesickness was first called melancholic during the period of Hellenism in the first century CE (by Aretaeus of Cappadocia), and thereby a tradition that has endured to the present day was born. According to Avicenna (eleventh century), love is an illness, a form of mental distress similar to melancholia; Arnaldus (thirteenth century) was of the opinion that love is a melancholic passion; Jason Pratensis (sixteenth century) classified erotic love among the diseases of the brain; Hercules de Saxonia (sixteenth century) reckoned that love-melancholy could be elicited equally by women and the excessive adoration of God; in Robert Burton's weighty tome, love-melancholy is the subject of a single long chapter; in 1612, Jacques Ferrand published a book in Paris with the title *Traité de l'essence et guérison de l'amour ou de la melancholie érotique*.

The lover, like a medieval melancholic, struggles in a double bind: on the one hand, he disputes with every fiber of his being that his amorous desires are in any way sinful, yet on the other hand, love fills him with a guilty conscience, since, after all, he is not supposed to evade a universal commandment. For him, love is a wonderful state in which the longings of body and soul are indistinguishable, yet at the same time, it is a sin—a sign of turning away from God. The lover would like to unite with his beloved, but he is afraid: all that remains is the longing, which gradually appropriates love to itself. *True love is nothing more than anguished desire that never attains its goal.* "Nothing is more enjoyable than love from afar," Jaufre Rudel wrote in the twelfth century; nothing is sweeter than love-to-death, said Wagner in the nineteenth century; and in the twentieth century, Thomas Mann wrote this in a notebook: "To long for love to the verge of dying for it, and yet nonetheless to despise everyone who loves. Happiness is *not* in being loved; it is satisfaction mixed with disgust for vanity. Happiness is loving and not making even the tiniest approach towards the object of one's love" (*Notizbücher 1–6*, 210). Pining love, which is essentially engaged with Nothingness, is a legacy of Christianity; the Romantics, both conceptually and in their way of living, were the most consistent in making twins of love and death. (Since early in the nineteenth century, modern love has lived on as Romantic rather than melancholic in the consciousness of nonlovers.) We have seen how, starting with the Renaissance, the notion of melancholia has been reinterpreted — in the case of love-melancholia, this has not happened in the same conspicuous way: the yearning, unfulfilled love of the Middle Ages is still alive and kicking in the present day, with only a shift in emphasis: what used to be a sin has become the principal value in modern times.[2]

"Modern" love is the love of people left alone. It is a matter of pure chance with whom they fall in love, but in a deeper sense it is nevertheless inevitable. For a lover's choice of his love object does not depend solely on his momentary frame of mind: the choice is influenced by forces that are linked to him, but also point beyond him. The past, personality, physique, mental constitution, sensitivity, temperament — all those play a part in deciding that out of a mass of people on a crowded beach one will pick out just one person, and no other, to be the object of one's love. That decision is so definite that it is open to question (though it cannot be decided) whether one was in love in the first place and just needed to pick the subject of that love

---

2. *De amore* (1484) by Marsilio Ficino is a notable example of the reevaluation of love intertwined with melancholia.

in retrospect. The choice is fateful, the meeting necessary. Of course, a lover will believe himself to be free in making his choice, and has a right to do so. Not in the Hegelian sense that freedom is the recognition of necessity, since that statement irretrievably incorporates the individual into a system of relationships and is true at most in the case of individuals of exceptional stature who genuinely do recognize the necessity but, having recognized it, treat it freely in accord with their own pleasure (Goethe). In the modern age, such a statement is downright cynicism. By making a choice, however, in spite of all the necessary and fatal constraints, lovers preserve their own freedom — the essence of love, after all, being irreplaceability, incomparability, and uniqueness. Therefore, lovers are *chosen* people, their bearing *aristocratic*, their position *peerless*. In the modern world, which strives for facelessness, love means a rupture: it can only assert itself against the world, and "introduction" into the world, the "taming" of the lover, that monster without any discretion, is in reality directed at the termination of love. "If one does not understand making love the absolute, in comparison with which all other topics are lost sight of," says Kierkegaard, "one should never get involved with, enter into love, even if one gets married ten times" (*The Concept of Dread*, 376). Love "takes away one's brains," "love is being beside oneself" — so talks the world of a lover, but scorn is all it gets back in exchange for the sympathetic pat on the shoulder: the lover has no intention of "returning" to the world, since only he knows that the world's primness and levelheadedness is all about the voluntary acceptance of limitations.

The emergence of love is a sudden appearance of the demonic, and is by no accident inexplicable:

> . . . nearing its desired end,
> our intellect sinks into an abyss
> so deep that memory fails to follow it.

(Dante, *Paradise*, canto 1, ll. 7–9)

How and why does one fall in love? The question is senseless, because when it comes down to it, the lover could only reel off the tangible reasons, even a million of them, but all that would not exhaust the sensual totality that is the object of love. The lover would protest most strenuously against the object of his love being reduced to a "sensual totality," because he would sense (rightly) that in doing so his own inner boundlessness was being forced between boundaries. "Love, on being delimited, evaporates," Unamuno wrote. The object of love cannot be spoken about, being almost unnamable. (I am in love with somebody, I will say, but in doing so I have said nothing about either the individual or my feelings.) In a certain sense, the object of love per se does not exist except as an object modified by movement and direction, and molded to the lover's own image. No one sees the beloved as the lover does, and that is why it is impossible to speak about the cause of love. The paradox of love: the object exists (after all, it is visible, can be induced to speak, can be violated) yet is nonetheless intangible, always slipping out of one's grasp. Uniqueness and perpetual vanishing from sight: that is the reality of love, a paradox of which unresolvability is the essence. It is another matter that although the lover is eager for resolution, would like to "grasp" the object of his love, doing so would immediately lead to a limitation (in the best-intentioned sense of the word), which contradicts the essence of love. Love does not brook resolution. Love cannot be fulfilled; man in love can only truly be in love if he has not gained his object—and vice versa: unattainability precludes the possibility of relief. Reciprocal love does not exist: two people cannot be in love with each other at the same time; mutual attraction is not love but affection. "If there is a kind of love," La Rochefoucauld writes, obviously speaking about the melancholia residing at the bottom of love, "that is pure and unmingled with our other passions, it is one that is hidden in the depths of the heart and unknown even to ourselves" (*Collected Maxims*, V: 69). The lover longs for and would like to appropriate the beloved, and thus is at the mercy of his beloved. It is no accident that one customarily talks about the *object* of love: in comparison to the inner vitality of the lover, an object is lifeless, neutral, and passive. The beloved ceases to be human and turns into an object. Thus, the lover always ends up in an excruciating trap: he creates for himself someone to be at the mercy of his creation; he falls in love with a person who will appear as an object, and that object, for all its defenselessness, subjugates him. The young Thomas Mann wrote as follows to his wife-to-be in June 1904:

> Silly little Katia, still going on with that nonsense about "overestimating" and still maintaining that she cannot "be" to me what I "expect" of her. But I love you—good Lord, don't you understand what that means? What more is there to expect and to be? I want you to "be" my wife and by being so make me madly proud and happy. . . . What I "make of you," the meaning I attribute to you, which you have and will have for my life, is my affair, after all, and imposes no trouble and obligation on you. Silly little Katia!

> (*Letters of Thomas Mann, 1889–1955*, 38)

The objects of love are "defenseless," since they permit themselves to be fallen in love with, and possibly are even unaware of it, yet they gain the upper hand over the "creator" (Pygmalion). Though the lover thinks of himself as the stronger, he is unable to avoid being enslaved. His irresistible masochism does not permit him to be on equal terms with the beloved. He longs for such equality, knowing full well that only it will afford a resolution, but since he is incapable of grasping the beloved, he cannot regard himself as equal in rank. Equality—the lover knows this, but cannot resign himself to it—is ruled out from the start, the physical differences alone foredooming it to failure. But even beyond the question of bodies, it is a pipe dream if, in calling someone my equal (for example, in friendship), I selectively accentuate only those of his or her qualities that are important for me, paying no attention to the rest. That, however, is precisely the result when one attempts to place divergence and dissimilarity in equality of rank. Equality in rank is conceivable only in theory (the formal aspects of political or legal equality are another matter), whereas the essence of love is that it strives for a very specific equality in rank, that is, wanting to make one's own, possess, devour, identify oneself with every particularity of the other. Those theories about the origin of mankind (Plato, Blake) according to which women and men were born from a hermaphroditic creature are very pertinent, since love, by its very existence, ought to believe in the possibility of this reunion. It does not yearn for marriage or procreation; it is at a loss when faced with the possibility of all kinds of practical solutions, because its intention runs beyond them into a world of imagination, faith, and, in the final analysis, nothingness ("Love expires as soon as gods have flown" [Hölderlin, *Death of Empedocles*, 1.4]). The lover strives for the other to exist solely for him in his or her entire concreteness, yet at the same time the other is a completely abstract being (that is, unattainable, unprocurable). He or she is something that cannot be had. The lover would like to combine perfect abstraction and blood-and-flesh uniqueness—that is why his fate is always tragic. In mundane life, the lover will usually achieve his goal, win the hand of the loved one, but that is already a compromise: he has renounced everything that sustained his love, sheer movement and longing having been altered into a closed position, faith into something evident.

The lover is in a state of constant inner turmoil; therefore, his ideal is well balanced. This, however, is unattainable, because as long as love lasts, it is necessarily fraught with dissatisfaction, and when it is fulfilled, it is no longer love. The lover sees equanimity as a compromise, and love must be perfectly free of any compromises. He does not know stability and is constantly suffering on that account—suffering because his love is not fulfilled, though if it were to be realized, it would no longer be love, since reality is always a result of compromises. Love is a peculiar state: its essence is movement and elusiveness, in contrast to all other relationships, which, even in the midst of the change and evolution typical of relationships, possess a kind of stability, bourgeois reliability, and verifiability. Love is not a relationship, but a one-sided disposition. All relationships presuppose a sort of objectivity, but in the case of love, even the object is not a "real" object, but rather a belief, an illusion. The lover is thus necessarily solitary, and besides suffering, that is the other cause of his melancholia. This solitude is at the same time delightful: the lover finds that through his feelings he conducts an intimate conversation with the absolute, which, due to its indefinability, he would justifiably call nothingness—*for to converse with the absolute, to be in love, is nothing other than to live from moment to moment with recognized nothingness*, to accept dispossession. For that reason, the lover's suffering is associated with autonomy of the highest order, all the more so because the existence of the other is not determining, not influential, just a "pretext." The object of his love does not have to do anything, does not have to behave in any particular way or reciprocate—love is in any case blind, though that blindness is like Teiresias's, giving rise to inscrutably profound knowledge. ("The lover would be more divine than the beloved because God was in the former but not in the latter," Thomas Mann puts in the mouth of Socrates in *Death in Venice*.) The lover "creates" the object of that love, who, were she or he not a heretic, would fittingly worship the lover as her or his own god and creator. No other person in the world would pay her or him so much attention; there is no one to whom she or he could turn with such confidence as the person in love with her or him. Man is "fragmented"; only God can be hoped to behold us as a "complete whole"—or our lover, since he is also our creator. "Only love (*l'amour*) is true knowledge," says Gabriel Marcel. "It is legitimate to approach adequate knowledge; for love, that is, and only for love, the individuality of the loved being is scattered into I know not what kind of heap of abstract motifs" (Marcel, *Journal métaphysique*, 63). For the object of love, it would be enough to glance into the lover's eyes to see his or her true nature. Yet the glance of a lover is just as devastating as God's; to be able to look God in the face, we must also become God. A true lover becomes frightening; the beloved is startled and runs away terrified; he or she is scared of the lover, in the same way that one, even while on earth, would rather choose hell than God when the time comes. The lover is a solitary god who in his own way is just as pitiable as anyone who fails to find his own god.

When one falls in love, one has been seduced; one falls in love with the other person with such force, losing oneself and one's place in the customary scheme of things to such an extent, that a doubt inevitably arises whether it is a matter of seduction. The object of love seduces the lover, even if the "object" knows nothing about what he or she has provoked. Just as a lover does not choose his object of love, but that person is chosen through the "machinations of the forces of hell" (Kleist, *Werke und Briefe*, 2:206), so the object of love is seductive in a deeper sense. Of course, this has nothing to do with mindless courting, breach of trust, or coquetry. Seduction is a manifestation of the attraction of the personality; the lover, who has been seduced, enjoys the plunge into love, by which he hastens from himself into the other. "I thank you from the bottom of my heart for all the desperation you have caused me and detest the tranquillity in which I lived prior to knowing you," wrote Mariana Alcoforado, a Portuguese nun, in a letter to her seducer (quoted in José Ortega y Gasset, *On Love: Aspects of a Single Theme*). Love appears as a never-ending pleasure, and the secret of the pleasure is that it is under these circumstances that our own uniqueness, inexhaustibility, and inscrutability present themselves most sensually. Doors open for a lover, chains fall away, and only then does he feel that he has finally found himself. Found himself, because he has experienced his world extending past where he thought it ended, beyond its borders, to a region that in his naïveté he had never noticed; a boundless space marks its start, inviting him to the hopeless task of conquering it. What else would this be but the accession of melancholia to the throne? The lover finds himself by glimpsing his own infinitude — but in doing so, he also loses himself (*Liebestod*). "Plato calls love bitter," Ficino wrote, "and not without justification, because death is inseparable from love" (Ficino, *De amore*, bk. 2, 4; quoted in Wind, *Pagan Mysteries in the Renaissance*, 161). The suffering and anguish, as well as superiority and bliss, derive from the same experience as the melancholic's simultaneous fear of death and death wish, from the intertwining acts of self-surrender and self-discovery. By contrast, in our everyday life we experience these emotions either as mere sacrifice or as our own invulnerability. The lover breaks out of the bonds of the customary world, and the beloved becomes a seducer, tempting him out of the world of trust into a world of which the essence is incessant delusion, elusiveness, and unappeasable craving.

Power is on the side of the beloved; the lover is helpless here. Thus, if one regards love as the highest form of an individual's self-enjoyment, then that pleasure is passive and paralyzing on the part of the lover. The object of love, on the other hand — insofar as she is aware at all of anyone being in love with her — is "active." Active because, as against the lover, she enjoys strength rather than defenselessness, which is latent in her personality. Only in love does she awaken to what her personality is capable of, what an effect it can provoke — and from the moment that she experiences her own strength, she is up to the game. According to her personality, the beloved will start to test her strength, test how far her power extends. It is a game, though one that is a matter of life and death for the lover. It starts with not looking back at her lover, and its most extreme boundary is to go along with a relationship only in order to be able to give it up. In the giving up, the demonic strength of personality equals the demonic power of love. Goethe's breakup with Friederike, Kierkegaard's with Regine Olsen, and Hamlet's with Ophelia: these were experiments, games, tests of strength for the personality. In those cases, the actions of the beloved formed the decisive factor; for the men (and there is little doubt that only men are capable of totally "unwarranted" break-ing off, which is not the same as infidelity or losing interest and is likewise a bridge to melancholia), it was no longer a matter of love.

Loneliness separates the lover from other people, and love from all other relationships. The lover is left to himself by the object of his love (the latter does not allow herself to be reached), but instead of seeking a cure, the lover derives pleasure from suffering and avoids every situation in which his solitude might be relieved in some way. He avoids people and does not speak about his love to others, for he thinks this would be a form of betrayal; words and fixed expressions would tie down, as it were, his love and its object, and he thinks this fixity would soil him, "lead him back" to the place out of which love had led him. For this is love's greatest gift: it makes it possible for the lover to rise above quotidian existence and, by constructing the ob-ject of his love, create a new world for himself. This is a world of lack. It is accompanied by suffering: the lover finds no place of abode or rest, other connections having lost value in his eyes. He disdains the world and neglects everything that had once been of value to him. He is neglectful of his life, and regards this carelessness as the most natural thing. There is no greater or more natural force than ruin-ing one's own fate, which is typical of the lover. He fritters away his energies—though from his point of view, this dissipation is actually a way to gather strength for enduring a higher-order life that affords a glimpse into the destructive power of nothingness. Faith in the other sustains him, and he feels that in that other person, a new world is realized, for which he must leave this earthly world.

> Faith is the substance of the things we hope for
> and is the evidence of things not seen.

> (Dante, *Paradise*, canto 24, ll. 63–64)

Yet that new world, needless to say, seems to be unstable and unat-tainable. A lover thinks that the new world will resolve all the contradictions and painful restrictions that torment him in the old world. Of course, we know full well that this is not what is going to happen. But one can sense just as well that once one has got over the suffering of the lover, love's greatest gift is not just wanting but faith as well. The lover is like a work of art in the process of being realized; love condemns him to solitude and crushes him but, by way of compensation, raises him out of this world so that he can pass beyond time and geographic boundaries for a while, and gain insight into a world that is at least as real and existent as our usual home, and look back on our home from that remoteness, rearranging the order of his world from afar. The new world in which the lover ends up is a world of melancholia, which slowly consumes everything—and by rearranging the order of this world, he helps smuggle nothingness, along with his love, into it. This makes the lover awe inspiring and uninhibited, but also extremely lamentable, since he has overstepped the boundaries that people who are not in love and nonmelancholics regard, in their own defense, so to speak, as the ultimate barriers of existence.

Chapter 8

ILLNESS

During the period of Romanticism, people not only reevaluated melancholia retrospectively but also sought to place the whole world in the parentheses of melancholia. The notion of melancholia, along with the related image of love, could be regarded as huge parentheses: according to the Romantics, it was only within these that the world had a chance to speak up. If the world sought nevertheless to assert its own right, then by doing so it would sooner or later bring about the death of melancholics as it became unable to set limits on their desires. The notion of melancholia was never so broad, nor so fragile: its huge dominion was girded by the closely set border markers of death. We see the last major efforts of melancholia: following the Renaissance, melancholia gradually shallowed out into a mood, an emotional state that—and hence its enemies' haughty self-assurance—was supposedly only a state of the soul, and for that reason it had no "objective" place in the world's scheme of things. It was pointless to waste much time on it. The Romantics, together with lovers who hastened to their assistance, strove once more, one last time, to make melancholia global, to conjure up a law out of a mood, something of universal validity out of a feeling. Their death and their failure pointed to the ultimate hopelessness and futility of their undertaking, as did the disapproving shakes of the heads of enemies girt with the armor of their scientific spirit; for the age not only allowed the individual to be omnipotent only in the sheer ardor of emotions and eliminated even the idea of striving for the unconditional—insisting deceitfully and misleadingly that anyone was free to choose among moods—but also impoverished those very moods by its own ever more ramifying scientific spirit: it claimed that the mood was unconnected with the world, that it was simply a manifestation of the soul, of unknown origin, that did not create a new world and even in the best case was merely an impression of what was already present.

In the eighteenth century, on the heels of research concerning the nervous system, the conviction grew that the cause of melancholia was the nervous system itself, which, in turn, was responsible only for itself. In this view, a person became melancholic neither because of his (physical or psychological) situation in the world nor because of his interpretation of existence, but because of his own narrowly understood physical constitution. The belief in black bile was shattered in the eighteenth century; the interpretation based on the pathology of humors was replaced by a neurophysiological interpretation that explained melancholia through the stimulation of nerve fibers. In 1765, Anne-Charles Lorry distinguished between *mélancolie humorale* and *mélancolie nerveuse*, the latter being derived from changes in the nerve fibers (*De Melancholia et Morbis Melancholicis*). It was in connection with melancholia and melancholics that medical science in the eighteenth century introduced the remarkably vague expression of a "weak" nervous system. It may be an imprecise term, but for the scientific mind it was not something to be brushed aside: it created an apparent connection (closed circuit) in which the affliction of the soul was derived from a weakness of the nervous system, and the disturbance of the soul was responsible for the weakness. Melancholia was stuck in a vicious circle, which came as a godsend for positivists: people who move in closed circuits are not in contact with the world, and anyone who has lost touch with the world can have only false ideas.[1] Physicians of the age unanimously complained about the excessively broad, elusive meaning of the term

---

1. Philippe Pinel, the most celebrated neurologist of the late eighteenth and early nineteenth centuries, called melancholia a "false diagnosis" and regarded the ideas of melancholics as idées fixes.

"melancholia"; indeed, two millennia of interpretations of existence were hard to squeeze into a concept that was supposed to have a well-defined and delimited scientific meaning. The term "melancholia" was replaced by new expressions: it was renamed "monomania" and, later, "lypemania" (by Philippe Pinel and Jean-Étienne Dominique Esquirol, respectively). Later, in the mid-nineteenth century, when the concept of the so-called unitary psychosis (*Einheitspsychose*) was developed, melancholia came to be seen as the initial stage of madness in general.[2] Despite being classified with mental disorders in the strict sense, melancholia still had an excessively wide signification: in Wilhelm Griesinger's classification, it still embraced certain aspects of the condition nowadays called schizophrenia. In *Die Melancholie* (1874), Richard Krafft-Ebing narrowed the broad scope of interpreting melancholia by identifying it as depression, and later as the depressive stage of so-called manic-depressive disease. (The illness, which had been described as far back as Aretaeus of Cappadocia, returned to the purview of psychiatry in the nineteenth century: it was introduced into the domain of psychiatry and neurology under the designation *folie circulaire* by Jean Falret and Jules Baillarger in the 1850s, independently of each other, whereas in 1864, Théophile Bonet had called it *folie maniaco-mélancolique*. At the end of the century, Kraepelin broke apart the previous unitary psychosis on the basis of clinical practice: he adopted a theory that identified depression and melancholia, specifying depression to be the physical symptoms typical of melancholia, but still retained the concept of melancholia.) Melancholia became one of the diseases attended by intellectual degradation, the increasingly severe variants of which were melan-

---

2. According to Wilhelm Griesinger, a German neurologist and psychiatrist, all mental illnesses were manifestations of one and the same madness, the stages of which were melancholia, mania, confusion, and dementia. In 1764, Karl von Linné classified melancholia, along with delirium, dementia, and mania, as one of the "ideal mental illnesses."

cholia simplex, melancholia gravis, paranoid melancholia, fantastic melancholia, and delirious melancholia. (Kraepelin, though unable to prove it, hypothesized that melancholia was produced by changes in the cerebral cortex.)

Identifying certain depressive symptoms (which had always typified melancholia) as being melancholia itself was a dethronement: a relatively well-circumscribed cluster of symptoms appropriated for itself the concept of melancholia, only for the original name to be banished and finally supplanted by that of depression. (Pinel, for example, did not mean by "monomania" a melancholic diathesis but a monoideatic depressive illness.) One cannot fail to notice the straining of the scientific mentality: for the sake of regularity and accurate description, science chops up phenomena and extends its attention merely to what it is capable of delimiting. Since in principle everybody possesses some kind of weltanschauung, and an interpretation of life is one of the preconditions of existence, a melancholic interpretation of being does not necessarily imply illness. Therefore, positivist minds since the nineteenth century have been obliged to distinguish two kinds of melancholy: one, despondency, does not call for medical intervention, but the other, an endogenous psychosis, belongs to the domain of psychiatry. To avoid misunderstandings, the latter is usually renamed depression. What had earlier been inconceivable took place: neither the notion of melancholia of antiquity nor that of the Renaissance or the Baroque recognized that kind of sharp delimitation of healthy and sick melancholia. (It was perhaps only the Middle Ages that dared to draw a boundary between health and sickness with a similarly firm belief.) Up until the eighteenth century, medical science undertook the task of interpreting existence openly, and therefore when it came to melancholia, it was just as unable to offer an unequivocal definition as any school of philosophy that had set itself the goal of explaining existence. (One may be put in mind of Robert Burton's treatise on melancholia: even after reading the more than one thousand pages of that work, one finds it impossible to define melancholia precisely—but having fought one's way through the labyrinths of the melancholic interpretation of life, one is nonetheless left richer in experience, if not in knowledge.) The medical science of the nineteenth and twentieth centuries likewise interpreted existence in its own way, but did it tacitly, *despite* its declared intention and its goal, as was recognizable first and foremost in its methodology. The slicing up of melancholia, the narrowing down of the concept, the absolutization of "bodily" symptoms, and the attempt to impose a closed, clinical systematization on the "psychological" symptoms—what else was this if not an obvious interpretation of human existence? Science, acting under the spell of facts that are held to be palpable, is inclined to eschew value judgments: the illusory nature of its methodology, however, is especially glaring in the case of psychiatry. And since the interpretation of being (whether that is overt or covert) is a process that cannot be closed, psychiatry, if it strives for definitive conclusions, commits violence against human existence. One can never describe the world per se, said Kant; whatever one might write down is always *inside* the world. The narrowing down of the concept of melancholia by science was a warning of an internal, unspoken dilemma of medical science itself. It seemed that medicine of old, which had no wish to describe melancholia (or any other medical condition) as being a closed, unitary disease to be interpreted mainly in physical terms, relating it instead to existence as a whole, knew more about melancholia (and the nature of diseases) than medical science of the most recent times, spellbindingly well-founded as it may be in scientific terms. This scientific method forwent from the very outset probing any of its own boundaries or setting the investigated disease and the ensuing changes in a broader context of being. The disruption of melancholia in the modern age is explicable by this imposed methodological confinement.

We say about one person that he is melancholic and about another that he is depressed. Who would fail to sense the difference? Depression has counted as an illness in every age, but the judgment

of melancholia has always been unsettled: on the basis of the kinship of its symptoms with those of depression, it was considered to be
an illness in the Middle Ages, and in antiquity or the Renaissance it
could mean "outstanding health." The depressive always experiences
his condition as a burden, an illness, in which his biological being
is extensively affected; the melancholic, on the other hand, is possibly unaware of his own melancholia: the melancholic experience
of fate does not necessarily rule out serenity. Everyday parlance is a
reminder of what science passes over in silence: melancholia offers a
deeper (and thus, less easily accessible) insight than depression into
the interconnections of existence. It is precisely that boundlessness
that disturbs science, which imagines that the ever-expanding horizons of humankind can be fenced in—after all, interpretations of
being cannot be diagnosed. It has been seen how the bourgeois mentality strove to tame and ransack melancholia following the Renaissance. In the nineteenth century, medical science took over the role
of the tamer, disputing the original meaning of melancholic attempts
to explain existence (the bourgeois world could not permit the world
to be explained, or even experienced, on the basis of a point of view
radically different from its own), and it referred them to the authority
of learned specialists. History is not a monolithic formation, however, nor was the human mind carved from a single block: horizons
cannot be caught up with. Just as the notion of melancholia has retained in everyday parlance the profundity and infinite openness of
the original meaning, down to the present day, the unitary diseases
born of the constraints of medical science and stipulated by the age
are always fragile and exposed to continual change. In Wilhelm Griesinger's 1845 classification, which became one of the foundational
works of psychiatry in the nineteenth century (*Pathologie und Thera-
pie der psychischen Krankheiten*, or *Mental Pathology and Therapeu-
tics*, as it became known in English translation), melancholia, or,
more precisely, the *stadium melancholicum*, assumed symptoms of
schizophrenia, which are in fact alien to it, and Griesinger himself

included the most diverse manifestations of mental disorders under the label "melancholia." There were, of course, plenty of precedents for that, going back to antiquity: melancholia had always been associated with a variety of mental illnesses. What was new was the restriction of melancholia *exclusively* to the ambit of mental illnesses, thus limiting its meaning as well. In Kraepelin's clinical taxonomy, which was supposed to eliminate the inaccuracies associated with unitary psychosis, it was the use of "depression" and "melancholia" that became inaccurate. In 1896, Kraepelin finally dropped the concept of melancholia altogether from his taxonomy and used the word "depression" instead (see Edward Shorter, *A Clinical Dictionary of Psychiatry*, 82). A few years later (in 1904), at a meeting of the New York Neurological Society, the Swiss-born American psychiatrist Adolf Meyer recommended that no further use be made of the term "melancholia": "[It] implied a knowledge of something that we did not possess and which had been employed in different specific by different writers. If, instead of melancholia, we applied the term depression to the whole class, it would designate in an unassuming way what was meant by the common use of the term melancholia" (quoted in Michael Alan Taylor and Max Fink, *Melancholia*, 6).[3] Yet depression

---

3. In his work *Darkness Visible* (1990), the American writer William Styron was loath to have his own depression confined within the conceptual framework of an illness called "depression":

When I was first aware that I had been laid low by the disease, I felt a need, among other things, to register a strong protest against the word "depression."

Depression, as most people know, used to be termed "melancholia," a word which crops up more than once in Chaucer, who in his usage seemed to be more aware of its pathological nuances.

"Melancholia" would still appear to be a far more apt and evocative word for the blackest forms of the disorder, but it was usurped by a noun with a bland tonality and lacking any magisterial presence, used indifferently to describe an economic decline, a true wimp of a word for such a major illness. It may be that the scientist generally held responsible for its currency in modern times, a

is not a uniform concept either: in *bipolar* depression (or "*dépression circulaire*"), the symptoms of "melancholia" alternate with those of "mania," whereas in *unipolar* or *recurrent* depression, the illness is characterized by the alternation of episodes of "melancholia" and episodes of "health only." According to recent observations, psychotic symptoms (delusions of grandeur or persecution, catatonic episodes, acoustic hallucinations, underlying schizophrenic symptoms) are present in 20–25 percent of patients in depressive periods, though American researchers reckon that nowadays the majority of depressions are not psychotic but neurotic in origin. Thanks to that, depression has become the most frequently diagnosed illness. It appears that melancholia is being finally expelled from the psychiatric vocabulary: the term, which had featured previously, was removed from the third (1987) edition of the *Diagnostic and Statistical Manual of Mental Disorders* (*DSM-III*—see Taylor and Fink, *Melancholia*) as "a term from the past," though in the fourth edition (1994) it reappeared as one of the subspecies of depression ("major depression with melancholia"). In the latest revision of the *International Statistical Classification of Diseases and Related Health Problems* (2012), melancholia crops up in the main category Mental, Behavioral and Neurodevelopmental Disorders, in the subgroup Major Depressive Disorder, Single Episode, within the group Other Depressive Episodes, partly as a self-standing entity (ICD-10-CM F32.9) and partly as "Involu-

Johns Hopkins Medical School faculty member justly venerated—the Swiss-born psychiatrist Adolf Meyer—had a tin ear for the finer rhythms of English and therefore was unaware of the semantic damage he had inflicted by offering "depression" as a descriptive noun for such a dreadful and raging disease. Nonetheless, for over seventy-five years the word has slithered innocuously through the language like a slug, leaving little trace of its malevolence and preventing, by its very insipidity, a general awareness of the horrible intensity of the disease when out of control.

(36–37)

tional Melancholia (Recurrent Episodes) (Single Episode)" (F32.8). "Psychosis" (codes 290–299) mentions "involutional melancholia" as a depressive subtype of "major depressive disorders" (code 296.2).

Mention of melancholia creates palpable unease; if psychiatry were to seek to return to the concept its due rights (V. E. von Gebsattel, L. Binswanger, E. Straus, H. Tellenbach), the closed system would be spectacularly thrown wide open. It is no accident that it was first and foremost the so-called Daseinsanalysis school of philosophical anthropologists that attempted to take into account the insoluble problem of melancholia. This approach has a prominent place within dynamic psychiatry as Daseinsanalysis; true to the old notion of melancholia, it does not strive for an instrumental classification of a psychophysiological condition, pegging it like an object, but aims instead at understanding the horizon unfolding within a given condition. A separation of melancholia and depression occurs here, too, but on the basis that depression is *describable* by its symptoms, while melancholia is at best only *interpretable*. According to this school of thought, only depression has a symptomatology, whereas melancholia is a peculiar state of being that is not apprehensible as a certain cluster of symptoms—just as no interpretation of being can be entirely set down, spelled out, or treated as an object.[4]

The Daseinsanalytical approach touched the weak point of mainstream psychiatry, and in doing so—as its critics emphasize—it

---

4. The Daseinsanalysis school, however, was also obliged to make use of the same language as other schools of thought, and if those who endure their condition as a burden are looked at from a medical standpoint, then despite the use of the word "melancholia," it is a matter of depression. That is just as much a trap of language as that of the present setup of the world: in talking about melancholia, it is not possible to be unambiguous. In this case, the ambiguity is not proof of the richness of the topic, but of its not having been clarified. A good example of this is the attempt by Julia Kristeva, who wanted to deepen the meaning of melancholia by introducing the category "*melancolio-dépressif*," though in reality she only concealed the obscurity of its relationship to depression.

has laid the groundwork for its own collapse as a closed psychiatric discipline. For if melancholics (or persons suffering from any psychiatric illness) construct for themselves an interpretation of existence that is just as valid and "homely" for them as that of persons who are free from similar conditions, then it becomes questionable whether a sharp boundary can be drawn between illness and health. Usually, a person whose notions do not conform with reality is held to be mentally ill—but that presupposes a view that is not at all typical of the world in modern times: that reality is unified, and its unity is guaranteed by an external power independent of us. For the Middle Ages, the boundary between madness and soundness of mind was obvious: doubt or belief in the divine order—*ordo Dei*—provided the proof. The evolution of the concept of melancholia in the modern age went hand in hand with the disintegration of the divine order: the closed uniform order and the sense of definitiveness backing up the notion of reality vanished, and the fragmentation, the "terrible dissolution" (Nietzsche) of the modern age altered the notion of reality itself: reality cannot be apprehended as an object. Facts become facts only in relation to humans; reality is not something existing, irrespective of us, to which we relate externally. The word "reality" is metaphorical to begin with. The physical existence of man is no more real than his intellectual existence; indeed, only with major qualifications can one make a distinction between the two. For the scientific mind, which contrasts subject with object, reality is identical with so-called objectivity, the world on the far side of the individual, and it fails to notice that what I perceive of the external world is picked up by my "soul" and "body"; or in other words, my "mental" state (for example, whether I am melancholic, in love, or, perhaps, perverse) is just as much "flesh-and-blood" reality as a stone lying by my foot. Ludwig Klages points out, with good reason, that a physicist who insists that the ultimate criterion of reality is its measurability is the victim of a delusion: his reality is measurable only because he has already filled it with concepts that are alien to reality (Klages, *Der Geist als Wider-*

sacher der Seele, 711). The common conception is that reality is what starts beyond me; yet anyone who doubts that (and, let us add, is melancholic) will sense that this idea of reality deprives consciousness and, along with it, a person's entire being of its validity. According to Aristotle, potentiality and actuality are two sides of the same reality: there is no actuality without further inherent possibilities, and there is no potentiality that is not in some way actual. The scientific mentality of the modern era has given up on searching for humanity's horizons; sensing that such research would open the way to ultimate inscrutability, it has narrowed reality down to a closed factuality. By the nineteenth century, the living cosmos had been disfigured into dead raw material. Paradoxically, the more lifeless and subservient it became, the more elusive and incomprehensible it turned out to be. No wonder—in the meantime, man forgot about his own "reality," the cosmic nature of his own being, and as a result the ground slipped ever further from under his feet. At least since the emergence of psychoanalysis, we know that so-called neutral reality is a pure fiction, and this was reinforced later by Wittgenstein, Roland Barthes, structuralism, and Jean Baudrillard, who has employed the category of the simulacrum to show that in some cases the representation of reality is more real than reality, as a result of which the real is not what is reproducible, but what has already been reproduced.

The ultimate unresolvability of the clinical classification of mental illnesses is a signal that even the most closed so-called actuality is unstable in principle because only a human being, living in uncertainty as he or she must, the *Homo insipiens* of Ortega y Gasset, can say about something that "this is a fact." Sooner or later, even facts deemed to be closed will reopen, and then one will be compelled to announce: what we hitherto believed to be fact is fiction, and what hitherto was fiction turns out to be fact. Dynamic psychiatry, and especially the Daseinsanalytical approach, considers this permanent openness to be definitive, and it seeks to understand mental illnesses on this basis: we can witness how philosophy stabs psychiatry in the back. In his own slightly scholastic, slightly fairy-tale-like, yet thought-provoking style, Schelling wrote the following about madness:

> What is the human mind? Answer: an existing entity that came into being out of the nonexistent, as intelligence came into being out of an absence of intelligence. So what is the basis of the human mind? . . . Answer: an absence of intelligence, and as the human mind relates to the soul, too, as a nonexistent entity, thus at one and the same time it relates as an unintelligent entity. The deepest essence of the human mind, therefore, if one looks at it separate from the soul, and thus from God, is madness. . . . What is called intelligence, insofar as it is a matter of genuine, living, and active intelligence, is, in point of fact, nothing other than madness hobbled by rules. . . . Those people in whom there is no madness possess a vacant, unproductive intelligence.

(quoted in Leibbrand, *Heilkunde*, 455–56)

If one does not interpret the words literally, then one will notice the following truth lying behind it: the human mind is not a divine, un-attached substance, and therefore it cannot be studied as an independent object (or consciousness). Madness is not something mysterious that suddenly envelops the mind from an unknown direction, but is a result of the *interaction*, the ultimate identity, of mind and being. (For Schelling, madness was very natural, by no means something fearful to be condemned.) Madness is not an "objective fact," irrespective of judgment (it does not fall onto one's head like a flowerpot), but a particular interpretation of existence that, in the end, strikes one as madness (or a sane judgment) in a dynamic, moving, constantly changing net of innumerable interpretations of existence in a given period. Naturally, this does not mean that madness and sanity are relative terms. There is unambiguous insanity as illness, and there is unambiguous sanity as health. Uncertainty of judgment relates, on the one hand, to their relationship, and, on the other hand, to intermediate states between the two. A London psychiatrist by the name of John Conolly, who in the middle of the nineteenth century did a lot for the humane treatment of the mentally ill, wrote in 1830 that very often individuals were locked up in lunatic asylums out of ignorance and failure to understand them. This could have disastrous consequences: "A man of undisturbed understanding, suddenly surprised by the servants of a lunatic asylum, with handcuffs ready, and a coach waiting to carry him off, would infallibly exhibit some signs, easily construed into proofs that he was 'not right in his head,'" adding: "Once confined, the very confinement is admitted as the strongest of all proofs," and visitors would tend to project (to use a modern term) certain symptoms of madness onto the persons in question—symptoms that in reality were nonexistent (Conolly, *An Inquiry Concerning the Indications of Insanity,* 4–5). Besides, he adds, those who are locked up among real madmen can easily lose their minds. And a hundred years later, at a time when systematic clinical psychiatry was gaining ground and the scientific way of looking at things was developing explosively, Freud wrote at the end of his career: "We have seen that it is not scientifically feasible to draw a line of demarcation between what is psychically normal and abnormal; so that that distinction, in spite of its practical importance, possesses only a conventional value" (*An Outline of Psycho-Analysis,* 195), and when he asserted that "a knowledge of the neurotic illnesses of individuals has been of good service in assisting understanding of the great social institutions," then, without having traversed that path himself, he outlined the methodological horizon for dynamic psychiatry: madness is not just a cluster of physical or psychological symptoms but also an autonomous interpretation of existence.

It is understandable that the scientific frame of mind is not inclined to make that view completely its own—not only in connection with diseases in general, but even regarding mental illness. Melancholia has always been accompanied by somatic symptoms (usually described similarly from Hippocrates through Diocles of Carystus to the present day), but unlike the medical science of antiquity, the Hellenistic period, or the Renaissance, the so-called nosological trend of modern psychiatry, oriented to brain pathology—in compliance with an interpretation of reality that is mesmerized by facts—perceives symptoms primarily as symptoms of the body, in a strictly defined sense, that is, it tries to derive the disease from the body itself, not from the broader context, the study of which characterized old-style medicine and is not alien to modern dynamic psychiatry, the Daseinsanalytical school, or psychosomatic medicine. In the first half of the eighteenth century, Friedrich Hoffmann held the view that melancholia was the result of a physiological change in the brain, a kind of *status frictus*, whereas Anne-Charles Lorry, in the latter half of that century, attributed it to a change in the nerve fibers. In 1804, the French physiologist Pierre Cabanis posed the poetic question: "How could [physicians] soothe that ruffled mind, that soul consumed by persistent melancholia, if they did not take notice of the organic changes that may cause such mood disorders, and to which functional disturbances they are connected?" (Cabanis, *Coup-d'oeil sur les révolutions et sur la réforme de la medicine*, 346). By the mid-nineteenth century, Wilhelm Griesinger was claiming that every mental illness was a disease of the brain. But if one takes into consideration that he reached this conclusion *before* the explosive development of research into the nervous system, the suspicion arises that it was just a matter of *faith*, of a supposition that empirical science has been unable to prove satisfactorily down to the present day in the case of endogenous psychoses, the commonest species of psychiatric diseases. That same faith was also given expression by Kraepelin and Carl Wernicke, and Hugo Münsterberg articulated it in 1891 almost as a moral dictum for medical science: "Breaking down the totality formed by the contents of consciousness into its elements, in establishing combinatory laws and particular combinations of these elements, and in seeking empirically, for each elementary psychic datum, its concomitant physical stimulus; in order indirectly to explain by the causally intelligible coexistence and succession of these physiological excitations, the combinatory laws and the combinations of different psychic data which are not explainable from a purely psychological point of view" (quoted in Wilhelm Dilthey, *Ideas concerning a Descriptive and Analytic Psychology,* 49). But medical science has failed so far to find an unequivocal, demonstrable correspondence between changes in the central nervous system, the mind, and the soul, nor has it managed to reveal the relationship between physical and psychological processes. The supposition that with the assistance of the electroencephalograph it would be possible to get nearer to the riddle of so-called endogenous psychoses, which may be independent of external causes, has not been fulfilled; though certain mental abilities or changes can be localized, others (mania, depression, illusions) cannot be. And even if the ability to concentrate, the loss of memory, or disorientation could be localized, the switchover of the body "into the mind" would remain a mystery. Certain physical lesions and changes can be coupled with the melancholic-depressive symptom cluster,[5] although no evaluable pathomorphological changes are detectable. A mutual change in body and soul is not regular and absolute: this is a myth that somatic-oriented medical science dreamed up in order to conceal the ultimately unexplained and inexplicable nature of the relationship of body and soul. After all, it can be in God's power only to make definitive pronouncements about human existence, which is surpassing itself time and time again. The admission of such inexplicability would radically undermine not just nosologically aligned medical science, but also the mentality of the cur-

---

5. Tumors of the third cerebral ventricle damage the rear area of the corpus mamillare at the back of the hypothalamus, and can provoke depression; endocrine conditions such as hyperthyroidism, castration, menopause, Addison's disease, Simmonds' disease, and poisoning by certain chemicals (carbon monoxide, alcohol, arsenic, mercury) are likewise accompanied by melancholic mental symptoms.

rent time, existing as it does under the spell of a practical universe. The instrumental mind seeks instant answers, but in spite of medicine having a degree of efficacy, it is unable to answer the most fundamental question, namely, what kinds of psychophysiological processes take place within an organism under the influence of drugs. It is a self-contradiction of nosologically directed psychiatry, which is exclusively concerned with pathological forms, that it *believes in matter* in roughly the same way that medieval medicine *believed* that illness was the *devil's* work. Faith in matter, especially since it has not managed to clarify satisfactorily the problem of the materiality and intellectuality of the human body, is a sort of tacit religiosity, a *diabolic theology*, and it is related to the modern undertaking of pushing God off his throne. This undertaking regards existence as an ultimately decipherable chain of practical connections, and believes that it is able to explain all the riddles in the world without any reference to God. Tamás Nyíri[6] indicated the self-contradictoriness of this way of thinking, which could be characterized as a perverse theology:

> Those who assert that all that exists is material, which in their opinion is the sole reality, ought to be asked what they mean by material. If the objects recognized by the senses are called material, then they are not talking about material but about various individual experiences, and they do not offer an answer to the question as to why they are being collected into a unified concept. Those, however, who assert that material is everything that exists objectively are doing nothing more than use the word "material" to designate whatever exists. Although that assertion is not false, it is nevertheless a nuisance, because it smuggles back the assumption that only what is perceptible to the senses exists.
>
> (Nyíri, *Antropológiai vázlatok*, 127)

---

6. Tamás Nyíri (1920–1994) was a Hungarian Roman Catholic priest, theologian, and philosopher.

Hegel called an unconditional trust in the material the "science of captivity" because it prevented people from discovering themselves in what is not themselves and so prevented them from admitting that mind and matter are inseparable from each other, whether it is a matter of the universe or the human body as a microcosm. It was no accident that classical German philosophy, with its idealism and trust in both human freedom and the omnipotence of the mind, strongly influenced those physicians who were looking for a way out of the internal contradictions of somatocentric medicine. Romantic psychotherapy and medical science[7] upheld the old conviction that diseases of the brain and mood disorders were not explicable only physically, and by considering environmental and cultural factors, they made psychotherapy dynamic and placed the mental disorders in a wider context. By doing so they not only preserved the pathos of freedom, characteristic of classic idealism, but also gave voice to the idea that human beings could not be divided into body and psyche but instead formed a body-psyche unit, the distinguishing mark of which was the ability to create a culture. The body-psyche-culture triad formed a context in which each member determined the others. Thereby the scope of diseases was broadened, and the diseases themselves were differentiated: in the latter half of the nineteenth century, Paul Möbius distinguished endogenous and exogenous diseases on the basis of whether the mental disorder had an external precipitating fact. So-called endogenous psychoses are those cases in which one does not know the precipitating and sustaining somatic processes and alterations, and the illnesses are not comprehensible from the life history or personality of the affected patient. In the end, every element in the body-psyche-culture aggregate acts on everything—and it appears that the broader the horizon in which an illness is set, the

---

7. Johann Christian August Heinroth, Carl Gustav Carus, and J. G. Langer-mann—the last, for all that he was a physician, had as an instructor the philosopher Johann Gottlieb Fichte and for a while was a teacher of Novalis.

less unequivocal the effects, and the greater the chance of endogeny holding good. If I declare of melancholics that, in the last analysis, the surrounding culture is responsible for their condition, what I have said is true (after all, animals cannot be melancholic),[8] but from the standpoint of medical practice, the statement carries little weight. If, on the other hand, I searched for exogenous traumata, I might be on the right path, but I would be deferring the etiological understanding of the disease. The essence of endogenicity, which the neurologist Hubert Tellenbach called "endon," spans and determines the entire personality. It is not identical with either the psychic or the somatic structure, but contains both, and it follows changes of the environment, too. The endon forms a complex network, influencing the overall personality and its dynamics at the molecular and cellular levels: gender, physique, and the individual forms of behavior are just as dependent on it as are abilities, character, and intelligence—that is, the endon is what enlivens the personality and makes it exclusive and unique. The relationship between endogenicity and exogenicity is cultural, and endon and world are imaginable only in close symbiosis. For that reason, Tellenbach sensibly supplemented the word "endogenous" with a new term: in writing about melancholia, he refers to its being an *endocosmogenic* illness. In other words, in contrast to the somatic approach, he links the body's inner state and the general state of culture: "We consider as being endogenous what steps forward as *a unit of the basic temperament in every occurrence of life. The endon is, in origin, the physis which evolves in endogenous phenomena, slumbering in them,* and by *physis* ('nature') we mean the basic imprint prior to the formation of the personality, its structure, so to say. . . . The way of being of the endon is not only *transsubjective,* and consequently *metaphysiologic,* but at the same time *transobjective,* and consequently *metasomatologic,* but the endon

---

8. According to medieval concepts, they could: one has to think only of Agrippa von Nettesheim's list.

materializes both psychically and physically" (Tellenbach, *Melancholy: History of the Problem, Endogeneity, Typology, Pathogenesis, Clinical Considerations*, 41; emphasis in the original). This bold train of thought, which puts even philosophers to shame, was the firm conviction of a practicing neurologist and psychiatrist. It is hard not to discover the medico-philosophical tradition behind this thinking, yet nosocentric medicine is just as uncomprehending of its medical aspects as positivism is of its philosophical considerations.

The interpretation of melancholia as endocosmogenic depression expands the concept so greatly that strictly objectivist medicine might justly feel that the ground has been cut from under its feet. It seems as though some kind of deadly relativism were not only obliterating the difference between physical and mental diseases, but also making the relation between illness and health relative. As far as melancholia is concerned, this might lead to a radical revision of the medical diagnosis of the last two centuries: is it possible, after all, that melancholia cannot be defined as an illness? To be able to consider this, it is necessary to make a few remarks about the role of the body-psyche problem in diseases. On the one hand, the physical consequences of the soul's functioning, or the influences that the physical state exercises on the soul, are undeniable; on the other hand, none of the sciences dealing with man is able to clarify satisfactorily what is actually taking place. I decide to do something, then get on my feet and carry it out—in all likelihood, it is the ultimate riddle of existence how a *thought* assumes the form of *will* and *physical action.* Science talks about interaction (that is, the relation of body and soul is causal) or parallelism (that is, body and mind behave in compliance with each other), but that does not take us a whit nearer to the solution of the problem, and in any case both those suppositions are unprovable. The inadequacy of language, and of thought adhering to language, arouses the suspicion that perhaps the way this question is posed is wrong: perhaps the reason we cannot find a solution to the problem is that we are posing a false problem. In all probability, the distinction between the *words* "body" and "soul" is one of the most fatal misunderstandings of our culture, and on the basis of what we have exposed so far, our conviction is that melancholia is precisely that gap (lesion) in human culture pointing to the fact that it is a matter of a misunderstanding, but an *inevitable* misunderstanding. The history of culture is a series of fatal misunderstandings: this melancholic assertion can be translated into our own language thus: the "essence" of man is that he is continually surpassing himself, and since he is unclosable, his essence is conceptually and objectively indefinable.

The ultimate indefinability of the relationship between body and soul points to this negativity, but even thinking about this relationship is a warning of the ultimate negativity: one may talk about body and soul, but this is obviously incorrect. Every moment of our lives proves that these apparently ultimate units are manifestations of an unknown, maelstrom-like chasm, of the foundations of our being, at which, for want of anything better, one is able only to hint. "Body" and "psyche" are mere *words*, references, and they have an allegorical role: whichever one speaks about, in reality one is not talking about that but about something else, in spite of one's intentions and convictions. One cannot overcome the inadequacy of language: the words themselves cannot be made more precise; at most, the relationship we have developed toward them can be modified and shaped. It seems that it was only ever possible to stammer about the body-soul problem: at all events, Aristotle's thoughts are like such stammering, though this stammering is precisely a sign that in fact he does not wish to make statements about the soul and the body but about the inaccessible human essence. "The soul is, in a way, all existing things," he says (*On the Soul*, 431b), and elsewhere: "The soul must be . . . capable of receiving the form of an object" (ibid.). Or: "All natural bodies are organs of the soul" (τῆς ψυχῆς ὄργανα) (ibid., 415b); "the soul is the first grade of actuality [ἐντελέχεια] of a natural body having life potentially in it" (ibid., 412b). The mind and soul, therefore, are simultaneously body and extracorporeality, whereas the body is soul and mind, or rather a reality that surpasses both. Both body and soul, then, are manifestations of an existing entity that points to itself and beyond itself at one and the same time.[9] (The aim of ἐντελέχεια—a compound of ἐντελής (full) and ἔχειν (to be in a certain condition)—is in itself; whereas ὄργανον is an organ, an instrument, so its goal is outside itself—it relates to something.) Only man is such an existing entity. Man is identical with himself and yet has a meaning beyond himself; he is simultaneously creature and creator (naturally, not in the sense that his body is creature and his soul creator); he is master of himself, but is also at the mercy of existence; he has very little command over that which can serve as the main proof of his existence: his life; and he is the one who has a human body and soul. In that sense, the definitive difference between human and animal bodies is not anatomical but existential. (One has in mind, for example, the upright stance, which is not primarily an anatomical but an existential property of man.) Man's eyesight is dimmer than that of a bird, yet he sees more; he runs slower than a cheetah, and yet he can call a greater territory his own. The secret of the human body is precisely that it lives in a human—that is, an intellectual—manner, and for that reason one can speak of it only as an *existential and functional unit.* If the body is examined and regarded purely as an anatomically definable set of morphological units, then it is not man that one is examining but a hunk of flesh (a pathologist, who analyzes humans after their death, is examining a body differing only anatomically from an animal's body); if only the soul is interpreted, on the other hand, then man is replaced by an angel, and thereby he is lifted out of the world to which he owes his existence as man.[10]

---

9. "Suppose that the eye were an animal—sight would have been its soul," Aristotle writes (*On the Soul,* 412b), and St. Thomas Aquinas writes, "If, therefore, the soul were not a body, it could not have knowledge of corporeal things" (*Summa theologica,* 75. q. 1. a. 1).

10. For Homer, the body (σῶμα) meant a corpse, whereas the soul (ψυχή) meant

Medicine of bygone times was always clear about the insepa-
rability (and indistinguishability) of body and soul; it appears that
a radical turning point was reached only when Descartes sharply
separated the provinces of *res cogitans* and *res extensa*. In antiquity,
the Hippocratic, empirical way of looking at things started from the
symptoms of the body to draw conclusions about the condition of
the soul (both the Greek word πνεῦμα and the Latin *spiritus* conjure up the bodily process of inspiration) and hence about a failure
of the cosmos as a whole: the Empedoclean philosophical and medical view of things descended from an examination of the general
laws of existence to an empirical understanding of diseases (cathar-
sis related to both body and soul—*KAΘAPMOI,* "Purifications," the
title that Empedocles gave to his medical work, signals that physical
nature and the intellectual world have identical dimensions). The
difference between body and soul was thus negligible in comparison
with the unity of the cosmos as a whole. This led to the notion of the
microcosm, which became crucial for medical science: to be healthy
meant to live in harmony (συμπαθέω) with the cosmos, and therefore
the nature of disease could not be unraveled solely on a physical basis.
Although the notion of a microcosm, which is also of decisive significance for today's psychosomatically oriented medicine, reflected
the effort to unify an original duality (only after there was a rift between human and natural law—νόμος and φύσις—did it become
possible to pose the problem conceptually; it was in the Hellenistic
period that the previously uniform view of being was conceptually
reconstructed), the metaphor pointed not only to a heroic skepti-

---

the soul of a dead person: body and soul could be imagined as a duality only after
death. According to Plato, though body and soul could be distinguished, both had
their own nature (φύσις), which was akin to the nature of the cosmos: both were nurtured from a shared root. Nor does one hear anything about an incorporeal soul in
the New Testament, only about a mind (πνεῦμα): the body is an organism animated
by the psyche, and the psyche is individual life itself.

cism concerning the ultimate insolubility of human existence, but also to the possibility of gaining a true understanding of disease. Reviving the antique notion, Paracelsus wrote that man is a small world with everything in him that the world at large contains, healthy and unhealthy alike (Lepenies, *Melancholie und Gesellschaft*, 172); and writing about melancholia, Robert Burton asserted: man is the most excellent and noble creature in the world because he is a "Microcosmus, a little world, a model of the world, sovereign lord of the earth, viceroy of the world" (Burton, *Anatomy*, partition 1, sec. 1, member 1, subsec. 1, 130); Thomas Browne, likewise a physician, one of the most melancholic minds of all time, laid down: "The world that I regard is my self; it is the Microcosm of my own frame that I cast mine eye on; for the other, I use it but like my Globe, and turn it round sometimes for my recreation" (*Religio Medici*, pt. 2, sec. 11). The Romantics tried to heal the Cartesian rift of body and soul (which would later be profoundly suitable for the bourgeois mentality),[11] and Romantic psychology, after laying a relatively brief theoretical groundwork, assumed the most intimate kinship between mood and body as a matter of common knowledge (Franz von Baader, Carl Gustav Carus). The conviction slowly grew that man did not get sick because he had a body *or* a soul, but because he had a body *and* a soul, or in other words, because he was born a man.

According to the radical school of psychosomatically minded medical science, it is not just specific diseases that are psychosomatic, *every* illness is psychosomatic in origin: there is no illness that could not be set in a wider context and investigated as a manifestation of the patient's anamnesis. The role of psychological (or, more correctly, anamnestic) causes is obvious in gastrointestinal disorders (gastric and duodenal ulcers, inappetence, vomiting, etc.), asthma, high blood

---

11. See Friedrich Schlegel: "Man is a microcosm: the characteristics of the universe are part of the characteristics of the individual" (*Kritische Ausgabe seiner Werke*, 18:229).

pressure, angina pectoris, hypo- and hyperthyroidism, diabetes mel-
litus, migraine, various dermatological diseases and menstrual disturbances, but extensive research is under way with respect to the
psychosomatic origin of all physical alterations, including cancer.
(Galen noticed that melancholic women developed breast cancer
a good deal more frequently than sanguineous ones, and in recent
times American researchers have reached the conclusion, based on
a comprehensive sample, that certain types of cancer—lymphomas,
leukemia, uterine cancer—are preceded by severe depression stemming from an insoluble situation in life: as a component of stress,
depression promotes hormonal changes in the immune system, and
cancer is related to, among other things, precisely such disturbances
of immune reactions.) The possibility of disintegration is inherent in
the organism (without this there could be no life), and according to
the psychosomatic approach, the environment and the life condition of the individual are able to induce, speed up, or slow down this
inevitable destruction: letting go of oneself psychologically leads to
losing all lines of defense, including the defensive role of the body.
As a result, the person in question can shortly come under attack by
a serious organic disease. (This may account for the "prophetic" capabilities of many physicians: they can foretell imminent death in the
case of certain diseases when no major organic changes are demonstrable; the patient is ready to accept death, which indeed, wasting no
time, arrives in some previously unsuspected form.) Physical symptoms and vital complaints accompanied by melancholia (a sensation
of pressure in the chest and the hypochondrium—so-called *globus
melancholicus*) can likewise be traced back to a change in the relationship of the individual to the world: *not only the mind, temperament, and mood, but the body as well plays a part in interpreting
existence.* One cannot be understood from objectively dismantled
elements of one's body or one's soul, but only from the position one
occupies in the world and in one's environment. One's view of life
and physical state cannot be picked out causally except from one's

situation, and one's organism cannot be described as a morphological but only as a functional unit. Neurologists (Gustav Ricker, Victor von Weizsäcker) showed that many neurological phenomena were incomprehensible on the basis of the morphological "objectivism" of the Cartesian concept of the body, and it was possible to explain them only if the researcher, instead of regarding the nervous system as a closed, object-like unit, accepted that objectivity contains cognitive subjectivity from the outset, and that biological acts are not independent, autonomous events taking place in space and time, but interactions in the course of which space and time are created and the functioning of the nervous system becomes *human*ized. At the bottom of this recognition lay a radically new picture of human beings (although that picture was not at all as alien to more ancient cultures as to our own): human illnesses can be interpreted only as part of a context that in principle assumes a general openness. (Just as you ought not to attempt to cure the eyes without the head, or the head without the body, so you ought not attempt to cure the body without the soul, writes Plato in *Charmides* [see 156b–c].) The cause (etiology) and course of development (pathogenesis) of a disease are not congruent: in the case of numerous diseases, we know why they came into being without knowing what the cause is. All kinds of things are known about allergies, for example, but one cannot say why X became ill at ten years of age, Y at the age of twenty, and Z not at all. Nosocentric medicine is usually able to supply explanations for cases in which man is the same as an animal (animal experiments), but it barely concerns itself with etiology. As was remarked by Arthur Jores, a German gastroenterologist who became one of the founders of psychosomatic medicine, in an age of technical civilization, the causes of most diseases are still as unknown as in the era of magic; only the spirits have vanished, and their place has been taken by impersonal (yet still unknown) forces. The nosological approach, since it starts out from the duality of body and soul (in other words, it overlooks all other factors in its practice), implicitly suggests that although we all possess unique, diverse minds, our bodies are never-theless uniform. Up to a certain point, all bodies are indeed similar; yet individuality is not a function of the mind alone: paradoxically, in police records people are distinguished on the basis not of their minds but of their bodies (fingerprints, descriptions)—that is, the body as an existential-functional unit, the vehicle of the endon, is the incarnation of individuality. It is not just the soul but also bodies that are different for everybody, and as existential-functional units, two bodies, like two souls, are merely reminiscent of, but not identical to, each other. If this is the case, the diagnosis and the examination of a patient naturally call for much greater prudence (and more money) than is currently used: it is necessary to establish what tangible disease a specific body is suffering from. Making the disease tangible means elucidating it in every respect, which entails no longer generalizing it. If no two humans are identical, then neither can be diseases; they can, at most, only resemble each other. A precondition of the appre-hension of a disease is a functional-existential interpretation of the human body: in the end, what has come about is a disturbance of the unique life history of an irreplaceable person. His illness is not my illness, but exclusively his, so it is his personal life that has to recover. In connection with brain physiology, Erwin Straus, a representative of the Daseinsanalysis school of psychiatry, wrote:

> I have to understand man, the subject of my observation, as an observing subject. Just as my brain renders me capable of seeing, observing, and describing, so does his brain render my fellow human being capable of similar achievements. Behavior and ex-perience are always my behavior and my experience, or yours or his, and that is how they come into relationship with my brain, or yours or his. Brain physiology does not much concern itself with this basic relationship. It takes no notice of the possessive relation: without its giving account of it even to itself, *a* or *the* brain substitutes for my brain, yours, and his. Physiology has no

choice. Reference to the possessive relation, however, cannot be brushed aside as a sentimental requirement. It is important that we realize and recognize that that substitution entails an unavoidable limitation of the research results. For by the elimination of the possessive relation, we distort phenomena, we restrict the scope of problems, we tacitly anticipate a theoretical decision. If one substitutes my brain, yours or his for *the* brain, then we do not view the brain at all as the organ of a living being but as the control mechanism of a moving body. The observer executes a physical reduction in the world accessible to him through scientific experience: in this physical system, the brain is postulated to be a bodily formation on which other bodies have an action, and which can act back on those. In the end, the observer is surprised to notice that processes in the brain are occasionally accompanied by conscious processes. . . . If it is justified to substitute my brain, or yours or his, for *the* brain, then the two brains ought in principle to be exchangeable, independent of their nature, structure, and life story.

(Straus, *Psychologie der menschlichen Welt*, 381–82)

There is a discernible skepticism about systems made up of closed, impersonal units of disease. The gradual narrowing of the concept of melancholia to depression in medical science could not prevent the survival of the notion of melancholy in its everyday sense, yet as a result of the rift, melancholia, both medically and as ordinarily understood, lost its earlier comprehensive, existential-functional signification. The scientific worldview could not permit notions to have the degree of flexibility that had characterized the description of melancholia up until the seventeenth and eighteenth centuries; it had to be narrowed down in order to be able to fit in. It speaks volumes that although for millennia medicine avowed that every illness was an unparalleled, unique phenomenon, from the seventeenth and eighteenth centuries it began to talk about general, impersonal sicknesses (in London, in the seventeenth century, diseases were being studied statistically), and in the eighteenth century the first big systems and classifications of diseases saw the light of day (Sauvages,[12] Cullen), from whence an unbroken path leads to the current WHO International Classification of Diseases, which is reviewed periodically. Such systems were always closed and yet were never shut down: every revision necessitated fresh categorizations. In the demand for a closed system, it is not hard to discern the objectified, alienated medical view of man, along with the conviction of rationalism in the modern age that man can be "described" within the frame of a system. Every classification of diseases as a method tacitly assumes that it is sufficient to highlight a few (often arbitrarily selected) symptoms, compare these with the symptoms of other psychological and physical conditions, set up reference systems and units of sickness, and interpret all of it as a system. Accordingly, it should be possible to describe, work out, and cure all diseases, for if the system is closed, then there must be a finite number of diseases (as among the ancient Persians, according to whom there existed 99,999 diseases). A system of diseases is fallible, however. It follows from the historicity of human beings and their continuous transcendence of themselves that *diseases are also existential and transcendental manifestations:* human beings develop their own diseases, unlike any other living being, from their own life situations, and they render those diseases not only historically determined (insofar as diseases are eliminated over time and hitherto-unknown ones spring up), but also existentially determined. Illness is a function of my unique, irreplaceable life history, and my own being (not just my will and consciousness, but my existential-functional mode of living) is responsible for what illnesses I have a share in or when I fall ill. The classification of diseases (that is, their

---

12. His treatise *Nosologia methodica systema morborum* of 1763 listed ten major classes of disease, further broken down into numerous orders, 295 genera, and 2,400 individual diseases.

instrumental interpretation) is not only incapable of defining them as a form of being, but can also lead to a dead end in regard to defining man. This is particularly noticeable in the case of classifying mental diseases, where the majority of present-day textbooks—indeed, the practice of psychiatry itself—try to satisfy standards set by Kraepelin's nineteenth-century taxonomy. The German psychiatrist, who had the professed goal of accomplishing a Linnaean-type "perfect scheme" (according to Linnaeus, there were as many species as God created at the beginning of the world), held three points of view to be fruitful: categorization on an anatomo-pathological basis (which, as he commented in 1896, was not yet possible); classification according to origin (this, he admitted, was likewise only at the start); and finally, arrangement on the basis of clinical symptoms. In ideal cases, those three points of view would match seamlessly, which is to say that diseases stemming from similar causes would be found to have the same symptoms, and the same changes would be observed in the cadavers (Kraepelin, *Lehrbuch der Psychiatrie*, 314).[13] The use of the conditional mode is telling: Kraepelin fixed his eyes on an ideal future in which every case would be closed and shut; framing the statement in the future tense refers to a *utopia* that lurks at the bottom of all systematizations. However, since history comes to an end in a utopia, living people have no business in it: the fact that Kraepelin should regard the anatomo-pathological examination of *cadavers* as an appropriate method for defining mental diseases showed that living man was left out of the classification of diseases, or rather that what was taken into account regarding man was no longer human.[14] The

---

13. Kraepelin was not only a major figure as a classifier but also a passionate botanist. In his old age, he gave up the principle of classification and concerned himself with the "construction" of individual diseases, accepting also the methods of empathy and sympathy.

14. Unlike Griesinger and Wernicke, who put forward strictly somatic explanations, the German neurologist and psychiatrist Karl Kleist was of the opinion as

human factor is unclassifiable: man cannot produce a system whose basis is not an open-ended understanding of being: every basis is supposed to conceal the gap, which, as it opens man's eyes to his own nullity, defenselessness, and unfathomability, manifests as bottomlessness. Self-knowledge too is an open-ended system; its infinity is not the objective infinity of science but that of man looking for his own horizons—and the infinity of the human horizon is a warning of its ungraspability. Melancholia, since it overtly gives voice to failure and hopelessness, is necessarily ousted from the system of mental diseases (or is constricted)—it is a suspicious phenomenon inhibiting the supposedly rational arrangements of life, and therefore ought to be disenfranchised. Melancholia smuggles chaos into man's well-ordered life; and yet there is no man without chaos, says Nietzsche. Chaos cannot be locked within borders, since it permeates the whole of existence. It has no definite place and cannot be tied to a definite time: it is always lying in wait, in everything. There is no telling from where it will swoop down on its victim, because it is invisible: it grows in the victim himself. The eyes of melancholics are met by chasms, covering all existence, from which, as from so many yawning gullets, an endless and unappeasable deficiency whistles. Chaos is an absence of existence, the absence that is wedged between the beginning and end of life; it is chaos, in the form of passing and death, that makes sure that life's uniqueness, to which melancholics owe their birth, will remain genuinely unique and unrepeatable.

If we conceive of man exclusively as a unit of body and soul, that leads not only to a dynamic reinterpretation of systems, but also to our seeing illness differently from nosologically oriented medical science, incomprehensibly optimistic as it still is (at least in its methods) in spite of its innumerable failures. A human body is a body by having a goal as an organism, seeking to fulfill something, and

early as 1913 that in investigating mental illness, one ought to adopt the criteria of "empathy" and "unintelligibility."

it carries within itself the unreachable horizon, which distinguishes man from all other existing entities. "The discernment," wrote Thure von Uexküll, a representative of psychosomatically oriented medicine, "that, in the case of corporeality, one is dealing not with an inflexible, invariable structure but with a mobile, provisional structure that is coordinated differently from one situation to another, in point of fact, confronts us with the task of the creation of a new anatomy. In that, the organs would no longer be described on the basis of purely morphological criteria but as a group of accomplishments that regroups itself again and again and possesses various presumed goals" (Uexküll, "Möglichkeiten und Grenzen psychosomatischer Betrachtung," 380). (Some of the body's organ systems, such as the hematologic, endocrinological, and immunological, do not form morphological units by their very nature, and can be characterized only functionally, in the more profound sense of the word.) The place of the earlier clinical diagnosis would be taken over by a structural analysis of body and soul. The doctrine based on functional units would not only render the concept of disease dynamic (and, in the last analysis, unclassifiable), but would also show the link between illness and health in a new light: illness, as the neurologist F. W. Kroll set forth, is rooted in healthy organisms: "In this sense one can speak of a *syndrome*, certainly as a foreground, as being *the centre of a clinical picture*, and one must distinguish the background, which is rooted in the reactions of a healthy, *premorbid* state of the *given individual*, and is not limited to the nervous system but much rather lies in every tissue and organ, and that is determined by all sorts of factors, both temporal and spatial, inner and outer world. We have thereby arrived not at a nervous illness but at the structural form of the nervous patient" (quoted in Leopold Szondi, *Experimental Diagnostics of Drives*, 451; emphasis in the original). The dynamic approach in medicine reaches the same point as philosophical anthropology: a disease affects only an individual patient, or to be more precise, the person's being induces the disease. An illness is always an illness of the *self*, similar to life and death, which means that an illness (even a simple toothache) is not merely a corporeal state but also an existential trauma. Sick persons see the world differently from others, and from the way they themselves do in their healthy state. In sickness the relationship between the individual and the world changes in the same way as the unity of the patient's body and soul, which is a reminder that an illness is not just a physical change, an unbending state in the patient's life, but a focal point in a system of relationships. Hippocrates distinguished illness, patient, and physician; in other words, the same phenomenon could be approached from three angles. Needless to say, the three viewpoints are not congruent; patients will always interpret their condition differently than their physicians (physicians may consider people who feel sick, healthy; and healthy, sick), and the concept to which their statements refer obviously does not mean the same for both parties.

Sickness is a peculiar state of being. Although there were times when sick people were killed,[15] illness has always meant an existential-functional change. One is justified in believing that the illness arrived from *outside* (as with the plague that the gods unleashed on humans in the *Iliad*), but at the same time, since it is oneself that has fallen ill, one is compelled to blame oneself: one is at one's own mercy. Disease-induced changes are not purely external lesions suffered by a body but are signs of the unstoppable deterioration and fatigue of existence manifesting in and through the body, the best proof of which is being at one's own mercy. In illness, the previously unnoticed becomes clear: life is merely a moment in the fulfillment of being, which eclipses life and brings annihilation. Illness is, at one

---

15. For example, at the end of the Middle Ages in England, lycanthropy, an illness in which patients believe themselves to be animals (Nebuchadnezzar in the Bible was one such), was considered to be one of the symptoms of melancholia, and hunting licenses were issued to destroy such patients.

and the same time, a physical and a metaphysical phenomenon: the individual being sickens, and yet a universal fate is fulfilled; an "injury" befalls the person, yet that is also a speeding up of inevitable disintegration. What is a lack there is fulfillment here: in illness, one always surpasses one's own healthy self (even when one evaluates the illness as "arrears"), since it makes one aware of what one is otherwise concealing: one's ability to be annihilated. Illness is therefore not a pure operational fault—or if it is that, then so too is existence, of which we cannot even establish the standard by which to measure failure. Would there be any illness, one wonders, if existence were flawless?

Heidegger demonstrated that death is not only an *exitus* in the medical sense, as with an animal, but an essential appurtenance of life itself, and irrespective of the body's biological dispositions, it may be slowed down or speeded up, and the relationship that is developed with it determines the conduct of life (death is not just an egress—an *exitus*—from life, but also an "ingress"). Disease can likewise be interpreted only from such an approach. To quote Thomas Mann: disease "has an intellectual and cultural side, connected with life itself and with its enhancement and growth, a side which the biologist and physician never fully understand"—and later on, speaking about possibilities inherent in sickness that few can draw on, he continues: "Certain attainments of the soul and the intellect are impossible without disease, without insanity, without spiritual crime, and the great invalids are crucified victims, sacrificed to humanity and its advancement, to the broadening of its feeling and knowledge—in short, to its more sublime health" ("Dostoevsky—in Moderation," xiv–xv). In illness, life as it were blooms: the physician Victor von Weizsäcker, with a boldness befitting a philosopher, appraised diseases of organs as achievements of the organism. One should look on disease as just as fundamental a state of being as health, regardless of how it is assessed. Illness is regarded by most people as not just a bad but an inferior state, a subspecies of health. The medieval approach reechoes in this: illness is a consequence of *sin*, and sin can be based only on the existence of non-sin, that is, sin is of a lower order than good. Evil is not an essential ingredient of existence, but pure negativity (in St. Augustine's wordplay, not a *causa efficiens* but a *causa deficiens*), and, mutatis mutandis, disease is not a substance but an accident: it is of a lower order than health. In sickness, man cannot dispose of himself, and this is a reminder of man's creatureliness. Sickness makes the chasm between God the Creator and created man unbridgeable. The everyday usage of the concepts of health and disease reflects the view of the Middle Ages: for us to really understand disease, it is necessary to eliminate the chasm wedged by the Middle Ages not only between the existence of the creature and the creator, but also between body and soul. From that point of view, *Philosophical Inquiries into the Essence of Human Freedom* by Friedrich Schelling is exemplary. Although not concerned with human illness, it nevertheless exchanges its central concept of sin for the word "disease." It is worth quoting at some length from this work; a new approach to disease emerges here, and Schelling expands the interpretation of melancholia.

"After the eternal act of self-revelation," he begins his discourse,

> everything in the world is, as we see it now, rule, order and form; but anarchy still lies in the ground, as if it could break through once again, and nowhere does it appear as if order and form were what is original but rather as if initial anarchy had been brought to order. This is the incomprehensible base of reality in things, the indivisible remainder, that which with the greatest exertion cannot be resolved in understanding but rather remains eternally in the ground. The understanding is born in the genuine sense from that which is without understanding. Without this preceding darkness creatures have no reality.

> (Schelling, *Philosophical Inquiries into the Essence of Human Freedom*, 29)

The essence of man, according to Schelling, is the yearning and aspiration to get out of that darkness into luminosity, but rootedness in the dark also belongs to that essence. For that reason, the root of evil is not lack, privation, or defect, as the early Church Fathers or the scholastics believed: "For the simple reflection that only man, the most complete of all visible creatures, is capable of evil, shows already that the ground of evil could not in any way lie in lack or deprivation. . . . The ground of evil must lie, therefore, not only in something generally positive but rather in that which is most positive in what nature contains" (36–37). Picking up an argument by Franz von Baader that is in much the same spirit, he continues: "If one asks from whence comes evil, the answer is: from the ideal nature of creatures to the extent that it depends on the eternal truths that are contained in the divine understanding, but not on the will of God" (36). Therefore, "we deny that finitude for itself is evil" (38). The finite, animal, physical part of man is held to be the root of evil by those who find freedom exclusively in intelligence and accordingly deny the freedom inherent in evil. "As it is, however, in no way the intelligent or light principle in itself that is active in the good but rather this principle connected to selfhood, that is, having been raised to spirit, then, in the very same way, evil does not follow from the principle of finitude for itself but rather from the selfish or dark principle having been brought into intimacy with the centrum; and, just as there is an enthusiasm for the good, there is a spiritedness [*Begeisterung*] of evil" (39–40). Schelling explains this boundless, Romantic tolerance as follows: "God as spirit . . . is the purest love: there can never be a will to evil in love just as little as in the ideal principle. But God himself requires a ground so that he can exist; but only a ground that is not outside but inside him and has in itself a nature which, although belonging to him, is yet also different from him" (42). Evil is comprehensible from this doubly committed nature: "For evil is surely nothing other than the primal ground [*Urgrund*] of existence to the extent that this ground strives toward actuality in created beings and therefore is in fact only the higher potency of the ground active in nature" (44). The ultimate cause of evil is nature as understood in the nonempirical sense, which, as a foundation, contains the divine essence, but not as a unity. Sin derives from the state that is outside God and yet related to God, for sin is manifested in the fact "that man transgresses from authentic Being into non-Being, from truth into lies, from the light into darkness, in order to become a self-creating ground and, with the power of the centrum which he has within himself, to rule over all things." He adds, "In evil there is the self-consuming and always annihilating contradiction that it strives to become creaturely just by annihilating the bond of creaturely existence and, out of overweening pride [*Übermut*] to be all things, falls into non-Being" (55). The multiple, constantly present contradictoriness of being outside God means that man, unlike God, "never gains control over the condition, although in evil he strives to do so; it is only lent to him, and is independent from him; hence, his personality and selfhood can never rise to full actuality [*zum Aktus*]. This is the sadness that clings to all finite life." The philosopher ends: "Hence, the veil of dejection that is spread over all nature, the deep indestructible melancholy of all life" (62–63).

Evil and sin are not accidental phenomena, not deformations or divestments of the good, but essential ingredients of existence. If, for the two concepts, one substitutes the concept of disease (one can do that all the more readily since Christian theology, by referring to a preoccupation with creatureliness, creates a kinship between sin and disease), the radical reevaluation of the concept of illness becomes apparent: disease is not a separation of creaturely being from the creative being latent in man (this view is based on a duality between body and soul), but a creative principle itself: *through it, the ineliminable endangerment of existence is revealed, which one will never be capable of surmounting in one's determined and determining being.* Therefore, disease is not merely a temporally circumscribed condition but also the unraveling of a constantly latent possibility; its symptoms are like the tip of an iceberg: deep down, invisibly, the possibility and the reality of annihilation are entwined with survival. "There is no such thing as health per se," Nietzsche avows, and one may add: there is no such thing as soul or body, creatureliness or creative principle per se either. "Health and disease," to quote Nietzsche again, "be careful! The standard must always be the efflorescence of the body, the resilience, courage, and cheerfulness of the spirit—but naturally also *how much morbidity it can absorb and conquer—*in other words, *make healthy*" (quoted in Mann, "Dostoevsky—in Moderation," xv; emphasis in the original).

According to one of the founding principles of our culture, man's mission is to take complete possession of himself, to become entirely master of himself. Is that his way of making up for the Fall, in the course of which, as Augustine saw it, the rational soul—*anima ratio-nalis*—lost its unlimited dominion over the body? We carry the tension and tribulation arising from the forced duality of body and soul down to the present day. Insight, comprehension, and the mind have the right of the last word. That is how culture seeks to persuade man to lift himself up by his own bootstraps: to break away from everything to which he owes his being, even his body, over which he has limited power. If he should succeed, however, and by raising himself into the region of the unimpressionable, untouchable mind he were able to have full command of himself, then there ought to exist a part that is foreign to him and yet homogeneous with him, that has him in its power. Yet would not the existence of a part like that, which belongs to the self and is nevertheless foreign to it, prove that man still failed to have command over himself, because he surrendered his self to universal mind, which seems to be beyond the self? Christianity may have tried to bridge that paradox, but by putting man at the mercy of God via the mediation of Jesus, it did not resolve the problem of self-determination. Nor could it, since self-determination, in itself a notion burdened with contradictions, was born of a one-sided hypothesis that had limited validity from the outset: death is not equal in rank to life but subordinate to it, and disintegration is merely a subordinate part of an organization furnished with a goal and sense. But the chaos that permeates life cannot be eliminated; it can at best be obscured. That concealment was served by introducing a general scale of values from which one could infer relatively easily that chaos and disintegration were "bad," whereas goal-directed intelligence was "good." Christian theology denied evil a self-standing foundation, ascribing that only to the good—the devil being just a vaudeville character. But by regarding only the beginning, and not disintegration, as definitive, did it not prevent man from contemplating himself and his world impartially? The concept of self-determination is high-sounding because hidden in it is the unspoken assumption that man is able to extricate himself from the universal chaos and flee from the completely senseless rhythm of beginning and disintegration. Nietzsche justifiably accused Christianity of having deprived humans of nihilism, but only from a standpoint of universal "censorship" and repression can one say that this nihilism suggests "pessimism." Nihilism means acknowledgment of the unacceptable. Not its acceptance, because one instinctively protests against chaos and destruction, but only its recognition. The idea of self-determination suggests ultimate reconciliation, to which there can be at most practical (technical, political, ideological, civilizational) obstacles, and these can be overcome in principle. Nihilism, in contrast, reports on indissoluble constraints (which is no obstacle to nihilists taking part in political and other sorts of struggles, working for "progress," etc.). According to the nihilistic (or Romantic or anarchist) viewpoint, there can be no ultimate reconciliation: man cannot have ultimate command of himself, since he does not simply exist, but existence pours through him: he is at its mercy. He lives his own life, but the death that awaits him is likewise his own.

Man is just as responsible for his illness as for his health. This ultimate self-dependency makes disease unfathomable and depressing. Man is always more than he is able to reveal of himself: everything that he says about himself is objectifiable—yet man cannot be entirely objectified. The infinity of his horizon, in the last analysis, imposes a limit on determination, and muteness is a sign of the ultimate incommunicability of personality, of the mysteriousness manifesting in individual death. Communication has validity only within the circle of objectifiability: whatever is not objectifiable about a disease is not communicable either. There can be no compromise here: the diagnosis of a bodily symptom,[16] along with its objectification, is not the same as a complete understanding of the disease: by merging etiology and pathogenesis, one proclaims that man's bodily-psychic reality is technically apprehensible.

The concept of disease is accessible, but since it belongs to the essence of man, it cannot be unraveled. This is displayed most spectacularly in connection with the suffering of a patient: the ultimate isolation and abandonment of the individual becomes evident in suffering; indeed, suffering is abandonment itself. (That is why sufferers crave to share their suffering with others.) Suffering reveals that man is in a state of being under perpetual threat. The incommunicability of suffering is a peculiarly human element: in contrast to the pain experienced by animals, it results in (not necessarily conscious) insight. Suffering, which originally meant a movement of the soul ($\pi\acute{\alpha}\vartheta\text{os}$), is as much a psychological factor[17] as a physical phenomenon (an object of pathology in the strict sense), and is thus one of the keys to the interpretation of human existence. For a long time, the science of pathology concerned itself only with the suffering evoked by bodily changes,[18] but in its very name, suffering ($\pi\acute{\alpha}\vartheta\text{os}$) and the spoken word, the law ($\lambda\acute{o}\gamma\text{os}$), are linked. Pathology in a broad sense

---

16. The verb "to diagnose" refers to communication: diagnosis—the communication ($\delta\iota\acute{\alpha}$) of knowledge ($\gamma\nu\tilde{\omega}\sigma\iota\varsigma$)—presumes a dynamic, dialogic connection between knower and known.

17. Hence the Latin *patior* (suffer, endure) and *passio* (intense emotion).

18. Inscribed on the façade of many institutions of pathology is the motto *Mortui vivos docent* ("The dead teach the living").

is *knowledge built up about suffering*, or rather, since suffering is not objectifiable, that is, an adequate knowledge of it cannot be gained, it is the *knowledge that emerges from suffering*. It is not just a play on words if, moving beyond knowledge, one also discerns in the notion of logos the Christian interpretation of that word: Logos is the son of God, that is, Jesus Christ (1 John 1:14), whose sufferings involved the acceptance of bodily torment as well as the transfiguration that emerged from that. His suffering not only referred to life, as against death, but also showed that suffering was inseparable from life. Man does not suffer by accident, but for one reason or another; suffering, which appears suddenly, signals the original fragility and unresolvable endangerment of human existence. Like disease, which is its most elemental manifestation, suffering does not arrive from outside but is latent in man, ready to burst out at any moment. Therefore, to deprive man of his suffering, however benign the hope, is to pronounce a death sentence (only in death is there no suffering). In Hölderlin's precise formulation: "Nothing causes greater pain . . . than riddling on our suffering" (*Death of Empedocles*, act 1, scene 4).[19]

If medicine seeks to clear up the existential notions of illness and suffering instrumentally, it forgets that technology itself cannot be defined technically. This once more raises the problem of infinitude and incommunicability, which the technophile outlook wishes to reject. One way or another, every sick patient is a mystic, Victor von Weizsäcker declared; they pose problems for which physicians are unprepared. In the vast majority of cases, however, medical science does not hear the question, or, to be more exact, it hears only the questions that it is able to answer. (Unlike pathogenesis, etiology has been a neglected area of medicine to the present day.) Questions implied by the answer are not questions, however. That is doubly true

---

19. It stands to reason that suffering caused by a given illness has to be alleviated: painkillers, however, can do nothing to alter the fundamental law that while there is life, pain will be bound to occur sooner or later.

in the case of illness because it is not possible to give unambiguous answers to the real questions relating to disease, just as human existence cannot be exhausted in a logical game of questions and answers. A physician wants to understand a disease, but it is precisely in the conceptual apprehension that a restriction presents itself, which was described by Kierkegaard in the following terms: "The secret of all comprehending is that the very act of comprehension is higher than every position which it posits. The concept posits a position, but the fact that it is comprehended means precisely that it is negated" (*The Sickness unto Death*, bk. 2, 3). Conceptual-logical understanding results in the same kind of split in the human phenomenon as the distinction between body and soul: the physician implicitly treats disease as an object to be explained, which seems like an external blow in its "objectivity," regardless of the position in life of both physician and patient. The relationship between comprehension and the object awaiting comprehension, however, is far from external; indeed, the fact that the two do not exist independently of each other indicates an inner relationship. It is a commonplace that the precondition for human understanding is some kind of profound identity between subject and object,[20] which means that the person wishing to acquire knowledge must possess some sort of foreknowledge, or to be more precise, a conjecture of the object to be known. "All knowledge

---

20. Empedocles put it this way:

For 'tis through Earth that Earth we do behold,
Through Ether, divine Ether luminous,
Through Water, Water, through Fire, devouring Fire,
And Love through Love, and Hate through doleful Hate.

(*Fragments*, 109)

This is cited approvingly by Aristotle, who himself writes elsewhere: "The organ which perceives colour is not only affected by its object, but also reacts upon it" (*On Dreams*, 460a).

is caused by means of a likeness," writes St. Thomas Aquinas. "The likeness of a thing known is not of necessity actually [*sit actu*] in the nature of the knower; but given a thing which knows potentially [*in potentia*], and afterwards knows actually [*in actu*], the likeness of the thing known must be in the nature of the knower, not actually, but only potentially" (*Summa theologica*, I. 75, q. 1. a. 2.). The modern idea and experience of the self-creation of man proved that man was, and the objective world could not be, separated into "contemplating subjectivity" and "neutral objectivity," independent of everything. It was not just the problem of body and soul that was radically reformulated but also, in close relationship to it, the question of knowing and understanding. The insight that man is a self-creating being who makes his own history goes hand in hand with the aforesaid transformation of the concept of reality. The "objective" reality waiting to be recognized is always a reality related to man and existing for him — the reality about which man knows nothing is, strictly speaking, unreality. The reality about which he knows, however, is a historical-existential existent resulting from his acquisitive activity (history), that is, even if it turns antihuman, it is never without humans. The relationship of man to the world (which includes the system of man-made institutions as well as nature and the cosmos) is determined historically and existentially. If I want to interpret and get to know reality, then I become part of the interpretation as an object and, at the same time, a subject: the understanding of a so-called objective phenomenon, if I press ahead consistently with my questions about revealing the *being* of the phenomenon, will eventually lead to understanding myself: I cannot acquire information about something without also gaining knowledge about myself and the life situation that defines the act of cognition. (Admittedly, truth is not just a substance but also a subject, phenomenology teaches; and the understanding of a chemical effect, although an "objective" process, suggests that the phenomenon depends on human interpretation.) "According to pre-dialectical logic, the *constitutum* cannot be the *constituens* and the conditioned cannot be the condition for its own condition," says Adorno. "Reflection upon the value of societal knowledge within the framework of what it knows forces reflection beyond this simple lack of contradiction. The inescapability of paradox, which Wittgenstein frankly expressed, testifies to the fact that generally the lack of contradiction cannot, for consistent thought, have the last word, not even when consistent thought sanctions its norm" (introduction to Adorno et al., *The Positivist Dispute in German Sociology*). Returning to Schelling's earlier thought: man is incapable of taking possession of the precondition of his own existence—hence the dejection that one might call the connective tissue of existence.

Technically minded medicine aims to eradicate all contradictions, and although efforts to cure result in insoluble problems every day for physicians and patients alike, strictly somatic medical science puts this down to an insufficiency of the conceptual and technical apparatus, not noticing that in practice insoluble cases are often due to the ultimate insolubility of human existence. (Toothache may seem mundane, death mysterious, and yet the case of Thomas Buddenbrook, who died of a toothache, shows that even an apparently ordinary event may have the potential for mystery.) The categories of cognition and the stockpiles of technical apparatus wish to fix unfixable human reality, and what could be more typical of the obstinacy of the objectivist spirit than the fact that in defense of its own tools, it seeks to force dynamic human-historical reality into its own closed, technically defined notion of reality. The categories of cognition and the reality examined do not coincide (human reality does not coincide with anything), but they can be approximated to each other. The precondition for doing this is to open up, which was in fact done by dynamic psychiatry and psychosomatically oriented medical science: cognition has to be linked with understanding, since, after all, the "object" of medical knowledge, human existence, is indissoluble from self-interpretation, following from historicity.[21] Understanding points to the way out of the apparently irresolvable conflict between technical dogmatism and an insoluble life situation. "Comprehension," writes Sartre, "is none other than my true life, that is to say, the totalizing movement, which contains my fellow human beings, my good self, and the neighborhood in the synthetic unit of in process" ("Search for a Method"). It is in understanding that the questioner and the questioned, the physician and the patient, recognize each other; it is only there that the infinite horizon is unfolded in their dialogue, the horizon that makes the concept of disease open, infinite, and, despite its insolubility, promising. The appropriate approach to a disease is the task of unraveling in practical conversation, since in the end every disease ought to direct attention to a particular individual's way of life. That means, on the one hand, that in every patient one can follow the individual structuring of a concrete human situation; on the other hand, that in every disease one is confronted by human existence in general. The two viewpoints twist spirally around each other: at each step, empirical medical science and the philosophical understanding of life have to recognize each other. Drawing on some words of Martin Heidegger:

> The totality of entities can, in accordance with its various domains, become a field for laying bare and delimiting certain definite areas of subject-matter (for instance, history, Nature, space, life, *Dasein*, language and the like), can serve as objects which corresponding scientific investigations may take as their respective themes. . . . Although research may always lean towards this positive approach, its real progress comes not so much from col-

---

21. This is the basis on which Dilthey contrasts explanatory and descriptive psychology; Jaspers, explanatory (causal) and cognitive psychiatry; the psychosomatic approach, the clinical and structural recognition of diseases. The demand for understanding emerged at the start of the twentieth century in connection with psychological phenomena that were not explicable on the basis of brain pathology.

lecting results and storing them away in "manuals" as from inquiring into the ways in which each particular area is basically constituted [*Grundverfassungen*] — an inquiry to which we have already been driven mostly by reacting against just such an increase in information. The real "movement" of the sciences takes place when their basic concepts undergo a more or less radical revision which is transparent to itself. The level which a science has reached is determined by how far it is capable of a crisis in its basic concepts. In such immanent crises the very relationship between positively investigative inquiry and those things that are under interrogation comes to a point where it begins to totter.

(*Being and Time*, §3)

The relationship of philosophy to empirical medical science is inexhaustible because of its intimacy: this follows from the endless amount of factual material of empirical science, from the transcendental nature of philosophical knowledge directed at the historicity of existence, but mainly from the personality of the patient, who is not only the object but also the subject of the examination. Until the evolution of medical science in the modern era, medicine never denied its kinship with the philosophical understanding of life, and man was never treated purely in his corporeal character. This was true of antiquity, when priest, physician, and philosopher regularly merged into one person; of Hippocrates and Empedocles, who may have approached patients with opposing methods but who both kept an eye on the cosmos as a whole; of Epimenides, who did not acquire his mastery of medicine from humans but from the gods and who also acquired the wisdom of the mysteries; of Caelius Aurelianus, who gave this advice for melancholics in the fifth century: "It is desirable that they take part in philosophical debates. . . . With their discussions philosophers help in dismissing the fear, sadness, and anger, which does the body a very, very great deal of good" (quoted in Starobinski, *Histoire du traitement de la mélancolie des origines,*

28); of Ficino, who was at once priest, physician, and philosopher; of Paracelsus, for whom a physician who called himself that while being wanting in philosophy and not understanding it was uncouth, and for whom a physician curing a melancholic patient ought also to be sorcerer, philosopher, and astrologist; of Robert Burton, who likewise called himself physician and priest, and who, like Sir Thomas Browne, was compelled by medical insight to reach the profoundest possible philosophical insights; of Romantic medicine, the philosophical roots of which are highly conspicuous; of Karl Jaspers, who united the medical and philosophical points of view in one and the same person; and of the representatives of the Daseinsanalysis school who, like many representatives of psychosomatic medicine, were not only physicians but philosophers as well. Not because they knew their way around philosophical disciplines, but because their way of looking at things and posing questions, free from the inhibitions of specialist sciences (inter alia, specialist philosophy), opened the doors to wonderment at human existence, which Plato reckoned to be the most important prerequisite of philosophy. The wisdom of disease—pathosophy (*Pathosophie*), the elegant term bestowed by Victor von Weizsäcker—opens up medical anthropology in the direction of philosophical anthropology. Anthropology, however, merits the name of science only if it abandons the claim to be a closed discipline; if, in discoursing about man, it is reconciled to being unable definitively to mark out and enclose in words the concept of being human; if it undertakes the far-from-risk-free venture of tackling secrets in such a manner that the secrecy remains intact. Only in that case can anthropology merit the epithet "philosophical"; otherwise, if it wishes to lock human phenomena in among finite concepts, there arises the natural human demand for questioning about "ultimate basic concepts." The exploration of diseases as anthropological phenomena, the uncovering of their concrete manifestations, assists in understanding man, so this understanding should lead to further immersion in the concept of illness.

Chapter 9

TREMBLING FROM FREEDOM

The radical reevaluation of body and soul, or health and disease, is necessary so that one may return to melancholia, a concept that over the past century has increasingly been sidelined and denied the rights that are its due. The segregation of the ordinary and the medical conceptions of the term commenced in the Romantic era, and the Romantics themselves played a large part in this. Melancholia was aggrandized into a life technique leading to death, and that was unacceptable to public opinion. A person who rushed to meet death, who courted it, as it were, could not be a sane member of society, and since a latent death wish was present in melancholia, it had to be classed in the increasingly rigid system of mental illnesses. Since one of the typical traits of melancholics was their inclination to suicide, after an expert removal of the notion of understanding existence, the diagnosis was instantly ready: the inclination to suicide pointed to mental illness. But the desire to understand existence that is manifested in melancholia cannot be abolished and annulled—and in most cases this understanding of existence does not necessarily indicate mental illness. Of course, no culture appreciates *all* kinds of understandings and modes of existence; moreover, the possibility is excluded theoretically, though the limits of tolerance vary from era to era. From this point of view, the tolerance of Western culture in most recent times has been low: the tolerance of which Western society is so proud is limited in two respects. Anyone can say or think anything, form an opinion—but society loses its patience if an ideology "comes to the boil," and is realized in practice, and it also loses its patience if ideology "freezes" and degenerates into a private interpretation of existence going beyond the bounds of any sort of social collusion. Anarchists, terrorists, and revolutionaries (and often even reformers) are just as suspect as mystics, prophets, or merely despairing people: the label of mental illness (or deviance, to put it more elegantly) can just as easily be branded on both those groups, and should the occasion arise the reformer and the desperate nihilist can be stuck in the same closed ward. That is not to say that there are no patients among the occupants of closed wards, but it depends on the tolerance of a society how far the limits of disease are stretched or narrowed down. This tolerance does not depend on medical attitudes: a physician's decision in so-called borderline cases is usually influenced from the outset by the cultural and political milieu, to which the medical practice is linked by a million invisible threads.

The history of melancholia over the past two millennia shows that bodily condition is inseparable from the understanding of existence. We have seen that one does not simply fall ill of "something," one's human nature is responsible for the illness. If we really feel the need to understand the concept of melancholy or depression, then that is possible primarily on the basis of examining a given individual's interpretation of existence and conduct of life. In departing from the strictly somatic interpretation of melancholia—or rather, the listing of certain "psychological" symptoms in a rather schoolmasterish, positivist spirit in the nineteenth century (an attitude that is still alive)—it was psychoanalysis that first attempted a more profound explanation. In comparing mourning and melancholia, Freud, making a decisive distinction between the two conditions, pointed out that the reason for mourning is known, whereas in the case of melancholia, the cause is unknown: "Melancholia is in some way related to an object-loss which is withdrawn from consciousness, in contradiction to mourning, in which there is nothing about the loss that is unconscious" ("Mourning and Melancholia," 245). The reason for this, as Freud explains, is that for a mourning person, "only" the world has been lost, whereas for a melancholic, it is also the "ego."

[An] attachment of the libido to a particular person had at one time existed; then, owing to a real slight or disappointment coming from this loved person the object-relationship was shattered. . . . The object-cathexis proved to have little power of resistance and was brought to an end. But the free libido was not displaced on to another object; it was withdrawn into the ego. . . . Thus the shadow of the object fell upon the ego, and the latter could henceforth be judged by a special agency as though it were an object, the forsaken object. In this way an object-loss was transformed into an ego-loss.

(249)

Since the ego as the object of libido is also an object of self-disparagement, melancholics will do all they can to get rid of the object—which leads to suicide. (Alfred Adler interprets melancholia in a similar spirit, albeit with a different conceptual apparatus: in his view, the melancholic is striving for authority and would like to gain an advantage. The melancholic's tactic is to be in touch with very few people and try to subjugate those around him by self-abasement and tears. If that works, then the melancholia abates, but if not, then he commits suicide and thereby escapes a hopeless situation or takes his revenge on those around him.) Freud attempted to loosen the rigid interpretation of melancholia, and by emphasizing the structure and dynamics of the personality, he shifted the discourse about melancholia from its positivist dead end. At the same time, however, he left basic questions untouched, even though these necessarily follow from the dynamic concept of personality. For Freud, like the exclusively scientific spirit of medical science, examines the state of the melancholic as a state of the ego, which is confronted neutrally by the world: "In mourning it is the world which has become poor and empty; in melancholia it is the ego itself" (246), and with this rigid, unacceptable separation he prevented himself from being able to unravel the interpretation of being inherent in melancholia.

Melancholia was thus associated with certain primary desires (narcissism, sadism, suicidal tendency, anal proclivity, etc.), and the goal was merely to satisfy each of these desires; the world is a lifeless *object* that is a suitable (or unsuitable, as the case may be) place for humans to satisfy their desires. Since, according to Freud, every psychological happening is determined primarily by the instincts, in interpreting melancholia he rigidly contrasts the ego and the world of objects: everything takes place in the ego, compared with which the outside world withdraws into neutral intactness.[1] This attitude, above and beyond the distinction between an internal and an external world being just as unfortunate as that of soul and body, decidedly impedes the understanding of illness as a phenomenon: it puts an end to the dynamic unity without which one cannot speak about an interpretation of being.

The sense of loss that Freud, showing a touch of genius, chose as his starting point is not a one-sided phenomenon: the essence of loss is not the bare fact that *the ego loses an object*, but that something that is part of the world, but is also in my possession, modifies the place it occupied in the collectivity of existing things, and thereby it is not just its position that has changed but my existence as well. Looked at from this angle, there is just a difference in degree between the loss of a pencil and the loss of a life: if I lose my pencil, the consequences ripple onward; I am unable to write, so I am compelled to look for a new pencil; maybe I have regrets about the old one because I had long wanted a pencil just like it; I shall take more care in storing the new pencil; I take note of where I put it away; perhaps I'll buy a pencil box; but even if I don't, it will occur to me that I once had a pencil that was lost, and by then I shall have not only a new pencil but a memory, too, etc. All that can be enacted in a matter of moments or might last an hour or two, but in no way more than a day or two in the case of a pencil. It could be that I do not think of any of these things: still, the

---

1. Erwin Straus considered psychoanalysis to be "anthropological solipsism."

loss of the pencil "in itself" brings about a change in my world; it is not as though this had ever become fixed, but the loss draws attention to the incessant changeability of existence. Usually, one notices a loss with annoyance; that annoyance, however, is proof that it is not about the lost item slipping back into a neutral, objective world, but about the intimate relationship (which of course had been seemingly neutral and external until the loss happened) between objects and people, which is transformed. I am annoyed because with the loss of the pencil a piece of my property, in the deeper sense of the word, a piece of me, however unnoticeable, is gone. Loss is not an analogue of arithmetical subtraction, but a human situation. In the loss and my ensuing annoyance there is a warning: something was unavoidably injured. What that was is normally not noticeable; we reach too quickly for a new pencil for us to realize what has happened. We can't say that the pencil has ceased to exist (it may be under the bed), nor did I die over the loss. All the same, something got muddled up just enough for me to suppress a quiet curse, with which, as in the case of all cursing, I conceal that this petty inconvenience is a harbinger of that certain, final, big inconvenience.

This is one of the most typical manifestations of melancholia, but it is also in melancholia that the sense of loss manifests its true reality. For while mundane practice teaches people not to get stuck for too long on losses that befall them (this relates not only to pencils but, as Claudius advises Hamlet, to the death of loved ones as well), and the loss is interpreted practically (including their own death, about which it is "best not to think"), the melancholic is incapable of that; an injury is discerned in the loss, injustice in the injury, and death, the chief injustice, in the injustice. The lost item is not an object but a part of myself, and the essence of the sense of loss — contrary to the Freudian notion — is precisely that there is an intimate relationship between ego and object. The more profoundly I experience the loss, the more irreplaceable the object, because all the more do I feel I have lost my footing. Among the reasons the melancholic is melancholic is because he sees the *personal* death awaiting him in the slightest loss of an object.[2] The symptoms observed in melancholics can be explained by the profound (mortal) experience of loss: the not primarily psychological but corporeal heaviness (vital depression); psychomotor inhibition, which can lead to total inhibition of action, stuporous melancholia; along with the related cognitive inhibition. Only the melancholic is capable of *experiencing* the sense of death that may result from loss: the physical symptoms signal that it is not just a matter of thinking death over. (In the view of psychosomatically based cancer researchers, it is precisely loss-induced depression that can promote the development of certain types of cancer.) The nihilistic ideas that melancholics report (everyone is dead, everything has been destroyed, all is bleak, etc.) are related to nihilistic sensations of the body (they feel that their brains have been replaced by feces, their veins have dried up, there are worms under their skin, their skin is too tight for their bodies, etc.). A sense of loss can also explain the frequent wavering uncertainty of melancholics when it comes to making decisions (in truth, it is not that they are unable to decide but that they have lost the ability to judge whether it is worth deciding at all), and the accompanying lack of ability to act.

(It is evident that we have also failed at the conceptual separation of depression and melancholia—the change in perspective over the past two centuries has permeated language so profoundly that no one can avoid it. The symptoms listed above are not new: they have been mentioned in regard to melancholia for two and a half millen-

---

2. A wealthy Swiss businessman suffered a significant loss of money in his business, though not one large enough to have an appreciable effect on his financial standing. Afterward, he was admitted to the hospital with the symptoms of melancholia, and there his every thought revolved around the lost sum of money. After a while, news came that there had been a mistake: the money had not been lost. Despite the prognostications of the physicians, however, the news did not make him happier; if anything, his depression intensified.

nia. What is novel is that the horizons revealed behind the symptoms rarely occupy medical science in the modern era. Even when it speaks about the symptoms of "melancholia," it understands that condition as depression. The two are not the same, however. Although the symptoms are unequivocally experienced as a burden by the affected person, under the pressures of the symptoms the melancholic possesses insights that point beyond his physical state and direct his attention to the place he occupies in the world. To put it another way, he can turn the body's symptoms to "profit," and that remains even if the physical complaints disappear. In the case of depression, that does not necessarily come to pass; indeed, by labeling the person in question as depressed, by the very fact of giving it that name and judgment, he is held back from striving for a deeper understanding of his condition. Melancholia is an opening; depression—a closing in.)

Melancholics have always been accused of laziness, and in former times that laziness was given as the explanation for melancholia.[3] Laziness, however, like the sense of loss, is not "objective," something of which one will take more or less, according to taste (if one defines laziness as work-shyness, that says nothing about it). Laziness is not some kind of "surplus" that is added to the personality, but like disease and suffering, it emerges from the innermost essence of the personality. Laziness is doing nothing; yet if laziness issues from us, then the mysterious attraction to nothing is also inseparable from our essence. *Laziness is an abnegation of life on a small scale*, and

---

3. A peculiar manifestation of laziness is the inarticulate prattle that can sometimes be observed in melancholics, which Aristotle commented on in the *Problemata physica*: the mind is slow in following the notions that crop up, it is too "lazy" to articulate clearly. In interpreting the medical symptomatology of depression, Julia Kristeva rightly highlights inhibition of speech and action: their behavioral rhythm has been disrupted, the semblance of the world having a coherent nature has ceased, everything has lost its sense, and depressed patients, immersed in their own pain, perceive acting and speaking, which automatically place actor and speaker in an interdependency, to be equally burdensome.

though not requiring conscious consideration, it is an evocation of death similar to a sense of loss. Physicians often report on the peculiar, alienated body movements of melancholics — deep down in this disjointedness lurks a kind of "negative laziness": although the person in question moves, the movement is not directed at accommodating the body to the surrounding conditions but at creating an autonomous internal space. The "laziness" of melancholics (for example, not getting out of bed for days on end) is a sign of retreat into an "internal world";[4] that "internal world," however, is utterly a world of death. Their thoughts are directed at death, and the structure of that world repudiates life.[5] So-called monoideism (concentration on a single idea) is not necessarily concomitant with degeneration of the mind: the melancholic is aware of everything, but he finds the same thing in everything: the loss that sooner or later is bound to be incurred. Hence the curious phenomenon, hard to interpret in strictly medical terms, that is typical of one and the same melancholic person — that of simultaneous oversensitivity and complete insensitivity. On the one hand, melancholics most commonly complain of pain-

---

4. The German romantic Achim von Arnim characterized his close friend Heinrich von Kleist as "extraordinarily singular, slightly eccentric in nature": "He is the most impartial of men, almost cynical. I have long been acquainted with him; there is something indefinable in his manner of speaking which is akin to stammering and is manifested in the course of his work as continual deletions and alterations. He has an odd way of living; he sometimes stays in bed for days on end so that, while smoking a pipe, he should be able to work without being disturbed" (quoted in Helmut Sembdner, ed., *Heinrich von Kleists Lebensspuren*, 347).

5. In the first half of the nineteenth century, Jean-Étienne Dominique Esquirol concluded from the frequent onanism of melancholics that this was one of the causative factors (see Thomas Szász, *The Myth of Mental Illness*, 185); in reality, however, the pressing need that melancholics have for masturbation — suicide on a small scale — is not the cause, but a symptom of a life oriented to death. Joachim Heinrich Campe, in his book *Kleine Seelenlehre für Kinder* (A short psychology for children, 1780) gives an impassioned warning to children about onanism, threatening that it would make them "dejected and melancholic."

ful feelings of senselessness (*anesthesia dolorosa*), of not being able
to be either glad or sad. (A melancholic was unable to grieve over her
son's death; she was considered *medically* cured only when she was
again able to feel sorrow and cry.) On the other hand, such insensitivity may be coupled with vibrant sensitivity: anxiety, hypochondria,
a perpetual inferiority complex, self-reproach, and sleeping disorders
can all be put down to hypersensitivity. This duality suggests that the
melancholic experiences the world as a continuous loss, that is, as a
continuous death: *nothing escapes his attention, and yet everything
blurs into one.* Depersonalization, with its experience of an internal void, is akin to melancholia, and the suffocating experiences of
paramnesia—*déjà vu* and *jamais vu*, *déjà parlé* and *jamais parlé*,
etc.—which are similar to the experience of death, may likewise be
connected with melancholia. The melancholic fears himself as well
as the world: he fears every event, since he is able to view genesis and
change only as incipient death, but he is afraid of himself as well,
because he knows that with the passage of time he will increasingly
ruin everything to the point that in the end he will irredeemably
ruin his whole life by dying. The reason for the frequency of suicide
among melancholics is impatience: the melancholic sees life as a
path leading to death (could he see it otherwise?), with everything
running downhill (a sense of insufficiency). No specific factor trig-
gers suicide: the sole cause, if one can call it that, is life. (There is a
story about a melancholic patient who, upon hearing that his grand-
son had been born, broke into inconsolable wailing.) Life itself is the
chief obstacle to true life; and since so-called true life can possess no
kind of objectivity, since the world of objects induces melancholia,
"true life" itself is pure negativity. As negativity, it can be realized only
through destruction or self-destruction; it is only the fulfillment of
the possibility of annihilation, latent in everything, that gives meaning to a melancholic's life. Either the melancholic sinks into himself
(in the case of stuporous melancholia, the inhibition may intensify
to the point of total immobility) or—which amounts to the same

thing—unable to find his place, he paces up and down, wrings his hands, makes a start of things without ever being able to carry them through (*melancholia agitata*), searching in vain for the thing that would satisfy him. The melancholic who wanders around restlessly and aimlessly (*melancholia errabunda*) becomes ever more desperate: the sense of futility that envelops everything turns into fear,[6] then the fear is transformed into wild attacks (*raptus melancholicus*): he races up and down and either commits suicide or, to spare others a torment-filled life, turns against those around him. (Krafft-Ebing knew of a case from 1851 of a young man in his twenties in the city of Lyon whom he considered to be melancholic, who stabbed a woman and then turned to her husband, "You did me no harm; neither did she. I don't even know you," before going on to demand that he be executed—Krafft-Ebing, *Lehrbuch der gerichtlichen Psychopathologie*, 85.)

A sense of loss escalating to destruction is a consequence of the depletion of the world: if the world is lost, then I am lost, too. The first sign of depletion is aimless yearning ("This unhappy inclination to all places where I am not, to things which are not mine, lies completely within me," admits the Romantic writer Annette von Droste-Hülshoff (quoted in Benjamin, "German Men and Women: A Sequence of Letters"), a prime manifestation of which is nostalgia: though the persons in question long for *home*, the pain felt is shoreless and unappeasable. They surrender to the attraction of nothingness. The word "nostalgia" originally meant "homesickness,"[7] and down to the present day it has been seen as one of the "causes" or sub-

---

6. His throat constricts and dries out, his breathing becomes labored, his extremities grow weak, he breaks out in a cold sweat, he is overcome by psychomotor inhibition.

7. The term was formed from the root words νόστος ("a return home") and ἄλγος ("pain") by Johannes Hofer in 1688 in his *Dissertatio medica de nostalgia oder Heimweh*.

species of melancholia (*melancholia nostalgica*). The narrow meaning of "homesickness"[8] was gradually altered, and it became synonymous with breaking away from orderliness in general.[9] The loss of something always results in "disorder" (the accustomed order breaks up), and it is always some unforeseen incident, suddenly breaking into order and threatening it, that the sense of loss implies. (One of Thomas Mann's finest and most melancholic stories, "Disorder and Early Sorrow," brilliantly portrays the profound kinship of order-upsetting disarray and grief.) The function of order is to fend off chance, to make the world cozy (one readily finds one's way about when things have been set right): "I would sooner commit an injustice than tolerate disorder," Goethe noted in his report on the siege of Mainz about his stopping a mob from lynching a person (quoted in Peter Boerner, *Goethe*, 67). In this instance, the disorderliness is death appearing in the form of a murder that even Goethe could only delay. No order is able to cover up disorder and threat forever. The greater the order, the more oppressive life is—that applies equally to totalitarian forms of state and petit bourgeois homes. The universal sense of loss that melancholics feel is manifested in their relationship to order and disorder: in his poem *The Spleen* (1737), Matthew Green advised those who suffer from spleen (that is, melancholia) to seek a cure far from town, in a tranquil, well-ordered rural environment. Writing about mental illnesses a century later, in 1838, Esquirol noted their correlation with social disorder: "In every century, the ruling ideas powerfully influence both the frequency and the charac-

---

8. Nostalgia, like the idea of melancholia, was eliminated from the lexicon of clinical psychiatry in the nineteenth century, only for it to become of interest again to the dynamic psychiatry of Karl Jaspers in the early twentieth century.

9. A fine example of the pairing of nostalgia and melancholia is the opening image of Hans Jürgen Syberberg's monumental *Hitler: A Film from Germany* (1977): the lower part of the picture is taken up by the word "melancholia," evoking the Düreresque inscription; above that, a tomb with the initials R.W. (Richard Wagner) on it, with a resurrected Hitler rising from the opening tomb.

ter of mental illness. . . . The ideals of freedom and reform disturbed the minds of many people in France, and it is noteworthy that in the lunacies which have been breaking out for the last thirty years one can recognize the characteristics of those storms which have brought our homeland into upheaval" (Esquirol, *Des maladies mentales considerées sous les rapports medical, hygiénique, et medico-légal*, 1:43). (Statistics show that between 1786 and 1813, the number of mental patients in France doubled.) Disorder, however, is not pure negativity: it is not an absolute opposite of order, just as illness is not an absolute opposite of health. Disorder is not a fait accompli (not just "disarray," chaos) but a threat: it appears only in relation to order, which, because it is not a divine formation but the result of human endeavor, is under threat from the very outset—if from nowhere else then from the direction of death, which raises man from the orderliness produced by life. Reinhold Bernhard Jachmann noted the following case with regard to the profoundly melancholic Kant:

> In the course of his lectures he would usually look at a nearby member of the audience in order, so to say, to read from the face if he had been understood. At such times he would be troubled by the most insignificant trifle, especially if it disturbed the natural or accepted order of things and thereby upset the order of his train of thought as well. In one of his lectures his absent-mindedness became singularly apparent. At noon Kant informed me that he was continually getting stuck in his thoughts because a button was missing from the coat of one of the members of the audience seated directly in front of him. His attention and his thoughts kept returning to it unwittingly, and that was why he became so absent-minded.
>
> (quoted in Groß, *Immanuel Kant*, 135)

Kant's near-pathological partiality for neatness was also noted by Wasianski, another of the biographers:

Over the long course of years he developed his own settled, in-variable way of living to such an extent that he was perturbed if a pair of scissors or a penknife lay on the table at another angle from the usual direction, especially if it had slipped an inch or two; and if the place of one of the larger objects, such as a chair, was changed in his room, to say nothing of the number of seats being increased or reduced, then he would become completely discomposed, with his attention continually returning to the place of the chair until order was fully restored.

(ibid.)

Disarray, an eternal threat to order, is the source of melancholia that undermines life at its foundations; but since sooner or later every-thing gets mixed up anyway, disorder is not so much the cause as the consequence of melancholia: obsessed with order, man comes across melancholia and ends up disrupting the ties of order himself. Kierkegaard was convinced that despondency would help the man who lived in secure circumstances in a crowded city to find his way back to the basic principles of life, which, in his view, were truly felt only by those who lived in solitude — and by sailors. Likewise, Walter Benjamin, in writing about well-ordered and planned metropolises, found that it was the prostitutes loitering in the gateways of Berlin tenements or on railway platforms who provided a glimpse into noth-ingness from a secure life. Beyond a certain point, order is not merely practical neatness but an intolerable prison. An angrily destructive melancholic carries out a kind of prison revolt. In *The House of the Dead*, Dostoevsky reports on murderers who for decades had been decent, reliable villagers; beyond their taciturnity, nothing about them indicated that one day, all of a sudden, they would pick up an axe and slaughter their best friends. There is no necessity to commit mayhem, however; there are other ways of revolting against order. According to Dr. Watson, "Save for the occasional use of cocaine, [Sherlock Holmes] had no vices, and he only turned to the drug as a protest against the monotony of existence when cases were scanty and the papers uninteresting."[10]

Melancholia is not an uprising, a revolt, or a reconciliation: the sense of the world is depleted in the eyes of the melancholic, and therefore, terrified as he is of disorder, he is also unable to become preoccupied with order. Günter Grass, who subjected melancholia to a searching inquiry, wrote in his journal that in our time, melancholia is to be found at the conveyor belt, discerning its cause in the fact that production quotas have become the determining principle of life (Grass, *From the Diary of a Snail*, 254).[11] Life at the conveyor belt does not necessarily lead to melancholia, however; apathy is not the same as melancholia: for that, a breakaway from order is also required. Whether the melancholic has to part with an object or a loved one, he feels that he is confronting nothingness: for him, the *possibility* of breaking away is proof that the coherence of the orderly world is just apparent, and sooner or later everything will fall to bits. Melancholia does not emerge from sheer order (which does not exist anyway) but out of the inevitable cracks concealed in order. One truly experiences the pain of loss only if one has a strong link to whatever has been lost, and that same response applies to a loss of order: the melancholic must make a superhuman effort to preserve order, he must be well aware of what has been lost, and he must perceive that he did everything he could on his part to protect his life from being threatened (before rebelling against his fate, Hercules first completed all his labors, set the world to rights in his own fashion). It is telling that

---

10. Arthur Conan Doyle, "The Adventure of the Yellow Face," from *The Memoirs of Sherlock Holmes*, 1893. That monotony can also be a source of a certain mysterious pleasure. "What is there more sad in this world than a Sunday afternoon in December in the barracks?" Céline writes. "And actually it takes me a great deal of effort to escape out of this melancholy. And it seems to me that my soul has softened and that I can only in such circumstances see what I really am" (*Cannon Fodder*, 83).

11. Analyzing the increasingly frequent phenomenon of melancholia in Japan, several Japanese psychiatrists arrived at the same conclusion.

in the Middle Ages, mathematicians and geometricians were considered to be melancholic.[12] Tertullian called the genii of mathematicians and astrologers fallen angels (in the Middle Ages, melancholia
was a sin), and Henry of Ghent differentiated two types of people:
those who are capable of stepping out of the domain of finitude and
of thinking about transcendent beings such as angels, and those who,
remaining prisoners of the empirical world, feel comfortable only in
a directly and transparently perceivable world. The latter will become
melancholics: "Whatever they think, it is something spatial (*quan-
tum*), or else it is located in space like a point. Such people are therefore melancholic, and make the best mathematicians, but the worst
metaphysicians" (quoted in Benjamin, *German Tragic Drama*, 227).
(Mathematicians are sad, Martin Luther said, and in Dürer's *Melencolia I* there are instruments alluding to geometry.) Mathematicians
organize the world and then become disconsolate: the only way out
of the prison leads to nothingness.

A change in a well-regulated life is perceived by a melancholic as
all-engulfing disarray. The more they cling to order, the more readily
they lose their footing: a torn-off shirt button is enough to reveal the
purposelessness of existence. In the unanimous opinion of psychiatrists, before the appearance of melancholia the majority of melancholics experienced an upsetting of order; this might have taken the
form of menopause, involution, menstruation, childbirth, release
from an oppressive psychological burden(!), a change in workplace,
a family breakup, or moving to a different house (even if the new
residence is better in every respect, since, after all, a home is not just
a physical space but also an existential arrangement). Melancholics
will do their utmost to ward off a change in life: from the outset,
they arrange their lives so as to avoid losses. Psychiatrists have observed that the "melancholic type" is brought up from childhood to

---

12. The psychoanalyst Alfred Winterstein likewise discerned a correlation between melancholia and mathematics.

be performance- and order-oriented, so later on he does everything for himself and does not let others do anything for fear that his non-viability will come to light—though it is likely that the real cause is terror that in the absence of his personal control extending to the minutest detail, a chink may be left in the fabric of existence that will subsequently lead to the disintegration of everything. The terror extends to everything and closes in on itself; the very possibility of terror paralyzes the melancholic. Terror is regarded as inseparable from the world, from which he would like to withdraw definitively. The melancholic strives to overcome every random accident or un-expected development, which is to say that he is willing to conceive of life only as orderliness, yet he is bound to experience that his own personality is the chief obstacle to ultimate orderliness. For if the per-sonality could be set in order existentially, then it would not be a per-sonality but a machine; on the other hand, if the ultimate disorderli-ness of life were to be recognized, then life would lose its meaning: why bother to sew on a shirt button if the ultimate prospect is dis-order? (According to Diogenes Laertius, Heraclitus did not complete some of his works due to melancholia, rather like the housewife who stopped washing clothes because of the same affliction.) The crack through which a melancholic steps out into nothingness comes into being within order: the compulsion to create order is attended by an intensified loathing, leads to respect for authority, commands adher-ence to family bonds, holds moral order in respect, implies a great demand for performance and for giving up striving for the impos-sible. (How much more docile today's melancholic has become com-pared with one from the Romantic era!) Hidden behind all this lies an unacknowledged dread: the melancholic, as was shown by Franz Kafka, does not respect authority because he fears it, but because if he did not respect it then existence itself would become meaning-less. Boundaries would cease to exist, and the alienation that he most fears would irrupt into his life. In this case, respect for authority is a flight from nothingness, from horror. Only melancholics feel true respect for authority: they will sincerely bend the knee to someone they may just as sincerely hold in contempt. And the same goes for the avoidance of conflicts, family, articles of faith, etc.: the seemingly mutually exclusive traits of perspicacity and resignation, sensitivity and willingness to compromise, merge in them, only to degenerate in the end into "incomprehensible" suicide, "mere" change, or "unwarranted" sorrow. *In point of fact, the melancholic is characterized by a simultaneous love of freedom and terror of freedom:* he does not feel free in his actions, because order binds him hand and foot, yet he does not dare strive for freedom — for unequivocal self-realization, fearless confrontation with mortality. A melancholic patient declared to her physician: "I have always looked for order, it is gratifying to me. It protects against disorder, uncontrolled behavior, anarchy, and against sin." The patient then meant to say, "Satan is the representative of disorder in the soul," but making a slip of the tongue said instead: "Satan is the representative of order in the soul" (quoted in Tellenbach, *Melancholy*, 209).

The melancholic fears order just as much as disorder; his fear and the attendant sorrow show that he has failed to find solace in order. Try as he might to achieve order, it nonetheless elicits from him the most profound unease: order is much too arranged; there is no place in it for the "indigestible," "inexpressible" character traits that utterly upset this order. The melancholic creates order but realizes that he has no place in it. And since he wishes to tidy up the whole world, he is forced to realize that his own person can appear in it only as a permanent deficiency, a great misunderstanding. But he is unable to regard deficiency as a normal condition, and in order not to be "alone" in his suffering, he makes deficiency the innermost essence of existence: his life is a misunderstanding, like existence itself. A state of anxiety characteristic of melancholia (*melancholia anxiosa*) is a fear of deficiency: but since the melancholic finds this not outside but in the very world of which it is the inner essence, the fear relates not only to deficiency, to nothingness, but to *something* as well. This paradox is painful for him, and consequently he experiences the world anew in an unprecedented manner: as a pile of ill-matched fragments that render the deficiency palpable. Although he lives in the world, he also moves along *beside* it, as it were, which is why the world gives the impression of being an external object, totally alien to the self. He is part of the world, but at the same time totally alien to it: left to his own devices, feeling homeless and expelled from everywhere, having no idea what purpose could be served by his unappeasable desire.

The desolation and terror that overwhelm the melancholic cannot be reduced to dejection or fear as they are commonly understood. He is sorrowful, but he also has an outlook on his sadness: he is well aware of the futility, the "'senselessness" of grieving, and he relates to his sadness as to an object. He is sad, but also has nothing to do with his own condition, so he cannot be comforted either. He has sunk so deeply into gloom that he is capable even of being cheerful. The ancients discovered an intimate relationship between melancholia and mania, which has remained valid down to the present day. An eighteenth-century comic by the name of Carlini was a severe melancholic, and Byron, too, was melancholic, though his depression did not hinder him from being the center of any company. And Keats wrote in his "Ode on Melancholy":

> Ay, in the very temple of Delight
> Veil'd Melancholy has her sovran shrine.[13]

The same goes for dread, which is akin to, yet not synonymous with, fear. The melancholic fears order, fears the world, and fears nothingness; however, since he both is *in* the world and also *embodies* it, he is not just afraid, but is also able to keep a distance from his fear, and though it does not cease, he is able to realize that it is groundless. The fear transforms into dread: he is afraid of everything, even though

---

13. An investigation of the fifty-five most famous U.S. comedians was carried out in 1974, and most of them proved to be suffering from depression.

his fears have no palpable cause. One may fear mosquito bites, but normally one does not dread them; the melancholic, on the other hand, like the figures standing on the cliffs of Rügen in the painting by Caspar David Friedrich, is not scared even of imminent death, though he may dread existence itself. Dread does not have a specific cause, and since it relates to everything, it blurs the world, making everything look homogeneous. But things can be made indistinguishable only if one finds something that they have in common. To do that, one must deprive them of their individuality, take their specific reality for nothing. Dread, like dogmatism, renders the whole world null and void; however, nothingness ensconces itself in those who dread: in the end, the melancholic comes to fear his own personality most of all. Such a personality ends up in a double bind: he dreads that the world has been annulled, and since he is the exclusive cause of his dread, he feels fragile and yet free. But he also dreads the nothingness lurking inside him, with the world (which is not nothing in the first place, even though he sees it as such) towering over him and crushing him to death. It has been seen that the love and the dread of freedom are equally typical of the melancholic — in that duality, the pitfalls of the medieval notion of melancholia are revived: dread of freedom is a sin (since I withdraw from realizing the infinitely many possibilities inherent within me), and in the love of freedom, love directed at God should be expressed. Kierkegaard was justified in thinking that dread was a manifestation in the individual of original sin: "Dread is not a determinant of necessity, but neither is it of freedom; it is a trammeled freedom, where freedom is not free in itself but trammeled, not by necessity but in itself. If sin has come into the world by necessity (which is a self-contradiction), then there is no dread. If sin has come into the world by an act of abstract *liberum arbitrium* (which no more existed at the beginning than it does at a later period of the world, for it is a nonsense to thought), neither in this case is there dread" (*The Concept of Dread*, 45).

People who fear are not free, because they are at the mercy of whatever they fear; those who are in dread are likewise not free, yet in this dread there is nevertheless a chance of absolute freedom: they are entirely at the mercy of themselves. People who dread do not look "outward," but focus inward, and they discover such a bottomless depth that they try to hold on to *something* at all costs. Yet anyone who has ever seen through everything can no longer be satisfied with the horizon of finitude; those truly in dread are unable to feel at home in the world. Faust is an embodiment of dread, and it takes narrow-mindedness not to discern the mainspring of his being in all-determining dread. Faust fears nothing, but he is in dread of himself: he dreads failing himself, and that is why he is incapable of reaching an agreement with anyone: his dread stems from his desire for everything, and his inner freedom from his dread. The nothingness, appearing on the finite-infinite boundary discoverable everywhere, is also a kind of no-man's-land for a person who lives in dread. The melancholic, who has reached insight into (and experienced) nothingness masochistically, enjoys the fact that no matter what he chooses, it will cripple him, and therefore he abandons himself to *vertigo*, which utterly removes him from the clockwork-like circulation of the world, bearing in mind Goethe's saying that true pleasure is to be had only where one feels vertiginous.

Vertigo concomitant with dread has nothing to do with fear; one fears a fall only if one is at the edge of a precipice and has solid ground beneath one's feet. In dread, the solid ground vanishes, so the vertigo is in fact the fall itself. One does not necessarily have to fall. Kierkegaard aptly says that the reason for the dizziness lies just as much in the eye as in the precipice. As with dread, this too has no "external" or "internal" reason: if the melancholic were able to say *what* he dreaded and what induced his thoughts to dizziness, he would not be melancholic but "merely" bad tempered, sad, or angry. Self and world are inseparable in a mood; it indicates the original unity of the two, which is further attested by the fact that one is always in some mood: having moods in general cannot be contrasted with moodlessness—one can discern only contrasts between individual moods. The common psychological notion that there is some sort of mood "inside" people, which is reflected onto the world, and vice versa, that a situation "external" to us arouses a mood in us, are both erroneous. Unlike a sentiment, which is always linked to something, a mood has no object (or subject), because, to follow Heidegger's train of thought, in moods one can discern the "how" of the situation of the human being; in a mood, existence unfolds before one as human existence. For the melancholic, this deep, original interdependence of the self and the world is obvious; and if he curses the world or himself, then behind the words one should notice something that cannot be referred to in words: he does not dread merely the world or himself, but also the fact that he is at the mercy of existence by virtue of his own life. Mood can at most be hinted at, but one cannot speak about it satisfactorily; as a matter of course, speech handles as objects things that are not only objects, and treats as subjects things that are not merely subjects. Speaking about one's own mood, one inevitably reassigns the interpretation of being to a sentiment. That makes the impatient reaction of others comprehensible: "Come off it. There's no need for the foul mood," or "This is no time to be so cheerful." Mood is incommunicable, and when someone is in a euphoric mood, he is just as isolated in his own way as the melancholic: the individual's ultimate self-dependence (even loneliness) is exposed in mood. Compared with other moods, melancholia has a special role insofar as it is the only one that confronts itself as a mood. European thinking has been struggling since the time of Heraclitus with the dual experiences of reality common to everyone and the reality granted to the individual alone: the search for truth and the desire for an explanation of existence suppose and reject both. Every mood is intermediate between the two poles, trying to bridge them at ever-shifting points (a happy person, for example, believes he is able to share his joy with everyone, but then comes to realize that in truth he cannot do so with anyone). The melancholic occupies an extreme pole: he has no ambition to step into a reality common to everyone (hence his taciturnity, which was noticed by Aristotle), but proclaims (not verbally, but by his being) that man is incapable of accounting satisfactorily for himself, is unable to communicate himself to others.

Consistently adopted uniqueness and self-reliance make the melancholic an isolated eccentric (ἰδιώτης) — an idiot. Yet even if he suffers from his situation, he experiences it quite differently from the way that external observers see it. The psychosensory disturbances experienced by the melancholic indicate the difference: he feels his head to be empty and his body to be an alien entity, his perspective and experience of time become disturbed, etc. — all that seems groundless ("unjustified") to an outside observer, yet it still helps the melancholic constructs his own world so that no one else can enter it. The illusions, visions, and psychosensory disturbances coupled with a perfectly intact consciousness are not just of "bodily" or "psychological" origin — they are harbingers of a singular experience of being (and that being does not necessarily have to be linked with pathological sensations and perceptions). The melancholic is perfectly free yet totally bound while creating a world where different laws apply from those in the "other," accustomed world. The new world of the melancholic is born of the insight that he has made a mess of what he deemed to be his own possibilities, thereby becoming a victim of a serious injustice: the possible became impossible, and what had looked impossible (that is, that he would become a prisoner of himself) came true. The notion of possibility acquires a new meaning here: as it fuses with the concept of impossibility, it takes on a meaning different from the colloquial sense. *For the melancholic, possibilities smuggle infinity into existence, and that, rather than the chance of their turning into reality, is their main value.* The melancholic knows what an opportunity is but cannot avail himself of it, because he missed it long ago; in his case, opportunity therefore means experiencing infinity within total, finite constraint—yearning without an object, futile hope. "My whole life is one great homesickness," Gustav Mahler wrote in a letter. And Kierkegaard noted the following: "What is sickness? Melancholy. Where is the seat of this sickness? In the power of imagination: and it feeds on possibility" (*Stages on Life's Way*, 356) Future-directedness, which elevates man above all living creatures, is for the melancholic a source of torment; the future is an unfolding of coming possibilities, but since from the outset he has let everything slip, there is nothing to unfold. *For the melancholic, the future does not signify the realization of opportunities but the possibility of real things passing:* the future relates to transience, that is, it is not a future but a *coming past* expressible in no verbal tense.[14] "I was already elderly when I was born," begins an entry in the journal of Kierkegaard, who considered it to be the truest mark of despair that *all* the past is preserved in it. "I skipped childhood and adolescence." The melancholic experiences opportunities and hope more deeply than anyone, since for him there is nothing to come true, nothing to hope for. Luther, who was not free from melancholia, wrote: "Hope directs the gaze to expected things, but that does not become visible. So the glance is directed at the unknown, the hidden, the inner darkness, in such a manner that it does not know what it hopes for, but knows what it does not hope for" (quoted in Rudolf Bultmann, "Humanismus und Christentum," 73). For the melancholic, the story of Pandora's box possesses the most profound truth: all manner of suffering was unleashed on the human race; only hope, Elpis, remained in the jar. At the bottom of the loss of hope one can discern a closure in the face of hope; hence the bad conscience of the melancholic

---

14. This makes comprehensible the observations made by psychiatrists that the melancholic concerns himself to a striking degree with past events, and his dreams are also linked to the past.

(he sees his life as a series of omissions) but also his clear-sightedness. After all, everyone has hope except the person who is omniscient: "For we are saved by hope; but hope that is seen is not hope: for what a man seeth, why doth he yet hope for?" (Romans 8:24). Only the omniscient is exempt from hoping; those who have no hope regard hopelessness, closure, and being deprived of all possibility as a normal state—and what else would that be but death?

The present is "open" solely toward evanescence; the future becomes past, whereas the past is synonymous with the present moment. For the melancholic, the extension of the present moment and its exclusivity are a result of glimpsing the essence of time: for him, time is not an "objective" entity to be measured with a clock, but a function of human situations; it is not external in relation to man, but a consequence of human activity and perspective. Time and the human condition are just as indistinguishable as body and soul: their relation is characterized as one of interdependence. (Aristotle, in anticipation of the interpretations of space and time by the most recent theories of physics, postulated that time is inseparable from the calculator (that is, the mind): "If nothing can count except consciousness . . . it is impossible that time should exist if consciousness does not" (*Physics*, 223a). That is why the melancholic experiences time differently from nonmelancholics: the transformation of time follows from his singular situation (loss of hope and purposeless yearning). If illness, suffering, and death are not blows arriving from outside but possibilities unfolding from within, then the duration of life also depends on the person (within the biological threshold), an extreme manifestation of this being the "speeding up" or "slowing down" of time (in the case of man, the "moment" of death is determined mentally as well: one can be ready to die but can also keep death waiting). The Middle Ages, which considered humans to be metaphysically determined in all respects, regarded time as a gift of God independent of them, and its "objectivity" was external in relation to the attitude of the observer.[15] It was no accident that time was a problem precisely for those who wanted to find their path to God alone, solitarily, without external help—or even to battle with him. If what we make of ourselves depends on ourselves, then the sense of time also depends on ourselves: this assumption perturbed mystics (who experienced the decline of the Middle Ages more keenly than anyone) just as much as it did melancholics, against whom one of the accusations brought up in the Middle Ages was precisely that they were constantly brooding about the past and casting glances at an unknown future instead of at eternity. The Middle Ages judged time on the basis of divine eternity, whereas mystics and melancholics contrasted time with eternity: the differentiation of endless time and timeless, living eternity follows from the human capacity to create time. Since the human intellect is infinite, and cannot reach its goal in time, it stands *outside* time, Marsilio Ficino stated. According to Pico della Mirandola, if we are raised to the most sublime heights of theology, "we shall be able to measure with the rod of indivisible eternity all things that are and that have been" (*Oration on the Dignity of Man*, 27). The ability to step outside time (a secret of melancholic Renaissance portraits!) means that human beings have mastered time: they bestow unique, irreplaceable meaning on their own existence, and thereby they also bestow upon themselves their own time, a rhythm of being typical only of themselves. The timelessness experienced by the mystic automatically presupposes that time is a function of the human situation: in the case of the melancholic, the melting (or rather, freezing) of the future and the past into the present moment is a consequence of the conversion of the lived present into a lived timelessness. Because of its slow circling around the sun, Saturn, the planet of melancholics,

---

15. On the instigation of Henry of Ghent, Étienne Tempier, the bishop of Paris, declared, "*Quod aevum et tempus nihil sunt in re, sed solum in apprehensione: error*" ("That age and time have no reality, but exist only in our perception, is an error").

embodies eternal time in certain Eastern notions, and "eternal time" is indeed the name given to the planet in Armenian texts (Zurvān = Zoroaster). Lived timelessness, although it may afford a glimpse of a new philosophy, results in a form of deprivation: the melancholic does not know the future as possibility; therefore, *timelessness* is not complete attainment for him but rather the opposite: a complete lack of attainment, a complete deficiency. The self-reproach typical of the melancholic corresponds to a religious sense of guilt: he feels that he has missed his appointed time, his *kairos*—which in the New Testament is the instant when man comes close to eternity—and has fallen hopelessly behind his own possibilities. The eternity experienced by the melancholic is a negative eternity: he is damned to eternal unfulfillment, to a constant experience of lack. A melancholic patient announced to his physician day after day that he would be executed that evening, and he was not convinced by the argument that he had already said that many times before. He had a sense of time that was different from that of nonmelancholics because the future could bring nothing new (for example, that he would not be executed after all). The melancholic's revaluation of the future, the loss (or rather, purposelessness) of hope, creates a tension characteristic of his makeup: he who has no hope sees everything clearly—but to have a simultaneous view of all events is granted exclusively to God, who is located outside the creaturely, temporal world. The melancholic, who lives within the creaturely, temporal world, is compelled to live in and through time, which is incompatible with the transtemporality of the divine clarity of vision: he yearns in vain to withdraw from the world (Bellerophon). Another melancholic patient hid his watch so as not to be obliged to "see" the passage of time. As he recounted his condition to his psychiatrist:

> I often think I am not ill but recognized something that others had not hit upon: I have developed in myself a miserable view of the world that others do not share and yet is perfectly logical; I

don't understand at all how one can think in any way differently.
. . . Those thoughts and feelings go hand in hand with dread.
. . . To me it is inconceivable to think in any different way after
having thought it over. . . . I wish to kill myself so as to rid myself
of these thoughts, but I have a great love of life. . . . The terrible
thing is that I can control myself to the extent that others notice
nothing; indeed, I can be cheerful and am able to laugh.

> (V. E. Freiherr von Gebsattel, *Prolegomena
> einer medizinischen Anthropologie*, 7)

The melancholic is condemned to continuous annihilation: his eternity is the eternity of the *right now*.[16]

The never-ending "now," despite all its negativity, is eternity, or
to be more precise, extratemporality. And if the melancholic suffers
from himself, then in point of fact he suffers from the recognition
that time, along with its infinite possibilities and infinite constraints,
depends entirely on man.[17] Existence in time makes man able to un-

---

16. The Hungarian poet Dániel Berzsenyi writes in his poem "Melancholia":

A vidámság csak a valóságnak
S szűk jelenvalónak szedheti rózsáit:
De te, karján a szép Álmodásnak,
Éled a jövendőt s a multnak óráit.

[Happiness can pick only the roses
of reality and the narrow present,
But you, on the arm of a fine dream,
You live the future and past hours.]

17. The teaching of Orphic theogony relating to Chronos, the god of time,
illuminates this problem with unsurpassable sharpness. The Orphics regarded the
Titan Cronus, who as Saturn became the incarnation of melancholia, as a seer and
soothsayer, and since soothsayers have an insight into *time*, they identified Cronus,
the father of Zeus, with the primordial deity Chronos. (According to some, the name
Chronos derives from the verb κραίνω, "to fulfill"!). The union of the god of melan-

fold his own possibilities, but being enclosed in time prevents him from uniting with God. Behind the closed horizons of practical life unfolds a world in which the melancholic is at home — if, indeed, one can call home a world that prevents a person from finding solace. The melancholic steps onto a path where we cannot follow, and therefore we see him, like all trailblazers, as possessing some unknown, mysterious knowledge. His knowledge, however, is not simply knowledge of this or that fact; if that were all, he would not be melancholic. His knowledge is directly linked with the original sin (the Tree of Knowledge) and is beyond preoccupation with practical matters. The three satanic promises of knowledge, as Walter Benjamin saw them, were the following: "What tempts is the *illusion of freedom* — in the exploration of what is forbidden; the *illusion of independence* — in the secession from the community of the pious; the *illusion of infinity* — in the empty abyss of evil" (*German Tragic Drama*, 230). The melancholic's knowledge is not true knowledge — but it is questionable whether there is any truer knowledge than his. For although his knowledge points beyond the practical world, that is possible only because he was once preoccupied with the mundane world and became acquainted with it. Just as only the experience of order makes the melancholic sensitive to disorder, so it is that knowledge of the everyday, practical world makes it possible for that knowledge to transcend the world and enter a place where there is nothing to which it can be directed. Profoundly melancholic Thomas Mann frequently wrote in his diary that he was tired of living — not for personal reasons, but because every life moves on prescribed tracks and every existence is finite, adding that the sense of the term "world-weary" (*Lebensmüde*) is general rather than personal (*Tagebücher 1933–34*, 121). The knowledge possessed by the melancholic tempts him onto unknown,

choly with the god of time corresponds to the similarly Orphic idea of Hellanicus of Mytilene and Hieronymus of Rhodes, which identified the likewise melancholic Hercules with timeless Chronos.

untraversable terrain—or at least that is how outsiders see it. Yet he is sure that he is proceeding on very familiar terrain indeed: the unknown unfolds here, in our world, and it is here, in our world, that the paths on which we are unable to follow the melancholic intersect one another. In his poem "The Veiled Image at Sais," Schiller tells the story of a young man who thirsted for the knowledge of *everything*. On reaching Sais, his gaze fell on a giant veiled image behind which stood Truth, and no one had till then dared lift the veil. One night the young man drew the veil aside—but we never find out what he saw:

> ... And ask ye what
> Unto the gaze was there within revealed?
> I know not. Pale and senseless, at the foot
> Of the dread statue of Egyptian Isis,
> The priests beheld him at the dawn of day;
> But what he saw, or what did there befall,
> His lips disclosed not. Ever from his heart
> Was fled the sweet serenity of life,
> And the deep anguish dug the early grave:
> "Woe, woe to him"—such were his warning words,
> Answering some curious and impetuous brain,
> "Woe—for she never shall delight him more!
> Woe,—woe to him who treads through guilt to Truth!"

> (*The Poems and Ballads of Schiller*, 71)

The youth glimpsed Truth, and he forgot to smile, because when he glanced behind the veil a terrible eye fastened on his frightened gaze. It was undisguised chaos, which Jakob Böhme called "the eye of the bottomless Abyss." The Truth that he chanced upon was infallible not-knowing: a manifestation of the anarchy of existence. The young man had become a victim of his own daring: if the quest for insight or knowledge oversteps the boundaries, it becomes boundless and is fulfilled in indeterminacy. It then turns out that truth does not mean the true character of a statement—with that, one merely testifies to a respect for boundaries. By staying within boundaries, one hides from another kind of truth, which is revealed when one transgresses the boundary: while living in the truth of correspondences, one forgets about the true nature of one's life, about how life can be fitted to nothing, subordinated to nothing, and that on account of life's uniqueness, any statements relating to it are also invalid and false. The sole truth of one's life is that no definite statement can be made about it, that the more one yearns for certainty, the more obvious one's elusiveness becomes. The paralyzing spectacle of chaos plunged the youth into anguish. Before arriving at Sais, he had supposed it was a matter of time and perseverance for him to find the truth. By pulling the veil aside, however, he realized that he would have to give up on his illusion of ultimate Truth. By transgressing the boundaries, he came to recognize the chaos engulfing him—which, until then, he had shied away from in fear and trembling, and which he had hoped to eliminate from his life by investing hope in an unknown, ultimate truth. This new "truth" no longer augmented knowledge: it opened one up to one's own abysmal depths.[18]

With every step he takes, man tries to smuggle some goal into nothingness. The melancholic is skeptical of those goals, seeing aimlessness as life's main motive force. Hence his bad conscience: after all, burdened with two thousand years of Christian culture, how else could he look on the collapse following aimlessness as anything but a sin? But he cannot be absolved of his sin: it does not have a definite location, but extends to everything, and like illness, it is not an external force. In sin, existence blossoms, as it were. "Let no man say when he is tempted, I am tempted of God: for God cannot be tempted with evil, neither tempteth he any man. But every man is

---

18. According to a note made by Plutarch, the inscription on the shrine of Isis at Sais read: "I am all that has been, and is, and shall be, and my robe no mortal has yet uncovered" (*On Isis and Osiris*, in *Moralia*, 5:9).

tempted, when he is drawn away of his own lust, and enticed. Then, when lust hath conceived, it bringeth forth sin: and sin, when it is finished, bringeth forth death" (James 1:13–15). This is what prompts the melancholic to despair when looking at the human condition, and to consider existence hopeless. From the seventeenth century on, it was precisely in arguing with God or with the explanation of existence offered by Christian theology that numerous thinkers sank ever deeper into their own despair: it was only against the context of expediency and order that aimlessness and chaos appeared enticing (Browne, Donne, Pascal, Schelling, Kierkegaard, Nietzsche, Bataille). Kierkegaard saw very clearly that melancholia, which he called "the hysteria of spirit," melts away as soon as the person "bows with genuine humility before the eternal Power" (*Either/Or*, trans. Swenson and Swenson, 193–94). He adds elsewhere: "The self is in sound health and free from despair only when, precisely by having been in despair, it is grounded transparently in God" (*The Sickness unto Death*, 28–29). Man, the unhappiest and most unfortunate animal (Nietzsche) is human precisely because he is unable to relate to God at every moment, and ultimately is incapable of rising above the limitations of his ego. That is why Kierkegaard says the following about despair: "The possibility of this sickness is man's advantage over the beast, and this advantage distinguishes him far more essentially than the erect posture, for it implies the infinite erectness or loftiness of being spirit" (11). The capacity for despair distinguishes man from animals, whereas what separates him from God is that he is unable *not* to despair — one way or another, everyone despairs at some point. And one does not necessarily have to think of "ultimate" questions; shades of an ultimate confusion can be felt in the least vexation, the slightest bother: "It was through dead fashions that Lola perceived the passage of time," Céline writes in connection with an insignificant prostitute. "The possibility that there would never again be races at Longchamp overwhelmed her. The sadness of the world has different ways of getting to people, but it seems to succeed almost every time"

(*Journey to the End of the Night*, 56–57). Melancholic Kierkegaard tried to fight his melancholia, which is why he introduced a distinction between good and bad despondency: if the good variety settles on a person, he loses his illusions, but in return he regains himself; if the bad despondency overpowers him, he loses himself along with the illusions.[19] Yet if the knowledge of nothingness relates to existence itself, and sin is an organic component of supposed innocence, then the melancholic is unable to find a way back from despair to the original unity but regards duality and discord as a natural basis of life. "All that comes to be," Schelling writes in the unfinished fragment *The Ages of the World*, "can only do so in discontent; and as dread is the basic feeling of each living creature, so is everything that lives conceived and born only in violent conflict," adding "dread is the basic material of every life and existence" (*The Ages of the World*, 211).[20] The true melancholic never recovers from his condition, and if he notices that things have an unknown face as well, he will feel eternal nostalgia for the unknown landscape toward which that face is looking. From then on, sadness, that "enigmatic pleasure," will not only catch hold of him every now and then,[21] but will attach to him like a shadow. Sadness, the attraction to evil (ill humor), cannot be

---

19. According to the astrological differentiation of benign and malignant melancholia, the conjunction of Saturn and Jupiter in Libra lead to benign, the conjunction of Saturn and the moon in Scorpio to malignant melancholia.

20. "All of existence, from the tiniest gnat to the secret of incarnation inclusively, fills me with dread," Kierkegaard wrote in his *Journal* from a far-from-Christian basic position.

21. Like Rosanette, the kept woman in Flaubert's *Sentimental Education*, who "even before going to bed always exhibited a little melancholy, just as there are cypress trees at the door of a tavern" (ed. Dora Knowles Ranous, 155). One wonders whether Flaubert was aware that in the Middle Ages, cypresses were held to be melancholic plants. Equally, one wonders whether people in the Middle Ages were aware that according to Pythagoras, coffins should not be made of cypress, because the "scepter of Zeus was made of cypress wood" (see Mansfeld, *Die Vorsokratiker*, 177).

clarified with the aid of reason; it is inexplicable (on the basis of sociology, anthropology, theology, or the philosophy of history) because the enigma of evil, of nothingness, is precisely that it is elusive: if one were to force it into concepts, one would be doing violence to oneself. The melancholic is incapable of hanging on to anything; he feels that existence has cast him out, and he takes the view that his life is a fatal mistake,[22] for which he condemns the whole of existence. The mysterious naïveté that separates him from everyone else is precisely what makes him incapable of distinguishing his self from existence. Whatever he touches, he is thrown back on himself; and if he looks into himself, he catches a glimpse of a miniature copy of the world. Endless deprivation makes his loneliness unbearable, but only he knows of what he had been deprived: for him, lack is a kind of fulfillment, just as in losing himself he arrives back at himself as an ever-more ephemeral imprint of his ego. As if we were looking through a telescope, bewildered, to see whether the outside world continued inside us, or as if we were looking back from outside at our ego, wielding the telescope in confusion. But let the telescope be reversed and aimed at the by-now barely discernible figure of the melancholic, letting our eye rest on him for a while — only then to reverse the perspective again and look out at the overpoweringly magnified world. Who is right? The melancholic or the world? It is no use swinging the telescope — like Nietzsche's restless boatman, we will never be able to decide whether we should feel that infinity is a cage or, in fact, freedom.

---

22. As when a typographical error comes to life and demands its rights, Kierkegaard might say.

BIBLIOGRAPHY

Adorno, Theodor W. *Kierkegaard: Construction of the Aesthetic.* Translated by Robert Hullot-Kentor. Minneapolis: University of Minnesota Press, 1989.

Adorno, Theodor W., Hans Albert, Ralf Dahrendorf, Jürgen Habermas, Harald Pilot, and Karl Popper. *The Positivist Dispute in German Sociology.* Translated by Giyn Adey and David Frisby. New York: Harper and Row, 1976.

Agrippa, Heinrich Cornelius, von Nettesheim. *Of Occult Philosophy.* 1510. Translated by J. F. London, 1651. Reprinted as *Three Books of Occult Philosophy or Magic: Book One—Natural Magic,* edited by Willis F. Whitehead (Chicago: Hahn and Whitehead, 1898).

———. *Three Books of Occult Philosophy or Magic.* 1533. Edited by Willis F. Whitehead, Chicago: Hahn and Whitehead, 1898.

Albertinus, Aegidius. *Lucifers Königreich und Seelenjaidt: Oder Narrenhatz.* Berlin: Spemann, 1900.

Angelus Silesius [Johannes Scheffler]. *Alexandrines.* Translated from the *Cherubinischer Wandersmann,* by Julia Bilger. North Montpelier, Vt.: Driftwind, 1944.

———. *Cherubinischer Wandersmann.* 1657. Jena and Leipzig: Verlag Eugen Diederichs, 1905.

Apuleius, Lucius. *The Golden Ass.* Translated by Eric Chaim Kline. www.poetryintranslation.com/klineasapuleius.htm.

Aristophanes. *The Clouds.* In *The Greek Classics: Aristophanes—Eleven Plays,* translated by the Athenian Society, edited by James H. Ford. El Paso, Tex.: El Paso Norte Press, 2006.

Aristotle. *Aristotelis qui ferebantur librorum fragmenta.* Edited by Valentin Rose. Leipzig: Teubner, 1886.

———. *Metaphysics.* Translated by W. D. Ross. Oxford: Clarendon, 1908.

————. *Nicomachean Ethics.* Translated by W. D. Ross. Oxford: Oxford University Press, 1925.

————. *On Dreams.* Translated by J. I. Beare. Oxford: Clarendon, 1908.

————. *On Prophesying by Dreams.* Translated by J. I. Beare. Available from the Internet Classics Archive, http://classics.mit.edu/Aristotle /prophesying.html.

————. *On the Heavens.* Translated by J. L. Stocks. Available from the Internet Classics Archive, http://classics.mit.edu/Aristotle/heavens.html.

————. *On the Soul.* Translated by J. A. Smith. In *The Works of Aristotle,* vol. 3, edited by W. D. Ross. Oxford: Oxford University Press, 1963.

————. *Physics.* Books 1–4.Translated by P. H. Wicksteed and F. M. Cornford. Rev. ed. Cambridge: Harvard University Press, 1957. Reprinted, 1996.

————. *Poetics.* Translated by Stephen Halliwell. Cambridge: Harvard University Press, 1995.

————. *Problemata physica.* Translated by E. S. Forster. Oxford: Clarendon, 1927.

Artaud, Antonin. "Tutuguri—poem." Partly translated in *Antonin Artaud: Selected Writings,* edited by Susan Sontag. Berkeley: University of California Press, 1976.

Augustine. *City of God.* Translated by R. W. Dyson. New York: Cambridge University Press, 1998.

————. *Confessions.* Translated by Albert C. Outler. Philadelphia: Westminster, 1955.

————. *The Confessions of St. Augustine.* Translated by Edward B. Pusey. New York: Collier and Son, 1909.

————. *Soliloquies.* Translated by Rose Elizabeth Cleveland. Boston: Little, Brown, 1910.

Bandmann, Günther. *Melancholie und Musik. Ikonographische Studien.* Cologne and Opladen: Westdeutscher Verlag, 1960.

Bataille, Georges. *Œuvres complètes.* Vol. 1. Paris: Gallimard, 1978.

Bayer, Walter von, and Richard M. Griffith, eds. *Conditio Humana: Erwin W. Straus on his 75th Birthday.* Berlin: Springer Verlag, 1966.

Benjamin, Walter. "A Berlin Chronicle." Translated by Rodney Livingstone. In Walter Benjamin, *Selected Writings,* vol. 2, pt. 2, *1931–1934,* edited by Michael W. Jennings, Howard Eiland, and Gary Smith. Cambridge: Belknap Press/Harvard University Press, 1999.

————. "German Men and Women: A Sequence of Letters." Translated by Edmund Jephcott. In Walter Benjamin, *Selected Writings*, vol. 3, 1935–1938, edited by Howard Eiland and Michael W. Jennings. Cambridge: Harvard University Press, 2002.

————. *The Origin of German Tragic Drama*. Translated by John Osborne. London: Verso, 2003.

Berzsenyi, Dániel. *Összes művei*. Budapest: Szépirodalmi, 1978.

Binswanger, Ludwig. *Melancholie und Manie: Phänomenologische Studien*. Pfullingen, Germany: Neske, 1960.

Boerner, Peter. *Goethe*. London: Haus, 2005.

Boethius. *Consolation of Philosophy*. Translated by H. R. James. London: Elliott Stock, 1897.

Böhme, Hartmut, and Gernot Böhme. *Das Andere der Vernunft: Zur Entwicklung von Rationalitätsstrukturen am Beispiel Kants*. Frankfurt am Main: Suhrkamp Verlag, 1983.

Böhme, Jakob. *Sämtliche Schrifte*. Facsimile of 1730 ed. 11 vols. Stuttgart: Fr. Frommanns Verlag, 1955–61.

Boll, Franz, and Carl Bezold. *Sternglaube und Sterndeutung: Die Geschichte und das Wesen der Astrologie*. Leipzig: Wilhelm Gundel, 1926.

Bovelles, Charles de. *Libellus de nihilo: Le Livre du néant*. Edited and translated by Pierre Magnard. Paris: Éditions Vrin, 1983.

Browne, Thomas. *Religio Medici* and *Hydriotaphia: Urne Burial*. In *The Works of Sir Thomas Browne*, edited by Geoffrey Keynes. Vol. 1. London: Faber & Faber, 1964.

Büchner, Georg. *Werke und Briefe*. Leipzig: Insel-Verlag, 1967.

Buhr, Manfred, and Gerd Irrlitz. *Der Anspruch der Vernunft*. Berlin: Akademie-Verlag, 1968.

Bultmann, Rudolf. "Humanismus und Christentum." *Studium Generale* 1 (1947–48): 70–77.

Burney, Charles. *The Present State of Music in France and Italy*. London, 1773.

Burton, Robert. *The Anatomy of Melancholy*. 1621. Reprint, New York: New York Review Books, 2001.

Byron, George Gordon. *Letters and Journals.* 6 vols. Edited by Rowland E.
    Prothero. London: John Murray, 1900–1904.

Cabanis, Pierre. *Coup-d'oeil sur les révolutions et sur la réforme de la medi-
    cine.* 1804. In *Œuvres Complètes de Cabanis.* Vol. 1. Paris: Claude
    Lehec et Jean Cazeneuve, 1823.

Caraco, Albert. *Bréviaire du chaos.* Lausanne: L'Âge d'Homme, 1982.

Cassirer, Ernst. *The Individual and the Cosmos in Renaissance Philosophy.*
    Translated by Mario Domandi. Oxford: Blackwell, 1963.

Céline, Louis-Ferdinand. *Cannon Fodder.* Translated by K. De Coninck and
    B. Childish. Rochester, Kent: Hangman Books, 1988.

———. *Journey to the End of the Night.* Translated by Ralph Manheim.
    London: Calder, 1988.

Cioran, Émile M. *Tears and Saints.* Translated by Ilinca Zarifopol-Johnston.
    Chicago: University of Chicago Press, 1998.

Conolly, John. *An Inquiry Concerning the Indications of Insanity: with Sug-
    gestions for the Better Protection and Care of the Insane.* London: John
    Taylor, 1830.

Cusanus, Nicolaus. *Complete Philosophical and Theological Treatises of
    Nicholas of Cusa.* 2 vols. Translated by Jasper Hopkins. Minneapolis:
    Banning, 2001.

———. *On Learned Ignorance.* Translated by Jasper Hopkins. Minneapo-
    lis: Banning, 1981.

Dante. *Divine Comedy: Inferno, Purgatory, Paradise.* Translated by Allen
    Mandelbaum. New York: Vintage, 2013.

Diderot, Denis. "Mélancolie." In *Encyclopédie ou Dictionnaire raisonné des
    sciences, des arts et des métiers,* vol. 10, edited by Denis Diderot and Jean
    Le Rond d'Alembert. Neuchâtel: Samuel Faulche, 1765.

Diels, Hermann, and Walther Kranz. *Die Fragmente der Vorsokratiker.* 3 vols.
    Berlin: Weidmannsche Verlag Buchhandlung, 1954.

Dilthey, Wilhelm. *Ideas concerning a Descriptive and Analytic Psychology.*
    1894. In *Descriptive Psychology and Historical Understanding.* Edited
    and translated by Richard M. Zaner and R. A. Makkreel. The Hague:
    Nijhof, 1977.

Diogenes Laertius. *Lives of Eminent Philosophers.* 2 vols. Edited and trans-
    lated by R. D. Hicks. Cambridge: Harvard University Press, 1991.

Donne, John. *Poetical Works*. Oxford: Oxford University Press, 1971.

Drieu La Rochelle, Pierre. *Geheimer Bericht und andere biographische Auf- zeichnungen*. Translated by Joachim Sartorius. Munich: Mathes & Seitz, 1986.

Dürer, Albrecht. *De Symmetria partium in rectis formis humanorum corpo- rum—Four Books on Human Proportion*. 1528. Translated into English by Silvio Levy. CD-ROM. Oakland, Calif.: Octavo, 2003.

———. *The Painter's Manual: A Manual of Measurement of Lines, Areas, and Solids by Means of Compass and Ruler, Assembled by Albrecht Dürer for the Use of All Lovers of Art, with Appropriate Illustrations Ar- ranged to Be Printed in the Year MDXXV* [1525]. Edited and translated by W. L. Strauss. New York: Abaris, 1977.

Eckermann, Johann Peter, and Johann Wolfgang von Goethe. *Conversations of Goethe with Eckermann and Soret*. With contributions by Frédéric Jacob Soret. Translated by John Oxenford. London: Bell and Sons, 1875.

Eckhart, Johannes (Meister). *Treatises and Sermons of Meister Eckhart*. Edited and translated by James M. Clark and John V. Skinner. New York: Harper and Row, 1958.

Empedocles. *Fragments*. Translated by W. E. Leonard. Chicago: Open Court, 1908.

———. *Fragments and Commentary*. Translated and edited by Arthur Fair- banks. CreateSpace Independent Publishing, 2012.

Eriugena, John Scotus. *Periphyseon*. In *Iohannis Scotti Eriugenae Peri- physeon [De divisione naturae, bk. 3]*. Translated by I. P. Sheldon- Williams. Dublin: Dublin Institute for Advanced Studies, 1981.

Esquirol, Jean-Étienne Dominique. *Des maladies mentales considerées sous les rapports medical, hygiénique, et medico-légal*. Vol. 1. Paris: Baillère, 1838.

Euripides. *Bellerophontes*. Translated by C. Riedweg. *Illinois Classical Studies* 15, no. 1 (Spring 1990): 39–53.

———. *Heracles*. Translated by E. P. Coleridge. New York: Random House, 1938.

———. *Iphigenia in Aulis*. Translated by George Theodoridis. Available at Poetry in Translation, poetryintranslation.com/PITBR/Greek /Iphigeneia.htm.

Fawcett, Benjamin. *Observations on the Nature, Causes, and Cure of Melancholy, Especially of That Which Is Commonly Called Religious Melancholy.* Shrewsbury: Eddowes, 1780.

Ficino, Marsilio. *Epistolae: The Letters of Marsilio Ficino.* 9 vols. Translated by the Language Department of the School of Economic Science. London: Shepheard-Walwyn, 1975–2013.

———. *The Letters of Marsilio Ficino.* Translated by Arthur Farndell. London: Shepheard-Walwyn, 1978.

———. *Meditations on the Soul: Selected Letters of Marsilio Ficino.* Translated by the Language Department of the School of Economic Science. Rochester, Vt.: Inner Traditions International, 1996.

———. *Platonic Theology.* Translated by Michael J. B. Allen. Vol. 2. Cambridge: Harvard University Press, 2002.

———. *Three Books on Life* [*De Vita Triplici*]. Translated by Carol V. Kaske and John R. Clark. Tempe, Ariz.: Renaissance Society of America, 1998.

Firmicus Maternus, Julius. *Ancient Astrology: Theory and Practice; Matheseos Libri VIII.* Translated by Jean Rhys Bram. Park Ridge, N.J.: Noyes, 1975.

———. *The Error of the Pagan Religions.* Translated by Clarence A. Forbes. New York: Newman, 1970.

Flashar, Hellmut. *Melancholie und Melancholiker in den medizinischen Theorien der Antike.* Berlin: Walter de Gruyter, 1966.

Flaubert, Gustave. *Sentimental Education.* Edited by Dora Knowles Ranous. New York: Brentano's, 1922.

Francis of Assisi. *The Little Flowers.* Translated by T. W. Arnold. London: Chatto & Windus, 1908.

Freeman, Kathleen, ed. *Ancilla to the Pre-Socratic Philosophers.* A complete translation of the fragments in Diels, *Fragmente der Vorsokratiker.* Oxford: Blackwell, 1948.

Freud, Sigmund. *A General Introduction to Psychoanalysis.* Translated by G. Stanley Hall. New York: Boni and Liveright, 1920.

———. "Mourning and Melancholia." 1917. In Freud, *The Standard Edition of the Complete Psychological Works,* vol. 14, edited and translated by James Strachey. London: Hogarth, 1957. Reprint, London: Vintage, 2001.

———. *An Outline of Psycho-Analysis*. In *The Standard Edition of the Complete Psychological Works of Sigmund Freud*, vol. 23, edited and translated by James Strachey. London: Hogarth, 1949.

Friedenthal, Richard. *Goethe: His Life and Times*. Translated by John Nowell. London: Weidenfeld and Nicolson, 1965.

Gebsattel, V. E. Freiherr von. *Prolegomena einer medizinischen Anthropologie: Ausgewählte Aufsätze*. Berlin: Springer-Verlag, 1954.

Gent, Werner. *Das Problem der Zeit: Eine historische und systematische Untersuchung*. Hildesheim: Olms, 1965.

Grabbe, Christian Dietrich. *Don Juan and Faust*. Translated by Maurice Edwards. In *The Theatre of Don Juan*, edited by Oscar Mandel. Lincoln: University of Nebraska Press, 1963.

Grass, Günter. *From the Diary of a Snail*. Translated by Ralph Manheim. New York: Harcourt Brace Jovanovich, 1973.

Groß, Felix, ed. *Immanuel Kant: Sein Leben in Darstellungn von Zeitgenossen; Die Biographien von L. E. Borowski, R. B. Jachmann und A. Ch. Wasianski*. Berlin: Deutsche Bibliothek, 1912.

Habermas, Jürgen. *Knowledge and Human Interest: A General Perspective*. Translated by Jeremy J. Shapiro. Boston: Beacon, 1971.

Handwörterbuch des deutschen Aberglaubens. 9 vols. Berlin, 1938–42.

Harvey, E. R. *The Inward Wits: Psychological Theories in the Middle Ages and the Renaissance*. London: Warburg Institute, University of London, 1975.

Hegel, Georg Wilhelm Friedrich. *Elements of the Philosophy of Right*. Translated by H. B. Nisbet. Cambridge: Cambridge University Press, 2003.

———. *Lectures on Fine Art*. Translated by T. M. Knox. Oxford: Clarendon, 1973.

———. *The Phenomenology of Mind*. Translated by J. B. Baillie. London: Swan Sonnenschein, 1910.

Heidegger, Martin. *Being and Time*. Translated by John Macquarrie and Edward Robinson. Oxford: Blackwell, 1962.

Helvétius, Claude-Adrien. *De l'Homme*. In *Oeuvres*, vol. 8. Paris: Didot l'ainé, 1795.

Hermes Trismegistus. "Pœmandres: The Shepherd of Men." In *Thrice-Greatest Hermes: Studies in Hellenistic Theosophy and Gnosis*, vol. 2, translated and edited by G. R. S. Mead. London: Theosophical Publishing Society, 1906.

Heyden-Rynsch, Verena von der. *Riten der Selbstauflosung.* Munich: Matthes & Seitz, 1983.

Hieronymus [St. Jerome]. *Des Heiligen Kirchenvaters Eusebius Hieronymus ausgewählte Schriften.* Munich: Kösel, 1936–37.

Hippocrates. *On Airs, Waters, and Places.* Translated by Francis Adams. London: Sydenham Society, 1849.

———. *On the Nature of Man.* Translated by W. H. S. Jones. Cambridge: Harvard University Press, 1923.

Hippolytus. *The Refutation of All Heresies.* Translated by J. H. MacMahon. Edinburgh: Clark, 1868.

Hobbes, Thomas. *Leviathan: Or the Matter, Forme, and Power of a Common-Wealth Ecclesiasticall and Civill.* Edited by by Ian Shapiro. New Haven, Conn.: Yale University Press, 2010.

Hölderlin, Friedrich. *The Death of Empedocles: A Mourning-Play.* Edited and translated by David Farrell Krell. Albany: State University of New York Press, 2008.

Homer. *Hymn to Demeter.* In Gregory Nagy, *Greek Mythology and Poetics.* Ithaca, N.Y.: Cornell University Press, 1990.

———. *Iliad.* Translated by Samuel Butler. London: Longmans, Green, 1887.

Jackson, Stanley W. *Melancholia and Depression: From Hippocratic Times to Modern Times.* New Haven, Conn.: Yale University Press, 1987.

Jehl, Rainer. *Melancholie und Acedia: Ein Beitrag zu Anthropologie und Ethik Bonaventuras.* Paderborn, Germany: Schöningh, 1984.

Jünger, Ernst. *Annäherunge: Drogen und Rausch.* Stuttgart: Ernst Klett Verlag, 1970. A chapter was translated as "Drugs and Ecstasy," in *Myth and Symbols: Studies in Honor of Mircea Eliade,* edited by Joseph M. Kitagawa and Charles H. Long (Chicago: University of Chicago Press, 1969).

Kahn, Charles H., ed. *The Art and Thought of Heraclitus: An Edition of the Fragments with Translation and Commentary.* Cambridge: Cambridge University Press, 1979.

Kant, Immanuel. *Critique of Pure Reason.* Translated by Patrick Frierson and Paul Guyer. Cambridge: Cambridge University Press, 1999.

————. *Observations on the Feeling of the Beautiful and the Sublime, and Other Writings.* Translated by John T. Goldthwait. Berkeley: University of California Press, 1960.

Kerényi, Karl. "Asterobléta Keraunos." *Egyetemes Philológiai Közlöny* 52 (1927).

Kierkegaard, Søren. *The Concept of Dread.* Translated by Walter Lowrie. Princeton, N.J.: Princeton University Press, 1944.

————. *Either/Or.* Translated by David F. and Lillian Marvin Swenson. Princeton, N.J.: Princeton University Press, 1944.

————. *Either/Or.* Vol. 2, *Equilibrium between the Aesthetical and the Ethical in the Composition of Personality.* Translated by Walter Lowrie. Garden City, N.Y.: Doubleday, 1959.

————. *The Sickness unto Death.* Translated by Walter Lowrie. Princeton, N.J.: Princeton University Press, 1941.

————. *Stages on Life's Way.* Translated by Walter Lowrie. Princeton, N.J.: Princeton University Press, 1940.

Klages, Ludwig. *Der Geist als Widersacher der Seele.* Bonn: Bouvier Verlag, 1981.

Kleist, Heinrich von. *Werke und Briefe,* 4 vols. Berlin: Aufbau Verlag, 1978.

Klibansky, Raymond, Erwin Panofsky, and Fritz Saxl. *Saturn and Melancholy: Studies in the History of Natural Philosophy, Religion, and Art.* London: Thomas Nelson and Sons, 1964.

Kollesch, J., and D. Nickel, eds. *Antike Heilkunst: Ausgewählte Texte aus dem medizinischen Schrifttum der Griechen und Römer.* Leipzig: Reclam Verlag, 1986.

Kraepelin, Emil. *Lehrbuch der Psychiatrie.* 4th ed. Leipzig: Meiner, 1893.

Krafft-Ebing, Richard von. *Lehrbuch der gerichtlichen Psychopathologie.* Stuttgart, 1875.

Krimmel, Elisabeth. "Naturgestalt und Kunstfigur." In *Darmstadt in der Zeit des Klassizismus und der Romantik,* edited by Bernd Krimmel. Exhibition catalogue. Darmstadt: Magistrat der Stadt, 1978.

Kristeva, Julia. *Black Sun: Depression and Melancholia.* Translated by Leon S. Roudiez. New York: Columbia University Press, 1989.

La Rochefoucauld, François de. *Collected Maxims and Other Reflections.* Translated by E. H. and A. M. Blackmore and Francine Giguère. Oxford: Oxford University Press, 2007.

Lasota, Jean-Pierre, ed. *Astronomy at the Frontiers of Science*. New York: Springer, 2011.

Lawätz, Heinrich Wilhelm. *Versuch über die Temperamente*. Hamburg, 1777.

Leibbrand, Werner. *Heilkunde: Eine Problemgeschichte der Medizin*. Freiburg im Breisgau and Munich: Alber, 1953.

Lepenies, Wolf. *Melancholie und Gesellschaft*. Frankfurt am Main: Suhrkamp Verlag, 1969.

Lucian. *Dialogues of the Dead*. In *The Works of Lucian of Samosata*, vol. 1. Translated by H. W. and F. G. Fowler. Oxford: Clarendon, 1909.

Lucretius. *On the Nature of Things* [*De rerum natura*]. Translated by Cyril Bailey. Oxford: Clarendon, 1947.

Mahnke, Dietrich. *Unendliche Sphäre und Allmittelpunkt: Beiträge zur Genealogie der mathematischen Mystik*. Halle: Niemeyer, 1937.

Malebranche, Nicolas. *Œuvres complètes*. Vol. 10, *Méditations chrétiennes et métaphysiques*. Edited by Henri Gouhier and André Robinet. Paris: Vrin, 1959.

Mann, Thomas. *Death in Venice*. Translated by Martin C. Doege. Wolf Pup Books, 2014.

———. "Dostoevsky—in Moderation." Introduction to *The Short Novels of Dostoevsky*. Translated by Gustave Otto Arlt. New York: Dial, 1945.

———. *Essays*. 3 vols. Frankfurt am Main: Fischer, 1977.

———. *Letters of Thomas Mann, 1889–1955*. Compiled and translated by Richard Winston and Clara Winston. New York: Knopf, 1970.

———. *Notizbücher 1–6*. Frankfurt am Main: S. Fischer, 1991.

———. *Tagebücher 1933–34*. Frankfurt am Main: S. Fischer, 1977.

Mansfeld, Jaap, ed. and trans. *Die Vorsokratiker: Auswahl der Fragmente*. Vol. 1. Stuttgart: Reclam Verlag, 1983.

Marcel, Gabriel. *Journal métaphysique*. Paris: Gallimard, 1927.

Michelangelo. *The Complete Poems of Michelangelo*. Translated by John Frederick Nims. Chicago: The University of Chicago Press, 1998.

Montesquieu. *My Thoughts*. Translated by Henry C. Clark. Indianapolis: Liberty Fund, 2012.

Nietzsche, Friedrich. "The Dionysian Worldview." Translated by Claudia Crawford. *Journal of Nietzsche Studies* 13 (Spring 1997).

————. *The Will to Power.* Translated by Walter Kaufmann and R. J. Collingdale. New York: Viking, 1968.

Norden, Edouard. *Agnostos theos: Untersuchungen zur Formengeschichte religioser Reden.* Leipzig and Berlin: Teubner, 1913.

Novalis. *Ausgewählte Werke.* 3 vols. Leipzig: Max Hesse, 1903.

Nyíri, Tamás. *Antropológiai vázlatok.* Budapest: Szent István Társulat, 1972.

Ortega y Gasset, José. *On Love: Aspects of a Single Theme.* Translated by Toby Talbot. New York: Meridian, 1957.

Parmenides. *Fragments.* In *Early Greek Philosophy,* edited by John Burnet. London: A & C Black, 1892.

Pascal, Blaise. *Letters.* Translated by Mary L. Booth. In The Harvard Classics, vol. 48. New York: Collier & Son, 1910.

————. *Minor Works.* Translated by O. W. Wright. In The Harvard Classics, vol. 48. New York: Collier & Son, 1910.

————. *Oeuvres complètes.* Edited by Jacques Chevalier. Paris: Bibliothèque de la Pléiade, 1954.

————. *Pensées.* Translated by A. J. Krailsheimer. Harmondsworth: Penguin, 1966.

Petrarch. *Letters on Familiar Matters,* vol. 2. Translated by Aldo S. Bernardo. Baltimore: Johns Hopkins University Press, 1982.

————. *The Secret.* Translated by Carol E. Quillen. Boston: Bedford, 2003.

Philo. *Who Is the Heir of Divine Things.* Translated by F. H. Colson and G. H. Whitaker. In *Philo,* vol. 4. Cambridge: Harvard University Press, 1932.

Pico della Mirandola, Giovanni. *Oration on the Dignity of Man.* Translated by A. Robert Gaponigri. Washington, D.C.: Gateway Editions, 2012.

Pindar. *Odes.* Translated and with notes by F. A. Paley. London: Williams and Norgate, 1868.

Platen, August von. *Die Tagebücher der Grafen August von Platen.* 2 vols. Stuttgart: J. G. Cotta, 1896, 1900.

Plato. *Apology, Republic,* and *Symposium.* In *The Dialogues of Plato,* vol. 1. Translated by Benjamin Jowett. Oxford: Clarendon, 1871.

————. *Phaedrus* and *Protagoras.* Translated by Benjamin Jowett. Oxford: Oxford University Press, 1877.

————. *Statesman.* In *The Dialogues of Plato,* vol. 4. Translated by Benjamin Jowett. Oxford: Oxford University Press, 1892.

————. *Timaeus*. In *The Dialogues of Plato*, vol. 3. Translated by Benjamin Jowett. Oxford: Clarendon, 1892.

Pliny. *Natural History*. 6 vols. Translated by John Bostock and H. T. Riley. London: Bohn, 1855.

Plotinus. *The Enneads*. Translated by Stephen Mackenna. Burdett, N.Y.: Larson Publications, 1992.

Plutarch. *De moralia*. Vol. 5. Translated by Frank Cole Babbitt. Cambridge: Harvard University Press, 1936.

————. *De moralia*. Vol. 6. Translated by W. C. Helmbold. Cambridge: Harvard University Press, 1939.

Rahner, Karl, and Herbert Vorgrimler. *Concise Theological Dictionary*. Edited by O. P. Cornelius Ernst. Translated by Richard Strachan. London: Herder and Burns & Oates, 1965.

Rilke, Rainer Maria. *Letters of Rainer Maria Rilke, 1892–1910*. Translated by Jane Bannard Greene and M. D. Herter. New York: Norton, 1945.

Ritter, Joachim, and Karlfried Grunder, eds. *Historisches Wörterbuch der Philosophie*. 7 vols. Basel and Stuttgart: Schwabe, 1971–84.

Sartre, Jean-Paul. "Search for a Method." Introduction to *Critique of Dialectical Reason*. Translated by Hazel Barnes. New York: Knopf, 1963.

Schalk, Fritz. "Diderots Artikel 'Mélancolie' in der Enzyklopädie." *Zeitschrift für französische Sprache und Literatur* 66 (1956): 175–85.

Schelling, Friedrich W. J. *The Ages of the World*. Translated by Frederick de Wolfe Bolman Jr. New York: Columbia University Press, 1942.

————. *Philosophical Inquiries into the Essence of Human Freedom*. Translated and with an introduction by Jeff Love and Johannes Schmidt. Albany: State University of New York Press, 2006.

————. *Sämtliche Werke*. 14 vols. Stuttgart: J. G. Cotta, 1856–61.

Schiller, Johann Christoph Friedrich von. *The Death of Wallenstein*. Translated by S. T. Coleridge. London: Longman and Rees, 1800.

————. *The Poems and Ballads of Schiller*. Translated by Edward Bulwer Lytton. 2nd ed. Edinburgh: Blackwood and Sons, 1852.

————. *The Poems of Schiller*. Translated by Edgar Alfred Bowring. New York: Crowell, 1873.

Schipperges, Heinrich. "Melancholie als ein mittelaltlicher Sammelbegriff für Wahnvorstellungen." *Studium Generale* 20 (1967): 723–36.

Schlegel, August Wilhelm. *Kritische Ausgabe seiner Werke*. Edited by Ernst Behler. Vol. 18. Paderborn: Verlag Ferdinand Schöningh, 1963.

———. *Kritische Schriften und Briefe*. Edited by Edgar Lohner. 7 vols. Stuttgart: W. Kohlhammer, 1963.

Schlegel, Friedrich. *Lucinde and the Fragments*. Translated by Peter Firchow. Minneapolis: University of Minnesota Press, 1971.

———. *Werke in zwei Bänden*. Edited by Wolfgang Hecht. Berlin: Aufbau, 1980.

Schönfeldt, Klaus. *Die Temperamentenlehre in deutschsprachigen Handschriften des 15. Jahrhunderts*. Heidelberg: A. Grosch, 1962.

Schreiber, Wolfgang. *Mahler*. Reinbek bei Hamburg: Rowohlt, 1971.

Schulte, Walter. "Das Glaubensleben in der melancholischer Phase." *Der Nervenarzt* 25 (1954): 401–7.

Schultz, Wolfgang. *Dokumente der Gnosis*. 1910. Reprint, Munich: Matthes & Seitz, 1986.

Sembdner, Helmut, ed. *Heinrich von Kleists Lebensspuren: Dokumente und Berichte der Zeitgenossen*. Munich: Deutscher Taschenbuch, 1996.

Seneca, Lucius Annaeus. "On Tranquility of the Mind." In *The Stoic Philosophy of Seneca: Essays and Letters of Seneca*, edited by Moses Hadas. New York: Norton, 1958.

Shelley, Mary Wollstonecraft. *Frankenstein, or, The Modern Prometheus*. London: Henry Colburn & Richard Bentley, 1831.

Shorter, Edward. *A Clinical Dictionary of Psychiatry*. Oxford: Oxford University Press, 2005.

Simmel, Georg. *Fragmente und Aufsätze aus dem Nachlaß und Veröffentlichungen der letzten Jahre*. Edited by Gertrud Kantorowicz. Munich: Drei Masken, 1923.

Sophocles. *"Electra," and Other Plays*. Translated by E. F. Watling. Harmondsworth: Penguin, 1953.

———. *The Theban Plays*. Translated by E. F. Watling. London: Penguin, 1974.

Starobinski, Jean. *Histoire du traitement de la mélancolie des origines*. Acta Psychosomatica 3. Basel: J. R. Geigy, 1960.

Storm, Theodor. *Briefe*. Edited by Peter Goldammer. 2 vols. Berlin: Aufbau, 1972.

Strabo. *Geography.* Edited and translated by Horace Leonard Jones. 8 vols. London: William Heinemann, 1924.

Straus, Erwin. *Psychologie der menschlichen Welt. Gesammelte Schriften.* Berlin: Springer, 1960.

Styron, William. *Darkness Visible: A Memoir of Madness.* New York: Random House, 1990.

Swift, Jonathan. *Travels into Several Remote Nations of the World: In Four Parts; By Lemuel Gulliver, First a Surgeon, and then a Captain of Several Ships.* 1726. Edited by Claude Rawson. Oxford: Oxford University Press, 2005.

Szász, Thomas. *The Myth of Mental Illness: Foundations of a Theory of Personal Conduct.* New York: Harper & Row, 1974.

Szilasi, Wilhelm. *Macht und Ohnmacht des Geistes.* Bern: Francke, 1946.

Szondi, Leopold. *Experimental Diagnostics of Drives.* Translated by Gertrude Aull. New York: Grune & Stratton, 1952.

Taylor, Michael Alan, and Max Fink. *Melancholia: The Diagnosis, Pathophysiology, and Treatment of Depressive Illness.* Cambridge: Cambridge University Press, 2006.

Tellenbach, Hubertus. *Melancholy: History of the Problem, Endogeneity, Typology, Pathogenesis, Clinical Considerations.* Translated by Erling Eng. Pittsburgh: Duquesne University Press, 1980.

Temple, William. *Five Miscellaneous Essays by Sir William Temple.* Edited by Samuel Monk. Ann Arbor: University of Michigan Press, 1963.

Thomas Aquinas. *Summa Theologica.* Translated by the Fathers of the English Dominican Province. New York: Benziger Bros., 1947.

Uexküll, Thure von. "Möglichkeiten und Grenzen psychosomatischer Betrachtung." *Der Nervenarzt* 26 (1955): 380–85.

Unamuno, Miguel de. *Mist: A Tragicomic Novel.* Translated by Warner Fite. Urbana: University of Illinois Press, 2000.

———. *Our Lord Don Quixote: The Life of Don Quixote and Sancho, with Related Essays.* Translated by Anthony Kerrigan. Princeton, N.J.: Princeton University Press, 1967.

Vasari, Giorgio. *Lives of the Most Excellent Painters, Sculptors, and Architects.* 10 vols. Translated by Gaston du C. de Vere. London: Macmillan, 1912–14.

Völker, Ludwig, ed. *"Komm, heilige Melancholie": Eine Anthologie deutscher Melancholie-Gedichte.* Stuttgart: Reclam, 1983.

Wackenroder, Wilhelm Heinrich. *Dichtungen, Schriften, Briefe.* Edited by Gerda Heinrich. Berlin: Union Verlag, 1984.

Walter, Bruno. *Gustav Mahler.* Translated by Lotte Walter Lindt. London: Hamish Hamilton, 1958.

Wellek, René. *A History of Modern Criticism, 1750–1950,* vol. 2, *The Romantic Age.* Cambridge: Cambridge University Press, 1981.

Wind, Edgar. *Pagan Mysteries in the Renaissance.* Rev. ed. Harmondsworth: Penguin, 1967.

Winterstein, Alfred. *Dürers "Melancholie" im Lichte der Psychoanalyse.* Leipzig, 1929.

Wittgenstein, Ludwig. *Tractatus logico-philosophicus.* Translated by C. K. Ogden. London: Routledge Kegan & Paul, 1922.

Wittkower, Rudolf, and Margot Wittkower. *Born under Saturn: The Character and Conduct of Artists; A Documented History from Antiquity to the French Revolution.* New York: Norton, 1963.

Young, Wayland Hilton. *Eros Denied: Sex in Western Society.* New York: Grove, 1964.

Zilsel, Edgar. *Die Entstehung der Geniebegriffs: Ein Beitrag zur Ideengeschichte der Antike und des Frühkapitalismus.* Tübingen: Mohr, 1926.

Zutt, J. "Über Daseinsordnungen." *Der Nervenarzt* 24 (1953): 177–87.

László F. Földényi (b. 1952) studied English and Hungarian philology and the philosophy of art in Budapest and spent several years in Germany and the Netherlands. He is now a professor at the University of Theatre, Film, and Television, Budapest, and holds the chair in the theory of art. His books on literature, art, and the history of ideas have been translated into more than ten languages. He has won many literary prizes in Germany und Hungary, including the highest state honor in Hungary, the Széchenyi Prize. In 2009, he was elected to the Deutsche Akademie für Sprache und Dichtung. He lives with his American-born wife, an architect, in Budapest, and has two daughters and a son.

Tim Wilkinson's translations include books by distinguished Hungarian historians such as Éva H. Balázs, *Hungary and the Habsburgs 1765–1800*, and Victor Karady, *The Jews of Europe in the Modern Era*, as well as works by literary memoirists and novelists such as Tibor Déry, Gyula Illyés, Dezső Kosztolányi, and Sándor Márai. He is the main English-language translator for Imre Kertész.

Alberto Manguel is a Canadian writer, translator, editor, and critic. Born in Buenos Aires, he has since resided in Israel, Argentina, Europe, the South Pacific, and Canada. He now lives in New York.